*Medicine Bundle*

# *Medicine Bundle*

Indian Sacred Performance and
American Literature, 1824–1932

Joshua David Bellin

**PENN**

University of Pennsylvania Press
Philadelphia

Published by
University of Pennsylvania Press
Philadelphia, Pennsylvania 19104-4112

A Cataloging-in-Publication Record is available from the Library of Congress

ISBN-13: 978-0-8122-4034-4
ISBN-10: 0-8122-4034-0

*For Geraldine Murphy*

# Contents

# Introduction

*Cultures are most fully expressed in and made conscious of themselves in their ritual and theatrical performances.*
—*Victor Turner, quoted in Richard Schechner and Willa Appel,* By Means of Performance (1990)

Some years ago, at the opening of the Pittsburgh American Indian Center, I met a man named Edward Hale, a Mandan/Hidatsa medicine man and promoter of Indian causes. Both aspects of Hale's dual role were on display at the inaugural ceremony. Called on not only to provide the mostly Anglo audience with a living example of Indian people's resurgence but also to supervise and interpret the enactment of Native dances, songs, and rituals, Hale, dressed in what I took to be a traditional costume of feathers and fringed leather, beating a drum and chanting in a soft voice that seemed too small even for the tiny Quaker meetinghouse in which the event took place, was at once the arbiter of Native mysteries and the vendor of a mystery as strong and strange as the medicine bundle he bore: the mystery of his people's presence and persistence. I acknowledge now that I too was beguiled by the promise of Hale's performance, that I was taken by the preposterous thought that I, at that time beginning to study Native American sacred traditions in antebellum literature, could make contact with that yet more distant mystery by fitting a lone hour's encounter with a lone contemporary healer into a hectic research and writing schedule. I imagined that I might talk with Hale at length—again, I meant an hour—about his practice, his people, his powers. I imagined that his medicine, ensconced within my pages, might live on through me.

As it turned out, my hopes were vain. Hale was distracted, the center of attention, rushing here and there, wearily answering questions and permitting his possessions and person to be admired and handled. Compounding

this problem, he seemed, in the few moments I was able to capture his notice, to be convinced that I was looking to participate in one of his ceremonies, which I was not. "I'll set you up," he said—meaning, I suppose, that
he would arrange for me to undergo a procedure similar to that of the older
woman who, after submitting to a few passes from his healing crystal, pronounced herself cured, though of what I don't know. Hale could not seem to
grasp that my interests were academic rather than therapeutic. He had come
to heal, to break down barriers between peoples through the immediate or
symbolic application of his medicine, while I—though I imagined my purpose to be somewhat the same—had chosen my medium in a secular, mate-
rialist, demystifying field, and neither of us was prepared or able to
appreciate the other's vocation. I left the meetinghouse both discouraged and
a bit annoyed. I imagine, as I recall myself dogging Hale, introducing the
same tired questions time and again, that he must have felt pretty much the
same.

Though I did not get from Hale what I was—absurdly—seeking at the
time, I have come to believe that my encounter with him was immensely productive for, as well as emblematic of, the project I begin with this reminis-
cence: the project of studying Indian sacred performance in its manifold,
conflictual, intimate relationships with American literature and culture.
What was being enacted in the Quaker meetinghouse, I now believe, was an
encounter between Native Americans and Euro-Americans that has pervaded American culture and shaped American literature throughout our
mutual history, an encounter with two complementary, inseparable acts. On
the one hand, it is an encounter involving Euro-American misapprehension
of, fascination with, and dispossession of Native American sacred performance: ceremony, healing ritual, dance, song. On the other hand, it is an encounter embracing Native American repossession of, and revitalization
through, the very acts by which whites have sought their dispossession: acts
including, most notably, the public performance of Indianness in scenes engineered and attended by whites. In this twinned performance space, neither
Native Americans nor Euro-Americans can escape the other's presence.
Thus, though Hale may have seemed the only one onstage that day, we were
all engaged in the performance, and not merely as spectators: not only did we
in the audience crave a taste of Hale's medicine but the very context of his
performance, the setting for the drama, was tuned to our desires. Conversely,
though Hale may have seemed the only one who was *not* playing a role, the
only one who was artlessly expressing Indian medicine rather than calculat-

ingly peddling or consuming it, the fact that our presence, our expectations, had brought him there necessitated his adopting a persona that met us (at least) halfway. In this regard, the performance space we created was an *intercultural* one, a space in which Indian and white traditions of sacred and secular performance circulated, collided, confounded, and compounded one another. This encounter of Indian and non-Indian traditions of performance, I argue, played a central role in producing American identities, American culture, and American literature during the period of my study—as, indeed, it does to this day.

In the following pages, I trace the forms, sources, and uses of Indian performance in American literature and culture from 1824, the publication date of Cherokee convert Catharine Brown's jointly authored *Memoir*, through the period of Indian Removal and the late century era of the Wild West show, and then into the opening decades of the twentieth century, my terminal date correlating with the publication of John G. Neihardt's *Black Elk Speaks* in 1932. In this book, I urge the reader to think of *Indian performance* as a complex, contested arena encompassing various interlocking acts and actors. On the one hand, Indian performance cannot be thought of without regard to the sacred performances enacted by Indian peoples, both before and during the era of intercultural contact: performances including ceremony, dance, song, visionary experience, and shamanistic ritual. The importance of such performances to Indian communities can scarcely be overstated. Paula Gunn Allen (Laguna Pueblo) captures their significance as sources of spiritual as well as cultural power, as sites of tradition and innovation, and as markers of Indian identity: "At base the ceremonials restore the psychic unity of the people, reaffirm the terms of their existence in the universe, and validate their sense of reality, order, and propriety. The most central of these perform this function at levels that are far more intense than others, and these great ceremonies, more than any single phenomenon, distinguish one tribe from another."[1] But during the contact period, such sacred performances were met by another form of Indian performance, one that was itself deeply significant in shaping the terms of encounter. This was the performance *of* Indianness, by both Indians and whites: acts of Indian portrayal, invention, and identity formation including conversion narratives, stage plays, bicultural autobiographies, traveling medicine carnivals, and Wild West shows. Generally speaking, I refer to the varieties of Indian sacred performance as *Indian medicine*, a phrase reflecting widespread usage among Indian peoples: *medicine* (or its Native-language equivalents) refers not only to healing remedies but also to sacred power or mystery, as well as to the invocation or performance thereof, by individuals ("medicine men") as well as by communities. Extending this usage, I refer to Euro-American systems and practices of power or mystery—including Euro-American acquisition of Indian medicine—as *white medicine*. In bringing together two forms of Indian performance that have been studied at length but in relative isolation—the former principally by anthropologists and ethnohistorians, the latter principally by historians and literary critics—I will illustrate that sacred performance *by* Indians and the performance *of* Indianness by Indians and whites alike have coexisted throughout American history, contending with each other, fighting and folding into each other, disrupting and determining each other. These processes of interaction and cocreation I name the *medicine bundle*, a phrase I adapt from its autochthonous sense—sacred objects bound together for ritual or ceremonial purposes—to designate the complex, conflictual, cross-cultural acts that lie at the heart of American life and literature.

My decision to focus this exploration of Indian and white medicine on the period from 1824 to 1932 reflects my belief that it was during this roughly one-hundred-year span that the convergence of certain developments in American history, culture, and literature fundamentally transformed the practice and representation of Indian performance in all its forms. It was during the nineteenth century that initiatives to undermine Indian sacred performance were formalized, legalized, and nationalized. Beginning in the colonial era, Europeans had attacked Indian shamanism and ceremonialism; because, in Francis Jennings's words, the Indian powwow or medicine man was "one of the strongest unifying factors in any Indian community," this religious figure "became the object of the most intense hatred of Europeans striving to weaken and dominate his tribe." Thus, in the 1648 list of "conclusions and orders" that Puritan missionary John Eliot imposed on his Indian converts, the following rule appears second from the top: "there shall be no more *Pawwowing* amongst the *Indians*. And if any shall hereafter *Pawwow* [Pawwows are Witches or Sorcerers that cure by help of the devill.], both he that shall *Powwow*, & he that shall procure him to *Powwow*, shall pay 20 *s.* apeece."[2] Yet as Ronald Niezen writes, it was not until the nineteenth century that "campaigns against native spiritual practices," including shamanistic healing and ceremonial performance, "developed not only from evangelical ambitions but also from, and at the same time as, territorial and ideological ambitions of the state." Such state-sponsored campaigns took a variety of forms: federal support of missionary programs that sought to squelch Native belief and ritual, the development of boarding schools (particularly off-reservation) in which young Indians were taught to relinquish and revile traditional spiritual practices, the removal and debarring of Indian peoples from sacred sites, and the funding of an anthropological profession that deprived Indian peoples of sacred materials in the name of science and progress. In 1824, Secretary of War John C. Calhoun established the Bureau of Indian Affairs, whose first commissioner, Thomas L. McKenney, was charged with "the administration of the fund for the civilization of the Indians"; the code word *civilization*, while embracing a variety of Euro-American ideals, was grounded in the conviction that Christianity must supplant the Indians' heathen beliefs and customs. The following year, in his address on Indian affairs, President James Monroe broached the subject of Indian Removal, suggesting that it might be the only means to "teach [the Indians] by regular instruction the arts of civilized life and make them a civilized people." In so doing, Monroe laid the groundwork for a federal assault not only on Indian lands and lives but also on the sacred traditions that Euro-Americans deemed irreconcilable with their own or the Indians' civilization.[3]

By the second half of the nineteenth century, the oppressive apparatus of Indian civilization had become entrenched on a continentwide basis. In 1869, as a central component of President Ulysses S. Grant's Peace Policy, Christian missionaries were licensed to set up missions throughout the reservation system; these missionaries, as Lee Irwin writes, "specifically targeted Native religions as the bane of all civilized Christian ideology. . . . Indian ceremonies were banned, religious practices disrupted, and sacred objects destroyed or confiscated." Additional support for this campaign came in 1883, when Secretary of the Interior Henry M. Teller established Courts of Indian Offenses to eliminate the "savage rites and heathenish customs" of the Indians, including "the old heathenish dances, such as the sun-dance, scalp-dance, &c. These dances, or feasts, as they are sometimes called, ought, in my judgment, to be discontinued, and if the Indians now supported by the Government are not willing to discontinue them, the agents should be instructed to compel such discontinuance." Teller likewise targeted Indian medicine men, arguing that "steps should be taken to compel these imposters to abandon [their] deception and discontinue their practices." In 1892, Commissioner of Indian Affairs Thomas Jefferson Morgan clarified the rules of the Indian courts, providing fines and prison sentences for "any Indian who shall engage in the sun dance, scalp dance, or war dance, or any other similar feast, so called," as well as for "any Indian who shall engage in the practices of so-called medicine men, or who . . . shall use any arts of a conjurer to prevent Indians from abandoning their barbarous rites and customs."[4] A latter-day John Eliot—but this time with the weight of the federal government and armed forces behind him—Morgan epitomized the nineteenth century's efforts to purge Indian medicine from the body of the nation.

Those efforts came to a formal close only in 1934. In that year, the Indian Reorganization Act, engineered by Roosevelt's commissioner of Indian affairs, John Collier, proclaimed an official cease-fire to the century-long, federally funded war on Indian medicine. And, indeed, the cease-fire was merely official: though Collier's Circular No. 2970, "Indian Religious Freedom and Indian Culture" (1934), asserted that "no interference with Indian religious life or ceremonial expression will hereafter be tolerated," Indian religious freedom continues to be threatened even after the 1978 passage of the American Indian Religious Freedom Act and its 1994 supplement, the Native American Free Exercise of Religion Act.[5] Nonetheless, the period from 1824 (the year of the publication of Brown's *Memoir*) to 1933 (the year after the publication of *Black Elk Speaks*) still stands as the time during which a combination of state-orchestrated suppression and a corresponding lack of legal recognition or redress made Indian medicine particularly vulnerable to attack. And as such, Indian sacred performance assumed a unique prominence in American print culture during this period: seen as the key to Indian character and the curse of Indian society, Indian medicine became a subject of intense scrutiny and hostility in the missionary, political, ethnographic, and imaginative literature of the time.

Yet against this background of incomprehension and recrimination, there emerged two further developments that played a decisive role in the circulation and representation of Indian medicine during this period. First, and perhaps as a necessary corollary to white actions against Indian peoples' practice of their own sacred traditions, white Americans in the first quarter of the nineteenth century began systematically to assimilate Indian medicine for their own ends: national and literary identity, personal health, and consumer spectacle. It is possible to trace such acts to an earlier time period: playing Indian, as scholars such as Philip Deloria have noted, had precursors in the Revolutionary-era theatrics of the Boston Tea Party, the Sons of Saint Tammany, and the white Indians or tenant gangs of border regions undergoing the throes of transition from a freehold system to one of landed aristocracy.[6] Indeed, tracking this tradition to its roots, one might go as far back as

Thomas Morton of Merry Mount, where European revelers and rebels "brought the Maypole to the place appointed . . . and there erected it with the help of Salvages," who joined in the dance.[7] The adoption of Indian medicine by whites had a long, if largely unrecognized and unheralded, history.

The nineteenth-century instance is, nonetheless, unique: there is a significant distinction between the situational performance of Indian medicine of an earlier time and the volitional, material, articulable consumption of Indian medicine that predominates in the nineteenth century. During the latter period, Euro-Americans began to perceive Indian medicine, in both its narrow and extended senses, as a potential panacea for a range of individual and societal maladies, from loss of primitive vigor to lack of national identity. Hence the rise during this period of the figure whom contemporary critics term the "whiteshaman" or "plastic medicine man"; hence too the rise of various, interlinked show spaces—carnivals, museums, theaters—in which Euro-American supplicants congregated to sample the white medicine man's wares. As with the federal attacks on Indian medicine, these acts may be seen as forms of desecration or desacralization: Indian medicine, stripped from its own cultural contexts, is reproduced in secular forums orchestrated by and for the benefit of non-Indians. Yet at the same time, these processes significantly complicated the relationship that Euro-Americans bore toward Indian medicine: as a medium for the production of intercultural theater, the taking of Indian medicine by whites not only changed the meanings and uses of Indian medicine but also transformed the participants who enacted, embodied, and consumed it.

This transformation was aided by a second, and equally significant, factor that affected the nature and function of Indian medicine during the period of this study: the entrance of Indian peoples into white-engineered performance spaces and the production of written works by or about these performers. Depending on one's definition, Indians had been performing their lives, identities, and medicine for Euro-American audiences from the beginning of the contact era, the most obvious example being the translated confessions and conversion narratives that appear in the writings of missionaries such as Eliot.[8] Yet it was during the era of Indian Removal, as Arnold Krupat writes, that "a conjunction of historicism and egocentric individualism first brought autobiography as a term and a type of writing to America," and it was during this period that autobiography became established as the most prominent literary genre of Indian self-expression.[9] Two of the most popular Indian autobiographies of the nineteenth century, Seneca captive

Mary Jemison's *Narrative* and Cherokee convert Catharine Brown's *Memoir*, were published in 1824. The work most critics consider the pinnacle of antebellum Indian autobiography, William Apess's *A Son of the Forest*, appeared shortly thereafter, in 1829. By the tail end of the period I consider in this study, Indian life stories had become a staple of the autobiographical genre, culminating in 1932 with the text that is, arguably, the single most widely read and influential work of American Indian literature: *Black Elk Speaks*. Written autobiography, then, played a central role in the construction and dissemination of the new forms of Indian performance that took hold in the nineteenth and twentieth centuries.

It was not only via the written word that Indian identities were being tested, contested, and forged anew during this period, however. At the same time, as the assault on Indian sacred performance escalated, corresponding movements arose among Indian peoples to revitalize their sacred traditions and, in so doing, to reinstate their identities as Indians. In the antebellum southeast, the Cherokees sought to contest Euro-American dominance through the development of both nationalist and nativist ideologies (as well as through the development of their own literacies, the most prominent of which was the syllabary designed by Sequoyah); in the late nineteenth-century northern and southern Plains, followers of the Paiute prophet Wovoka were dancing (as well as trading tales of the prophet via written and pictorial missives) in an effort to bring about the return of the buffalo and their traditional way of life. The connection between these varieties of Indian performance and the autobiographies that paralleled them may not seem an obvious one, other than the fact that some of the autobiographies were written by or about participants in these acts. Yet the life writings and the various forms of collective cultural reinvention were powerfully linked in at least two, if seemingly contradictory, ways. On the one hand, both represented attempts to reinvent sacred performance, to re-sacralize what had become, within the dominant culture, either a despised relic or a desired commodity. On the other hand, both sought to reanimate Indian medicine in large part by deploying the very language, ideologies, and performative practices—the white medicine—by which Euro-Americans had sought to dispossess Indian peoples: Christianity, nationalism, literacy and Anglo education, sentimental and racial theory, and Wild West performance all played a role in the constitution of revised and revitalized Indian identities. The interaction of Indian and white medicine in the works of nineteenth- and twentieth-century Indians thus represents a particularly complex form of Indian performance, one that, as Simon J. Ortiz (Acoma Pueblo) writes, evidences "the creative ability of Indian people to gather in many forms of the socio-political colonizing force which beset them and to make these forms meaningful in their own terms."[10]

To Ortiz's point, I would add one further: it was by gathering the other's "forms" and investing them with meaning that Euro-Americans, no less than Native Americans, constituted their cultures and identities. There are, of course, substantial differences between the response of Indian peoples to a colonizing force and the response of Euro-Americans to those they colonized, and it will be one of the concerns of this book to explore those differences. At the same time, it is one of my principal claims that there is no *absolute* difference between the performance of medicine by Indians and by whites, that manifestations of Indian and white medicine couple and blur in the words and works of all peoples involved in the encounter. This is the concept of the medicine bundle: the bringing together of diverse medicine acts, all of which derive their form and power through contact with their others. The culture of Indian performance is a dynamic and inventive arena from which neither party, Indian nor white, can emerge without sharing and shaping the other's medicine.

> There is no more an "Ur-*performance*" than there is an "Ur-*text*." Only the systematic study of performances can disclose the true structure.
> —*Dell Hymes, "Breakthrough into Performance" (1975)*

To understand the culture of Indian performance in America, however, it is necessary to explore in greater depth the relationship of Indian *performance* to American *literature*. Though I am concerned in this book with varieties of performance, I rely heavily on textual representations of those performances: records drawn from the nineteenth and early twentieth centuries, on the one hand, and more recent reconstructions by ethnohistorians and literary critics, on the other. That these textualizations of performance differ from their originals need hardly be belabored. A moment's reflection calls to mind a great range of performative features that do not translate literally—and that may not translate at all—in written sources: tone of voice, facial expression, gesture, costume, props, music and song, performers' interaction with each other and with an audience, setting, time of day—the list could be extended indefinitely. All of these factors may be embraced by the word *context*, a term that not only signifies the presence of such variables in a particular performance but also, and just as importantly, emphasizes that each performance is unique *because* no context can be perfectly reproduced. Written records, then, do not simply leave out features of the original performance; more comprehensively, they leave out the emergent, nonreplicable nature *of* performance.[11]

In the case of Indian sacred performance, moreover, the disconnect between event and account assumes a particular gravity—for what is sacred about such performances *is* the event. As Christopher Vecsey writes: "Indians believe through their practices, in ways that often transcend verbal formulation. Indian beliefs are performed and embodied by living communities." German traveler Johann Georg Kohl, one of the few white observers during the period of this study to mistrust written records of such embodied performances, employed a striking image to express the impossibility of conveying sacred act via verbal artifact: Indian song, ceremony, and dance, he wrote, "very frequently resemble polypi and certain molluscs, which, while floating on the sea, have splendid colours and interesting forms, but which, when seized, prove to be a lump of jelly, and dissolve in the hand." Kohl's terms are particularly apt, inasmuch as his language suggests the reckless destruction of Indian sacred performance that characterized Euro-American practices during the nineteenth and twentieth centuries. In this respect, it could be said that literature (or, more broadly, the literate) was itself a principal means by which the dominant culture effected the desacralization of Indian medicine. Performance theorist Richard Schechner asks rhetorically but—given the history of Indian-white relations—urgently: "What happens when performances tour, playing to audiences that know nothing of the social or religious contexts of what they are experiencing?"[12] The answer, it seems, is obvious. Indeed, one might say that *any* account of Indian performance written in a European language is by definition a touring performance, playing to audiences that know and care little of its unique cultural contexts, emergent characteristics, or sacred properties.

If, however, it is necessary to approach textualized performances with care, it is also possible that drawing too absolute a distinction between event and account produces a misleading, reductive portrait of Indian-white encounter. For one thing, as recent developments in performance theory have demonstrated, lived performances and written texts are *not* absolutely opposed in either form or function; rather, in W. B. Worthen's words, "both texts and performances are materially unstable registers of signification, producing 'meaning' intertextually in ways that deconstruct notions of intention, fidelity, authority, present meaning." Performance, according to this view, is, like text, inherently mediated, enmeshed within a host of social and ideological pressures (including, importantly, other performances) through which any one performance is read, by its participants no less than by its recorders. Schechner includes within this network of performances not only prior acts but also acts that have not yet come into being: "it is this 'performative bundle'—where the project-to-be . . . governs what from the past is selected or invented (and projected backward into the past), . . . that is the most stable and prevalent performative circumstance. In a very real way the future—the project coming into existence through the process of rehearsal—determines the past."[13] What such a model suggests is that it is vain to designate a performance original to which all other versions or variants—written or reenacted—are beholden (and subordinate); for what we term performance originals—as opposed to secondary, ancillary copies or even distortions—are inseparable from the very representations or reenactments to which we colloquially oppose them.

And this model holds true not merely for spontaneous but also for emplotted performance, not merely for secular but also for sacred performance. As Herbert Blau writes, "there is something in the very nature of performance which . . . implies *no first time*, no origin, but only recurrence and reproduction, whether improvised or ritualized, rehearsed or aleatoric, whether the performance is meant to give the impression of an unviolated naturalness or the dutiful and hieratic obedience to a code." Even in the case of sacred performance, which places a premium on being the original, non-replicable act, there *are* no performance originals, in the sense of stable, self-contained occasions that one can extricate from the tangle of past and future reenactments, cultural contexts and references, and reproductions and revisions through which all performances are contrived. Rather, even in this most specialized of cases, any one performance necessarily emerges in relation to its others; each act within the performative bundle is constituted by what it is not. And so, as Joseph Roach sums up, "the relentless search for the purity of origins is a voyage not of discovery but of erasure": erasure of the multiple, competing, compelling acts of which any performance is constituted. Roach thus envisions a "genealogy of performance"—an attempt to track the development of performative traditions—not as a quest for origin but as "an intricate unraveling of the putative seamlessness of origins. It is at once a map of diasporic diffusions in space and a speculation on the synthesis and mutation of traditions through time."[14]

Roach's *Cities of the Dead: Circum-Atlantic Performance* (1996), from which the preceding quotations are taken, is one of a number of recent works to apply the insights of performance theory to early American texts and contexts. Other examples include Jay Fliegelman's *Declaring Independence: Jefferson, Natural Language, and the Culture of Performance* (1993), David Waldstreicher's *In the Midst of Perpetual Fetes: The Making of American Nationalism, 1776–1820* (1997), Sandra Gustafson's *Eloquence Is Power: Oratory and Performance in Early America* (2000), and Susan Castillo's *Colonial Encounters in New World Writing, 1500–1786: Performing America* (2006). What these works demonstrate is that the interplay among diverse performative and written traditions enacted by America's diverse peoples does indeed call into question the seamlessness of cultural origins and the demarcation between (secular) text and (sacred) act.[15] At one level, performative traditions challenge this distinction by demonstrating the presence of multiple literacies and the emergence of oral-literate crosses among Indian peoples. As Gustafson writes in her study of the power of eloquence in colonial and Revolutionary-era texts, including those that involved the meeting of Indian and Euro-American speakers within ceremonial settings such as mission towns and treaty councils: "viewing speech and text as symbolic and performative forms of language rather than as discrete and hierarchical entities" challenges the "teleological understanding of language in which textual forms displace oral ones. . . . Recognizing the flexible boundaries and considerable overlap between oral and textual forms, as well as the persistence of oral genres, we must attend to the symbolic and performative meanings attached to speech and writing." Gustafson coins the phrase "the performance semiotic of speech and text" to capture this interbreeding of oral-performative and textual forms within American culture and literature, and she calls attention to Indian devices—such as pictographs, wampum strings, and so forth—that evidence the interaction of scriptlike forms and nonliterate, bodily behaviors within Indian sacred performance. Approaching the issue of performative-literate practices from another direction, Phillip Round explores the ways in which Indian authors sought "to preserve oral and pictographic traditions and extend them into the new world of U.S. print culture"; he shows that Native print culture was impacted by authors' incorporation of alternative literacies within written works.[16] Rather than viewing the act as primary and the text as ancillary, then, such studies call attention to the interplay and interpenetration of text *and* act in the emergence of Native American culture, identity, and literature.

At the same time, and of particular importance to this study, it was not only among Indian peoples that the text bore the mark of sacred, oral-performative practice. Rather, the impact of Indian sacred performance is evident throughout the texts of encounter, the majority of which, of course, were authored by Euro-Americans. Gustafson phrases the performative-literate juncture this way: in situations of cultural contact, "oral encounters" become "a residue that the colonial Imaginary produces but cannot fully assimilate."[17] The conflictual, productive exchange between text and act generates an intercultural performative bundle, what I am calling the medicine bundle: a literate-performative network within which all elements are shaped by their others, becoming what they are through their encounter with what they are not. As such, rather than rejecting the texts of Indian-white encounter as a derivative or diminishment of a sacred original—or accepting these texts only as a regrettable concession to the futility of rescuing an oral-performative prototype—I view these texts as a necessary aspect of the medicine bundle, existing in tension and relation with other aspects within the larger performative network. This does not mean, of course, that these texts are identical to the sacred performances with which they coexist; given the emergent nature of performance, they could not be so. It does mean, however, that these texts could not exist as such without the sacred performances they are unlike. In this respect, the literature of encounter is itself an emergent form, born as Indian and white medicine vie and breed, relativizing and revitalizing one another.

Indeed, in this respect, the interaction of Indian and white medicine can be seen as both medium and metaphor for the intercultural relations that bound Euro-American and Indian peoples during the period of this study (and that bind them still). The intercultural, as ethnohistorians have argued in recent decades, is rooted in specific contexts of encounter; though it has proved all too easy from a summary point of view to ignore the presence of Indian peoples in the shaping of American history and culture, in the eyes of the intercultural critic all cultural productions bear the marks of the dynamic interrelationships among peoples. As Richard White put it in his landmark *The Middle Ground* (1991): "The meeting of the sea and continent, like the meeting of whites and Indians, creates as well as destroys. Contact was not a battle of primal forces in which only one could survive. Something new could emerge." Indeed, as Scott Michaelsen writes in his study of the intercultural origins of anthropology, "to White's account one must add that cultural *difference* is a product, too, of the same encounter and that cultural difference is produced at the very same moment as the most minimal 'middle ground.' A middle ground, in fact, is culture's very condition of possibility, of visibility. Culture quite literally cannot appear until such a space is opened. And today Anglo and Amerindian identities remain wedded within a contentious shared space," such that "there are no separate, secured 'cultures' to which one might have recourse or to which one might nostalgically return." In this sense, as James Clifford concludes, "difference is an effect of inventive syncretism." This understanding of encounter as a site for cultural reinvention—or for the invention of culture as such—is inherently performative, in that it treats culture as the emergence of "something new," a set of acts made and remade within particular contexts. To view culture in this way is not to deny conflict and inequality in the transaction of Indian and white (a charge that has, in fact, been leveled against the concept of the middle ground); as Rosemarie Bank cautions, the performative paradigm, "in its insistence that from the beginning red and white cultures acted upon, influenced, and appropriated each other, erasing the possibility of a return for either race to an untouched ('originary' or 'real') condition, is perilous if it is assumed that the cultural stakes for red and white peoples in the internal imperialist scenario were the same."[18] Rather, to view culture in this way is to recognize that the forces that mark American history and literature are the same that marked the interaction of Indian and white medicine: forces of struggle and settlement, violence and rapprochement, destruction and creation.

Moreover, it is to recognize that these forces evolved, and survived, from earliest contact to the present. Most ethnohistorians cite the onset of the American Revolution—or, at latest, the close of the War of 1812 and the collapse of Tecumseh's intertribal confederacy—as the death knell of intercultural accommodation, exchange, and emergence. In White's words, "the final dissolution of this world came when Indians ceased to have the power to force whites onto the middle ground. Then the desire of whites to dictate the terms of accommodation could be given its head. As a consequence, the middle ground eroded. . . . Americans invented Indians and forced Indians to live with the consequences of this invention." Such a portrait of unilateral invention is based on the reasoning that "a rough balance of power, mutual need or a desire for what the other possesses, and an inability by either side to commandeer enough force to compel the other to change" are the necessary constituents of meaningful cultural interaction.[19] To follow this reasoning would mean that my book must end here, before it begins.

Needless to say, I dispute this reasoning, which seems to me both arbitrary and unwarranted. White, for example, wraps *The Middle Ground* with an anecdote picturing Tecumseh's spiritual ally, the prophet Tenskwatawa, as an abject figure whom time and circumstance have passed by, a superannuated relic pathetically narrating his visions of power to ethnologist C. C. Trowbridge, who casually seized these once-sacred materials, "recorded them, filed them away, and forgot them." Yet Tenskwatawa makes a particularly poor choice for such a coda. His sacred performances persisted long after the defeat at Tippecanoe and the disbanding of Prophet's Town; in physical form as pictographs and other nonalphabetic literacies, as well as in intangible form as an ideology of Indian unity and resistance, the Shawnee prophet's medicine reappeared throughout the nineteenth century (though, to be sure, in novel configurations) among both Indian revivalists and white conspirators in Indian decline. Writing of the flourishing of a middle ground in what might seem a sheer act of imperialist nostalgia—the Revolutionary-era celebrations of the white Indians who called themselves the Sons of Saint Tammany—Roger Abrahams argues that "even in the midst of the most belligerent interactions, both sides are deeply affected by the other's presence. And once put into practice, these culturally transferred effects continue to ripple through the lives of those involved and of those who inherit the memory of these occasions," reemerging with particular force during "ritual and festival" occasions. In numerous, demonstrable ways, through acts of imitation, adoption, and adaptation, Indians and whites left what Abrahams terms "traces on the skin of the other" throughout the period of this study; indeed, they leave such traces still.[20] As such, I reject any claim that the productive (as well as destructive) cross-fertilization of Indian and white medicine that is the legacy of all Americans came to a close during the era of removals, reservations, Wild West shows, and state-sponsored massacres. To the contrary, by illustrating that it was during this relatively late period that Indian medicine became most fiercely debated, defended, and redefined, I demonstrate that Indian performance in all its forms has long played a significant, indeed a definitive, role in the constitution of America.

> *Oral tradition . . . becomes central to Native political analysis and the development of Native literary theory rather than fodder for backing up critics' pet theses on performance and translation, a discussion that has become largely redundant.*
>
> —*Craig Womack,* Red on Red: Native American Literary Separatism *(1999)*

Before moving on to this demonstration, however, there are several matters of definition that need to be addressed. The phrase *Indian sacred performance*, it seems to me, needs to be clarified; none of its terms is without controversy. To begin with the least contentious of the three, the term *performance*: I must say that I am leery of current usages in which this term becomes synonymous with most if not all human activities. As Elin Diamond enumerates, "'performance' can refer to popular entertainments, speech acts, folklore, political demonstrations, conference behavior, rituals, medical and religious healing, and aspects of everyday life."[21] It is the final item in this series that most gives me pause; though in a certain sense meeting one's neighbors or tying one's shoes may constitute a performance, I fear that so pliable a definition renders the term meaningless. For the same reason, I am resistant to using the word *performance* as a mere substitute locution for *text*. Though I am engaged in studying *how* texts relate to the performances with which they coexist, though I view texts as constituted by and constitutive of their contexts, and though I believe that certain texts are self-consciously or distinctively performative, I worry that calling *all* texts performances may obfuscate the very relationships I am seeking to excavate.

Accordingly, in an attempt to limit what counts as a performance in this book, I follow the definition offered by James Peacock: "performances [are] set apart, marked by various signals as distinct from ordinary routines of living. . . . A performance is not necessarily more meaningful than other events in one's life, but it is more deliberately so; a performance is, among other things, a deliberate effort to represent, to say something about something."[22] In practice, this means that I reserve the term *performance* for two classes of events: ritual or ceremonial experiences in which individuals break the flow of everyday life to engage in heightened forms of behavior in the presence of an audience (even an audience of one), and textual instances that exhibit comparable, heightened moments of self-presentation or self-invention for their reader(s). I am not altogether certain that I have succeeded in keeping performance within these bounds, but I hope that readers will approach the book with such restrictions in mind.

If it is difficult to define performance, it is even more difficult to fix the sacred. Indeed, applying my own definition of performance as "heightened forms of behavior," one might argue that *all* performances are sacred. And in fact, in the case of Indian performance, this might well be true. As Deward Walker writes, though the "division of the world into two domains, the one containing all that is sacred, the other all that is profane, is a distinctive trait of most religious traditions," among Indian peoples the sacred is "founded on the idea that it is an embedded attribute of all phenomena." Christopher Vecsey lists (some of) the practices that might fall under the heading of the sacred for Indian peoples: "Indian religious practices include what foods can be eaten, what names can be addressed. Since languages are usually gifts from the spiritual realm, the speaking of the native tongue can be a religious act. Hunting, farming, the gathering of herbs can all take on religious significance, as can the deference paid to an elder, the care paid in tending a fire, or the averting of one's eyes before strangers. In short, a whole way of life has religious potential."[23] In this respect, my previous qualm about the term *performance*—my sense that to apply it to the ordinary or the everyday is to empty it of meaning—would in the Native American context be precisely wrong: in the Native American context, the ordinary or the everyday (in common if not in absolute equivalence with the extraordinary and the numinous) *is* the realm of meaning, the realm of sacred performance.

The broader implications of this culturally distinctive sense of the sacred should be obvious. For in the largest sense, it has been the failure of Euro-Americans to grant the universality of the sacred in Indian lives that has facilitated the outlawing of Indian sacred performances, the expulsion of Indians from sacred sites, the plundering of Indian sacred objects, and more generally the blindness to or denial of Indian sacred traditions. And in this respect, my own work can be said to be guilty of a similar failure of understanding. For with one major exception—that of the life of Catharine Brown—I do *not* focus on the performance of everyday life as a site for the sacred among Native American peoples; holding to the previous definition of performance, I focus on performative occasions that are clearly marked as existing outside the quotidian. In part, I believed this was necessary in order to concentrate my attention on particular examples among the countless examples I could have selected. But at the same time, my decision to highlight performative occasions that are "clearly marked" as exceptional can only mean that I have selected those occasions that were clearly marked as such not just for my sources but also for *me*. And in this respect, in singling out only those manifestations of the sacred that struck my sources' and my own consciousness or interest, this book plainly perpetuates the history of incomprehension and misrepresentation it critiques: a history of Euro-American textual experts determining which instances of Indian sacred performance are suitable for reproduction and display and which can be ignored or left to die.

It is with this thought in mind that I turn to the final term in the triad of *Indian sacred performance*: the term *Indian*. In this case, my mere use of the term is not so much in question: I use the term, as well as others such as *Native American*, *Native*, and *indigenous*, simply because both Indian and Euro-American peoples did and do. What is in question, rather, is whether in this study of Indian sacred performance and American literature there is, in the end, anything truly Indian. Native American critics such as Craig Womack (Creek), whom I cite in the previous epigraph, would seem to argue that there is not; Womack would seem to suggest that in applying my and other critics' "pet theses on performance" to Indian sacred materials, I strip these materials not only of their performative qualities and their sacredness but also of their Indianness.

Womack is one of many Native American critics who, beginning with the revolutionary work of Vine Deloria Jr. (Standing Rock Sioux) in the 1960s and 1970s, have called for an end to the near monopoly over Indian materials that non-Indians have held in the public consciousness and the academic community. Insisting, in Deloria's words, that "each ethnic group must, in effect, form its own interpretation of itself," these critics have sought to apply traditionally Native epistemologies, theories, and methodologies to the study of Indian history, culture, and art. M. Annette Jaimes Guerrero (Juaneño/Yaqui) describes this project as one that involves no less than "the displacement of Eurocentrism and its replacement by an indigenous worldview," the building of "an autonomous Indian tradition of scholarship and intellectualism that carries a viable conceptual alternative to Eurocentrism and its institutions." Womack, similarly, seeks to rally "radical Native viewpoints, voices of difference rather than commonality," to "disrupt the powers of the literary status quo as well as the powers of the state"; he envisions a Native literary criticism grounded in "ceremony" and "oral tradition," constitutive—sacred—elements of indigenous culture that must be liberated from secular, scholarly norms.[24] As I understand these critics, many if not all of the theories with which I have built a case for the study of Indian sacred performance in American literature are precisely those that must be overturned: deconstruction, performance theory, and the like merely extend the reign of Eurocentrism over what is, at root, *Indian* sacred performance. According to this view, I have advanced little, if at all, beyond my meeting with Edward Hale many years ago: now as then, I am eager to ingratiate myself to the bearers of Indian sacred performance in order to make their medicine my own.

This strikes me as a perfectly reasonable way to view my book, and I think it behooves the reader (as it does the author) to keep such a characterization in sight as we proceed. At the same time, however, an alternative view of the book is possible, a view based on two considerations: first, that indigenous theories of Indian sacred performance are themselves interrelated with the Euro-American theories they contest, and second, that Euro-American studies such as mine are themselves interrelated with the Indian sacred performances they seek, with whatever success, to represent. Thus, following a long history of indigenous separatism through interaction represented most dramatically by the prophetic tradition of Tenskwatawa, each of the Native critics I have cited seeks to recover "an autonomous Indian tradition" that "carries a viable conceptual alternative to Eurocentrism and its institutions" and to achieve the "displacement of Eurocentrism and its replacement by an indigenous worldview" through selective use of the white medicine they reject. A Native critic who perceives such an interplay of indigenous and Western traditions is Greg Sarris (Pomo/Miwok), who asks, "How do scholars see beyond the norms they use to frame the experiences of others unless those norms are interrupted and exposed so that scholars are vulnerable, seeing what they think as possibly wrong, or at least limited?"[25] Sarris's question, which presumably applies to Native and non-Native critics alike, challenges not only the strict separation of Indian and white theoretical constructs but also the blanket indictment of Euro-American writers on Indian subjects. As I have discovered in writing this book, many of the authors I discuss, such as James Mooney, Jeremiah Evarts, and for that matter George Catlin and Buffalo Bill Cody, were individuals whose experiences with Native peoples deeply, if in most cases unconsciously or ambivalently, shaped their outlooks, their writings, and even their efforts on behalf of those whom they met. All of these writers came to Indian country certain of the inherent superiority of white over Indian medicine; but none left without Indian medicine having left its mark on their lives and works. They had become, as it were, part of the medicine bundle they had set out simply to study, to usurp, or even to destroy.

And in this respect, Sarris's question has assumed particular force for me as I have joined the long and mostly inglorious tradition of Euro-Americans writing on Indian medicine. For coming into contact with Native writers and Native performative traditions, even when those traditions were mediated by Euro-authored texts and Euro-critical theory, has interrupted my own critical norms, affecting the ways in which I have conceived of not only Indian sacred performance but also my own project. That I have been led to read the written works and public acts of Removal-era Euro-Americans through the lens of Native American sacred medicine bundles is one sign of this transformation; that I have been convinced that Euro-critical identity politics are inadequate to understanding the conversion experiences of Catharine Brown and her Cherokee peers is another; that I have been persuaded Indian performance in late century Wild West shows must be seen as a form of revitalization along the lines of Tenskwatawa's intertribal, nativist vision is yet another. If, then, I depart from critics such as Deloria, Guerrero, and Womack in my belief that Indian sacred performance speaks not solely in indigenous terms but also in terms that are mediated, negotiated, and mutually constituted by Indians and whites, I concur with them in my attempts to understand how indigenous theories of the performative have shaped both the texts I study and the text I write. As an intercultural critic, I have insisted that all persons in the cultural encounter, myself included, are profoundly affected by each other's medicine. And in this respect, my book should itself be seen as another aspect of the medicine bundle, its shape determined by those other acts that it cannot pretend or hope to be.[26]

This book consists of three chapters. The first focuses on writings by, and issues central to, Euro-Americans; the second and third focus on writings by, and issues central to, Native Americans. In each chapter, however, the necessary counterpart to, indeed the inescapable atmosphere for, the principal actors is the presence of the other. Chapter 1, "George Catlin, Te-ho-pe-nee Wash-ee," situates the writings, paintings, and performances of impresario Catlin within the early nineteenth-century quest for an authentic national identity that was to be achieved through the acquisition or imitation of Indian medicine. Chapter 2, "Being and Becoming 'Indian,'" considers the case of the Cherokee Nation and, in particular, Cherokee convert Catharine Brown in light of the attempts of Removal-era Indian peoples to forge or renew a sacred identity through the agency of white medicine. The final chapter, "The Acts of the Prophets," examines the late century participation of Indian peoples in two distinct yet interconnected spaces for Indian performative revitalization: Buffalo Bill's Wild West and the prophetic revivals that would culminate in the Plains Ghost Dance.

*Chapter 1*

# George Catlin, Te-ho-pe-nee Wash-ee

*My friend, then, is something like what the Indians call a Great Medicine, is he? He operates, he purges, he drains off the repletions.*
—*Herman Melville,* The Confidence-Man: His Masquerade *(1857)*

A funny thing happened to George Catlin, antebellum exhibitor, interpreter, and impersonator of the American Indian. As a privileged observer of the O-Kee-Pa (okipa), the annual initiation/earth renewal ceremony of the Mandan Indians, Catlin seized on this rare opportunity to view an Indian sacred performance from the inside, to "put the whole of what we saw" on paper and canvas for an inquiring Euro-American audience.[1] Yet at a critical juncture in the ceremony, just at the point at which the personage Catlin takes to represent "the Evil Spirit" (1:167) is sent packing by (presumably) the forces of good, Catlin offers his audience neither insight nor moral but, instead, what appears to be pure gibberish: "Then, to proceed: I said that this strange personage's body was naked—was painted jet black with charcoal and bear's grease, with a wand in his hands of eight feet in length with a red ball at the end of it, which he was rubbing about on the ground in front of him as he ran. In addition to this he had—*ung gee ah waheea notch,t oheks tcha, ung gee an ung hutch tow a tow ah ches menny. Ung gee ah to to wun nee, ahkst to wan ee eigh' s ta w*" (1:168). And again:

After repeated attempts thus made, and thus defeated in several parts of the crowd, this blackened monster was retreating over the ground where the buffalo-dance was going on, and having (apparently, par accident) swaggered against one of the men placed under the skin of a buffalo and engaged in the "bull dance," he started back, and placing himself in the attitude of a buffalo,—*hi ung ee a wahkstia, chee a nahk s tammee ung s towa; ee ung ee aht gwaht ee o nunghths tcha ho a, tummee oxt no ah, ughstono ah hi en en ah nahxt gwi aht gahtch gun ne. Gwee en on doatcht chee en aht gunne how how en ahxst tehu!* (1:168)

George Catlin, it seems, was overcome by a sudden, savage Pentecost while he took in the Indians' strange ceremonial; George Catlin, who elsewhere shows no fluency in Indian languages, was stricken with Mandan while he watched. George Catlin spoke in tongues.

This weird moment in Catlin's *Letters and Notes on the Manners, Customs, and Conditions of the North American Indians* (1841), the author-artist's account of eight years' peripatetic travel among the Indian peoples east and west of the Mississippi, I take to be emblematic of the complexity of Indian performance during the era of Indian Removal. On the one hand, the passage typifies the cagey showmanship that permitted Catlin and his Gallery of Indian portraits, precursor of P. T. Barnum's big top and Buffalo Bill's Wild West,[2] to captivate audiences in the eastern United States and Europe throughout the 1830s and 1840s: Catlin is emphatically, spectacularly *not going to show* what he witnessed, and this coy come-on promises more than revelation ever could. (Originally published serially, as dispatches from the field, *Letters and Notes* seems to have been worked up by Catlin as both marquee and script for his traveling show. Though it is hard to envision him spouting stylized red-speak onstage, one can imagine such devices as integral to, perhaps cues or keys to, his live performances.) Yet if Catlin's calculated theatricality confirms his directorial, not to say dictatorial, command of Indian sacred performance, at the same time the unarticulated scene, the barbarous idiom, suggest precisely the opposite: a breakdown of control, a failure to compass the performance he has witnessed. The impenetrability of the transliterated passages announces either that the Mandans' medicine *cannot* be domesticated—that it lacks or refuses English equivalents—or that it *should not be,* that it is too foreign, perilous, or repugnant to be penned by civilized lines.[3] Whatever was going on, Catlin was stymied in his efforts to transmit it, whether literally, pictorially (*Letters and Notes* contains no image marking the scene), or, once he had taken to recruiting Indian players to reenact their songs and dances, dramatically. The okipa eludes not simply disclosure but closure; Catlin's representation of Indian sacred performance is confounded by the performance he claims to represent.

And this tension between Indian sacred performance and its representation has profound implications for our understanding of Catlin's art and, more broadly, of the struggle over Indian medicine in the Removal era. Catlin is representative of a shift in the attitude white Americans bore toward Indian medicine during the early nineteenth century. Where for previous generations Indian medicine could only be sinful, blasphemous, too terrible to be reproduced and too dire to be (consciously) imitated, for Catlin's kind Indian medicine, while still gross and uncouth in actual practice, formed in its genteel appropriation a veritable *rite de passage* of the individual, and national, character. As Philip Deloria puts it, "to understand the various ways Americans have contested and constructed national identities, we must constantly return to the original mysteries of Indianness," which "provided impetus and precondition for the creative assembling of an ultimately unassemblable American identity."[4] Thus, as in Catlin's lecture-hall and salon tours, patrons paid for the experiential (and in some cases material) possession of Indian artifacts, costumes, simulacra, and performers. At the same time, by consuming these commodified objects, persons, and performances, audiences were prompted to invest themselves in the spirit of the Indian, to become its repository or embodiment. Distilled, bottled, and swallowed by whites, Indian medicine—whether as liquid potation or as spirit force—became a tonic that braced the white nation, recaptured its essence, secured its right of place. In Catlin's case, the relationship between the staging and selling of Indian spirits was particularly intimate and intricate: for the entertainer's claim to fame rested on his purportedly having been honored with the title of *Te-ho-pe-nee Wash-ee* or "medicine white man" by the Mandans, for whom, he said, his image-capturing art represented a mystery far greater than theirs. As such, his self-proclaimed initiation into Indian sacred space was parlayed into a performance in which spirituality and spectacle, shaman and showman, blurred in a peculiar expression of the nineteenth-century cult of Indianness. In Catlin's show space as in countless others, Indian sacred performance was profaned: stripped of its sacred quality, transplanted to masquerades and marketplaces, and transformed into the titillating, totemic object of white American identity.

Traditionally, the explosion of white Indian play in the nineteenth century has been glossed in terms of a simple, and seemingly natural, causal relationship: into the vacuum left by the removal of real Indians poured the gaseous bubbles of white "Indians."[5] Yet however tempting this reading, Catlin's case should instruct us in skepticism. Though the artist insisted that Indian peoples in toto, and the Mandans in particular, had succumbed to the adverse forces of civilization—the latter, in his words, holding "nowhere an existence on earth" after an 1837 smallpox epidemic—it becomes evident that it was Catlin's *need* to represent himself as the sole and uncontested heir to (and handler of) the Indians' spirit that determined his representation of Indian peoples, performers, and performances as absent.[6] For not only was

Catlin quite simply wrong on both counts—neither Indians as a body nor the Mandans as a tribe had vanished in his time[7]—but his claims of Indian evanescence were fundamental to the processes of desacralization in which he participated, processes that sought to engross Indian healers, ceremonies, ritual objects, and sacred sites in a quest to deliver Indian medicine to his own kind. Like many an artist, ethnographer, and exhibitor to follow, Catlin relied on the illusion of representational totality to pull off his effects, and such an illusion could not be validated if the original bearers of the medicine he was vending had *not* vanished. So cause and effect are confused in his works and in the critical literature that follows: for all the conceptual and material damage that people like Catlin did to Indian sacred performance, we must resist furthering that damage, resist treating Indian sacred performance as the superseded relic Catlin claimed it to be. As David Mazel notes, "Catlin cannot, in a book that is after all *about* Indians, banish [them] entirely," and thus "the repressed native presence remains perilously close to the surface," erupting, as his okipa ellipsis intimates, to thwart the incursions of the white trafficker.[8]

And as such, the okipa suggests an alternative reading of nineteenth-century white medicine play. Rather than supposing the player's freedom from the sacred performances he or she assumes, this reading starts from the premise that the player bears a relationship to, or—better—a dependence on, those performances. According to this line of reasoning, white Indian play, far from being immune to Indian medicine, is deeply and powerfully informed by it: the peoples on whose supposed absence white Indian performers ground their acts are the peoples whose central and ongoing participation in, opposition to, and revision of those acts underlie, and belie, the white performer's authority. And just as the erasure of Indian sacred performance constitutes the central claim of white medicine play, so does the restoration of Indian sacred performance constitute the central claim of the medicine bundle: the claim that each performance exists not in isolation but through the interaction of multiple, competing, interpenetrating performances. To quote Joseph Roach on the intercultural foundations of American performance, though the acts of displacement that ground the production of white identity "conceptually eras[e] indigenous populations," these acts simultaneously "carry within them the memory of otherwise forgotten substitutions," for the "vast scale of the project of whiteness—and the scope of the contacts among cultures it required—limited the degree to which its foils could be eradicated from the memory of those who had the deepest motivation and the surest means to forget them."[9] Catlin and his kin cannot do away with Indian sacred performance, for the nature of their quest means that their own acts will be incorporated within the medicine bundle, will emerge from this intercultural, performative meeting ground.

Catlin's life and works thus provide particularly productive sites within which to examine both Euro-American attempts to strip Indian medicine from its indigenous, sacred contexts and the ways in which white medicine was involved in, inextricable from, and indeed constituted by those contexts. In seeking, as Roach puts it, both "to embody and to replace" their originals, to conjure themselves "into illusory fullness of being by acting out what they think they are not," white Americans achieved otherwise than they intended.[10] They became not possessors of the Indians' medicine but, more ambiguously, possessed of that medicine. Exploring Catlin's works thus demonstrates that deep into the nineteenth century, Euro-Americans and Native Americans remained locked in a struggle for the meaning, control, and use of Indian sacred performance, a struggle in which both parties grounded their being on the absent presence of the other.

## Medicine Show

> *"Yes, yes; it is not every imitator that knows natur may be outdone easier than she is equalled."*
> —Natty Bumppo *on playacting the medicine man, in James Fenimore Cooper,* The Last of the Mohicans *(1826)*

Catlin's multiple artistic performances—verbal, visual, and *vivant*—span a long and (to use his own favorite adjective) toilsome career. Indeed, in his case, it is anything but a cliché to say that his life and art were inseparable, for the artist made sure the two would be seen as such. Notoriously and, it seems, intentionally slipshod in itemizing his activities and whereabouts, Catlin encouraged the reading of his career as a nonstop, rollicking road show, always in flux and in the process of fine-tuning, none of it to be held too closely to account or isolated from the total effect. A frustrated lawyer turned failed portraitist in 1820s Philadelphia and New York, Catlin had snatched an opportunity in 1830 (the year of the Indian Removal Act) to travel among the western tribes, whose visages, costume, and ways of life had not yet been fixed in the popular mind as the pan-Indian norm.

Throughout the 1830s, Catlin mounted a series of western tours during which he amassed his canvases of Indian personages and performances, totaling roughly five hundred images and representing approximately fifty tribes, including Pawnees, Sioux, Crows, Blackfeet, Osages, Choctaws, Comanches, Assiniboines, Omahas, Kiowas, Sauks, Ojibwas, Tuscaroras, Cherokees, and Seminoles. In 1832, he had the good fortune to visit the Mandan villages on the Upper Missouri and there to record white America's fullest textual and graphic depiction of the occult okipa; four years later, he was among the first white artists to view and paint the sacred red pipestone quarry of the Santee Sioux. Among the Indian notables who sat for Catlin were the Seneca orator Red Jacket, the Shawnee prophet Tenskwatawa, Principal Chief of the Cherokee Nation John Ross, Sauk rivals Keokuk and Black Hawk, and, most famously, the imprisoned Seminole leader Osceola, who died mere hours after his audience with Catlin. When Catlin concluded his travels in 1837, he seemed poised to make a killing among eastern audiences and—his ultimate hope—to secure congressional approval for the purchase of his truly national artistic undertaking.

For a brief time, Catlin seemed to make headway toward these goals: his works were well received during stops in New York, Albany, Boston, Philadelphia, Pittsburgh, and Cincinnati, and his petitions garnered the support of Whig heavyweights Henry Clay and Daniel Webster. Yet in 1839—whether hoping to force the issue or seeing the writing on the wall after his lobbying failed to bear fruit—Catlin crated his canvases and set sail for London. There, finding himself in competition with such lifetime showmen as Barnum and his diminutive, sprightly drawing card, Tom Thumb, Catlin cast about for ways to advertise and supplement his Gallery: publishing *Letters and Notes* on subscription, hiring white performers to act out scenes of Indian life, and finally staging the living alternates of his painted simulacra in the form of parties of Ojibwa and Iowa dancers. None of these novelties, however, ensured a steady business, and Catlin gradually sank into debt. Personal tragedy next overtook him: his wife died in 1845, his only son in 1848; every bit as devastating, his beloved Gallery was sold in 1851 after repeated motions for its purchase had been tabled or defeated in Congress. In the last twenty years of his life, Catlin undertook a flurry of trips—to California, Mexico, and South America—that produced additional, though largely ignored, paintings and cartoons; authored a handful of publications on subjects ranging from sleep disorders to antediluvian geography; tilted with the nation's leading ethnologist, Henry Rowe Schoolcraft, over the authenticity of his okipa representations; and, at last, gained a berth for himself in the Smithsonian in 1871, one year before his death and ten years before the Institution finally purchased his Gallery. In his own life, Indian medicine had been the source of both triumph and disaster; it had made and, in the end, unmade him.

In their various permutations, as well as in their overarching thematics and theatrics, Catlin's productions unite all of the dominant public forums in which antebellum Americans saw fit to convey and consume Indian sacred performance: the medicine show, the ethnologic museum, and the Indian drama. (The late century spectacle of the Wild West show, which—like Catlin's acts—combined all three forums but—unlike Catlin's—achieved the notoriety of a mass-market juggernaut, will be addressed in a later chapter.) In each of these (themselves overlapping) performance spaces, Indian-white relations were framed in particular contexts of power, visualized, and more to the point realized, in participatory exchanges between audience and exhibitor that turned Indian medicine into a desirable, manageable, and salable commodity. Each of these performances, then, relied at once on cultural fulfillment—on a principally Euro-American audience that bore a certain relationship of authority toward the Indians—and on cultural lack—on the same audience perceiving itself to be in need of some essential quality that could be met through the consumption of Indian-themed spectacle or the merchandise affiliated with it. In addition, and for my purposes definitively, all of these performances relied on the notion of the achieved or impending disappearance of the Indians and thus on the presumed desuetude of the original sacred performances of which these shows served as reconstructions or replacements. All of these shows, of course, contributed to the loss they mourned: not only did all three deny the presence of Indians save as tutelary vestiges, but the medicine show bastardized Indian healing practices, the museum made a living despoiling Indian sacred materials, and the drama sanitized and glorified the conquest of Indian sacred space. Removing Indian sacred performance from its own contexts and reproducing it as reified object or essence, these shows announced that whites were free to partake of the Indian spirit because the Indians in whom such medicine power had originally been vested were hastening toward oblivion.

Of the various performances, the aptly named Indian medicine show most directly illustrates the promise of white renewal through the consumption of a portable, and potable, Indian essence. In the nostrums sold at such venues, white customers literally imbibed what they took to be the healing remedies of Indian medical wisdom. The roots of the medicine show lay in the colonial tradition of herbal and botanical healing that, some scholars suggest, may have blossomed from early contacts between Indians and Europeans. Even an inveterate foe of shamanistic healing such as Cotton Mather found occasion to praise Indian herbal treatments, which he claimed had effected cures that "are truly stupendous."[11] During the Revolutionary period, physicians such as Benjamin Smith Barton carried on the quest for knowledge of the Indians' healing arts, asking eagerly, "What treasures of medicine may not be expected from a people, who although destitute of the lights of science, have discovered the properties of some of the most inestimable medicines with which we are acquainted?" Whatever their basis in scientific theory and observation, these early inquiries into Indian medicine were buttressed by the primitivist notion, articulated in 1774 by Barton's colleague Benjamin Rush, that the Indians, who "obey the gentle appetites of nature," were free of the diseases that plagued the besotted members of civilized communities: "may we not look for a season when fevers, the natural diseases of the human body, will be lost in an inundation of artificial diseases, brought on by the modish practices of civilization?"[12] The terms of this contrast—the natural and healthy versus the artificial and wretched—persisted into Catlin's time, with whites identifying Indian medicine as a wellspring of vitality in which the civilized had only to immerse themselves to be healed.

In the early nineteenth century, popular health journals took up the chorus. "The natural appetites of man," they counseled their clientele, had "become perverted from their original simplicity, by an improper indulgence," and "liberty and happiness thus sacrificed by a departure from the plain and obvious laws" of Nature. What differentiated the nineteenth-century hunt for Indian healing from that of earlier times was both its scope and its spin. No longer did white practitioners claim simply to employ Indian medicines, but increasing numbers, as Virgil J. Vogel notes, professed "to have absorbed their knowledge directly from contact with the Indians" or even "to be at least partly of Indian descent." Lone white Indian healers had appeared during the eighteenth century: according to Richardson Wright, the earliest known patent medicine, a 1711 cure for consumption, was branded "Tuscarora Rice," while a late century Massachusetts "squaw," Peter Benes has learned, carried on an itinerant practice in which she claimed "the ability to cure cancers with an external application and internal administration of herbs." By the antebellum period, the phenomenon of Euro-Americans marketing their pills and powders—as well as their persons—under the banner of Indian healing had assumed the proportions of a full-fledged cultural craze. Products as varied in name (though probably identical in composition and effectiveness) as Indian Expectorant, Red Jacket Stomach Bitters, Old Sachem Bitters, and Indian Compound were sold through catalogues and itinerant salespeople, while books as uniform in both title and contents as Peter Smith's *The Indian Doctor's Dispensatory* (1813), Jonas Rishel's *The Indian Physician* (1828), S. H. Selman's *The Indian Guide to Health* (1836), Robert L. Foster's *The North American Indian Doctor* (1838), William Daily's *The Indian Doctor's Practice of Medicine* (1848), and James Cooper's *The Indian Doctor's Receipt Book* (1855) rolled off New England and midwestern presses and were available for purchase at traveling carnivals.[13] The confessional autobiography of one antebellum "Indian" healer, Henry Tufts, gives some inkling of the true relationship characters of his stamp bore toward the Indians they claimed as tutors. Ridiculing as "not much removed from a farce" the Native "ceremonies" he—farcically—exploits for gain, Tufts reveals the cynical uses to which Indian medicine was put by its white practitioners. As Herman Melville recognized when he featured the Indian root-and-"yarb" doctor as one of the iterations of his protean, scurrilous confidence man, Indian medicine was big business, and big bunco, in the nineteenth-century culture of sickness and health.[14]

If Catlin's full-fledged stage show, which included costumed Indian performers and the (sometimes costumed) artist as combination tour guide and barker, mimicked the medicine show in form, it likewise echoed the medicine show in function and philosophy. For clearly enough, more was being sold at such venues than bottles of snake oil. What was being sold, at the same time and as a necessary ingredient in securing the customer's faith in chemically inert remedies, were two seemingly contradictory but actually interdependent messages. On the one hand, the medicine show played on deeply rooted convictions about primitive health versus civilized sickness. On the other hand, it touched off equally staunch beliefs about Indian cultures' enfeeblement when confronted with Euro-American cultural prowess (or, as evidenced by the wildfire spread of epidemic diseases among Indian peoples, with Euro-American maladies). "Society has advanced upon them like one of those withering airs that will sometimes breathe desolation over a whole region of fertility," Washington Irving wrote in "Traits of Indian Character" (1819). "It has enervated their strength, multiplied their diseases, and superinduced upon their original barbarity the low vices of artificial life." In an early and glowing review of Catlin's Gallery, James Hall applauded the artist's decision to ignore such dissipated, artificial Indians and to focus on the original Indian "as he exists in his own wide plains": "There is a curse in our touch that withers them. Whenever we come in contact they perish, or are contaminated—they are swept from the face of the earth, or live in degradation."[15]

Catlin's own spiel was perfectly in keeping with this twinned theme of Indian sickness and vigor. Dressed in a Blackfoot medicine man's castoff robe, parading portraits and pantomimes of robust Indian bodies while citing the Mandans' supposed extinction as a synecdoche for the baleful effects of civilization on Indian peoples everywhere, Catlin ballyhooed the therapeutic value (for whites) of contact with a people to whom such contact brought disease, disaster, and death. In this light, it is unsurprising that in 1861 Catlin, his exhibiting days past and his Gallery held hostage to creditors, should publish the quack-healing treatise *The Breath of Life; or, Mal-Respiration* (cutely retitled *Shut Your Mouth and Save Your Life* in later printings), a hand-printed pamphlet that would have sold briskly at a traveling medicine show. Here, noting the "healthy condition and physical perfection of [the Indians], in their primitive state, as contrasted with the deplorable mortality, the numerous diseases and deformities, in civilized communities," Catlin traced the Indians' exemplary health to the fact that they "strictly adhere to Nature's law" in sleeping with their mouths closed. By contrast, civilized sleepers' "enervating and unnatural habit" of sleeping gape-mouthed he blames for idiocy, croup, fatigue, nightmare, decay of the lungs, curvature of the spine—in short, the whole range of afflictions that supposedly beset his fellows. If this balmy diagnosis seems to indicate that, in his later life, Catlin, wracked by sorrow over the loss of his family and Gallery, had gone off the deep end, in truth *Breath of Life* completes the arc of his career as medicine-show front man—or, put another way, without a Gallery to muddy the picture, his medicine-show bent could at last appear in its barest guise. Through all his whoppers and showstoppers, Catlin was hot on the trail of an elusive Indian elixir, a saving residue that could be culled before the "dissipations and vices" of civilization had wholly "corrupted" the original Indian. Thus his conviction in *Breath of Life* that Indian habits "might be adopted with good effect in civilized life," promising a "*Re-generation* of the Human Race," was but the capstone of his lifetime faith in Indian medicine as the vanquished savage's deathbed bequest to his civilized usurpers.[16]

Viewed in these terms, as an inverse exchange of white for Indian health—or as an emptying of Indian medicine's sacred contents and contexts for Euro-American consumption—the medicine show can be seen not merely as a discrete phenomenon but as the medium underlying a host of practices that appear to have little to do with Indian remedies in their narrow sense. What binds these performances, rather, is their claim to have assimilated the Indians' spirit as a panacea for the society that has undermined and overwhelmed once-sound Indian cultures. Consider, in this light, the testimonials concerning Indian medicine from another, better-known Henry T., who writes in *Walden* (1854): "Those plants of whose greenness withered we make herb tea for the sick, serve but a humble use, and are most employed by quacks." The remedy? "If, then, we would indeed restore mankind by truly Indian, botanic, magnetic, or natural means, let us first be as simple and well as Nature ourselves, dispel the clouds which hang over our own brows, and take up a little life into our pores." Though enough of a patrician to disdain the street shows that fleeced the unthinking multitude, Thoreau too dispenses primitivist bromides, prescribing Indian medicine as the cure for civilized society's sickness of body and soul. Nor does Thoreau (his multiple admonitions in *Walden* notwithstanding) recommend this course solely for himself. Rather, so great is his enthusiasm for Indian medicine, the "tonic of wildness" that promises to revivify the withered roots of civilization,[17] that in *The Maine Woods* (1864), he recommends its repackaging on a national scale:

not only for strength, but for beauty, the poet must, from time to time, travel the logger's path and the Indian's trail, to drink at some new and more bracing fountain of the Muses, far in the recesses of the wilderness.

The kings of England formerly had their forests "to hold the king's game," for sport or food, sometimes destroying villages to create or extend them; and I think that they were impelled by a true instinct. Why should not we, who have renounced the king's authority, have our national preserves, where no villages need be destroyed, in which the bear and panther, and some even of the hunter race, may still exist, and not be "civilized off the face of the earth,"—our forests, not to hold the king's game merely, but to hold and preserve the king himself also, the lord of creation,—not for idle sport or food, but for inspiration and our own true recreation? or shall we, like villains, grub them all up, poaching on our own national domains?[18]

For the poet to promote this nationalist utopia, Indians must be doubly erased: not only are their habitations excluded from Thoreau's reckoning of what constitutes a village, but their cultures are to be, if not literally destroyed, then radically restructured as objects of white vassalage and the white tourist trade. In a spiritualized version of the commodity fetishism the Concord seer most scorns, the essence of a vanishing race of natural men is stoppered as a renewable resource for white sufferers (or a tonic for white sufferers' renewal). "I am not sure but all that would tempt me to teach the

Indian my religion would be his promise to teach me *his*," Thoreau enthuses upon his discovery in the Maine woods of the transcendentalist equivalent of a gold mine: chunks of phosphorescent wood that he takes to represent the indigenous "spirits" he has been tracking all along. In his assumption of these spirits, Thoreau may be seen not only as a practitioner but as a perfecter of the medicine show, a pitchman who to this day has convinced white buyers that his medicine will salve or save their souls, even if what ails them are the acts of spiritual subjugation he is selling.[19]

Whether Thoreau knew it or not, his national park project had been pioneered by Catlin a few years before the poet-naturalist traversed the Maine wilderness, and with a virtually identical rationale. Closing a particularly bitter rebuke of the civilized cupidity that is desolating Indian communities, Catlin suggests a way of salvaging the essential Indian for posterity: "they *might* in future be seen, (by some great protecting policy of government) preserved in their pristine beauty and wildness, in a *magnificent park*, where the world could see for ages to come, the native Indian in his classic attire, galloping his wild horse, with sinewy bow, and shield and lance, amid the fleeting herds of elks and buffaloes. What a beautiful and thrilling specimen for America to preserve and hold up to the view of her refined citizens and the world, in future ages! A *nation's Park*, containing man and beast, in all the wild and freshness of their nature's beauty!" (1:261–62). Like Thoreau, Catlin rests a forward-thinking environmentalist impulse on a banal, retrograde premise of racial arrogation. As his talk of preserving Indian "specimens" makes clear, this mummified medicine show—what Mark David Spence calls "a monstrous combination of outdoor museum, human zoo, and wild animal park"—sustains Indian life principally so that the refined citizens of the white nation do not, through overrefinement, lose touch with the invigorating power of unspoiled wild(er)ness.[20] Catlin's national park, like Thoreau's, thus represents a particularly subtle (if sizable) commodification of Indian performance: "the native Indian in his classic attire" is folded into white national identity, yielding (in Thoreau's phrase) "our own true recreation."

Considerable debate has been expended, over the course of Catlin's career and in the years following it, on the question of whether the man was sincere or a hypocrite, a progressive who identified with Indians or a huckster who despoiled them. Where some critics, such as Richard Drinnon, maintain that Catlin "never looked on native peoples as so many red objects to be consumed or exploited for enormous personal gain," others, such as Catlin's contemporary, the Ojibwa missionary Peter Jones, dismissed the

artist as "a thorough blue Yankee [who] makes great professions of attachment for the Indians" solely to line his pocket. But as activities such as his national park scheme make clear, one does not need to choose between Catlin
the sympathizer or swindler, advocate or advertiser. If, as Philip Deloria aptly
puts it, Indian play "modeled a characteristically American kind of domination in which the exercise of power was hidden, denied, qualified, or
mourned," then Catlin, a characteristic American if ever there was one, can
swindle the Indians through sympathy and mourn their passing while reap-
ing its rewards. Brian Dippie writes that "Catlin might be emotionally involved with the Indians, but like their most unfeeling usurpers he could be
coldly selfish." It might be better to say that Catlin's involvement with the Indians was of a piece with his selfishness; to identify with them was for him,
as for the majority of his fellows, to make off with Indian medicine for his
own profit.[21]

Toward this end, it is plain that the most vital application to which
Catlin put Indian medicine was as a balm for his own ailing artistic career.
The artist himself was relatively frank about the role an idealized Indian
essence played in his professional regeneration. Though silent about the financial woes and critical scorn he had suffered as a miniaturist in Philadelphia and New York, he does provide a revealing, if probably apocryphal,
anecdote to explain his pursuit of Indian subjects: "my mind was continually
reaching for some branch or enterprise of the art, on which to devote a whole
life-time of enthusiasm; when a delegation of some ten or fifteen noble and
dignified-looking Indians, from the wilds of the 'Far West,' suddenly arrived
in the city, arrayed and equipped in all their classic beauty,—with shield and
helmet,—with tunic and manteau,—tinted and tasselled off, exactly for the
painter's palette!" (1:2). In Catlin's recollection, the allure of these pristine
primitives proved irresistible: "Black and blue cloth and civilization are destined, not only to veil, but to obliterate the grace and beauty of Nature. Man,
in the simplicity and loftiness of his nature, unrestrained and unfettered by
the disguises of art, is surely the most beautiful model for the painter,—and
the country from which he hails is unquestionably the best study or school
of the arts in the world" (1:2). Catlin's newfound resolve to travel West, "thus
snatching from a hasty oblivion what could be saved for the benefit of posterity" (1:3), appears in this origin story as a quest for Indian medicine to heal
the civilized sickness that has overcome Catlin's, and his country's, art—a
quest for an art without art, without artifice, artfulness, the artificial.

That quest, as John Cawelti notes, appealed widely to artists of Catlin's generation: "one of the most important and vital images of the West was as a place where one might escape from the artificial and corrupting boundaries of society into a spontaneous and open relationship with nature." Thus, though few undertook enterprises as ambitious as Catlin's, many, including those of the influential Hudson River school, pictorial historians of the American sublime, subscribed in spirit to the principles Catlin pursued.[22] In seeking out the haunts of unspoiled Nature, this medicine-show truism held, the painter might instill a natural sinew into the stale canons of drawing-room art, and thus experience the plastic rebirth Catlin ascribes to his western odyssey: "I have become so much Indian of late, that my pencil has lost all appetite for subjects that savour of tameness. . . . I take an indescribable pleasure in roaming through Nature's trackless wilds, and selecting my models, where I am free and unshackled by the killing restraints of society; where a painter must modestly sit and breathe away in agony the edge and soul of his inspiration. . . . Of this much I am certain—that amongst these sons of the forest, . . . I have learned more of the essential parts of my art in the three last years, than I could have learned in New York in a life-time" (2:37). Here again, Catlin's ravenous appetite for Indian medicine marks the emergence of a new mode, a new art, a new man. The transfusion into the painter-patient of that most essential marrow of a vanishing race, its wildness, inspires Catlin not only to reproduce Indian subjects for posterity but also to embody those subjects in his own person: "I have become so much Indian of late." In this respect, Catlin's slapdash style, which has rightly been attributed to his frenzied production schedule and technical deficiencies, at the same time suggests his attempt to distill an artless tonic for the benefit of civilized art. His hasty brush-strokes, raw pigments, limited palette, and contour-only human frames picture the Indians as unpolished, untainted, instilling new vigor into the ordered mannerisms of the studio. His painting of the Pawnee La-doo-ke-a, for instance, one of his few seated figures to be framed full-length, consists of a well-rendered but shockingly red face and neck shading into the cartoon outlines of a classically proportioned body, the very symbol of an unvarnished (but vanished) race that, "devoid of the deformities of art" (1:16), offers up its unblemished form for the recovery of its de-formed conquerors.

In order for Catlin to advance this aesthetic twist on the medicine show, to represent the Indians as raw material to be sublimated to the nation's art, certain preconditions must be met. Foremost of these is the Indians' inability to produce art themselves. Not only are natural men precluded from practicing anything that smacks of the artificial, but the presence of artistic conventions in Indian society might challenge the white aficionado's claim to representational authority. In pursuing the theme of Indian artlessness, Catlin's thoughts flow within a channel well laid by others; removalist testimonials from his decade of western travel, for example, pronounced the Indian unable to "imitate the arts of his civilized neighbors."[23] In Catlin's case, the certainty that Indians, originally lacking art, can acquire the rudiments of it only at the cost of forfeiting their authenticity—and ultimately their lives—leads to his censuring its merest appearance in Indian society. Thus, reviling the "half-polished (and half-breed) Cherokees and Choctaws, with all their finery and art" (2:82), he insists that those who have left the pure state of Nature are not "civilized" but "*cicatrized*" (2:101), scarred beyond a possibility of reconstruction. Though whites may—or must—imbibe Indian medicine to ensure their own health, a reverse act of cultural osmosis, by which Indians take on the white man's medicine, is in Catlin's view invariably fatal.

The fullest statement of Catlin's aversion to Indians crossing the nature-art frontier appears in his painting and preachifying on the Assiniboine brave Wi-jun-jon, Pigeon's Egg Head (or, properly translated, the Light). As Catlin tells the tale, this man traveled to the nation's capitol in search of the secret of white power. The only painting in *Letters and Notes* to narrate a series of events, a diptych representing an unaffected, westward-facing warrior arrayed in his native garb back-to-back with a debauched, eastward-facing dandy bedecked in civilized duds, the painting of Wi-jun-jon graphically conveys the absolute opposition between Natural Man and Artful Man, and consequently the absolute folly of Indians' dabbling in the white man's medicine. This opposition is driven home when, noting that Wi-jun-jon had "travelled the giddy maze, and beheld amid the buzzing din of civil life, their tricks of art" (2:196), Catlin grimly notes that the hapless fellow was murdered upon his return home by his distrustful, but still unsullied, people. Even granting that, here and elsewhere, Catlin's purpose may be a polemical one, that of exposing the abuses visited upon the unsuspecting Indians in the name of civilization, his allegory is congenial to the rhetoric and practices he may be trying to critique. That is to say, viewing the Indian as a purely a-cultural being—"a beautiful blank," as he comments in each volume of *Letters and Notes* (1:184), on which "anything might be written, if the right mode were taken" (2:245)—Catlin prepares the Indian for inscription or conscription by the civilization that so utterly ruins the natural man. The logic of the medicine show dictates that Catlin, though condoning the spiritual draining of Indian life, must damn its material base—for only in their undiluted, unmixed state can Indians provide succor for the civilized nation whose infirmities deplete them.[24]

The affinity of Catlin's paintings with the rhythms of the medicine show is further evident in another staple of his art, one that has received less attention than his portraits: his western landscapes. Though his vistas of the bluffs and valleys of the Upper Missouri and the grasslands of the northern and southern Plains look amateurish when contrasted with the dramatic chiaroscuros of the Hudson River school, they achieve a similar project of natural or national identity formation through the erasure and assimilation of the Indian presence. Depicting a land invitingly open and green, dotted with solitary dwarf Indians and—thanks to his invariable choice of visionary high-angle perspectives—affording the civilized eye an unencumbered prospect of the far horizon, Catlin's images, in a textbook example of what Albert Boime terms the "magisterial gaze," promise release from the ugliness of physical conquest in favor of a rhapsodic communion with the spirit of the land. As Gareth John writes, Catlin's landscapes "contributed to an imperial discourse on the Native American West," promoting "a view of the West as prospect, as the site of future national expansion and settlement, as land to be colonized by the westward advance of 'civilization.'" If, then, Catlin's work "embodies a deep ambivalence concerning his country's imperialist design on western lands and, in particular, its treatment of the Indian tribes both east and west of the Mississippi," such ambivalence can be viewed in the same light as that which surrounds his national park proposal or his tale of Wi-jun-jon: as the necessary melancholy of the medicine show, which required Indian dis-ease to secure white health. Indeed, in this light his landscapes may be seen as a visual accompaniment to—or even promotional brochure for—his projected nation's park: reducing Indians to microscopic "specimens" in a land open to white gambles and gambols, Catlin's landscapes graphically depict the Indian's vanishing as the precondition for the white nation's recreation.[25]

In characterizing Indians as "specimens" to be displayed (and displaced) by white painters, profiteers, and prospectors, Catlin's work falls in line with another of the major forums in which Indian medicine was exhibited and consumed by whites: the Indian museum, or more broadly, the newfound science of ethnology to which the museum gave visual, architectural, and popular embodiment. The premier midcentury statement of ethnologic science, Lewis Henry Morgan's *League of the Iroquois* (1851), formalized the view of Indian culture as a "beautiful blank" that *Letters and Notes* had intimated a decade before: "Civilization is aggressive, as well as progressive—a positive state of society, attacking every obstacle, overwhelming every lesser agency, and searching out and filling up every crevice, both in the moral and physical world; while Indian life is an unarmed condition, a negative state, without inherent vitality, and without powers of resistance."[26] What ethnology proposed to do, therefore, was to fill in the blanks, (re)producing for civilized audiences the essence of Indianness before the positive force of civilization obliterated all trace of the essential Indian.

Though the sedate, scholarly displays of ethnology may seem distant from the riotous chicanery of the medicine show, in point of fact ethnology originated in, and continued throughout the nineteenth century to draw inspiration from, comparable forms of white Indian performance. As Philip Deloria shows, Morgan came to his profession and his masterwork through a fraternal society, the Cayugas (founded in 1842 from the remnants of an older society, the Gordian Knot, and later renamed the New Confederacy of the Iroquois), that paralleled Catlin's exhibitions of the same period. "Garbed in Indian costume," the members of Morgan's troupe "called one another by Indian names" as they imagined themselves the spiritual heirs to the Iroquois on whose lands they stood. Gaining admission to the order, Deloria reveals, involved what Morgan termed an "Inindianation" ritual, in which "the spirits of departed Indian fathers" recited a lachrymose history of Indian decline and informed new members that "the only way to placate the mournful Indian shades" was for their white substitutes "to preserve their memory and customs." The ceremony concluded "by offering the initiate complete redemption and a new life through mystic rebirth as an Indian child."[27]

This textbook case of white medicine performance can, of course, be written off (in William Fenton's words) as "boyish enthusiasm," unrelated to Morgan's mature inquiries. Yet Morgan remained affiliated with the New Confederacy throughout his researching and writing of *League of the Iroquois*, on one occasion hosting Henry Schoolcraft, who read an address pronouncing America "the tomb of the Red man," sacred spoils for the white inheritor's reincarnation. Not surprisingly, then, the principles of "Inindianation" reemerge in *League* itself: in Morgan's poetic laments on Indian decline ("Obscurity next advanced with stealthy mien, and quickly folding the incidents of this sylvan pageant in her dusky mantle, she bore them, with their associations, their teachings, and their remembrances, into the dark realm of Oblivion") as well as in his hints that the vanishing Indian spirit may be reclaimed and displayed by white science: "if the sustaining faith, and the simple worship of the Iroquois are ever fully explored, and carefully elucidated, they will form a more imperishable monument to the Indian, than is afforded in the purity of his virtues, or in the mournfulness of his destiny." Morgan's medicine play thus appears to have shaped his entree into Indian society not only at the outset—for it was his activities heading the New Confederacy that led to his introduction to principal informant Ely S. Parker—but also in the output: given the close acquaintanceship and apprenticeship with living Indians from which *League* sprang, it is particularly striking that the book still leans so heavily on the stereotypical drama of Indian evanescence and white inheritance.[28] Morgan's life and work thus suggest that the science of ethnology—and the museum that housed its products—constituted a performance space in which Euro-Americans not only preserved Indian manners and customs but enacted the manners and customs of the medicine show: coming into intimate contact with, and departing in the symbolic or material possession of, the fading spirit of Indian medicine.

It comes as no surprise that another of the Indians' intimates, George Catlin, deeply—if, as always, ambivalently—was immersed in the discourse and practice of this new science. The most obvious example of his ethnologic aspirations—and embarrassments—is *O-Kee-Pa: A Religious Ceremony and Other Customs of the Mandans* (1867), published to refute Schoolcraft's charges that his okipa interlude was a fabrication, and addressed to the "gentlemen of science who study, not the *properties* of man, but *Man*." But Catlin's efforts to gain admission to the museum were lifelong, inseparable from his Indian infatuation. To begin with, not only did the nature of his activities make him as much curator of Indian lives as captor of their likenesses, but his exhibitionary practices dovetailed perfectly with those of ethnologic display. His penchant for imagining Indians as installations—as "living models" (1:2), "living monuments" (1:16), or (once again) "specimens" (1:22)—found expression in his variegated (and, as receipts grew thin, increasingly gimmicky) staging of Indian images, objects, and impersonations. As Catlin described his premier in London's Egyptian Hall, the motley appurtenance surrounding the main exhibit transformed his Gallery into a museum artifact: "The main hall was of immense length, and contained upon its walls 600 portraits and other paintings . . . and also many thousands of articles of their manufacture, consisting of costumes, weapons, &c. &c., forming together a pictorial history of those tribes, to preserve as a record of them, to be perpetuated long after their extinction. In the middle of the room I had erected also a wigwam (or lodge) brought from the country of the Crows. . . . " Likewise, the *tableaux vivants* Catlin arranged once interest in his Gallery started to flag signify the translation of Indian lives into the equivalent of museum displays: clusters of costumed white players rigged into scenes of warfare, ceremony, and domesticity, these literal living monuments represented bodily forms of ethnologic exhibition. By coming into contact with these taxidermic dummies, white audiences were presumably able, in a manner similar to Morgan's "Inindianation" recruits, to take the Indians' place or the Indians' trace: as one reviewer wrote, this "museum of Indian curiosities" would "serve as useful and agreeable souvenirs" to visitors "already familiar with the actual specimens."[29]

If, moreover, Catlin's museological collection paralleled the medicine show in its mechanisms of display, so too did it recall the medicine show in its manner of acquisition. Detailing the continental acts of plunder that spanned the nineteenth century, the period of ethnology's greatest and unchecked growth, George W. Stocking Jr. makes the obvious but easily forgotten point that the collecting of exotic objects situates the museum within a history of "imperial domination": "Since the objects thrown in the way of observers in museums were once those of others, there are relations implicit in the constitution of the museum which may be defined as relations of 'power': the expropriation (not only in an abstract etymological sense, but sometimes in the dirty sense of theft or pillage) of objects from actors in a particular context of space, time, and meaning and their appropriation (or making one's own) by observers in another."[30] Such acts of ex- and appropriation were fundamental to the medicine show, and they were likewise Catlin's stock-in-trade: along with picture taking, his western tours were marked by orgies of looting to outfit his exhibitions. Though at regular intervals he turns indignant at the scavenger hunts that fed the ethnologist's craft and the public's curiosity, as when he decries the Indians' having been forced to surrender "their bones to be dug up and strewed about the fields, or to be labelled in our Museums" (2:256), one can hardly be impressed by this judgment when he himself makes a practice of ransacking Indian burial sites "for the use and benefit of the scientific world" (1:91), or when, on the page facing the previously mentioned recrimination, there appears a plate representing "a Mandan robe in Catlin collection." In his account of his European tours, likewise, his outrage that "thousands of Indian graves" have been "thrown open by sacrilegious hands for the skulls and trinkets they enclosed" clashes with his loving enumeration of the Indian paraphernalia in his own potpourri, which includes "Skulls from different tribes, of very great interest."[31] Like the medicine show, the ethnologic collection made both available and necessary a steady stream of Indian dead for white perusal and—at least in programs, reproductions, and souvenirs—purchase.

It is possible, indeed, to see the cross-fertilization of the museum and the medicine show in terms of even more sinister forms of Indian (dis)play. C. Richard King argues that the museum "secured colonial contexts" in ways commensurate with the principal site wherein nineteenth-century Native cultures were simultaneously preserved and subverted: the reservation. As King writes, both "exhibitionary spaces developed as bounded sites of difference, energized by asymmetrical power relations, which confined Native Americans, seized their property, and constrained their cultural practices and precepts within EuroAmerican categories." Nor was this resemblance simply coincidental, for the museum relied explicitly on Euro-American military and administrative authority. To cite only one instance with particular relevance to Catlin, his first and firmest supporter, William Clark of the Lewis and Clark expedition, maintained a St. Louis residence that doubled, in John Ewers's words, as "an Indian council chamber and a museum," containing not only artifacts but also portraits of Indian dignitaries who came to treat or entreat with Clark. Sometimes visitors and their painted effigies could be hard to distinguish, as in one report of a disciplinary council with the Sauk Indians following their defeat in the Black Hawk war: "The rooms contain, likewise, portraits of the most distinguished Indian chiefs of different nations. General Clarke, with his secretary, was seated opposite to the Indians, who sat in rows along the walls of the apartment," a gallery of living curiosities awaiting their final, formal confinement to canvas, to prison, and ultimately to reservations.[32] Though Catlin preferred to do his work in the field, on numerous occasions he enjoyed such captive audiences: Black Hawk, Tenskwatawa, and Osceola were among the reservation-bound Indian luminaries his association with men such as Clark made available to his brush. Catlin thus benefited from, even as he furthered, the establishment of the bounded sites of difference within which Indian cultures could be contained and—in the manner of the medicine show as well as in a more literal sense—consumed. Whether collecting mementos or men, Catlin duplicated the museum's practice of harvesting endangered Indian artifacts (or art-facts) for the edification and amusement of those who had rendered these cultural materials perishable to begin with.

It is in this respect, in its production for a Euro-American audience of Indian objects and individuals alienated from their sacred origins, that one perceives the deepest resemblance between the ethnologic museum and the medicine show, which resembled Catlin's exhibitions, which resembled both. In his critique of museum culture, James Clifford traces the process whereby exhibits "create the illusion of adequate representation of a world by first cutting objects out of specific contexts. . . . The *making* of meaning in museum classification and display is mystified as adequate *representation*." Museums, in other words, provide tangible support of the medicine show's central conceptual dodge: the wresting of sacred performance from its indigenous contexts and its transformation, through representation, to consumable object. As such, though collectors attribute incontestable authenticity to the works they strip from local settings—an authenticity predicated on the conviction that within no time at all the original will have succumbed to the ravages of history, leaving only the captured object or image to attest to its existence—in reality, Clifford writes, "authenticity is something produced, not salvaged"—or, even more precisely, the authenticity that attaches to such collections is produced by the operation of salvage itself. As Clifford elaborates this process, "Ethnography's disappearing object" is "a rhetorical construct legitimating a representational practice: 'salvage' ethnography. . . . The other is lost, in disintegrating time and space, but saved in the text. . . . The recorder and interpreter of fragile custom is custodian of an essence, unimpeachable witness to an authenticity. (Moreover, since the 'true' culture has always vanished, the salvaged version cannot be easily refuted.)"[33]

This is sounding more and more like Catlin, whose acts of salvage—like his national park scheme or landscape paintings—were utterly reliant on the claim of the Indians' impending disappearance and on his own corresponding representational authority. Hence his and his boosters' obsession with the fidelity of his artworks, an obsession marked by the profusion of certificates affixed to *Letters and Notes* lauding the portraits as "faithful representations" of their lost originals (1:11–13). Vouchers such as these enact the museological shorthand of devising new, authoritative contexts of exhibition that occlude the local contexts within which the represented "specimens" performed, the circumstances of their collection, and—most importantly—the ongoing existence of the peoples from whom they were made. Hence too Catlin's double coups of Osceola's timely death and the Mandans' supposed extermination. Not only did these individual and cultural deaths confirm the baneful influence of civilized sickness on Nature's children, but the former definitively, and the latter at least presumptively, positioned Catlin's portraits as perfect representations, utterly replacing an absent original.[34] Lewis Cass, one of Catlin's early supporters (and, as secretary of war during the thirties, the man who presided over Andrew Jackson's removal policies), praised Catlin's Gallery in terms that buttressed the artist's twin claims of the Indians' evanescence and his own representational authority: "Unfortunately [the Indians] are receding before the advancing tide of our population, and are probably destined, at no distant day, wholly to disappear; but your collection will preserve them, as far as human art can do, and will form the most perfect monument to an extinguished race that the world has ever seen." For his own part, Catlin's most grandiose design, his projected "Museum of Mankind," a bargelike behemoth that would troll the waterways of the world collecting and exhibiting the fragile traces of "declining and vanishing races of man," epitomizes the belief in the imminent disappearance of authentic native culture that keeps such institutions, as it were, afloat.[35] No matter the venue, Catlin hammered away at the same script: mounting displays of pure (because otherwise lost) Indian relics and facsimiles for the benefit of white science, white history, and white identity, he was at the forefront of a museum movement that was rooted in the logic and logistics of the medicine show.

And if this is so of the museum, it is equally so, if not more, of a final forum for the production of ethnologic theater, one that bore a particularly striking resemblance to Catlin's live performances: the Indian drama, the most popular Removal-era example of which was John Augustus Stone's *Metamora; Or, the Last of the Wampanoags* (1829), immortalized by the actor who had solicited its composition, tragedian Edwin Forrest.[36] The origin of the Indian drama lay in the same impulse that gave birth to the Hudson River school (and, to a lesser extent, the museum, particularly in its civic form of the Smithsonian): in all the arts and sciences, the period following the War of 1812 saw an efflorescence of nationalistic feeling manifesting itself in the search for a distinctively American voice and vision. As James Kirke Paulding explained in 1827, the aim of the "native American" drama was to "create an identity of our own," an "original" American character "properly naturalized" to the soil and soul of the land. Yet to achieve such an identity, Paulding counseled, playwrights were to forge an adopted persona—to "personate an original character," in his wacky formulation—via proxy Indianness.[37] John Neal, hoping to stimulate the arrival of an "original" American character on the world stage, issued a similar plea in 1825: "We did hope . . . that some native, bold writer of the woods; a powerful, huge barbarian, without fear, and without reproach, would rise up to the call." Neal dilates:

Why go forth at all, if you may not go forth, in your own shape? . . . Were Tecumseh himself, the great Indian warrior and prophet; were he alive now, we should say to him this,—If you are going to the *city* of London, . . . away with all imitation, with all awkward restraint; away with your white kid gloves, and every other badge of servitude—(for, to *you*, every such thing *is* a badge of servitude)—on with all the rude pomp of your office, with all the barbarious dignity thereof:—Do all this, or keep away. Let your carriage be natural: Bear upon your very forehead, if you may, the sign of power, strange, though it be; the name of your country, savage, though it be. . . . All this we would have urged, if we had come in the way of such a noble creature as Tecumseh; . . . and all of it, we now urge to the writers of America.[38]

In this remarkable, perfervid passage—remarkable not least for its anticipation of two opposed yet inseparable moments in the Catlin mythos, his playing about London in Indian guise and his rebuke of the Indian who has done the reverse, the citified dandy Wi-jun-jon—Neal's vision of the truly natural American dramatist as a counterfeit Indian, rigged up in the "real costume of his tribe," exemplifies the unselfconscious lunacy of American literary nationalism. A decade after Neal's column appeared, Catlin and his nephew followed his prescription to a T. Decked out in chiefly robes borrowed from his collection and having "painted our faces and hands of a copper colour, in close imitation of the colour of the Indian," the two revelers beguiled an unsuspecting audience of British nobles with slapdash renditions of "the wardance and the scalp-dance of the Sioux." In the stagecraft logic of the medicine show, Catlin and company, by passing themselves off as "*real* Indians," secured "our original characters" as Americans."[39]

The folk story surrounding the origin of *Metamora*, the play that incited a flurry of copycat Indian dramas in the 1830s and that provided Shakespearean actor Forrest with his first and most celebrated "native American" role, provides a more extended illustration of the part Indian medicine plays in the Indian drama. According to his late century biographer, William Alger, Forrest—"the first great original American actor," a man "home-born on our soil, intensely national in every nerve" and "thoroughly American"—found in the idealized form of the Indian a spark of recognition and a source of artistic regeneration. "The North American Indian," Alger reflects, "is a picturesque object. . . . The freedom of savages from the diseased vices of a luxurious society, the proud beauty of their free bearing, the relish of their wild liberty with nature, exempt from the artificial burdens and trammels of our complicated and stifling civilization, appeal to the imagination." It is no wonder that Forrest, having fallen in with (if not in love with) a company of Choctaws, assumed the role of Indian understudy before essaying the lead: "He adapted himself to their habits, dressed in their costume, and, as far as he could, took part in all their doings, their smokes, their dances, their hunts, their songs. . . . He seemed to come into contact with the unwritten traditions of the prehistoric time, and to taste the simple freedom that prevailed before so many artificial luxuries, toils, and laws had made such slaves of us all." The culmination of this offstage rehearsal, and the immediate inspiration for Forrest's scripted role of Metamora, occurs when his closest Indian companion, the Choctaw chief Push-ma-ta-ha, consents at his bidding to strip and parade before him. "My God," Alger reports Forrest's transports upon viewing the chief's classic form, "what a contrast he was to some fashionable men I have since seen, half made up of false teeth, false hair, padding, gloves, and spectacles!" Under the trance of Push-ma-ta-ha's remembered perfection—of a body divested of the false covering that so rankled Neal—Forrest is empowered to perform the real: "Never did an actor more thoroughly identify and merge himself with his part than Forrest did in Metamora. He was completely transformed from what he appeared in other characters, and seemed Indian in every particular." Accordingly, "when he came to impersonate Metamora, . . . it was the genuine Indian who was brought upon the stage. . . . [T]he counterfeit was so cunningly copied that it might have deceived nature herself." Indeed, Alger concludes, natural Indians *were* deceived by Forrest's mimicry. When a "delegation of Western Indians" was ushered to a performance of *Metamora*, they "were so excited by the performance that in the closing scene they rose and chanted a dirge in honor of the death of the great chief."[40]

What Forrest has accomplished, in Alger's reconstruction of it, is the miraculous—yet for votaries of the medicine show, essential—act of trumping the actual Indian through a performance so magisterial as to ascend to the real. Through his Catlin-like sojourn among the Indians and, most blatantly, his scrutiny of the stripped-down, bare-bones Indian body, Forrest incorporates into his own flesh and blood the spirit of that native, naked race. In so doing, Forrest claims for himself not only the sexual thrill of ogling the chief's undraped form but also the proprietary rights to the chief's unburdened wildness. Notwithstanding the layers of paint and art, camouflage and makeup necessary to carry off the illusion, Forrest defrauds his way into an open, unmediated relationship to the spirit of the original America(n). When one recalls that all of this reality is staged—the western Indians who applaud Forrest's genuine acts are dramatis personae, while the spellbound savages who, Catlin writes of his European troupes, "advanced to the portraits of their friends and offered them their hands" are, after all, performers—it becomes clear that, for all the condescending talk concerning the Indian's need to "imitate the arts of his civilized neighbors," such imitative arts appealed to the civilized with at least equal force. "Despise not the red man's gift," Forrest's Metamora counsels his conquerors; their descendants took the hint.[41] Orchestrating elaborate masquerades of Indianness in order to bully and bluff their way into a native identity, Catlin and his codramatists set the stage for a national theater that was nothing less than (an) Indian play.

The principal rhetorical function (or fiction) of this medicine drama—the erasure of real Indians from the Removal-era theater, except as naked sidekicks or opera-box toadies, so that whites may consume the spirit of a departed race—persists, in one form or another, to this day. In the simplest variant of this rhetoric, theater critics have long denied the Indians any role in the development of American performance art. Whether maintaining categorically that "our theatre owed nothing in its beginnings to [Indian] sources," which "do not belong in a history of American drama," or granting that Indian rituals are functionally "dramatic" while minimizing their significance in (again) "our" theater, such readings treat Indian performance as a superseded, primitive relic. The more recent trend of naming the Indians' physical disappearance from the national stage as the necessary condition for their fancied reappearance in the national theater is no improvement. Writing that the Indian dramas "displace the actualities—the putative referents—that inspire them," for instance, Jeffrey Mason reenacts the script of Catlin, Forrest, and Alger, entitling white actors to inhabit the discarded husks the Indians have left behind. Similarly, when Susan Scheckel argues that Indian lives "had literally become a performance produced by whites, a performance from which [the Indian] as independent 'actor' was entirely excluded," she turns the Indians into what Morgan claimed they were: "passive and silent spectators" of nineteenth-century history and culture. As Rosemarie Bank points out, to read the plays solely "as an extension of U.S. government Indian removal policy" simultaneously "empties out 'the Indian,' reinscribes the myth of the omnipotent state, and reinserts the white man as the center of the reading," (re)producing the plays' own amnesiac version of national identity and destiny.[42] Thus the medicine-show allegory of total representation remains unchallenged: Indians still must be savaged to be salvaged, lost to be found.

An alternative reading is possible. The Indian drama, make no mistake, was part of the oppressive apparatus by which whites devoured the Indian spirit at the expense of Indian performers. And in the following years, the dense web of Indian representations—visual, verbal, and virtual—spun by Catlin and his contemporaries has congealed even further: however one might question the artist's particular take on things, his underlying claim, according to which his performances were simple displacements of a denatured, disposed-of Indian original, has been harder to shake. What would it mean, then, to reject this medicine-show mantra, to see that Catlin's acts of spiritual theft are riddled with the sacred performances he sought both to consume and to efface? What would it mean to restore the pressure that living Indian performances exerted on Catlin's staged Indian performances (even when, in some cases, those living performances were staged by Catlin)? What would it mean, in brief, to recognize that Catlin's medicine act was not the only show in town?

## Medicine Bundle

> *Every Juggler pretends to have a familiar spirit who pays him frequent visits when his attendance is required & . . . directs by his answers which are generally as dark & ambiguous as those of the ancient Oracles among the heathens, and which may be interpreted many different ways.*
>
> —John Macdonnell, *from a late eighteenth-century view of the Mandans*

Catlin's stay among the Mandans focuses the foregoing questions, exemplifying both his claims to representational authority and the ways in which Indian sacred performance complicates those claims. Though modern ethnohistorians have documented that the Mandans had been in contact with European traders for a good half-century before Catlin's stopover, they remained to many of Catlin's day emblems of unspoiled, original Indianness. An earlier visitor, for example, had described them as being "absolutely yet in a State of Nature," in "their primitive Simplicity not being hardly able to distinguish good from Evil."[43] Catlin himself promoted this illusion, asserting that the Mandans as he found them "were living entirely according to their native modes,"[44] and he hinted further of their being a specially, quintessentially aboriginal people: "The Mandans . . . are perhaps one of the most ancient tribes of Indians in our country. . . . Their traditions and peculiarities I shall casually recite in this or future epistles; which when understood, will at once, I think, denominate them a peculiar and distinct race" (1:80). Catlin's contention that the 1837 smallpox epidemic had rendered the Mandans "extinct; leaving in my hands alone chiefly, what has been preserved of their personal looks and peculiar modes" can be read not only as showman's patter. More fundamentally, this romance of Mandan alterity and extinction clinches his claim to ownership of the Mandan mystery, a medicine that is wholly "American,—indigenous, and not exotic."[45] And in turn, the Mandans' singularity boosts Catlin's authority to "lead [the reader] through a maze of novelty and mysteries to the knowledge of a strange" and "peculiar" people (1:94), whose essential character he alone has had the sagacity to preserve before they succumbed to "the fell disease" of "civilizing devastation" (1:95).

Catlin's authority as the repository of the Mandans' spirit is signalized by his initiation into two interrelated medicine performances: he becomes, according to him, both the greatest of all Mandan medicine men and, by virtue of this title of *Te-ho-pe-nee Wash-ee*, the sole white man to witness in its entirety the awesome okipa. Relating his prior reception by the tribes of the Upper Missouri, Catlin introduces the reader to the power the Indians attribute to his artworks: "I am a 'medicine-man' of the highest order amongst these superstitious people, on account of the art which I practice; which is a strange and unaccountable thing to them, and of course, called the greatest of 'medicine'" (1:35–36). The Indians, Catlin writes, are dumbfounded by the eerie power of his representational portraits; they believe that his canvases actually incorporate the spirit, if not the body, of those he paints: "They pronounced me the greatest *medicine-man* in the world; for they said I had made *living beings*,—they said they could see their chiefs alive, in two places— those that I had made were a *little* alive—they could see their eyes move— could see them smile and laugh, and that if they could laugh they could certainly speak, if they should try, and they must therefore have *some life* in them" (1:107). Later, he elaborates on the tribute the Mandans pay to one possessed of such extraordinary power:

Perhaps nothing ever more completely astonished these people than the operations of my *brush*. The art of portrait-painting was a subject entirely new to them, and of course, unthought of; and my appearance here has commenced a new era in the arcana of *medicine* or mystery. . . . I was christened with a new and a great name—one by which I am now familiarly hailed, and talked of in this village; and no doubt will be, as long as traditions last in this strange community. . . . I took the degree (not of Doctor of Laws, nor Bachelor of Arts) of Master of Arts—of mysteries—of magic, and of hocus pocus. I was recognized . . . as a "great *medicine white man;*" and since that time, have been regularly installed *medicine* or mystery, which is the most honourable degree that could be conferred upon me here; and I now hold a place amongst the most eminent and envied personages, the doctors and conjurati of this titled community. (1:105–6)

Catlin's transformation into medicine man was not, in truth, one of his more original acts. The minidrama of the white man passing as, mistaken for, or dabbling in the mysteries of Indian medicine was replayed in a substantial body of antebellum texts, including some that backed the nation's literary identity and ratified its literary canon: James Fenimore Cooper's *The Last of the Mohicans* (1826) and *The Prairie* (1827), Robert Montgomery Bird's *Nick of the Woods* (1837), Nathaniel Hawthorne's *The Scarlet Letter* (1850) and unpublished "elixir of life" manuscripts, and Herman Melville's *The Confidence-Man* (1857) all play variations on this theme. Nor was Catlin alone in treating his initiation into Indian medicine as an opportunity to score points at the Indians' expense. As his onetime patron Cass wrote in a typical attack on Indian medicine men and their devotees, as well as on those white reporters gullible enough to buy into their act: "The eating of fire, the swallowing of daggers, the escape from swathed buffalo robes, and the juggling incantations and ceremonies, by which the dead are raised, the sick healed, and the living killed, have been witnessed by many, who related what they saw, but who were grossly deceived by their own credulity, and by the skill of the Indian *Waubeno*."[46] Though Catlin's contribution to this tradition is fairly genial, his winking, tongue-in-cheek delivery accomplishes a diminishing effect comparable to the burlesques of a Melville or a Cooper. Despite the time he has spent "immersed in the Indian country, mingling with red men, and identifying myself with them as much as possible" (1:3), Catlin assures his readers that he has not been so unmindful of the prerogatives of his own race as to suffer Indian credulity before the healer's supposed power.

And yet, as is evidenced by his salesman's device of announcing, even while mocking the medicine man, that he has spirited away both the character's likeness and his costume—"You must see my painting of this strange scene before you can form a just conception of real frightful ugliness and Indian conjuration—yes, and even more: you must see the magic *dress* of this Indian 'big bug' (which I have this day procured in all its parts), placed upon the back of some person who can imitate the strides, and swells, the grunts, and spring the rattles of an Indian magician" (1:40)—Catlin's transformation into the great medicine white man plays a vital role in his operation. In a literal sense, Catlin's conversion ensures his veracity, because (he reports) it provides him immediate, unfettered access to those aspects of Indian culture that lie hidden from the remainder of his race: his title, he writes, "has been an easy and successful passport already to many strange and mysterious places; and has put me in possession of a vast deal of curious and interesting information, which I am sure I never should have otherwise learned" (1:106). In a larger sense, Catlin's metamorphosis symbolizes his identification with the mysteries he reports, visualizes, and dramatizes; his claim to have been (con)fused with the power of Indian medicine underwrites his validity as a conduit of that power to white audiences. Moreover, Catlin's strategic deployment of Indian credulity furthers his own credibility. As with the reports of awestruck Indian onlookers being taken in by the fidelity of Forrest's performance—or Catlin's own accounts of Indian performers gawking at his Gallery—the artist presents his Indian paintings as such immediate transcriptions, such perfect copies of their originals, that the Indians (who as artless men cannot dissemble) must acknowledge that he has indeed held the mirror up to Nature. Catlin's medicine paintings thus epitomize his unilateral and perfect power over Indian lives, a power—quite literal to the Indians as Catlin sees it—of spirit capture. It is not, then, to the Indians alone (or even primarily) that Catlin's paintings are medicine. More importantly, the Indians' authenticating gestures signify his ability and his right to collect, cultivate, and circulate the curative power of Indian medicine for his own kind. And, judging from the surfeit of reviews trumpeting his Gallery as a "complete and fascinating panorama of savage life," one in which "the very spirit of savage existence is unsphered before us," his medicine-show gambit paid off.[47]

But significantly, it is within the source of Catlin's representational authority, his art's supposed medicine power, that his authority shows signs of unraveling. For it is within this source of power that one begins to witness the competing claims to authority, to the performance of Indian medicine, that shape Catlin's own medicine performances. Indeed, reviewing the litany of attacks on the medicine man in the antebellum era, it becomes apparent that as a body these constitute struggles over spiritual, cultural, and representational power. Cass's disparaging remarks cited earlier, for example, are framed as a death match between those who succumb to and those who resist the medicine man's incredible acts. And for the moment, Cass's side appears to be losing, or at least losing its grip:

We have ourselves, in the depth and solitude of our primeval forests, and among some of the wildest and most remote of our Indian tribes, gazed with ardent curiosity, and perhaps with some slight emotion of awe, upon the *Jongleur*, who with impudent dexterity performed feats, which probably it is wiser to witness than to relate. And when the surrounding naked and painted multitude, exulting in the imposing performance, and in the victory obtained over the incredulity of the white strangers, fixed their eyes upon us, and raised their piercing yell, breaking the sounds by the repeated application of the hand to the mouth, and dancing around us with the activity of mountebanks, and the ferocity of demons,

"We dare not say, that then our blood,
Kept on its wont and tempered flood,"

nor that, under less favorable circumstances, the scene might not have been terrific, and impressed us with recollections, equally difficult to reject and to account for.[48]

A curious confession, if such it is, this account of Indian medicine retracts as much as it reveals. Shamelessly theatrical, laden with negatives and qualifiers ("perhaps," "slight," "under less favorable circumstances," "dare not, "might not"), and retreating, at the crux of the unsettling moment, to quotation—at once a sign of civilized composure and of a failure or unwillingness to name the experience—Cass's fevered synopsis deflates Indian medicine while at the same time exalting it to a degree so creepily potent that it infects not only his viewing but also his re-viewing of it. It is not so much that Cass fantasizes coupling with the "naked and painted" company (though given Catlin's and Forrest's wilderness reveries, I would not rule this out altogether) as that his exposure to their performance introduces a discordant note in his otherwise cocksure arrangement of Indian credulity versus white credibility. For the moment, it is Cass who stands gape-mouthed before the parlor tricks of savage charlatans, Cass whose credulity is laid bare. As in Catlin's okipa tongue-tie, Cass's spell demonstrates the power of Indian sacred performance to arrest the medicine show, to strip it of its veneer of civility, necessity, and inevitability, and in so doing to expose its workings as no better than Cass and company deemed Indian medicine, no more than artful deception.

Cass, of course, could gloss over the conflict between Indian and white medicine in ways that Catlin could not. For the latter, resting his authority largely if not wholly on his re-creation *as* "white medicine," it was essential to fulfill the offices assigned to him. "'Medicine,'" Catlin proclaims when introducing the concept, "is a great word in this country; and it is very necessary that one should know the meaning of it, whilst he is scanning and estimating the Indian character, which is made up, in a great degree, of mysteries and superstitions" (1:35). Their mystery, his mastery: Catlin must plumb the depths of Indian medicine to maintain his power over their lives and spirit, to unveil "the true modes and meaning of the savage" (1:84). Yet what becomes increasingly evident is that, medicine man or no, Catlin's attempts to divine the secret of Indian life are thwarted or baffled at every turn. In the letter following his first missive on medicine, Catlin hints at his inability to comprehend it: "The Letter which I gave you yesterday, on the subject of 'medicine' and 'medicine-men,' has somewhat broken the 'thread of my discourse;' and left my painting-room . . . and all the Indians in it, and portraits, and buffalo hunts, and landscapes of these beautiful regions, to be taken up and discussed" (1:42). In this introductory foray into native mysteries, Catlin acknowledges—or, deadpan as usual, attempts not to—that Indian medicine escapes him: breaking (or breaking into) his discourse, it challenges his claim to harbor all meaning, all power, in the transaction between Indians and whites. As Catlin concedes at a later point, the "most striking features in [Indian] character" are "valued, cherished and practiced . . . for reasons which are difficult to be learned or understood; and which probably will never be justly appreciated by others than themselves" (1:56–57). Indian medicine, rather than being a beautiful blank, the absent precondition for civilized revitalization, possesses stores of information, rules, and values that cannot be culled or uncovered by the white medicine collector.

At the same time, as the word *justly* indicates, it is not merely its inaccessibility that makes Indian medicine problematic to the white collector, interpreter, or performer. Rather, this inaccessibility draws attention to the fact that the white medicine man's acts are not "just"—are not innocent but are implicated in practices of corruption and coercion, not least through their attempt to mask these practices under the illusion of representational self-sufficiency. Indian medicine is thus less unveiled by Catlin than unveiling of him: it not only exposes his project as a partial act masquerading as the whole truth but also highlights the dubious tactics by which that project carries off its effects. This unmasking function appears surreptitiously in Catlin's comments on the various Indian prophets he interviews. For example, writing of the (to his thinking) underhanded activities of Kenekuk, the Kickapoo prophet, Catlin reports: "he commenced preaching and instituted a prayer, which he ingeniously carved on a maple-stick of an inch and a half in breadth, in characters somewhat resembling Chinese letters. These sticks, with the prayers on them, he has introduced into every family of the tribe, and into the hands of every individual; and as he has necessarily the manufacturing of them all, he sells them at his own price; and has thus added lucre to fame, and in two essential and effective ways, augmented his influence in his tribe" (2:99). Clearly akin to Catlin's own business and marketing techniques, the practices Catlin attributes to this enterprising Indian artist uncover the chicanery behind his own medicine acts: both men, peddling nostrums to allay what their audiences perceive as spiritual lack, are riding on acceptance of their representations as legitimate, truthful, and unique. Similarly, in his character sketch of Tenskwatawa, Catlin remarks on the man's "extraordinary cunning" in devising a stratagem to draw a crowd: "He carried with him into every wigwam that he visited, the image of a dead person of the size of life; which was made ingeniously of some light material, and always kept concealed under bandages of thin white muslin cloths and not to be opened; of this he made a great mystery" (2:117). The "images of dead people" that Catlin describes Tenskwatawa foisting upon his followers are, plainly enough, analogues to the medicine paintings Catlin himself offered his hometown and overseas fans; indeed, as I have said, it was by representing the Indians as dead—or at least dying—that Catlin wrapped his own images in an aura of mystery calculated to appeal to the tastes of his coterie. In these episodes, Catlin's representations, to cite Joshua Masters's provocative reading of *Letters and Notes*, "suggest an awareness of their own limitations, for the Indian 'lives' on only as long as he is repeatedly consumed—in museums, galleries, sideshows, and cigar stores—by a voracious public in a fickle cultural marketplace."[49] While implicating Indian healers in the marketing of Indian medicine, Catlin's text registers an awareness not only of Indian forms of self-representation but also of the ways in which the medicine show relies on acts of imposture, aggrandizement, and domination to secure the faith of its paying customers and to finagle its own appearance of legitimacy.

In this respect, there is another and, for Catlin, even more worrisome sense in which Indian medicine flags his project as one of imperialism passing for inheritance: revealing the complex, integral, undisclosed depths of Indian societies, Indian medicine reveals that whites can never justly obtain the "key to Indian life and Indian character" (1:36), for the mere attempt to do so constitutes an assault on Indian cultural and spiritual integrity. Catlin thus must confront his inability to separate his art from the rapacity of civilized intercourse with the Indians, his failure to secure a posture of aesthetic detachment. "It may be," he writes scathingly at the end of the first volume of

*Letters and Notes,* "that *power* is *right,* and *voracity* a *virtue;* and that these people . . . are *righteously* doomed to an issue that *will* not be averted. It can be easily proved—we have a civilized science that can easily do it, or anything else that may be required to cover the iniquities of civilized man in catering for his unholy appetites" (1:260). Abjuring the fatalistic reading on which the medicine show in all its forms relied, Catlin here traces such self-serving science to its roots. Yet toward the close of the work's second volume, this critique turns on itself, and his own artistry becomes enmeshed in the unholy appetites he arraigns: "Long and cruel experience has well proved that it is impossible for enlightened Governments or money-making individuals to deal with these credulous and unsophisticated people, without the sin of injustice; but the humble biographer or historian, who goes amongst them from a different motive, *may* come out of their country with his hands and his conscience clean, and himself an anomaly, a white man dealing with Indians, and meting out justice to them; which I hope it may be my good province to do with my pen and my brush, with which, at least, I will have the singular and valuable satisfaction of having done them no harm" (2:225). Catlin's italicized *may* is singularly ambivalent, disclosing a troubled recognition that his pen and brush are in fact agents of the "enlightened" governments who impel the Indians inexorably westward so that money-making individuals—himself among them—may profit from their enforced absence.

For it is evident that his pen and brush, far from doing no harm, leave a trail of desolation in their wake. An early—and, thanks to the intercession of Catlin's interpreter, amicably resolved—instance of his art's trespassing on Indian cultures occurs in a near fracas over his choice of sitters. Struck by the appearance of an Indian *"beau* or *dandy"* (1:112), Catlin begins to render the man's likeness: "He was truly a beautiful subject for the brush, and I was filled with enthusiasm," he recalls. "I had thus far progressed, with high-wrought feelings of pleasure, when the two or three chiefs, who had been seated around the lodge, and whose portraits I had before painted, arose suddenly, and wrapping themselves tightly in their robes, crossed my room with a quick and heavy step, and took an informal leave of my cabin. I was apprehensive of their displeasure, though I continued my work; and in a few moments the interpreter came furiously into my room, addressing me thus:—'My God, Sir! this never will do; you have given great offence to the chiefs—they have made complaint of your conduct to me—they tell me this is a worthless fellow—a man of no account in the nation, and if you paint his picture, you must instantly destroy theirs' " (1:113–14). Superficially no more than a quarrel between an ornamental and a sacramental view of art, what this aesthetic spat suggests is how profoundly out of step Catlin is with Indian conventions. For all his claims to have gained entrance to the Indians' world through his medicine art, Catlin remains oblivious to the power of such medicine in the communities where he practices it, the power of medicine both to create *and* to destroy. His art can hardly avoid doing harm, as he has no idea of its significance in Indian terms.

Nor is it merely misguided ebullience that marks Catlin's art as a risky presence; his project, as his own text reveals, necessitates—indeed constitutes—violence against the secret and the sacred in Indian lives. That this is so breaks into consciousness via a repeated motif, what I call the "pen/gun complex," that likens the scene of painting to the force of armed occupation. "I drew from my pocket my sketch-book, laid my gun across my lap, and commenced taking his likeness" (1:26); "my easel stands before me, and the cool breech of a twelve-pounder makes me a comfortable seat, whilst her muzzle is looking out at one of the port-holes" (1:29); "the Frenchmen in the Fort . . . seized their guns and ran out. . . . I, at that moment, ran to my painting-room" (1:38); "I armed myself with my pencil and my sketch-book" (1:199). So frequent are these references that one reviewer of *Letters and Notes* found the artist's gun more worthy than his pen of top billing: "Mr. Catlin went on with his rifle and his pencil, sketching and noting whatever he saw worthy of record."[50] And indeed, when Catlin writes that "I slipped my sketch-book and pencil into my hand, and under the muzzle of my gun, each fellow stood for his likeness" (2:142), he erases the distinction between recording device and firearm, suggesting not only that the portraits have been secured at gunpoint but also that they have been taken—muzzled, as it were—by the gun itself. In scenes such as these, representational fidelity becomes what it purposes to deny: a vehicle for the reconstruction of Indians to serve colonial authority. With its patina of innocence removed, the medicine-show logic of Catlin's project is uncovered: his cherished pose of championing the Indians by capturing their similitude is revealed as the means by which he furthers and sanctifies—or furthers *by* sanctifying—the violence he claims to despise.

That this unveiling of Catlin's art operates through the artist's relation to Indian medicine cannot be doubted—for it is precisely as an agency of oppression that, he claims, the Indians view his medicine paintings. "The squaws generally agreed," he writes, "that they had discovered life enough in [the portraits] to render my *medicine* too great for the Mandans; saying that such an operation could not be performed without taking away from the original something of his existence, which I put in the picture" (1:107–8). Catlin goes on: "they commenced a mournful and doleful chaunt against me, crying and weeping bitterly through the village, proclaiming me a most 'dangerous man; one who could make living persons by looking at them; and at the same time, could, as a matter of course, destroy life in the same way, if I chose. That my medicine was dangerous to their lives, and . . . that I was to take a part of the existence of those whom I painted, and carry it home with me amongst the white people' " (1:108). Catlin's characteristically patronizing tone cannot counter the fact that what the Mandan women are said to fear is spookily astute: Catlin does indeed intend to capture the spirit of the real Indian—why else the certificates of authenticity?—and carry it home among his own people. What's more, on a number of occasions the women's prophecy concerning Catlin's medicine paintings appears to be fulfilled; disaster dogs his footsteps as surely as if his brush truly were a weapon of destruction. At one point, having completed a round of sittings at the Mandan village, he is pursued by a party of Indians, who plead with him to return one painting in particular: "'Mi-neek-e-sunk-te-ka' (the mink), they exclaimed, 'is dying! the picture which you made of her is too much like her—you put so much of her into it, that when your boat took it away from our village, it drew a part of her life away with it' " (2:181). That the first to be struck down by Catlin's medicine brush is one of the "squaws" who railed against him cannot have escaped the artist's notice; for all his disdain for Indian superstition, their beliefs seem here to have been uncannily on the mark.

The signal instance of the damage dealt by Catlin's medicine brush occurs in the story of the Sioux chieftain "the Dog," a story to which Catlin twice alludes (including in the episode of the Mink) before relating it in full. At the start of the second volume of *Letters and Notes*, as he reacquaints readers with his exploits, Catlin writes: "I painted the portrait of a celebrated warrior of the Sioux, by the name of Mah-to-chee-ga (the little bear), who was unfortunately slain in a few moments after the picture was done, by one of his own tribe; and which was very near costing me my life for having painted a side view of his face, leaving one-half of it out of the picture, which had been the cause of the affray; and supposed by the whole tribe to have been intentionally left out by me, as 'good for nothing' " (2:2). Later in the volume, he fleshes out the events of the tragedy: "I had in progress at this time a portrait of *Mah-to-tchee-ga* (little bear); of the *Onc-pa-pa band.* . . . I was painting almost a profile view of his face, throwing a part of it into shadow, and had it nearly finished, when an Indian by the name of *Shon-ka* (the dog), chief of the *Caz-a-zshee-ta* band . . . entered the wigwam in a sullen mood, and seated himself on the floor in front of my sitter, where he could have a full view of the picture in its operation. After sitting a while with his arms folded, and his lips stiffly arched with contempt; he sneeringly spoke thus:— '*Mah-to-tchee-ga* is but *half a man*' " (2:190). The fatal consequences of this insult are quickly played out: an argument ensues, an ambush is planned, and at its execution "Little Bear lay weltering in his blood (strange to say!) with all that side of his face entirely shot away, which had been left out of the picture; and, according to the prediction of the Dog, '*good for nothing*,' carrying away one half of the jaws, and the flesh from the nostrils and corner of the mouth, to the ear, including one eye, and leaving the jugular vein exposed" (2:191–92). The murderer of Little Bear, the Dog, is himself pursued and killed—but not before Little Bear's brother is claimed by the ensuing internecine violence, and not before Catlin, accused of wielding a power too terrible to entertain, is himself marked for death, a fate that, he reports, he narrowly and fortuitously escapes. "Thus," the artist concludes, "terminated the affair of 'the Dog,' wherein have fallen three distinguished warriors; and wherein *might* have fallen one '*great medicine man!*' and all in consequence of the operations of my brush" (2:194).

In explicating the story of the Dog, it is important not to reduce the complex ways the episode operates in Catlin's recitation. On the one hand, as a piece of theater, the gruesome tableaux of tribal violence was plainly meant to appeal to patrons, registering not only as visceral thrill but also as proof, as William Dunlap wrote in his review of the Gallery, that "these people are savages and barbarians. They delight in war and murder; they inflict tortures on themselves through pride, and on others to satiate revenge."[51] It is not for nothing, then, that the showman twice provides, as it were, teaser trailers before screening the main event. Indeed, the whole story is carefully framed by Catlin to achieve two effects: shock value and moral instruction. Ending the previous letter with the warning that "there is *blood* and *butchery* in the story that is now to be related" (2:186) but insisting nonetheless that "it should be read by every one who would form a correct notion of the force of Indian superstitions" (2:186–87), Catlin withholds the full telling until the next letter, forcing readers to wait with bated breath for both the graphic and the edifying payoffs. Aside from providing insight into Catlin's stage strategy—he skillfully employs both verbal and pictorial elements to keep his audience in suspense as the tale builds to its awful denouement—the presentation of this story emphasizes the claims of representational authority that underlay Catlin's performance as a whole. "As my brush was the prime mover of all these misfortunes, and my life was sought to heal the wound, I must be supposed to be knowing to and familiar with the whole circumstances" (2:187), he states in the story's preface, insisting on his veracity as eyewitness or (however reluctantly) participant-observer.

And yet, if the devices by which Catlin distances himself from the tragedy while asserting his right to mediate it are familiar poses of the medicine showman, familiar too is the impression that neither of these poses is failsafe. Catlin has been at once too close to the power of Indian medicine and not close enough, both the agent and the pawn of forces he can neither control nor comprehend. As such, in this blood-drenched crescendo of the chaos his paintings cause within Indian communities, his medicine is exposed as an invasive force, a foreign entity that quite literally takes away the lives it professes to preserve. In the story of the Dog, aesthetic choices—a profile rather than a frontal view—have ideological, and material, implications. Cultural incompetence, in this instance, can kill.

To grasp more fully the ways in which the story of the Dog marks Catlin and his works as "invaders of a sacred soil" (2:47), it is helpful to place the saga in its wider context. The story of the Dog is embedded within a more sweeping tale of the artist's involvement in and incursion into Indian medicine, a tale that dramatizes the white man's discovery of, and subsequent coming into conflict because of, an essential space for the performance of Indian mysteries: the sacred Sioux red pipestone quarry. As with his pronouncements concerning Indian medicine generally, Catlin offers his portraits of the quarry as an invaluable find for American science, history, and nationalism. Indeed, capping his triumph here as in so many cases, he manages to carry off "specimens" (2:203) of the red pipestone, which was subsequently christened "catlinite" in honor of his securing and documenting the mineral. However, in marked contrast to the majority of his experiences, Catlin appears in his own narration as anything but an honored guest at the quarry. On the contrary, he is a renegade, a pillager and despoiler of the Sioux sacred site, who, accused by the Indians of having "come to trespass on their dearest privilege,—their religion" (2:166), is held as their prisoner while they engage in a passionate attempt to dissuade him from his quest: "As 'this red stone was a part of their flesh,' it would be sacrilegious for [']white man to touch or take it away'—'a hole would be made in their flesh, and the blood could never be made to stop running'" (2:166). Unswayed, Catlin proceeds to the quarry, where, in contrast to "the poor Indian," who "in humble supplication" to the spirit of the place "solicits permission to dig and carry away the red stone for his pipes" (2:203), he fulfills the Indians' prophecy that the white man would take without giving in return: "I resolved to procure specimens of every variety, which I did with success, by . . . breaking small bits from them with my hammer; until I had something like an hundred different varieties, containing all the tints and colours of a painter's palette. These, I at length threw away" (2:203–4).

As with most of Catlin's exploits—indeed, as with his story of the Dog—how much of this episode is reliable is anyone's guess.[52] The impression Catlin strives to convey of himself as a dauntless explorer, determined to track down this unique material against all resistance, suggests that he featured the story to appeal to the nationalistic fervor of his American audiences (and to convince his European audiences that he was a true representative of the American pioneer spirit). Nonetheless, for all its air of having been dressed up as a dramatic set piece, the scene of Catlin's ravages at the pipestone quarry emphasizes the literally ungodly power he possesses to violate the sacred spaces of the peoples he claims to celebrate. As such, Catlin's fallback rhetoric of "anti-conquest," the term Mary Louise Pratt applies to the language by which pioneer-explorers "secure their innocence in the same moment as they assert European hegemony," collapses as his art confronts its role in extending Euro-American might over the territorial, spiritual, and representational contact zone.[53] The fact that Catlin turns the pipestone into an aesthetic object—"containing all the tints and colors of a painter's palette"—does not mitigate the fact that, like the "mixture and medley of unintelligible trash" (1:88) to which he likens the fruits of Mandan culture, he disposes of this emblem of Sioux culture as worthless. On the contrary, by revealing the way Indian sacred materials are consumed and discarded to serve the white man's art, this episode exposes in its barest guise the dire gaps of comprehension, the grievous conflict of ideologies, aesthetics, and spiritual sympathies that enables even a professed conservationist and friend of the Indian to treat with truly civilized savagery the peoples to whom he looks for civilization's savage cure.

A crucial distinction needs to be made at this point. Were the issue simply that Catlin's own works expose his ruthlessness or hypocrisy, it would be sufficient to end here; though there is a wealth of additional evidence tending toward the same conclusion, producing it would smack of overkill. More significant than its role in lambasting Catlin, however, are the ways in which his troubled relationship to Indian medicine enables one to probe and contest the very basis of his project and of the medicine show itself: the assumption that the Indians, fast on their way to oblivion, were at best passive bystanders in the performances by which Indian medicine was disseminated throughout American culture. By disclosing the presence of powers and depths within Indian cultures that resist the white interloper's authority, episodes such as those of the Mink, the Dog, and the pipestone quarry reveal the medicine show to be founded on the Indians' presence, not their absence—on a displacement that is both dependent on and in denial of the performances it seeks to displace. This is evident, indeed, in the nature of Catlin's role as medicine white man: far from rolling over before the power of his brush, the Indians, whether seeking to harness, propitiate, or assimilate its mystery, have brought his art into uneasy contact with their own. Likewise with the pipestone quarry: though Catlin may discard it, the pipestone remains a tangible sign not only of the ravages of the medicine show in Indian country but also of the residuum of sacred performance on which the medicine show relied. This writing of a European name over the remains of an Indian sacred substance, like the founding of an American identity on the mysteries of Indian medicine, indicates that the Indians and Catlin alike are responding to the other's presence, creating intercultural medicine performances that cannot be completed, or even conceived, in the absence of the other.

One way to think of the complexities within Catlin's performance of Indian medicine, then, is to consider these factors in light of the emergent nature of performance itself: however authoritative one performance may appear, it is best to view any one performance as a variant or a version, and the performative bundle as the sum and interrelation of a potentially infinite number of versions. So with Catlin: though he strives for the impression that alternative (much less competing) performances are unimaginable, the full outlines of his performance are in fact imaginable only in their relationship to the alternative performances he disdains. Perhaps nothing better illustrates this truth than the social performance of Indian medicine: that is, not individual conjurors but the "conjuring" of Indian culture through collective forms of artistry, pageantry, and ceremony. In such performances, where the Indians manifest the meanings and meaningfulness of their cultures publicly, the insufficiency of considering Catlin's medicine performance in isolation comes to the fore; in such performances, where the entire community forges intricate ensembles of material and symbolic activity, Indian medicine becomes most problematically present within Catlin's own medicine acts. The pipestone quarry, a physical, public site for the collection and enactment of medicine performance, is one such communal space that contests Catlin's surveying and merchandising eye, revealing the inadequacy of any study of white medicine that fails to account for the Indians' presence. Even more telling in this regard, however, are two interrelated scenes of sacred performance on which Catlin reports minutely and (in one case) near maniacally: the phenomenon of Indian dance generally, and the combination of performative elements—dance, drama, song—that forms the Mandan okipa ceremony. In both cases, Indian sacred performance leaves its mark on the white player, even as he tries to create an origin free of the performances on which his are built. In the case of the okipa, Indian sacred performance fundamentally informs—indeed transforms—Catlin's art and act, instituting an alternative model of performance in which Indian and white medicine interact and interbreed, each complicating, complementing, and completing the other.

Catlin's interest in Indian dance was long-standing and, for his time, relatively free of overt bias. For these virtues, he has been lavishly praised. Richard Drinnon, for instance, argues that Catlin, "a most exceptional Anglo-American," "respectfully painted [Indian] dances and even sensed" in them "forms of sacred play." In their study of Plains Indian dance, meanwhile, Reginald and Gladys Laubin assert that "George Catlin had more to say, and show, about Indian dances than any other writer before him, and more than most writers after him. . . . Catlin certainly . . . took liberties, as most artists do, in some details of his paintings. But he was really *there*, for the best part of eight years, and most of his observations still hold true in light of what we know today." This emphasis on firsthand experience—"he was really *there*"— was, of course, the basis of the artist's own claims to authority; it was what enabled him, in the dances he hosted in the 1840s, to convince the *Illustrated London News* that his companies exhibited "by far the most pleasing and just representation of the North American Indians ever seen in England."[54] Yet in light of the preceding discussion, it is worth asking how "just" Catlin's representations of Indian dance really were. As Barbara Kirshenblatt-Gimblett points out, indigenous performance enacted within the auspices of the museum suffers the same effects of desacralization and ossification that infect the display of nonliving artifacts:

The living quality of [native] performances does not obviate the issue of artifactual autonomy, for songs, tales, dances, and ritual practices are also amenable to ethnographic excision and to presentation as autonomous units. . . . Through the kind of repetition required by stage appearances, long runs, and extensive tours, performances can become like artifacts. They freeze. They become canonical. They take forms that are alien, if not antithetical, to how they are produced and experienced in their local settings, for with repeated exposure, cultural performances are routinized and trivialized. The result is events that have no clear analogue within the community from which they purportedly derive and that come to resemble one another more than that which they are intended to re-present.[55]

Evidence of this alienating process comes, to cite one example, from Charles Dickens's obtuse, disparaging description of Catlin's Ojibwa troupe "dancing their miserable jigs after their own dreary fashion," a "pantomime" the novelist considers devoid of "any power of truthful dramatic expression." But even positive notices reveal that when sacred performance is enacted out of cultural context, it may become little more than stagnant carnival. Thus the *London News* wrote that Catlin's Ojibwa company "performed in succession, with all their wild and startling effect, the Medicine Dance, the Pipe Dance, and the War Dance," a series of oddities stripped of their sacred character and left only with the power to appeal to thrill seekers. Proof that these were routinized numbers comes from Catlin's comparable summaries: the "*wa-be-no* (or mystery) dance" is little more than an "eccentric and droll dance" that "caused much merriment among the audience," while the "*pipe-dance*" becomes a "spirited and picturesque" dance given "with great effect," just another of the artist's flashy showpieces. This transformation of the Indian dance's sacred spirit into a secularized, "spirited" frolic is exemplified by an episode involving an audience member's unscripted entrance onto the dance floor. Not only does this apparently spontaneous departure from routine rapidly become standard operating procedure, as the same woman (whom Catlin christens the "jolly fat dame") appears at later performances to reprise her impromptu interruption, but such an intrusion of a white comic interloper into a putatively sacred performance makes of Indian dance the equivalent of the minstrel show, a redface romp designed to tickle and stimulate the masses.[56]

Yet if Catlin's dance numbers, as mass phenomena that cemented white identity through racist impersonation, operated in ways similar to the minstrel show ("nobody here but us Chickasaws"), they did not fall so readily under the impresario's or his audience's control. Catlin, needless to say, had a decided interest in representing Indian dance as fully within his purview, incapable of escaping him in the slightest, much less of overtly challenging his authority. Thus a typical passage from *Letters and Notes* reads: "These exercises [the Mandans' dances] are exceedingly grotesque in their appearance, and to the eye of a traveller who knows not their meaning or importance, they are an uncouth and frightful display of starts, and jumps, and yelps, and jarring gutturals, which are sometimes truly terrifying. But when one gives them a little attention, and has been lucky enough to be initiated into their mysterious meaning, they become a subject of the most intense and exciting interest. Every dance has its peculiar step, and every step has its meaning; every dance also has its peculiar song, and that is so intricate and mysterious oftentimes, that not one in ten of the young men who are dancing and singing it, know the meaning of the song which they are chanting over" (1:126). Catlin repeats this medicine-show refrain, according to which the Indians require whites to mediate their own cultural acts, in his comments on an Ojibwa song: "they are generally as ignorant of the translation and meaning of the song, as a mere passing traveller" (2:248). Yet in this instance, Catlin concedes that he is not much better than his hypothetical "passing traveler" in cracking the code: "I was not initiated far enough in this tribe, to explain the mysteries that are hidden on this little [song] chart" (2:248). Catlin's unstated follow-up is patent: *had* he been fully initiated into the Ojibwa tribe—as he was into the Mandan—no mystery could long have eluded him.

In fact, however, this was *not* the case with the Mandans. Writing of a Mandan song and dance, Catlin gripes that the performance consists of a "strange manœuvre, which I did but partly understand" (1:55) and of "half-strangled gutturals, a sort of song, which I did not get translated to my satisfaction, and which might have been susceptible of none" (1:55). As with his bewilderment concerning aspects of Indian medicine, the breakdown of Catlin's comprehension of the Mandan dance steps and song vocables signals the presence of conventions and rules, intricate and mysterious elements of Indian culture that may indeed be insusceptible of straightforward translation but that are not, for that reason, meaningless within the context of the performance. "It would actually seem," Catlin marvels at one point, "as if they had dances for every thing" (1:244); an astute observation, signaling his awareness that dance signifies variously, infinitely, within its cultural contexts, this statement at the same time underlines the presence of an Indian performative tradition that cannot be fathomed by a traveler merely passing for one of their own.

Nor does Catlin's denseness regarding Indian dance lessen when he shifts from the prairie to the parlor. Here, as opposed to his work in the field,

Catlin is presumably in complete command; here, he is neither a passing traveler nor a frustrated tyro but a certified authority whose reputation rides on the accuracy of his interpretations. For this reason, perhaps, Catlin presents Indian dance in the same terms he applies to his paintings: purely representational or pantomimic, the dance as he sees it perfectly mirrors, prefigures, or imitates action drawn from some other sphere of activity. As he describes "the *discovery-dance*" of the Iowa Indians, "This curious mode forms a part [of] the commencement of the war-dance, and is generally led off by one of the War-chiefs, who dances forward alone, pretending to be skulking and hunting for the track of his enemy, and when he discovers it he beckons on his warriors, who steal into the dance behind him, and follow him up as he advances, and pretends at length to discover the enemy in the distance, ordering all to be ready for the attack."[57] Indicative, to Catlin, of the Indians' inability to create art that does more than rehearse the real—a trait that is at once laudable in their character as natural men and pitiable in their low capacity as primitives—such play-by-play coverage of Indian dance has a proto-ethnographic density meant to exhibit Catlin's full initiation into the ways of the tribe. However lucid the Indians' gestural language may be, viewers lacking the adequate cultural context would presumably be at a loss to match each (repeated) action with its original referent.

Yet even this apparently unambiguous bodily discourse is capable of disconcerting Catlin's promise to provide "a number of dances and other amusements, all of which I would render instructive by my explanations." For instance, in his effort to clear up the Ojibwa mystery dance, Catlin falls short: "After my explanations and their pipe were finished, they arose and gave the *Wa-be-no* dance, as they call it. *Wa-be-no*, in the Ojibbeway language, means mystery, and their mystery-dance is one of their choicest dances, only given at some occasion of their mystery-feasts, or for the accomplishment of some mysterious design. This dance is amusing and grotesque, and made much merriment amongst the audience. I explained the meaning of this also." The word *this* in Catlin's final sentence marks the limits of his authority: by "I explained the meaning of this," he appears to mean that he explained *that* the dance is "for the accomplishment of some mysterious design," not *what* that design is. (Syntactically, he could also mean that he explained to the audience its own merriment—a tempting interpretation in light of the self-referential nature of his explanations.) What Catlin cannot explain is the core or key of the mystery dance: he cannot explain its mystery, its medicine. In his study of contemporary Plains Indian dance, William Powers argues that "since the turn of the [nineteenth] century, Plains music and dance have become symbolic of American Indian resistance to wholesale adoption of Euroamerican culture, and it is partly through these particular cultural forms that American Indian values manifest themselves." Catlin's experiences suggest that the use of the dance to resist Euro-American culture—or, more narrowly, the cultured Europeans who took in the dance—was not an end-of-century but, at latest, a midcentury development, one that in all likelihood was spurred by the marketing of canned native dances that would otherwise seem to spell a dying culture's concession to the inevitable. The medicine man who belonged to Catlin's troupe of Iowa dancers characterized the showman in terms that suggest such backstage opposition: "he does not know our thoughts." A fellow player agreed: "He does not know any thoughts but his own."[58] While Catlin's thoughts were on making a killing, his dancers were subtly denying him and his audiences full possession of the sacred in their lives and arts.[59] Whatever combination of necessity and desire had led these players to join the medicine show, they refuse to yield to the whimsy that the deepest mysteries of Indian performance can be penetrated by the white initiate and represented for his audience's instruction or self-identification.[60]

It was precisely this assumption that underwrote Catlin's representation of the okipa: the very deepest mystery of the most singular, wild, original Indian tribe on the continent was to be laid open by the Medicine White Man's pen, brush, and act. Positioned critically as the climax of *Letters and Notes'* first volume, the okipa went on to become the centerpiece of Catlin's show, his most remarkable and, according to him, most inimitable find—the one area in which his arts and yarns absolutely supplanted, stood in for, the irrevocably and irrecoverably lost Mandans. As Brian Dippie comments, "Catlin rested his reputation, and his expectations of financial success, on his Mandan revelations. . . . The O-kee-pa was Catlin's greatest 'discovery,' and he exploited it shamelessly." Reviewers unanimously acclaimed the okipa as Catlin's coup, the most incredible and yet veracious of his representations. In Dunlap's view, "the picture of the inside of the medicine-lodge" was by far "the most interesting portion of Mr. Catlin's exhibition"; Hall, likewise, praised the power of Catlin's okipa images: "our notice was forcibly attracted to a series of four pictures, exhibiting the successive scenes of a grand religious ceremony of the Mandans. . . . Mr. Catlin was particularly fortunate in being permitted to be present at a solemnity from which strangers are usually excluded; and we have no doubt that he has sketched with fidelity those ferocious rites which are known to attend the *graduation* of a warrior, but of which we have not before had so authentic and minute a description." A quarter-century after the publication of *Letters and Notes*, the okipa remained a hot property—though by this time, rumors of Catlin's infidelity to fact (and of the Mandans' resurgence) having accumulated in the interim, it behooved the artist to publish his less sensationalist, more scholarly companion volume, *O-Kee-Pa*. Here, he defended his allegations concerning the Mandans' singularity (and extinction) against those who "represented" claims "contrary to my representations" and produced a further slew of testimonials from Indian experts endorsing the work's seemingly surreal images.[61] Clearly enough, the okipa brought Catlin both glory and grief among his own people; the ceremony became a focal point of controversy concerning his representations and reputation.

At the same time, Catlin's battle to patent the okipa was waged not solely against white auditors but against Indian actors. For if the okipa—as the supreme manifestation of Indian medicine—should have been the signal victory of Catlin's career, the okipa—as the supreme manifestation of Indian medicine—posed the greatest challenge to his dominion, highlighting the presence of resilient, alternative performances both contesting and undergirding his own. In the okipa, the troubles that plague Catlin's authority over Indian medicine come to a head: the okipa simultaneously exposes the limits of the artist's knowledge, underscores the violations of Indian sacred space that his project entails, and announces the lasting presence within his own medicine acts of the sacred performances he pronounces dead and gone. Demonstrating the inability of any single representation—and particularly one conducted by a cultural outsider such as Catlin—to speak authoritatively of Indian medicine performance, the okipa makes Catlin's text the bearer of a new (and for his era, undreamed of) relationship between Indian and white medicine, according to which the two are coeval and coequal, vying with, shaping, and restructuring one another.

To Catlin, so foreign and unsuspected is this relationship that he insists the okipa can be plotted—or better scripted—according to the customary terms of Western drama. Thus he presents the ceremony as another expert piece of stagecraft, too macabre for polite company, but fit, with proper packaging, for genteel consumption. "There are," he writes, "a great number of characters engaged in giving the whole effect and wildness to this strange and laughable scene, each one acting well his part, and whose offices, strange and inexplicable as they are, I will endeavour to point out and explain" (1:165).[62]

Within the master metaphor of the ceremony-as-stage, Catlin has recourse to an equally familiar, though in some respects contradictory, set of domesticating allusions: he reads the okipa as a botched or incipient Judeo-Christian allegory, one proving that the Mandans have "preserved and perpetuated an imperfect knowledge of the Deluge—of the appearance and death of a Saviour—and of the transgressions of mother Eve" (1:180). Indeed, in the plight of the young men undergoing the initiation rites, Catlin sees parallels to the essence of the Christian mystery: hung by skewers and ropes from the rafters of the medicine lodge and "crying forth a prayer to the Great Spirit to support and protect him in this dreadful trial" (1:171), the initiate at last "hangs, apparently, a still and lifeless corpse" whom the officiants pronounce "entirely dead" (1:171), only to be reborn as the ordeal proceeds. Catlin's painting of the interior of the lodge, which pictures young men hanging limply, their bodies flooded with light from above and pestered from below by devilishly red figures armed with pikes, completes the association: whether connoting the Crucifixion, with Christ's flank split by the centurion, or the pit of Hell, with Satan's imps harrowing the unregenerate, this image emphatically marks the Mandan ceremony as an abortive prefiguration of a drama divine in scope. Reading the ceremony thus, Catlin seeks to secure his authority as high priest of this ultimate expression of Indian medicine, to place his worshipful witness beyond all possibility of gainsaying.

But in fact, as with his comments on the dance, the quarry, and other manifestations of Indian medicine, Catlin's authority is hedged, scuttled, on the outskirts of true competence or comprehension. Though he prides himself that his visit institutes "the first time that their devotions had ever been trespassed upon by the presence of pale-faces" (1:161), and though he exults in the action of the "*master of ceremonies*," who, "taking me with a firm *professional* affection by the arm, led me into [the] *sanctum sanctorum*" of the okipa medicine lodge (1:161), it is within the lodge that Catlin experiences the fate of the physically present but spiritually alien:

On the centre of this little frame rested some small object, which I could not exactly understand from the distance of twenty or thirty feet which intervened between it and my eye. I started several times from my seat to approach it, but all eyes were instantly upon me, and every mouth in the assembly sent forth a hush—sh—! which brought me back to my seat again; and I at length quieted my stifled curiosity as well as I could, upon learning the fact, that so sacred was that object, and so important its secrets or mysteries, that not *I* alone, but even the young men, who were passing the ordeal, and all the village, save the conductor of the mysteries, were stopped from approaching it, or knowing what it was.

This little mystery-thing, whatever it was, . . . seemed, from the devotions paid to it, to be the very nucleus of their mysteries—the *sanctissimus sanctorum*, from which seemed to emanate all the sanctity of their proceedings. . . . This strange, yet important *essence* of their mysteries, I made every enquiry about; but got no further information of, than what I could learn by my eyes, at the distance at which I saw it. . . . I tried with all the doctors, and all of the *fraternity* answered me, that that was "*great medicine*," assuring me that it "could not be told." So I quieted my curiosity as well as I could, by the full conviction that . . . this little, seemingly wonderful, relic of antiquity . . . might have been at last nothing but a silly bunch of strings and toys, . . . which, when called upon to describe, they refuse to do so, calling it "*Great Medicine*," for the very reason that there is nothing in it to reveal or describe. (1:162–63)

Catlin's typical move of attributing ignorance to the Indians cannot overcome the fact that the "little mystery-thing" at the nucleus of the okipa—the "essence," as he writes, of the medicine that he and his customers long to obtain—mounts a firm, indeed invincible, campaign against his unwelcome advances. Noting twice the failure of his eyes to decipher the mystery, and indicating further that *he* becomes the exhibit, the anomaly ("all eyes were instantly upon me"), when he violates whatever codes govern the relationship one is supposed to maintain toward this sacred object, Catlin is reduced from eyewitness to witless, from mediator of Mandan medicine to meddler in mysteries far deeper than he can drain. Nor do his attempts to resolve the riddle through the showman's faith in the almighty dollar bring him closer to satisfaction: "I made several propositions, through my friend Mr. Kipp, the trader and interpreter, to purchase one of these strange things by offering them a very liberal price; to which I received in answer that these, and all the very numerous articles used in these ceremonies, being a *society property* were *medicine*, and could not be sold for any consideration; so I abandoned all thoughts of obtaining anything, except what I have done by the *medicine* operation of my pencil, which was applied to everything, and even upon that they looked with decided distrust and apprehension, as a sort of theft or sacrilege" (1:163–64). The Mandans' insistence on maintaining the ceremonial significance of these sacred materials exhausts the medicine showman's resources: neither enlightenment nor savage art-object is to be his for the asking, bargaining, or taking.

What Catlin has confronted, in fact, is the essence not merely of the okipa ceremony but of the cultural complex according to which such ceremonies were possible, or even imaginable, within Mandan society. Modern students of Plains Indian ceremonial life have noted that among the Mandans and other Plains tribes, sacred medicine bundles—mystery objects associated with, or to speak more properly necessary to, the operation of an aspect or aspects of ritual performance—functioned as physical conduits linking the sacred to the larger network of social relations. That is, the bundles recapitulated on a microcosmic scale the society that produced them and in so doing lent their power toward that society's self-identification and perpetuation. In his study of Plains ceremonialism, Lee Irwin notes that "the vitality of the medicine bundle, its sacred quality, was wholly dependent upon a shared context of religious discourse that both heightened and specified its place in the religious life of the community." In this sense, the bundle embodied the sacred character of Indian culture. The medicine bundle, as Irwin concludes, "expressed the heart of Plains religious life"; its mystery, as inaccessible as it was fundamental, was the mystery of the emergence and persistence of society itself.[63]

As such, for Catlin to breach the rules of bundle possession and revelation was for him to upset the imperative of sustaining social order through sacred action. As Alfred Bowers writes in the fullest study of Mandan ceremonialism available, "There were in each of the Mandan villages a large number of families owning or controlling important tribal bundles. These families were considered the authorities on tribal lore and custom." Within this system, "each Mandan ceremony was secret, and rules providing for the performance of and acquaintance with the secret rites differed somewhat between bundles. In general, it was not possible to complete the study of a ceremony with a single informant, owing to overlapping rights in the bundle, one informant being unwilling to divulge information belonging to another." Martha Warren Beckwith's study of Mandan and Hidatsa ceremony finds similarly that "informants were reticent about speaking of any ceremony to which they had no right" through "transference by purchase or inheritance"; Frances Densmore's work on Mandan music, furthermore, reports that only those possessing the "hereditary right to sing" sacred songs were permitted to do so. According to this system, infringing on the "prescribed rules of behavior when in the presence of [a] bundle or while it was open" was tantamount to rejecting the sacred, which is to say the social, itself.[64] Catlin's failed quest to wedge himself into the Mandan mystery thus reveals the poverty of his medicine-show assumption that the white insider can gain access to the sacred core of Indian life. Lacking an "in" not only to the bundles but also to the rules of the society that created them, the white medicine performer can only watch passively the unfolding of mysteries radically beyond his ken.

But it is not merely by removing Catlin from the lines of power within

Mandan society that the okipa revises the artist's representations. More comprehensively, the presence of sacred knowledge, conduct, and belief utterly
beyond Catlin's capacity opens a space within his text for an alternative reading *of* that text. The great mystery at the hub of the okipa, by announcing that
there is a fullness to Mandan culture, a depth that militates against the white
artist's power and that blocks the white man's ability to claim Indian medicine as the source of his own regeneration, performs in Catlin's works what
Neil Schmitz terms "the Mee-sham effect, or the Mee-sham trope," referring
to the central Mesquakie (Fox) medicine bundle: "It marks what is averted
from Euro-American knowledge, what will not be captured, and as such
marks the present text, the present explanation, as captured knowledge, as
captive utterance. As such it infallibly ironizes the present statement. It marks
the profanation, catches the folklorist, the ethnographer, in the stupidity of
her or his colonial discourse. . . . It puts the entire text in brackets. It desig-
nates as Indian freedom that which always escapes the captures of Euro-
American knowledge and translation, a 'mysterious something.'"[65] In
Catlin's case, what this means is that the undecipherable, unobtainable mystery lodged at the heart of the okipa unmasks for good the colonizing operations of his medicine performance, manifesting the literal and
epistemological violence whereby Indian cultures are stripped of their sovereignty, their spirituality, indeed their existence, to serve the needs of the white
actor and his nation. The mystery object of the okipa, in its defiance of
Catlin's scrutiny and speculation, names his presence in the Mandan ceremony an outrage, an affront to the medicine of which he presumes to partake. Or to put it another way: just as Catlin reads the okipa in terms of his
own or his culture's devising, so does the okipa "read" Catlin, marking his
representations as subordinate and fallacious, the Mandans' own as primary.

And intriguingly, in *this* reading of the okipa, Catlin appears not as an
honored guest, much less as the eminent Medicine White Man, but as the figure who occasioned such befuddlement that the artist was unable to choke
out the words in proper English: "the Evil Spirit," as Catlin names him (1:167),
or as Bowers more properly identifies him, "Foolish One," the representation
of "those who did not respect sacred things."[66] In Catlin's own words, the role
of this being was to allow "us to draw . . . the following beautiful moral:—
That in the midst of their religious ceremonies, the Evil Spirit (O-kee-hee-
de) made his entrée for the purpose of doing mischief, and of disturbing
their worship—that he was held in check, and defeated by the superior influence and virtue of the *medicine-pipe*, and at last driven in disgrace out of the

village, by the very part of the community whom he came to abuse" (1:169).
From the Mandan point of view, perhaps no more perfect representation of
white medicine could be staged. That Catlin's own works become the arena
in which his transgressions are exposed, and his unholy powers expunged, is
ironically appropriate, for it is essential to those works to represent the Indians as the absent ones, the impotent puppets to be manipulated by the master showman.

And in its ability to frame Catlin's project, to disclose his ignorance of
the Mandans' medicine and the ignoble aims and effects of his, the okipa performs a final, and revolutionary, act. The inaccessible secrets of the Mandan
grand ceremonial demolish the underpinnings of the medicine show, its
need to represent Indian cultures as either nonexistent or fast on their way to
nonexistence, vacating the scene so as to allow their white heirs to nourish
themselves on the lees of the Indian spirit. Largely in spite of itself, Catlin's
performance of Indian medicine inscribes the very thing that is most antithetical to the medicine show's authoritarian claims: the enduring presence
of Indian cultures that are anything but beautiful blanks, that are as replete
with self-regulating forms, as tenacious of their integrity, as fiercely resistant
to their displacement, belittlement, and desacralization, as his own. What
emerges from his texts and acts thus comes as close as any work of the pre-
modern era (with the possible exception of Morgan's *League of the Iroquois*)
to encompassing the paradigm of culture that has predominated since the
advent of Boasian cultural relativism: an emic, semiotic, or (as we might say)
performative paradigm. According to this view, culture consists of an infinitely complex system of signs, each of which is meaningless in itself and
thus no better than barren or bizarre when (re)presented to the outsider, but
all acquiring meaning through their actualization in the social arena, in the
multifarious rituals of the everyday as well as in the exceptional rituals of the
sacred. Here, for instance, is Catlin's disquisition on Indian and white
costume:

It is from the observance of a thousand little and apparently trivial modes and tricks
of Indian life, that the Indian character must be learned; and, in fact, it is just the
same with us if the subject were reversed. . . . A wild Indian thrown into the civilized
atmosphere will see a man occasionally moving in society, wearing a cocked hat; and
another with a laced coat and gold or silver epaulettes upon his shoulders, without
knowing or enquiring the meaning of them, or the objects for which they are worn.
Just so a white man travels amongst a wild and untaught tribe of Indians, and sees
occasionally one of them parading about their villages, with a head-dress of eagles'
quills and ermine, and elevated above it a pair of beautifully polished buffalo horns;

and just as ignorant is he also, of their meaning or importance; and . . . will presume that horns on an Indian's head are nothing more nor less (nor can they be in [his] estimation), than Indian nonsense and stupidity. (1:102–3)

An interesting commentary in its own right, particularly in that Catlin comes to his discovery of cultural relativism while reflecting on role-playing or playacting, his analysis of cultural form and function can be compared to that of Lévi-Strauss: "when one takes account of the wealth and diversity of the raw material, only a few of the innumerable possible elements of which are made use of in the system, there can be no doubt that a considerable number of other systems of the same type would have been equally coherent and that no one of them is predestined to be chosen by all societies and all civilizations. The terms never have any intrinsic significance. Their meaning is one of 'position'—a function of the history and cultural context on the one hand and of the structural system in which they are called upon to appear on the other."[67] Such a definition, with its emphasis on the necessity of context to activate and make sense of the otherwise random terms of the cultural system, illustrates why Catlin's "just representations" of Indian culture are, after all, just representations: culture cannot be represented; it can only be performed. Paradoxically, then, what makes Catlin's representations so rich in the final analysis is their implicit, inadvertent acknowledgment that there *is* no final analysis of culture, that any culture's repertoire can be performed with equal legitimacy and that no one culture can hope to install its particular performance as the one and only.

    In itself, this insight—however undreamt of by Catlin's contemporaries—will not strike modern readers as particularly momentous. But stretch it to its conclusion, and it arrives at a place few even today would recognize. The basis of the medicine show was the objectification of culture: poached as salable commodity, so the sales pitch went, Indian medicine could be endlessly reproduced, represented, and redeemed in venues not of its making. But what Catlin's works illuminate is that when Indian medicine is brought into contact with white, something far stronger and stranger than a simple change of hands occurs: in the medicine show space, the performance remains incomplete, indeed incoherent, without the sacred Indian performances that white America sought to master, to replace, to reinvent for white consumption. This is culture as medicine bundle: peoples bound to (or bound to be) who they are not. For the medicine bundle, to repeat Bowers's words, entails such a binding: "it was not possible to complete the study of a ceremony with a single informant, owing to overlapping rights in the bundle." In this Mandan model of sacred performance, the bundle cannot be reconstructed via a single source; rather, all sources gain shape and power through their bundling with their others. And so the various specimens of sacred performance that Catlin assembles all leave their mark: the pipestone, the dance, the images of dead people by Tenskwatawa, the deaths of the Mink and the Dog, the audience with Osceola, the okipa—this "mixture and medley of unintelligible trash" with which Catlin comes into reverent, poisonous contact makes his text, his art, and his act what they are through the transfers of power binding them as one. So too with Morgan's "Inindianation" postulants, the Iowa dancers' rapt marks, the eager grabbers of the medicine show—all are shaped by the mystery of the other. According to this Mandan performative theory, restoring Indian sacred performance to the culture of white medicine is anything but an act of courtesy or compensation. Quite the contrary, inasmuch as the two were at once deeply conflictual and mutually constitutive, recognizing the presence of Indian medicine is essential if white medicine is to be understood at all.

Our portrait of Catlin—and of the culture(s) within which he operated—thus needs to be redrawn. To this point, discussion of Catlin and his era has focused on whether the white man's representations are faithful depictions or dangerous fabrications: for every testimonial asserting that "we can trust George Catlin to show us things just as he saw them,"[68] there is an imprecation charging that his productions "mask Indian realities."[69] Yet the premise binding both these positions is the same, and it is the same that drove Catlin: the belief that his representations of Indian performance, his performances of Indianness, existed outside the contexts from which they arose. Vincent Crapanzano's discussion of Catlin's okipa idyll epitomizes this position. Though the modern ethnographer challenges his progenitor's claim of "objectivity," terming it a mere ploy to "constitute his authority," Crapanzano's conclusion that the Mandans are wholly displaced by Catlin—that they are "sacrificed to their rhetorical function in a literary discourse that is far removed from the indigenous discourse of their occurrence"—effectively restores Catlin's authority, making him the "definitive" arbiter of the encounter.[70] Though I agree with Crapanzano that contextual factors are central to performative meaning—this is precisely why Catlin cannot make sense of the okipa—for the same reason, I believe it is critical to consider the context of a performance such as Catlin's an *intercultural* one, a context shaped by the relationships among Indian and white. Indeed, when it comes right down to it, this is the only way that Catlin's performances *can* be seen. For though there is no question that the okipa, the quarry, the dance, and other manifestations of Indian medicine had an autonomous existence beyond Catlin's observational or representational powers—this was, again, precisely his trouble—it is impossible to gauge whether Catlin's representations of Indian medicine are authentic with respect to some stable, essential other they seek to represent. What we can say, instead, is that his performances, taken together with their many others, *create* the antebellum scene; they are not post facto records of that scene, more or less reliable, but the very stuff of antebellum history and culture.

As a final illustration of this point, let us revisit one of the many sites in Catlin's bag of tricks in which his performances intersect and are interdependent with the alternative performances of those he sought to represent and replace. I have noted the frequency with which Catlin and his backers plead for the "faithfulness" of his "representations"; and to this point, I have argued that such appeals work in the interest of his authority, emphasizing his art's ability to capture the essential spirit of the Indian. But in light of my claims that Catlin's art reveals the futility of faithfully representing culture, it is possible to turn this appeal around: to argue that what is faithful about Catlin's art is not that it captures, but that it is captivated by the spirit of Indian medicine. Writing of Catlin's contacts with the Mandans, John Ewers argues that the artist's "strongest medicine" was in fact his art, which effected a transformation in Plains artistry: "I have found no evidence to indicate that before white artists visited the Plains tribes the Indian painters of this region had any knowledge of perspective, of color modeling, or of how to combine a number of pictorial elements into an integrated composition. . . . Is it any wonder then that these Indians were awed by the magic of a George Catlin?"[71] I have no doubt that Catlin's presence—or the "magic" of his medicine—made its mark on the artistic conventions of the Plains. But I have every reason to doubt that the transaction was, as Ewers suggests, unidirectional.

Earlier, I wrote that "the most vital application to which Catlin put Indian medicine was as a balm for his own ailing artistic career." To put it this way, however, may be badly to understate the case. For it is evident to anyone who has studied Catlin's productions before, during, and after his western travels that the time he spent in the West (and particularly among the Mandans) absolutely revolutionized his art both thematically and technically. Where Catlin's early and late works resemble (oddly enough) Ewers's description of pre-Catlin Plains Indian figure drawing, which "represented the human being by a featureless, knob-like head atop a blocky body, from which projected linear, stick-like arms and legs," the portraits, vistas, landscapes, and dreamscapes of the artist's Western period are so utterly stunning one can hardly believe the same man painted them.[72] We can explain this metamorphosis any way we like, but perhaps we should explain it as Catlin did: in his culture's most cherished terms of religious conversion. As Catlin wrote, his brush "has been an easy and successful passport . . . to many strange and mysterious places; and has put me in possession of a vast deal of curious and interesting information, which I am sure I never should have otherwise learned" (1:106). Catlin, it may be, emerged from these strange and mysterious places not only playing Indian but also "praying Indian," not only in possession of but also possessed by the spirit of Indian medicine.

I do not make this suggestion lightly. It seems clear that Catlin, though raised by a mother who was "a Methodist and devout Christian," entertained an at best prickly relationship to the dominant religious ideology of his day. Thus, if in *Letters and Notes* he mouths the requisite pieties about Christian civilization frequently enough to escape censure, his later *Notes of Eight Years' Travel* suggests that he may have been searching for just such an alternative as Indian medicine offered. In this book, Catlin's chafing at the framework of Christianity emerges in his regular reporting of his dancers' sacrilegious comments; in the tradition of Montaigne's cannibals, Lahontan's Adario, Chateaubriand's Atala, and Freneau's Tomo-Cheeki, Catlin marshals Indian foils to deflate his own society's self-congratulatory rhetoric. Thus he writes of one enterprising Indian's response to Christian charity: "The Bibles they had received, and were daily receiving, as 'the most valuable presents that could be made them,' he had supposed must of course have some considerable intrinsic value." But when the Indian attempts to sell these icons, "nobody would buy, but one had been *given* to him by a lady; so he came home with one more than he took; and he said to us, 'I guess em no good—I no sell em, but I get em a heap.'" Paralleling Catlin's realization in *Letters and Notes* that cultural "value" arises not intrinsically but from context, this episode at the same time reduces Christian conversion to a seamy sales pitch. Even more suggestively, Catlin reproduces a pictographic chart, ostensibly copied from an Indian original, that represents "their ideas of white man's paradise, and the six different modes of getting to it." Strikingly similar to the pictographic scriptures produced in the eighteenth and nineteenth centuries by Indian revivalist prophets, Catlin's "*fac simile*" shows Indians ascending to their own afterlife via a straight and easy path, while Christians encounter a snarl of ladders guarded by Bible-toting ministers and stopping, maddeningly, just short of Paradise.[73] An engine of Indian critique, this image simultaneously resonates with the artist's own balked religious longings: like the hapless soul stranded atop one ladder, he surveys the Promised Land but cannot enter it.

Yet if Catlin was ultimately no more successful in scaling an Indian Elysium than his pictographic petitioner was in entering its Christian counterpart, his frustrated, in-between position is more revealing of the complexities of Indian medicine in the Removal era than a more satisfyingly complete conversion could have been. As always, Catlin's encounters with the okipa provide a key to understanding the quality of his spiritual rebirth. Consider in particular his meditations following the ceremony: "I took my sketchbook with me, and have made many and faithful drawings of what we saw, . . . and since the close of that horrid and frightful scene, which was a week ago or more, I have been closely ensconced in an earth-covered wigwam, with a fine sky-light over my head, with my palette and brushes, endeavouring faithfully to put the whole of what we saw upon canvass" (1:155). Despite—or because of—his revulsion for the perceived cruelties and crudities of the okipa, Catlin is determined to be faithful to his experience. And when he pictures himself "ensconced in an earth-covered wigwam, with a fine sky-light over my head," ritualistically laboring to fulfill his painful duty to his supreme faith, he fuses his act of reconstructing the okipa with his paintings of the Mandan faithful undergoing the initiation rites. Could it be, then, that Catlin was indeed an initiate, though not in the voracious, stockpiling manner he favored—that he was, instead, a proselyte, neophyte, or acolyte of a new faith, one that existed precisely in the meeting-ground of Indian sacred belief and white? Could it be that his testifying to the fidelity of his works shades over into another sense of "testifying"—praising the prodigies of "what we saw," bearing witness to the works of another Artist's hand? Again, one might refer to his paintings of the okipa, wherein the foreignness of Indian ritual meets the traditional Western imagery of Gehenna or of Golgotha. In moments such as these—however uneasily or ambivalently—Catlin represents the greatest white medicine of all, Christian civilization itself, as beholden to, or even indistinguishable from, the Indian medicine it was meant to brush aside.

And the Mandans? They too were transformed by Catlin's presence; the course of their arts, their ceremonies, and their lives was forever altered by the power of white medicine. This transformation, however, was otherwise than he imagined. Due in large part, Bowers theorizes, to the rules of bundle inheritance and apprenticeship that so bedeviled Catlin, the Mandans "were successful in preserving most of their rich ceremonialism," including the okipa, after the death of 80 percent of the tribe in the 1837 smallpox epidemic. Thus, almost exactly one hundred years after Catlin's visit to the Mandan villages, tribal artists survived to produce an artwork that reveals, however equivocally, their relationship to the arts of the white man. Published in Beckwith's *Mandan-Hidatsa Myths and Ceremonies* (1937), this is a Mandan Winter Count, a traditional, tribal record in which major events of each year are represented by pictographs. This particular Winter Count more or less overlaps the years of Catlin's stop and subsequent affairs: it begins in 1835 (three years after his arrival), covers the period of his American and European tours, the publication of *Letters and Notes*, and the loss of his family and Gallery, and ends in 1870 (two years before his death, and about the time that he spent lodged as a charity case at the Smithsonian, stone-deaf and as silent as the Indian portraits that would adorn the Institution's walls years after). Catlin is not, however, represented in this Winter Count, and one would not expect him to be; Winter Counts, as Chadwick Allen notes, offer "an Indian point of view on contact with intruding Whites," a "distinctly indigenous perspective on American Indian history," and as such they "can appear 'incoherent' to Western sensibilities."[74] The Winter Count thus represents yet another evidence of Mandan performative, representational, or sacred practice—another sign system that, though dismissed as unintelligible trash by Catlin and his fellows, gave shape and structure to Mandan society.

In this Winter Count, accordingly, whites are featured only as antagonists, intruders, carriers of disease and disorder. In 1837, the record reads, "Next summer there was small-pox." In 1851, we learn that "the United States government by executive order took away from the Indians approximately 11,000,000 acres of land without any compensation." In 1867, it is noted that "eight years later Custer was killed." In 1869, the news is that "the following winter Wolf-sleeps-long was killed by a white man." Nor is Catlin's artistic influence evident in this Winter Count; however valid Ewers's point may be about the upheaval in Plains art stimulated by Euro-American painters, the Winter Count in Beckwith's text utilizes traditional iconography, relying on clusters of nondimensional figures and series of nonrepresentational symbols impenetrable to any but the Mandan interpreter.[75] And so we have a Mandan reading of Euro-America, its medicine, its artistry, that effectively turns the tables on performances such as Catlin's: here it is the whites who are represented as vestiges, vacant figures consigned to the fringes of the Mandan world. According to this version of Mandan history, culture, and medicine, George Catlin, the great Medicine White Man, was not destined to be "talked of as long as traditions last in this strange community." No: his fate was to be simply absent, a beautiful blank whose banished presence animates every line those who erase him draw.

*Chapter 2*
# Being and Becoming "Indian"

*My friend Mr. Payne and myself will do ourselves the honor of calling this
evening for you & Sister, to attend Mr. Catlin's lecture.*
—*John Ross, principal chief of the Cherokee Nation, note of 10 April
1838*

It speaks volumes about the ubiquity of Indian performance in
the nineteenth century that John Ross, lobbying Washington in a last-ditch
effort to stay or at least soften the 1835 New Echota removal treaty, should pen
the above lines. Indeed, 10 April was little more than a month away from
what Ross's biographer terms the "ominous deadline of May 23, 1838," on
which date the New Echota treaty would go into effect; as Ross himself had
written several months earlier to his friend and sympathizer John Howard
Payne, with whom he would later attend Catlin's talk, "the dark cloud and
threatening storm, which has time past been gathering in the horizon o'er my
native land, seem now to be fully charged & is on the eve of exploding its
combustible elements."[1] For the whole of the preceding decade, Ross had
fought representations of Indian backwardness and dissipation: when, for
example, an 1836 performance of George Washington Parke Custis's play *Pocahontas* featured a contingent of (supposedly) real Cherokees exhibiting
their entrenched and hopeless savagery by enacting a "real INDIAN WAR
DANCE," Ross responded in print, denying that any of his people had performed the dance attributed to them.[2] But now, whether seeking reprieve
from his people's tumultuous affairs, maneuvering to acquire white allies, or
despairing of a positive outcome after unproductive meetings with Martin
Van Buren, he found himself attending a show where such representations
held front and center.

Ross left no record of how Catlin's dumb show of wild western tribes
struck him. (The closest we can come is a letter of 1837 in which he remarks

of a delegation of Sioux Indians, "These people are more in the primitive state than any tribe of Indians I have ever before seen, excepting the Osages. Paint, Feathers & Skins are their principal dress, and their bodies generally bear [bare]."[3] We can, however, make a pretty good guess as to how Ross's presence would have struck other attendees. In his 1833 review, James Hall had strongly hinted that mongrels such as the Cherokees had no place in a gallery devoted to Indian likenesses:

We lingered in this gallery of portraits with a melancholy pleasure. The day will come when the pictured sketches of painted warriors and dark maidens, will be gazed at with intense curiosity. The race is melting away as the winter snow before the vernal breeze. In a few years more we shall know them only in tradition and song, in painting and history. . . . Could even the fairest dream of the philanthropist be realized in the civilization of the Indian, the effect of such memorials as those to which we allude, will be the same; for the savage will have ceased to exist as such, and only on the canvass will he be seen clad in the barbarian pomp of aboriginal finery, armed with the relentless tomahawk, and decorated with scalps and skins, the bloody trophies of war and the chace.[4]

Hall's belief that Indianness and civilization were irreconcilable—that the Indian ceased to *be* Indian when he succumbed to the power of white medicine—was, as Roy Harvey Pearce established in *Savagism and Civilization* (1953), utterly typical of the time. Catlin played a variation on this theme in *Letters and Notes*. Though he praised the Cherokees as being "very far advanced in the arts," and though he was only too happy to depart town with Ross's portrait tucked in his trousseau, his suspicion of Indians who had left "their primitive state" is signified by his waffling reflections on the Removal tragedy: "it is not for me to decide, nor in this place to reason, as to the justice or injustice of the treatment of these people at the hands of the Government or individuals; or of the wisdom of the policy which is to place them in a new, though vast and fertile country, 1000 miles from the land of their birth, in the doubtful dilemma whether to break the natural turf with their rusting ploughshares, or string their bows, and dash over the boundless prairies, beckoned on by the alluring dictates of their nature, seeking laurels amongst the ranks of their new enemies, and subsistence amongst the herds of buffaloes."[5] This may be a swipe at the hypocrisy of Removal. Even so, it falls prey to that policy's principal argument: that civilized arts could not coexist with savage nature.

The most obvious point to be made about John Ross's dilemma is that it was impossible for nineteenth-century Indians, no matter how acclimated to Euro-American-style civilization, to avoid being swept up in the vortex of the medicine show. But just as white medicine play was a far more complex matter than simple imposition, so was Indian performance in the medicine show more trenchant than it might appear. After all, the Cherokees in 1838 were hardly rookies in the play of white medicine; they had lavished years of public and print appearances on promenading, serenading, and masquerading it. Let us recall that the New Echota treaty was itself bound to the representations of Indians that circulated within the space of the medicine show: promising the agricultural Cherokees "a good Country," as Ross's brother Lewis bitterly reported Andrew Jackson's words, with "plenty of game there Buffaloes, Deer &c," the treaty conjured regressive images of Indian savagery to satiate Removal-era policy. Thus, when Ross fought back against the theatrical misrepresentation of his people, he was surely aware that disowning such images was coextensive with his struggles to overturn the New Echota treaty: protesting that "the meeting at New Echota did not fully represent the Cherokee Nation"—that the treaty produced there was a "pretended compact" signed by renegades and miscreants who "arrogated to themselves the style of Chiefs"—Ross insisted that the *real* Cherokees "rejected this spurious treaty, and disclaimed it as their act."[6] The geopolitics of Removal were rooted in the medicine show carnivalesque: the debate over how a Cherokee *did* act—or of what it meant to act Cherokee—was fundamental to both.

And in this debate over Indian performance, Cherokees such as Ross played as subtle and salient a part as did their opponents. Catlin's audiences came to the medicine show in search of "the Indian as Indian," to quote Arnold Krupat in a somewhat different context, as opposed to "the 'civilized' or Christianized Indian"; they wanted Indians, not "Indians"—realities, not images, constructs, or conventions. That what they took to be Indian realities were precisely the images, constructs, and conventions they shunned is plain enough. Perhaps less plain is the fact that John Ross, the civilized or Christianized Indian, was himself an "Indian," and not only in the blinkered eyesight of those who attended Catlin's show: he was a trader in images, constructs, and conventions, a model Indian in white performance spaces. As Paul Gilmore writes of the ethnologic museum, Removal-era Indian displays "did not simply detach Native Americans and their objects from some original cultural context—thus fragmenting and embalming such cultures"; at once, these reenactments "*constructed* [Indian] cultures as authentic, so that both whites *and* Native Americans could re-appropriate Indianness for different political and aesthetic ends." Louis Owens (Cherokee/Choctaw) states starkly what those ends (and means) were for Indian peoples: "In order to be recognized, and to thus have a voice that is heard by those in control of power, the Native must step into [the] mask and *be* the Indian constructed by white America. . . . In short, to be seen and heard at all by the center . . . the Native must pose as the absolute fake, the fabricated 'Indian.' "[7] However unwelcome such fabrication may be to the critical impulse to celebrate Indian voices of protest, autonomy, and self-identification, it remains that the autobiographies and political writings that were the mainstay of the first Native American literary renaissance of the early nineteenth century were not Indian after all but "Indian," written by and about "Indians," not Indians.

To say this is not to say that these acts of Indian display were mere confidence games crafted to gain approval of, or advantage over, sucker whitefolks. That such feints took place I do not doubt. But to accuse all Indian performers of such subterfuge—an approach most strongly identified with the work of James Clifton, the title of whose *Being and Becoming Indian* (1993) I ironically adopt here—strikes me as shortsighted on two counts.[8] Not only does it slight the limits on a colonized people's self-representation, but also it ignores the possibility that the colonized might be, as surely as those who flocked to the medicine show for a draught of Indianness, legitimately shaped by the colonial relationship. The natural, the necessary, condition of intercultural encounter is that one forms oneself by performing one's other; just as whites of Catlin's generation found or founded their identities through the imitative acts of the medicine show, so did Indians model themselves on the very people from whom it was their purpose to establish their difference. Such a history of ethnic identity as invented, emergent, or performed implies, in the words of James Clifford, that "one is always, to varying degrees, 'inauthentic': caught between cultures, implicated in others. . . . If authenticity is relational, there can be no essence except as a political, cultural invention, a local tactic."[9] According to this view, Indian identity, like all American identities, is inevitably a *product* of encounter rather than an evasion or casualty of it.

At the same time, however, this crossing of identity posed challenges for Indian peoples of which majority-culture mimics knew little. For if it is true, as Philip Deloria writes, that "as they shifted, altered, crossed, and recrossed cultural boundaries," native peoples "demolished those boundaries, rendering their own identities slippery and uncertain in the process," one might ask whether traditional, sacred forms of identity were demolished as well. In her study of modern-day Indian identity, Eva Marie Garroutte (Cherokee) calls attention to the risky fuzziness in anthropological accounts such as Clifford's, which concludes that "all the critical elements of identity are in specific conditions replaceable: language, land, blood, leadership, religion. Recognized, viable tribes exist in which any one or even most of these elements are missing, replaced, or largely transformed." Garroutte rejoins: "If we agree that [Clifford] is correct, the whole idea of culture seems to slip through our fingers. How could we ever know if it were present or absent? If all the elements that compose a culture can disappear, while the cultural identity somehow remains, is there anyone who is *not* Indian?" Clifford himself troubles over such questions, writing that he is "straining for a concept that can preserve culture's differentiating functions while conceiving of collective identity as a hybrid, often discontinuous inventive process. Culture is a deeply compromised idea I cannot yet do without." And if Clifford cannot do without culture, is it any wonder that the Indian peoples of Ross's time, or the present, should consider cultural continuity something that, in Garroutte's words, "affects the well-being (perhaps even the survival) of their communities"?[10] Is it surprising that Indian peoples should be less disposed to concede that ethnic identity is up for grabs when for centuries they have been faced with a conqueror bent on obliterating all traces of Indian culture, on the one hand, and on assimilating all remnants of Indian culture, on the other? To rephrase Garroutte's question: If Indian identity is so labile and featureless that anyone can occupy it, what prevents one from furthering the processes of desacralization represented by the medicine show?[11]

In this chapter and the one following, I seek to address this question by exploring two seemingly irreconcilable but actually inseparable forms of Indian performance in the nineteenth and early twentieth centuries. First, I examine the capacity (indeed necessity) for Indians to construct novel identities through imitation of the dominant culture. Second, I explore the efforts of Indian peoples to renew sacred performance traditions, and the identities affiliated with them, not despite but through such imitative acts. In this investigation, I argue that Indian performance balances these seeming opposites not by reproducing the traditional or the sacred in any simple sense but by turning the elements of which it is constituted, even elements committed to *de*sacralization, to sacred use. Such an argument is itself an attempt to balance theoretical perspectives often seen as opposed: Euro-American performance theory, with its argument that every performance, sa-

cred or not, is "reinvented or recreated at each appearance," and Native theoretical orientations such as Garroutte's concept of "Radical Indigenism,"
which "assumes that scholars can take philosophies of knowledge carried by
indigenous peoples seriously," which "suggests resistance to the pressure
upon indigenous scholars to participate in academic discourses that strip Native intellectual traditions of their spiritual and sacred elements," and which
endeavors to utilize sacred philosophies and traditions "to reframe the questions we ask about Indianness." In particular, where Euro-American performance theory rejects essentialist notions of identity, arguing, as in Judith
Butler's comparable discussion of gender, that "the *appearance of substance* is
precisely that, a constructed identity," Native theory welcomes such "essentialist ideas," "ideas presupposing a connection to ancestry rooted in the individual's fundamental nature." To adopt this orientation—to utilize Indian
traditions to determine what counts as traditionally Indian—leads to the
finding, as Garroutte writes, that among Indian peoples, "tradition is fundamentally a *sacred* concept": Indianness consists not in a fixed quality or
quantum but in one's relation to sacred belief and action.[12] Viewing Indian
identity through these twin lenses thus allows for both restoration *and* reno-
vation, intention and invention; in the manner I have defined as characteristic of the medicine bundle, this intercultural model roots Indian identity in
the dynamic interplay of prior (sacred) enactments and ongoing reenactments. Put simply, this model supposes that to be Indian means to perform
Indianness in a traditional, which is to say a sacred, way. And if such a model
offers neither any ultimate criteria for establishing Indian identity nor any
absolute proof against the abuses of the medicine show, it does, I believe,
offer a significant reevaluation of the complex experience of being and becoming "Indian" in America.

   To test this model, I apply it in this chapter to what might seem an im-
probable case: that of the Cherokee Indians, and in particular one of their
number, Catharine Brown, subject of and contributor to *Memoir of
Catharine Brown, a Christian Indian, of the Cherokee Nation*, published in
1824 by American Board of Commissioners for Foreign Missions secretary
Rufus Anderson. (In the following chapter, I explore an equally unlikely example: that of the "show Indians" who traveled with Buffalo Bill Cody.) For
both past and present observers, Brown has epitomized the nineteenth-
century Cherokees' extensive and intimate contact with Euro-American civilization. The first Native convert at the American Board's Brainerd station,
which served as the hub of Congregationalist-Presbyterian missionizing to

the Cherokees from 1817 to 1838, she became a symbol of the successes of the Gospel among the Cherokees and of the tragic implications of the Cherokee Removal. A martyr to the missionary cause, dying of tuberculosis at about the age of twenty-three, the young convert was as close as Protestant America could come to the seventeenth-century Mohawk saint, Catherine (Kateri) Tekakwitha. The posthumous memoir based on Brown's life was remarkably popular in the years before the Civil War; it went through multiple printings in New York, Boston, Cincinnati, and London, was distributed by the American Sunday School Union, and was cited in antiremovalist pleas.

Yet where the stock of some antebellum Indian autobiographers (William Apess most prominently) has soared, Brown's has soured; to my knowledge, no single sustained literary reading of her life and *Memoir* exists.[13] By reconsidering Brown's life and life story, I seek to achieve a number of objectives. First, to the extent that it is true, as Daniel Heath Justice (himself a Cherokee scholar) writes, that "Cherokee identity," by virtue of certain Cherokees' highly publicized adoption of Euro-American customs and beliefs, "is often seen as conveniently porous and easily appropriated, diluted from an ideal Indigenous purity," I propose an alternative model of nineteenth-century Cherokee identity formation, one that emphasizes contact with, indeed imitation of, Euro-America but that rejects accusations of "ethnic fraud" or stereotypes of the Cherokees as "civilized savages or washed-out wannabes."[14] At the same time, by reevaluating a figure who might be placed in one or more of these categories, I challenge the tendency to admit Indians to the literary canon only if they seem vividly and vociferously to contest colonialist conventions or to reveal evidence of "precontact" traditions in their writing.[15] And so, finally, I hope Brown's life will show that the many possible subject positions within the Cherokee Nation, as within Indian nations as a whole—convert and traditionalist, follower of white medicine and practitioner of Native sacred performance, Indian and "Indian"—were themselves overlapping, interpenetrating, and coexisting, even within a single life. The newly struck identities claimed by Brown and her people were not, in any common sense of the word, *traditional*; they were shaped by, channeled through, or composed of cultural conditions that had no place in the past. And yet, in an *un*common sense, these performed identities *were* traditional. They were sacred; they were medicine; they were part of the bundle.

Wearing the Mask

> *The Christian religion is the religion of the nation.*
> —David Brown (Catharine's brother), describing the Cherokee Nation
>   in 1825

On the face of things, it is little wonder that Catharine Brown, unlike Apess and the other antebellum Indian autobiographers who have received scholarly attention and approbation in recent years, should remain largely absent from this critical rediscovery. To begin with, notwithstanding editor Anderson's expressed wish to allow Brown to "speak for herself as much as possible," her actual words, in the forms of letters and excerpts from her diary selected and arranged by Anderson, occupy a mere 50 pages of the book's roughly 120, or just over two-fifths of the whole.[16] Nor, as is typically the case with white-authored Indian autobiographies, is there the slightest pretense of Brown's having initiated contact with her amanuensis. Black Hawk, whose *Life* appeared in 1833, was said by his interpreter, Antoine Le Clair, to have expressed "a great desire to have a History of his Life written and published, in order, (as he said) 'that the people of the United States . . . might know the *causes* that had impelled him to act as he has done, and the *principles* by which he was governed." Meanwhile, Seneca captive Mary Jemison (whose *Narrative* was published the same year as Brown's) was represented as at least willing to hand over her history, having "tarried almost three days [with the editor], which time was busily occupied in taking a sketch of her narrative as she recited it."[17] By contrast, the most the *Memoir* can muster is the boilerplate pledge that "the author is not conscious of having exaggerated a single fact, nor of having made a single statement not drawn from authentic documents" (preface, n. pag.) and the even more blasé assurance that "alterations" in Brown's excerpted letters "are never made; and corrections in the grammar, but rarely" (29).[18]

It is, no doubt, this evident lack of agency that led Krupat, in an initial, quizzical reading of Apess, to pair him and Brown as similarly compromised (non)Indians: "if there is a Cherokee dimension to Brown's text and to her sense of herself . . . or a Pequot dimension to Apes's, these are not apparent to me." (Indeed, initiating a critical tradition of coupling Brown with Apess at the former's expense, Krupat adds in a footnote that "Brown's use of salvationist language is not only regular, as I have claimed of Apes's, but constant.") Barry O'Connell, whose edition of the writings of Apess sparked the

Pequot artist-activist's elevation, uses Brown as a means of emphasizing, by contrast, the unparalleled nature of Apess's achievement: writing that "the narrative voice" of Brown's *Memoir* "is unmistakably that of a Euro-American self-consciously presenting the life of an 'Indian,'" he concludes that "Apess begins a long and complex practice of Native American 'autobiographies' and does so in apparently complete control of his own narrative."[19] To these critics, Brown is entirely a colonialist construct or convention, a product of Euro-American social, religious, and literary mores brought back from the grave not to sustain but to subvert whatever "Cherokee dimension" might still be left to her people.

There is no point in denying that Brown's life exists within a colonialist context. When the *Memoir* digresses to ask "that the reader may be duly sensible of the singleness of heart and Christian devotedness of the men, under whose instruction this interesting female had placed herself" (16), or prays that "this little volume will augment the courage, animate the zeal, and invigorate the efforts, of the friends of missions, in their benevolent attempts to send the Gospel of Jesus Christ to all nations" (preface, n. pag.), one receives the unmistakable impression that the text's ultimate purpose has little to do with this "interesting female" after all. Yet the fact that the *Memoir* is mediated, even dominated, by white designs does not cancel its indigenous "dimension"; quite the contrary. It is only if one opposes Indian identity to colonialism and its constructs—including the construct of the text—that one will have to conclude, as Krupat does in another place, that "we will not learn of Cherokee lifeways in the early nineteenth century from Catharine Brown." If, by contrast, one considers Brown's life in light of the self-positioning of Indian persons and polities during the Removal era, a positioning that necessarily involved contact, struggle, and negotiation between Indian cultural identity and white discourse and interests, then one will find her works and acts fully expressive of, indeed exemplary of, the "Cherokee lifeways" of her time. In her study of Brown's late century heirs, Charles Alexander Eastman and Sarah Winnemucca, Malea Powell argues that these Native autobiographers compose "texts in which they 'consume' and reproduce nineteenth-century 'beliefs' about Indians in order to create 'something else,' a new kind of Indian-ness which allows them to 'maintain their difference in the very space that the occupier' has organized."[20] Brown's *Memoir* represents an early example of this pattern whereby Indians "consume" white medicine, (re)producing civilized discourse to sustain a traditional Indian identity.

In this respect, Brown was no different from the many Cherokee authors who published autobiographical, ethnographic, and political writings during the Removal era, authors including John Ross, Elias Boudinot, John Ridge, and others. For all of these writers, Cherokee identity emerged in relation to Euro-American beliefs about Indians (and non-Indians). As Cheryl Walker writes in her study of the foundations of Indian nationalism, "the general assumption in the critical literature has been that Native Americans were the victims of nationalist discourse pure and simple, that they resisted attempts to impose an idea of nation that derived from European models on their native and essentially tribal structures of governance and knowledge, because such ideas obviously threatened many aspects of their cultures. But the truth is more complicated than this view allows for, because by the end of the first third of the nineteenth century, there were several understandings of nation in play among both Euro-Americans and Native Americans."[21] All of these understandings of nation—as political entity, as land base, as traditional heritage, as racial or ethnic descent, as sacred space—were in play during the rise of the Cherokee Nation, and all were put into practice in the writings of Cherokee nationalists during the 1820s and 1830s.[22] In so doing, these authors fostered a version of Cherokee identity that embraced the twin heads of antebellum Indian performance, one in which their difference from the dominant culture was achieved through their resemblance to it.

And that resemblance was strong. In a memorial sent to the Senate and House of Representatives in 1824, the year Brown's *Memoir* was published, Ross had sought to dispel accusations that it was the Cherokees' white allies, not the Cherokees themselves, who stood behind an organized resistance to encroachment on the Nation's lands: "the *disposition* and *determination* of the nation, *never again to cede another foot of land*, is *positively* the *production* and *voice* of the *nation*, and what has been uttered by us, in the communications which we have made to the Government, since our arrival in this city, is expressive of the *true sentiments* of the *nation*, agreeably to our instructions"; "not *one word*," Ross concluded, "has been *put* into *our mouth* by a *whiteman*." But Ross's statement, however literally true, minimizes the extent to which the production and voice of the Cherokee Nation had been shaped by whites. For not only did the Cherokees adopt the language of their Euro-American supporters, but the very basis of their claims rested on Euro-American ideologies of nation and civilization. Indeed, so tightly were the claims of Cherokee spokespersons interwoven with those of Euro-America, it might be best to speak not of Indian and white voices at all but of a "Cherokee rhetoric" that had become the common property of both. A way of speaking about what it meant to be Cherokee, this rhetoric sought to resist removalist ideology by producing the Cherokees as simultaneously a sovereign state and a mirror image of the United States. The Cherokee rhetoric, then, represented a national program of imitation or simulation—terms I use not in any opprobrious sense, but simply to suggest the "process of self-invention and rhetorical boundary-crossing" that, as Thomas Hallock writes, the rhetoric entailed.[23] And by the same token, those English-literate Cherokees who employed the rhetoric can be seen as imitations or mimics—not, again, in any narrow or belittling sense but in the sense that the Indian identities they claimed, for themselves and their Nation, emerged through the terms of dominant discourse.

One can gain an appreciation of how deeply conventional, how narrow in range, and how reliant on Euro-American discourse the Cherokee rhetoric was by paralleling two Cherokee authors who have often been seen as opposites: Ross, the steadfast adversary of Removal, and Brown's fellow convert, Gallegina (Buck) Watie or Elias Boudinot, first editor of the bilingual *Cherokee Phoenix* and, as one of the signatories to the treaty of New Echota, notorious in his own time and ours for having forfeited—or sabotaged—Cherokee lifeways. Of the two writers, Boudinot initially had the greater opportunity to press his people's claims before a Euro-American populace. Thus in his 1826 "Address to the Whites," delivered during an eastern tour dedicated to drumming up support for a printing press and publicity for the Cherokee cause, Boudinot proposes an alternative to removalist rhetoric:

You here behold an *Indian*, my kindred are *Indians*, and my fathers sleeping in the wilderness grave—they too were *Indians*. But I am not as my fathers were—broader means and nobler influences have fallen upon me. . . . A period is fast approaching when the stale remark—"Do what you will, an Indian will still be an Indian," must be placed no more in speech. With whatever plausibility this popular objection may have heretofore been made, every candid mind must now be sensible that it can no longer be uttered, . . . for the present history of the Indians, particularly of that nation to which I belong, most incontrovertibly establishes the fallacy of this remark.[24]

In this passage, Boudinot sounds the refrain of Cherokee national identity: Indianness is distinct from savagery or heathenism, such that it is possible to imagine an Indian individual or Nation embracing non-Indian culture. As Boudinot's schoolmate (and, subsequently, fellow signatory at New Echota) John Ridge wrote in a report on Cherokee civilization prepared in the same year as Boudinot's address: "all Nations have experienced change. Mutability is stamped on every thing that walks the Earth." Ross, similarly, professed belief in the plasticity of human nature, writing in an 1822 letter to Catharine Brown's brother David that "Indians are endowed with mental capacity fully adequate to receive the highest branches of temporal and spiritual improvements, under the influences of civilized life."[25] In such passages, Cherokee spokespersons developed a notion of Indian identity as slippery, developmental, and above all performable: to be Indian, they argued, was necessarily to act out a part against a backdrop of civilization.

Such a position, it is needless to say, represented a denial of the discourses of racial fixity and monolithic Indianness that predominated at the time. Yet what it did *not* represent was a distinctively Cherokee addition to Removal-era thought. The debate over Indian improvability, as scholars such as Bernard Sheehan and Robert Bieder have shown, was rooted in a larger quandary concerning racial permanency versus racial permeability; in turn, this argument reflected both theological quarrels over the validity of the scriptural creation and philosophical investigations, most strongly identified with the Scottish Enlightenment and in America with Jeffersonian republicanism, concerning the stages of human social development.[26] The missionaries by whom Boudinot, Ridge, and other literate Cherokees were educated stood at the frontlines of this debate, which they saw not only as a challenge to their work but as a test of their faith. Keenly aware, as those who staffed the Brainerd station wrote in the mission's journal, that "the sentiment very generally prevails among the white people near the southern tribes (& perhaps with some farther to the north) that the Indian is by nature radically different from all other men, & that this difference presents an insurmountable barrier to his civilization," these laborers subscribed just as fervently as their flock to the belief that racial difference was of no account in determining a person's or a people's earthly success, much less future state.[27]

Parallel incidents recorded in the Brainerd journal disclose the missionaries' convictions. On the one hand, they describe a family of Cherokee nonbelievers: "We had this evening a melancholy proof of mans proneness to degenerate into the savage state, & [lose] the knowledge of the truths as it is revealed in the scriptures. A mother advanced in life & a son apparently about 25, who would not from their appearance or their language, be suspected to have one drop of Indian blood in their veins, tarried with us for the night. The[y] said they were part cherokee, though the son could not speak the language at all, & the mother but poorly. They were free to converse, &

manifested almost a total ignorance of every thing relating to religion or a future state, & differed in nothing but colour & speech from the sons of the forest." On the other hand, they exhibit the difference between a family of Cherokee Christians and one of nonobservant whites: "Mr. Hoyt again visited families. He found a striking, and an affecting contrast between two families visited to day—One a Cherokee (mixed blood) children instructed in letters, and religion, acquainted with family prayer, decent and orderly in all family duties, christianized and civilized.—The other a white family, raised on the borders of the nation, and now residing in it—children totally ignorant of letters, & of religion—not one could tell who made them; who made the world, or who is the Saviour—unchristianized, and sinking into the savage state, if not already there. Such a difference does the blessed gospel make even in the time of one generation: & (in the former instance) within a very few years."[28] In both of these passages, the porousness and reversibility of cultural barriers is the salient point; the savage state has nothing to do with racial nature but with *human* nature, with the proneness of all humans to revert to sin.

Given this shared understanding of race as superficial and, for all practical purposes, variable, supporters of the Cherokees, whatever their color, were equally deft at subverting the discourse of racial immutability. Their attacks often took the form of trading riffs on the language of civilization and savagery. "Nations cannot be civilized unless they renounce every inducement that tends to their deterioration," Ridge slyly suggests. "As a whole, I cannot call the Cherokees a civilized people and perhaps in this respect it would baffle our expectations if we were to look for it, in any Nation on the face of the Earth." In his 1830 condemnation of the Removal Bill, George Cheever played a comparable angle, asking, "to whom now does the imputation of savage inhumanity belong—to the Indian, or the white man?" He was seconded in the year of the New Echota treaty by Ross's friend Payne: "Well! So much for the beautiful state of our national legislation and morals, as civilizers and protectors of the red-men," he wrote after viewing a Cherokee Green Corn Dance. "It was a melancholy reflection for ourselves, that, comparing the majority of the white and red assemblage there, the barbarian should be so infinitely the more civilized and the more interesting of the two."[29] For white advocates of the Cherokee cause as for those they defended, racial identity was just part of the act.

That the Cherokees' benefactors did not always practice what they preached is all too apparent. For Boudinot, the most painful betrayal occurred when he became engaged to a white woman, Harriett Gold, during his days at the Foreign Mission School in Cornwall, Connecticut. The town—indeed, the region—erupted in a firestorm of racist protest, including the burning of the couple in effigy. Clearly, Ridge spoke prematurely when he predicted a peaceful intermarriage of Indians and whites: "in the lapse of half a Century if Cherokee blood is not destroyed it will run its courses in the veins of fair complexions who will read that their Ancestors under the Stars of adversity, and curses of their enemies became a civilized Nation." Ross was no more prescient in his suggestion that "the day would arrive, when a distinction between [the Indian] race and the American family, would be imperceptible; of such a change, the nation can have no objection. Complexion is a subject, not worthy consideration, in the effectuation of the great object." But if "Christian principles only thinly cover[ed] over firmly entrenched racism," as Theresa Strouth Gaul characterizes the response to the Boudinot-Gold engagement, this was hardly confined to the missionaries. Not only did Gold's own brother mastermind the burning in effigy of his sister and her suitor, but Catharine Brown's brother David, who complained to the missionaries that he saw the outcry against Boudinot as "an expression of abhorrence to the Indian character," had written the year before in praise of an institution that many Cherokees (including Ross) practiced: that of African chattel slavery.[30] The point, then, is not the inconsistency of such enlightened rhetoric but the fact that the rhetoric (as well as the failure to live up to it) was the common heritage of Cherokee and non-Cherokee alike.

Indeed, it was precisely the purpose of the Cherokee rhetoric to call attention to this common heritage: just as there was no absolute difference between Indian and white, the rhetoric went, neither could there be any absolute difference between the Cherokee Nation and the Euro-American nation that surrounded it. Thus in his "Address," Boudinot enumerated how closely the Cherokees had modeled themselves on the larger nation: "it cannot be doubted that the [Cherokee] nation is improving, rapidly improving in all those particulars which must finally constitute the inhabitants an industrious and intelligent people," he asserts before reeling off a list of farms, industries, schools, ferries, roads, libraries, courtrooms, churches, and other signs of his people's impending or achieved civilization. Ross took the same tack in a post–New Echota appeal, invoking the triad of truisms—Christianity, civilization, nationalism—that girded the Cherokee rhetoric: "This people have become civilized, and adopted the Christian religion. Their pursuits are pastoral and agricultural, and in some degree, mechanical," he writes, proceeding to catalogue the same attainments that his onetime associate and current nemesis had named. For his part, Boudinot went even farther in playing the civilization card by exhibiting his mastery of vanishing-Indian discourse: "There are, with regard to the Cherokees and other tribes, two alternatives; they must either become civilized and happy, or sharing the fate of many kindred nations, become extinct"—a truth he drove home by quoting from Washington Irving's "Traits of Indian Character" (1820): "they will vanish like a vapour from the face of the earth, their very history will be lost in forgetfulness, and the places that now know them will know them no more."[31] If, Boudinot insisted, the Cherokee Nation was to avoid this fate, it could only be by blurring racial lines beyond the vanishing point.

And as with their construction of race, in their construction of their Nation Cherokee authors broke no new ground. Andrew Denson, who has studied the Cherokees' petitions to the federal government in the years both preceding and following the 1838 Removal, argues that while "Cherokee political writing in the removal era accepted the basic terms with which European Americans identified Indian people," especially "the notion that Native Americans faced a choice between emulating white civilization and disappearing," it nonetheless deployed these terms in unique and resistant ways. In particular, he suggests that the Cherokee authors tailored the rhetoric to support Indian autonomy against not only the agents of Removal but the gospel of civilization: "Cherokee leaders claimed for themselves . . . the authority to decide the path that Indian civilization would take, insisting that there could be no progress without autonomy." Yet this argument overstates the distinctiveness of the Cherokee leaders' arguments. Cheever, for instance, takes a position identical to theirs: having established that "the first fair trial of the possibility of bringing an Indian tribe into the full perfection of civilization, and under the full influence of the redeeming power of Christianity, is here fast and auspiciously advancing to its completion," he concludes that Indian nations represent "*distinct communities*, and, in a certain and very important sense, *independent sovereignties*."[32] The Cherokees' white champions, it seems, were just as comfortable, and just as steadfast, in arguing that the Cherokee Nation, having made itself over into the white image, was not only capable of but also entitled to separation, self-determination, and self-identification *as* an Indian nation.

Even more forcefully, American Board member Jeremiah Evarts devotes his *Essays on the Present Crisis in the Condition of the American Indians* (1829), first published serially under the pseudonym "William Penn," to proving that

Cherokee *difference* is necessary to Cherokee *identity*: "The wisest men, who have thought and written on this subject, agree in the opinion, that no tribe of Indians can rise to real civilization, and to the full enjoyment of Christian society, unless they can have a community of their own; and can be so much separated from the whites, as to form and cherish something of a national character." Evarts is insistent on designating the Cherokees a sovereign nation. Indeed, his entire argument hinges on a reading of treaties entered into between the Cherokees and the United States (in particular, the foundational treaties of Hopewell and Holston) in which the Cherokees were designated as such: "It appears from this article, as well as from the preamble, that 'Indians' may constitute a 'nation.' The word *tribe*, when used to denote *a community living under its own laws*, is of equal force with the word nation; and in this sense it is to be taken, wherever it occurs in the course of my remarks." But this etymological nondistinction is moot in any event, for, Evarts continues, "as the seven clans, or tribes, of the Cherokees were united under one government, they were all comprehended under the phrase of '*the whole Cherokee nation of Indians*;' and the word *tribe* is not found in the treaty of Holston. The word nation is applied to the Cherokees, in this single instrument, no less than twenty-seven times; and always in its large and proper sense."[33] With a Euro-American editorialist taking so staunch a stand in defense of Cherokee sovereignty, it is difficult to agree that the writings of the Cherokees represented Indian-inflected departures from the canon. Indeed, if one wanted to make an issue of this, one might argue that in pioneering the strategy of grounding indigenous sovereignty in the treaty relationship, Evarts's approach was fundamentally *more* radical than Boudinot's, and possibly more than Ross's. For what Evarts implied was that Cherokee autonomy was based not on their emulating of white civilization but on their inherent rights *as* Nations, "civilized" or not. The tendency of Evarts's thesis, in other words, was to divorce nationhood from civilization (the Cherokees were "nations" long before they became "civilized"), whereas the tendency of Boudinot's (and to an extent Ross's) rather more timid claims was to exalt civilization as nationhood's stipulation.[34]

There is, at that, a final reason to suspect any argument that attributes a particularly radical or distinctively Indian bent to the Cherokees' use of the Cherokee rhetoric, or even that tries to tease the Cherokees free from that rhetoric: it is impossible to distinguish in either Cherokee-authored or Anglo-authored materials exactly *who* is responsible for what. In some instances, Euro-American production of or contribution to Native American materials is a certainty. For example, Evarts drafted almost in its entirety the "Address of the Cherokees" that was delivered to Congress in 1830. Thus, when the Cherokees of this address announce that "we wish to remain on the land of our fathers," it may be that such ceremonialized, conventionalized flourishes, which recur like clockwork in subsequent memorials, sounded to audiences then (and sound to audiences now) like authentic examples of Indian address because they are such perfect examples of "Indian" address. But even in a seemingly open-and-shut case like this, ascertaining where the Cherokees' voices end and the editor's begins is a fruitless task; as is always the case with bundles of performance, each strand is written over or interlaced with its others. Evarts was an accomplished ventriloquist, who threads a (constructed?) Cherokee voice throughout his "William Penn" essays: "To every application made for their lands within the last ten years, the Cherokees have said, 'We are not disposed to sell any more. We have betaken ourselves to an agricultural life. We are making progress in civilization. We are attached to our schools and our Christian teachers; to our farms; to our native rivers and mountains. . . .' This language," Evarts nods, "has been repeated in many forms, and with every indication of sincerity and earnestness."[35] This language had indeed been repeated in many forms—note its use by Boudinot and Ross—and as such its reemergence in Evarts's 1830 "Address" tells us not of its racial origins but of its capacity to erase racial origins (the erasability of which was precisely the point *of* the rhetoric). Boudinot's mature writings encompass the chorus of voices, Indian and white, that claimed a share in the Cherokee rhetoric:

The "Great Father" of the "red man" has lent his influence to encourage [the Cherokees'] difficulties. The *guardian* has deprived his *wards* of their rights—The sacred obligations of treaties and laws have been disregarded—The promises of Washington and Jefferson have not been fulfilled. . . . Is not here an array of *difficulties*? The truth is, while a portion of the community have been, in the most laudable manner, engaged in using efforts to civilize and christianize the Indian, another portion of the same community have been busy in counteracting those efforts. Cupidity and self-interest are at the bottom of all these difficulties—A desire to *possess* the Indian land is paramount to a desire to see him *established* on the soil as a *civilized* nation.[36]

This passage stitches together the various strands that had come to bear on the Cherokee crisis. Sounding overwhelmingly like Evarts—not to mention Boudinot's soon-to-be foe Ross—in adopting the "sacred" language of the treaty relationship, Boudinot plays as well with the patriotic language of the Fathers, echoes Chief Justice John Marshall's position in *Cherokee Nation v.*

*the State of Georgia* (1831) that the Indians' "relation to the United States resembles that of a ward to his guardian," and parrots Lewis Cass, whose 1830 essay on Cherokee Removal had complained of the "difficulties to be encountered in any effort to produce a radical change in [the Cherokees'] condition."[37] On first thought, the seamlessness with which this Cherokee editor voices dueling parts makes one wonder whether his writings were composed by dual parties—whether, that is, missionary coaching or even ghostwriting might have helped him to construct an "Indian" persona. But a second thought succeeds: no lone Cherokee's voice needed to be shaped by an editorial board, for the voice of the Cherokee Nation had been shaped by the American Board. Thus the crux of the Cherokee Nation: its identity (difference) as an Indian nation was founded on its identity (sameness) to the American nation.

To view the Cherokee Nation in this light is to raise what has been the dominant plaint among Euro-American critics from the nineteenth century to the present: that the Cherokees' literate spokespersons, if not exactly traitorous, had so fully consumed white medicine as to be consumed by it. In the Removal era, lobbyists of the Jacksonian persuasion were shameless in applying a racial reading to the supposed divide between these counterfeit "Indians" and the mass of their people. Thus Jackson, who fumed that the "real Indians, the natives of the forest," had been duped by "designing halfbreeds," was echoed by Cass, who scoffed at reports of a general Cherokee renaissance that might warrant rolling back Removal: "That individuals among the Cherokees have acquired property, and with it more enlarged views and juster notions of the value of our institutions, and the unprofitableness of their own, we have little doubt. And we have as little doubt, that this change of opinion and condition is confined, in a great measure, to some of the *halfbreeds* and their immediate connexions." Georgia representative Wilson Lumpkin laid on an even heavier dose of sarcasm, sneering during the House debates over the Removal Bill: "those [Cherokees] who have emigrated are delighted with their new homes, and most of their brethren who remain in the States would gladly improve their present condition by joining them: but their lordly chiefs, of the white blood, with their northern allies, 'will not let the people go.'"[38] This self-serving screed, employing an allusion both scriptural and (for Georgia's slaves) spiritual, provides a particularly ugly example of the uses of racial impersonation in the Removal battle.

Needless to say, modern critics are careful to avoid the language of bleached versus genuine Cherokees favored by Jackson and his conspirators.

In addition, the focus of modern criticism lies not in discrediting those Cherokees who resisted Removal but in fathoming those who ended up on the disastrous road to New Echota. Still, trace elements of the earlier critique can be found. For example, Boudinot's modern editor, Theda Perdue, views him as a "tragic figure" not solely for his part in paving the Trail of Tears but for his having "abandoned" the Cherokees' "traditional way of life"; "a product of colonization" unable to "accept his people, his heritage, or himself," Boudinot, in his desire "to create a homogeneous 'civilized' nation" bereft of its Indian identity, "may well tell us as much about our own culture as about nineteenth-century Cherokees." In a recent reevaluation of Cherokee nationalism, Mark Rifkin perceives a similar opposition between Cherokee traditionalism and the nation-state engineered by the literate elite. Writing that "the categorization of indigenous peoples as 'nations' privileges certain forms of native self-representation over others, often figuring 'autonomy' in ways overdetermined by U.S. political norms (including centralized forms of governance and capitalist economic development) and at odds with traditional beliefs, processes, and modes of identification," Rifkin argues that the rhetoric of Cherokee nationhood sought not only to contest United States hegemony but also to establish a hegemony of its own, one that disguised the heterogeneity of the Cherokee population in the interest of the elite, planter-capitalist class. Thus, "forms of Native American national self-representation such as the Cherokee Constitution . . . need to be read not only for the ways in which they resist U.S. territorial incursions but for their simultaneous construction of class-specific narratives of collective identity that, far from being ironic, serve as the basis for institutionalizing capitalist ideology and production and delegitimizing tradition." Rifkin is careful to define "tradition" in ways that have nothing to do with cultural backwardness or stasis (much less with blood quantum) but with "a sense of cultural distinctiveness" that operates "against the colonialist/capitalist pressure to assimilate to other norms."[39] Nonetheless, his argument sustains the long-standing terms of the debate, posing a total divide between a "distinctive"—that is, traditional— Cherokee culture and the "assimilated"—that is, colonialist/capitalist—Nation that committed acts of symbolic and literal violence in despite of, though in the name of, the majority of its own people.

To question this model is not to deny that Boudinot and other prominent Cherokees, including Ross, underestimated—or, to apply Rifkin's argument, purposely suppressed—the sizable percentage of their population who bypassed or refused Euro-American civilization; as critics have demonstrated in recent years, the homogeneity of the Cherokee Nation was indeed a trick of the rhetoric, not a fact of life.[40] In this respect, Rifkin's analysis is potentially revolutionary, for it seeks to restore to view forms of Cherokee personhood and peoplehood that were erased by the discursive hegemony of the Cherokee rhetoric—forms of imagining and acting what it meant to be a Cherokee that were rooted in traditional (which again I use as a synonym for *sacred*) bonds of being and belonging. Where I depart from Rifkin is in his insistence on sequestering these two forms of Cherokee individual and collective self-definition, thus reproducing the structure of the nineteenth-century argument: the Nation's leaders were elitist progressives alienated from the traditionalist majority. As I see it, this is no improvement over the Cherokee leaders' own vision, and it may in fact do violence to that vision. For if the Cherokee Nation illustrates anything, it is that tradition and civilization, though they could and did function as rivals, could and did function as a joint means of constituting the identities and writings of nineteenth-century Indian peoples.

Our problem in conceiving the Cherokee Nation lies in the deeply rooted suspicion that performance, mimicry, and imitation have a taint of the artificial (if not artful) about them: whether seen positively—as a triumph of covert resistance—or negatively—as a truckling to false consciousness—Cherokee "Indian" play is pictured as a deviation from, rather than a version of, real Cherokee-ness. Thus O'Connell, who reads Indian mimicry in terms of Henry Louis Gates Jr.'s concept of African American "signifiyin(g)," suggests that "straightforwardness is impossible" for Indian writers, whose need to dodge "the culture of domination" leads them to rely on "mimicry, parody, the pretense of stupidity, exaggerated irony," and other "devices" of "duplicity." But if imitation is recognized not as an aberration but as the necessary medium of intercultural encounter, then one will see that Cherokee imitation is deep imitation, not surface, imitation borne not in the word alone but in the blood and bone. This is imitation more in the manner of Homi K. Bhabha's much misunderstood and misapplied concept of colonial mimicry, which involves nothing so purposive as parody but which issues from the depths of colonial relation and representation: "It is as if the very emergence of the 'colonial' is dependent for its representation upon some strategic limitation or prohibition *within* the authoritative discourse itself. The success of colonial appropriation depends on a proliferation of inappropriate objects that ensure its strategic failure," such that "mimicry rearticulates presence in terms of its 'otherness,' that which it disavows." Or it is mimicry along the lines of Robert Cantwell's concept of "ethnomimesis," "that unconscious mimicry through which we take the deposits of a particular influence, tradition, or culture to ourselves and by which others recognize them in us."[41] Ultimately, this is mimicry inherent in the performative act: all performance is iterative, yet no performance is an exact copy of its presumed original. Just such mimicry characterized the medicine show, where white identity emerged through Indian sacred performance. It would be wonderful, then, if Indian sacred identity did not emerge through the performance of white.

The case of Ross is instructive. The man who attended Catlin's lecture and viewed, with whatever reaction of affront or assent, the images of painted barbarians assembled there was not by any conventional measure a traditionalist. Indeed, his writings reveal a man largely dismissive of Cherokee tradition, which he tended to represent as an impediment to the Cherokee Nation's experiment in civilized identity. Thus in an 1824 message to James Monroe (whose edict of the same year set the stage for Removal), Ross wrote positively of the passing of the older, traditionalist generation: "there are many who have been raised under the native habits of their ancestors, who cannot be expected to abandon wholly the favorite customs which have been imbibed in their youth, their partiality and prejudices in favor of their Fathers are naturally strong, but under the present aspect of improvement, they will not fail to encourage their children to adopt the prevailing habits of industry and civilizations; therefore as the old stubbles disappear, the new sprouts will flourish under cultivation." Ross's attitude toward Cherokee tradition might be symbolized by a letter on the subject that he wrote to Payne: "Mr. [Daniel S.] Butrick [of the American Board] asked me for letters of introduction to such persons as were familiar with the tradition, original customs & manners of their nation—[torn page, words missing]. . . ."[42] Though it is intriguing to speculate what might have been on the torn page, when it came to discussing his people's traditions, Ross's words were indeed missing.

Yet for all Ross's disregard for Cherokee tradition defined as a body of custom and belief transmissible through time, he was a traditionalist in the sense in which I have used the term here: a proponent of an enduring Cherokee identity that *could* be passed on from generation to generation, even if that identity was promoted through the agencies of white civilization that were intent on the Indian's ruin. And I can do no better than to suggest that such a quality, simultaneously intangible and durable, was a sacred quality—an essential quality that imitation did not destroy but, on the contrary, of which imitation became the vehicle. Ross's own use of the term *sacred* helps clarify the enigma of Cherokee traditionalism. At the start of his long career of public service, addressing the General Council of the Cherokees, Ross wrote: "The trust which you have reposed in me has been Sacredly maintained and shall ever be preferred." In the year of the Removal Act, he urged his people to "stand united & firm in the maintenance of these sacred rights, which we have enjoyed, and our interests & happiness would thereby be promoted."[43] In neither of these usages should one read the word *sacred* as applying to what Ross himself, and most commentators of his time and since, have termed Cherokee "tradition." Nonetheless, in both of these usages one perceives Ross invoking an essential—sacred—quality that survives despite (or because of) its flexibility, a quality that remains constant (and constantly Cherokee) even as it takes on the face of Euro-America.

Ross's imitative traditionalism should be seen, moreover, not as an exception, not as the halfway measure of a politico, but as a key to the exercise of tradition among the Cherokees as a whole. In another letter to Payne, Ross announced the discovery of some of his people's traditions and insisted that these sketchy materials "have not been received from whitemen," for the informants from whom they were harvested "have been from their childhood, most entirely secluded from the whites, having no direct communication with them."[44] As with Ross's denial that his people's resistance to land sales had anything to do with white influence—indeed, as with his denial of his people's performance in white show spaces—this representation of traditionalist Cherokees as utterly cut off from whites cannot be strictly true; the majority Cherokees who led traditional economic, spiritual, and domestic lives were, like all Indian peoples, affected by Euro-American civilization. Thus in Cherokee lives, as in the Cherokee rhetoric, tradition was achieved not solely by resisting the hegemony of the dominant culture but by working *through* it—a preposition I use advisedly, to suggest both traditionalism's dependence on and its transcendence of the acts by which it operates. That such traditional work was not unequivocally triumphant goes without saying; had it been so, no Removal would have taken place. But the failure of Indian tradition to rout its opponents should not lead us, in a vain attempt to preserve it, to abstract tradition from the varied forms it took, forms ranging from open resistance to equally open emulation. If we do so, we support the logic of Removal, with its image of a happy hunting ground outside white culture that is the sole and final resting place of real Indians. If, by contrast, we view tradition as an emergent process that took multiple forms—indeed, that could take any form, the point being not the form it took but the relation it sustained—then we will see that Ross, Boudinot, and other Cherokees were striving, though in different and frequently competing ways, to forge an identity as people of a sacred nation.

Such a definition of Cherokee sacred tradition as essential performance is vital if one is to overcome the image of Catharine Brown as a plaything of civilized-Christian hegemony. Reading her through this revised definition, it becomes clear that her Cherokee-ness arises not from her distinctive use of the Cherokee rhetoric—for in this respect she is a pure, indeed consummate, mimic—but from the ways in which she achieved sacred objectives through such mimicry. Writing of the violence done to medicine bundles by the agencies of colonialism, Neil Schmitz argues that "to reanimate a sacred pack, to have it turned on, would presumably take a religious tribal repossession, require some appropriate respiritualizing ceremony."[45] Such acts of tribal repossession occurred on a regular basis throughout the period of the Cherokee Nation's rise; in many cases, women were at the center of these ceremonies. But the reanimation of the medicine bundle did not take place solely in such manifestly traditional ways. It could also take place in the confines of a mission, in the toils of a domestic.

## Weaving the Cloth

> *The elevation of our race does depend upon the manner in which woman executes [her] commission. Nor does the destiny of man as an individual, alone depend on female influence, but that of nations, kingdoms, and empires.*
>
> —Qua-Tsy, "Female Influence," *an article published in* Cherokee Rose Buds, *the newspaper of the Cherokee Female Seminary in Oklahoma*

As a woman, Catharine Brown held a clearly defined role in the Cherokee Nation and its rhetoric. That role was expressed in a 1796 letter to her people from George Washington: "your wives and daughters can soon learn to spin and weave." In the decades following, the president's recommendation was put into practice not only in individual homes but in the regimen of domestic discipline carried out at Brainerd and other stations. "The girls certificate to day," an 1823 entry in the Brainerd journal reads, "contains the following summary of their labor between schools since monday of last week, viz. They have made fifty hunting frocks, besides hemming a number of handkerchiefs & some other sewing, in addition to their usual work in other branches of labor which is assisting in the dining room, in the milking, in all the washings, doing the whole of their own washings & ironing, most of the ironing for the mission family & boys, & mending the boys clothes." Cherokee authors joined the missionaries in identifying the spinning and weaving of cloth as the Cherokee woman's principal if not exclusive attainment in her people's surge toward civilization. As Charles Hicks, assistant principal chief of the Nation from 1817 to 1827, announced in an 1822 report compiled by Jedidiah Morse for the War Department, "the Cherokees may be considered in a progressive state of improvement, more particularly those in the middle part of the nation, for there is scarcely a family but what understands the use of the card and spinning wheel. . . . The arts of weaving and knitting have become part of the female attention of this nation." In his 1826 memo, John Ridge stressed this point as well: "for the family [the women] sew, they spin and weave and are in fact a valuable portion of our citizens."[46] Equating women's "value" with weaving, Ridge suggests the association—one might say identity—of the Cherokee woman with this domestic art.

But to these men, the value of women's weaving was not measured mainly in utilitarian terms. Rather, Jane Simonsen writes, women's domestic activities were seen as "an engine of civilization," not merely accompanying but steering the Nation's rise. As Ridge related: "The females were the first who were induced to undertake domestic manufactures," and as an anecdote of a chief initially opposed to Washington's civilization program illustrates, they were likewise foremost in influencing those around them to pursue the same course: "this Chief . . . came to the Agent and said, that he was going on a Hunt, should be gone six Moons, and hoped during his absence [the agent] would not mention to his family [the civilization] plan; that it would do for the white people, but not for Indians. While this Chief was absent, the Agent prevailed on his wife and daughters to spin and weave cloth, and it was done to that extent, as to be more valuable than the Chief's Hunt at his return. Pleasantly disappointed he immediately came to the Agent and accused him for making his wom[e]n better Hunters and requested a plough, which was given to him, and from that time he became a farmer." To Ridge, the lesson to be gleaned is plain: "mankind must yield to the tender sex. Woman civilized man or makes him barbarous at her pleasure. If Ladies gave us universally the smiles of approbation in our extravagancies we would be extravagant—in murder, we would delight to kill—if in cruelty we would be cruel"—and if in civilization, civilized. In his 1826 "Address," Boudinot had prophesied: "methinks I can view my native country, rising from the ashes of her degradation, wearing her purified and beautiful garments, and taking her seat with the nations of the earth"; by 1837, Ross assured, this vision had been fulfilled: "Our people [have] abandoned the pursuits, the habits and the tastes of the savage, and put on the vestments of civilization."[47] Literalizing these images of the Cherokees draping themselves in civilized suits, men such as Ridge invested women's everyday role as weavers with the godlike power to turn the savage civilized.

This image of woman as civilizer, exerting a pervasive if private influence over her partner and her people, is surely familiar, and it provides additional evidence of how intimately the Cherokee rhetoric was itself woven into the Removal era's dominant discourse. Ten years after Ridge offered his analysis of the Cherokee woman's special and crucial cultural office, and on the eve of John Ross's futile pre-Removal trip to Washington, D.C., minister Jonathan Stearns cast the women of his own nation in the role of civilization's savior, urging in his discourse on *Female Influence* (1837), "On you, ladies, depends, in a most important degree, the destiny of our country. . . . Yours it is to decide, under God, whether we shall be a nation of refined and high minded Christians, or whether, rejecting the civilities of life, and throwing off the restraints of morality and piety, we shall become a fierce race of semi-barbarians, before whom neither order, nor honor, nor chastity can stand." In her *Essay on Slavery and Abolitionism*, also published in 1837, a better-known Catharine B.—Catharine Beecher—presented a less hysterical yet essentially identical portrait of the awesome responsibility that was laid before the Christian women of the land: "to American women, more than to any others on earth, is committed the exalted privilege of extending over the world those blessed influences, which are to renovate degraded man, and 'clothe all climes with beauty.'" This conviction that Christian women were charged with the vital task of civilizing their people was the cornerstone of the nineteenth-century ideology of domesticity. In sermons, didactic tracts, and domestic literature, women imbibed—and in benevolent associations and writings of their own they acted out—the belief that like their patient, long-suffering, self-sacrificing Redeemer, civilized women—though removed from the political process proper—could by virtue of their very distance from the squalid affairs of men exert a heavenly influence that might effect "the moral regeneration of a fallen world."[48] In this respect, domestic ideology concurred with the Cherokee rhetoric in constructing identity as emergent not fixed; safe passage from the savage to the civilized state was guaranteed to those who could weave a new identity, refashion themselves in the civilized style.

This was, of course, the central conceit of Brown's *Memoir* as well: that Christian domesticity could transform the savage woman, whose life (and death) could in turn transform a savage nation. Thus, though editor Anderson devotes little attention to his subject's household duties, he structures Brown's life story to accentuate the total transformation from savage to civilized (domestic) state. The *Memoir*'s early pages present the pre-Brainerd Indian girl as a Catlinesque tabula rasa, a beautiful blank awaiting the touch of the missionary brush: "Her mind, like the wilderness in which she had her home, was uncultivated" (104). And that wilderness, as one of the few episodes taken from Brown's early life testifies, illustrates the vast distance the Cherokee ingenue must travel to enjoy the blessings of domesticity: "Considering the looseness of manners then prevalent among the females of her nation, and the temptations to which she was exposed," it is "remarkable" that, "during the war with the Creek Indians, [when] the army of the United States was stationed near her father's residence," she managed to escape defilement by Indian or white: "Once she even forsook her home, and fled into the wild forest, to preserve her character unsullied" (12). This passage conjures slantwise a familiar image: that of the Indian woman as the antithesis of the civilized, a thrall to male warlords and to her own bottomless sexual appetites.[49] In either case, as James Hall sermonized in the *History of the Indian Tribes of North America* (1836–1844), the savage woman's peculiar condition—indeed, the peculiar condition of savage life—could be traced to the perversion of domestic arrangements:

The savage woman is debarred of the prerogatives, and deprived from exercising the virtues, of her sex, by her wandering life. The fireside, the family circle, all the comforts, luxuries, and enjoyments which are comprised in the word *home*, are created and regulated by female affection, influence, and industry—and all these are unknown to the savage. He has no home. The softening and ennobling influences of the domestic circle are unknown to him; and the woman, having no field for the exercise of the virtues peculiar to her sex, never appears in her true character, nor is invested with the tender, the healthful, the ennobling influence which renders her, in her proper sphere, the friend and adviser of man.[50]

The Indian woman's sorry state exemplified the need for benevolent intercession on her people's behalf: if women were the fulcrum on which the fate of the Nation rested, then the reordering of gender relations was necessary to swing the balance toward civilization. Hence the force of the *Memoir*'s parable: home, the place where the Christian woman remains unsullied by the sordid traffic of the world, becomes in the morally rudderless savage state the place of woman's greatest peril; and Brown, for whom the Christian home is yet unattainable, must pursue salvation by fleeing to the wild forest, site of heathen revels and (as those familiar with the captivity tradition would know) pagan lust. For the Cherokee woman, domestic order is abrogated: to avoid rape in the home she must seek succor in the wild.

For Brown to adopt the habits of Christian domesticity, then, no less than "a revolution" in "the general course and tenor of her life" (115) will avail. The action that signals Brown's acceptance of the gospel of domesticity is one that fuses rejection of heathen things with rejection of female impropriety. "She had a high opinion of herself, and was fond of displaying the clothing and ornaments in which she was arrayed" (14), Anderson notes sourly, reminding the reader of this objectionable trait pages later: "she was vain, and excessively fond of dress, wearing a profusion of ornaments in her ears" (24). But "since she became religious, her trinkets have gradually disappeared, till only a single drop remains in each ear. On hearing that pious females have, in many instances, devoted their ornaments to the missionary cause, she has determined to devote hers also" (25). Putting aside worldly things was, of course, a conventional sign of the soul's regeneration. Yet for Brown, being "willing to give up every thing in this world to Christ" (30) carries a cultural connotation as well. "We find new aims, new plans, new habits of action," the *Memoir* exults. "'Old things are passed away'" (115). For Brown, the removal of Indian costume signifies the emergence of a civilized identity.

Having shed her heathen ornamentation, Brown appears in a wholly new guise "as a member of the domestic circle" (57). As one of Anderson's correspondents effuses: "She was not now the wild, untutored girl she was then. She was graceful and polite, and humility and benevolence beamed from her countenance" (69). Her outstanding qualities as a convert are picture perfect: "modesty and reserve" (23), "sweetness of temper, meekness, gentleness, and forbearance" (57), and "unfeigned piety" (68). Where earlier she had bridled at the commands of male authority figures, never more will she be guilty of what her Euro-American namesake, in *A Treatise on Domestic Economy* (1842), termed the sin of "unsubmissive murmurs": "Dear friends, I weep," Brown writes when forced to move with her parents to

Arkansas; "my heart is full; tears flow from my eyes while I write; and why is it so? Do I murmur? God forbid" (32). Anderson reads such submissiveness as a sign of her faith: "in this very way, God has given her an opportunity to set an example of filial obedience, by submitting to the authority of a father, in a most painful requisition, and of manifesting love to the Saviour, by her willingness to forsake all for him" (36). Indeed, submission to father figures, mortal and divine, is the premier quality that Brown strives to muster. "O may I be submissive to thy holy will," she pleads in her diary, as she wrestles with her brother John's impending death (67); on her own deathbed, she expresses a "hope to bear the chastising rod with humble submission" (90). Brown reveals the gratitude beseeming a woman who has escaped her sisters' fate: "When we consider what woman . . . is, in barbarous and savage lands," Stearns wrote approvingly and reprovingly, "darkened and degraded, without knowledge, without influence, without honor, the mere drudge of society . . . and contrast with this dark picture, the happier scenes which christianity presents, . . . we cannot wonder that *she* should exhibit peculiar attachment to a faith which has bestowed upon her such blessings."[51] Little wonder, either, that Brown appears to have shed her savage skin entirely: "some of my acquaintance," Anderson's correspondent concludes, "were unwilling to believe she was an Indian" (69).

In keeping with this equation of Christian domesticity with the erasure of Indian identity, the greatest triumph of Brown's "self-abasing" career (108) comes with her ultimate act of submission: her death, which is described, suggestively, as "her removal from the world" (87). The *Memoir*'s description of this exemplary convert as she awaits transfiguration indicates both her acceptance of and longing for removal: "The natural mildness of her features seemed lighted with a beam of heavenly hope, and her whole aspect was that of a mature Christian, waiting, with filial patience, the welcome summons to the presence of her Lord" (92). In a telling reference, Carolyn Ross Johnston suggests that Brown's deathbed scene "resembled that of Little Eva in *Uncle Tom's Cabin*. . . . Dying chaste, young, and beautiful, Brown became a symbol of true womanhood."[52] The arc of Brown's *Memoir* thus traces the loss of one racial/gendered identity—the girl-child given over to the perils of the pagan wilderness—and the assumption of its antipode, the Christian woman on the verge of entering her heavenly "Father's house" (94). As is typical of domestic literature, the *Memoir* closes with the reconstitution of a family, in this case one that folds the domesticated heathen into the family unit. Or, more ambitiously, Brown's beatifying heralds the spread of a continental domestic paradise, and thus the ultimate restoration of divine domesticity in heaven. "Let the life of Catharine Brown operate as an appeal to the benevolence of the Christian community," Anderson beseeches in the *Memoir*'s closing pages. "Though dead, she speaks; and oh, let her voice fall with persuasive and irresistible eloquence upon every ear" (121), urging the evangelization of all heathen people: "O let sloth be driven away; let the grasp of avarice be loosed; let benevolence assume the dominion; let a spirit of enterprise be kindled; let the messengers of salvation be quickly sent to every tribe that roams the western wilds" (123).

With sentiments such as these displayed so prominently throughout the *Memoir*, it is impossible not to note the ways in which the ideology of domesticity, for all its vaunted liberalism, supported a cultural absolutism as total as, indeed agreeable to, that of the removalist camp. The affinity of domestic and Jacksonian ideology can be perceived in Justice Marshall's use of domestic analogies to structure the Cherokee case. Beginning his opinion in *Cherokee Nation v. the State of Georgia* (1831) in the sentimental mode, with the observation that "if courts were permitted to indulge their sympathies, a case better calculated to excite them can scarcely be imagined," he went on, famously, to designate the Cherokees "*domestic* dependent nations" who "acknowledge themselves . . . to be under the protection of the United States," who "admit that the United States shall have the sole and exclusive right of . . . managing all their affairs as they think proper," and who therefore lack the rights of sovereign nations.[53] Given this casting of Indian nations in the role of the dependent domestic, it is at once understandable and lamentable that during the Removal crisis writers should so regularly plead sympathy to abet atrocity. One need only read the following lines from Lydia Sigourney's *Traits of the Aborigines of America* (1822), a text that plays a minor role in Brown's *Memoir*, to observe domestic ideology burnishing what it claimed to oppose:

Blot from th' accusing scroll
Those guilty traces, with repentant tears:
Teach thy red brother in the day of wrath
To stand before the Judge, and plead, "Forgive!
Forgive! For he hath sent thine holy word,
Hath told me of a Savior, and diffus'd
The day-beam o'er my darkness. His kind voice
Taught me to call thee Father. Oh! forgive
Those earthly wrongs which he hath well aton'd
By pointing me to Heaven."[54]

In what appears a rationale for domestic imperialism, the civilized woman's moral suasion operates here to justify the violence from which civilization has supposedly spared her, a violence now directed not against her but against those she professes to serve. Noting this bitter contradiction, Amy Kaplan christens domestic ideology with the perhaps more appropriate phrase "manifest domesticity": "the empire of the mother . . . shares the logic of the American empire; both follow a double compulsion to conquer and domesticate the foreign, thus incorporating and controlling a threatening foreignness within the borders of the home and the nation."[55] The paradox of domesticity—empowerment through removal—appears in this light anything but an idle one: by removing *themselves* from battle, Christian women sanitized or sanctified the removal of *others*, whose removal clinched domestic ideology's power while broadening the field for their labor of love. Sign and assurance of civilization's triumph over barbarism, domestic ideology became the basis of a blessed barbarism in the name of woman, Indian and white.

That Catharine Brown's *Memoir* arises from the same noisome mix of benevolence and butchery as Sigourney's poem cannot be doubted—for an excerpt from *Traits of the Aborigines* wraps the *Memoir*'s portrait of the heathen woman as Christian convert:

Modest, tender, kind,
Her words and actions; every vain desire
Is laid obedient at the feet of Christ.
And now no more the gaiety she seeks
Of proud apparel; ornaments of gold
She gladly barters for the plain attire
Of meek and lowly spirits. (117)

Lines well chosen to limn the woman who emerges from the pages of the *Memoir*—right down to the detail of her relinquishing her heathen ornaments—this passage indicates the extent to which the *Memoir* is beholden to the domestic imperialism of its day.[56] For if the Indian woman's acquisition of domestic influence is, as the *Memoir* urges, predicated on her repudiation of any vestige of herself *as* an Indian woman, then the same "influence" that raises her people into civilization justifies her people's removal from it. Officially, the American Board remained opposed to Removal (though individual members diverged from this mandate); missionary-activists at Brainerd, including Samuel Worcester and the station's doctor, Elizur Butler, suffered the hardship and ignominy of prison rather than accede to Georgia's takeover of the Cherokee country; and the *Memoir* itself, in a modest way befitting its female subject and its form of spiritual autobiography, adds its tithe to the budding anti-Removal movement, pleading for public support and action against the "unpropitious causes [that] press heavily upon the poor Indians" (120). Yet the series of removals Brown suffers on the road to redemption—removal from her family, removal to Arkansas, removal of her ornaments, removal from life—opens rifts within the Board's public position, enabling one to see how the *Memoir* replicates, albeit in a spiritualized form, the brutal logic of Jacksonian removal, which held that the Indians needed to be turned out to be brought in. The ideology of domesticity, as K. Tsianina Lomawaima (Creek) sums up, was "a clear surface manifestation of the gender- and race-based fault lines segmenting American society" during the Removal years; under its spell Cherokee partisans, red and white, lost their bearings, confused means and ends, courted the agents of hell in heaven's cause.[57]

It is possible, of course, that Brown was supportive of (or submissive to) the program of manifest domesticity; to refuse an Indian the right to adopt such a program is to restore the oppositions I have claimed the Cherokees challenged. Anderson reports that Brown "read accounts of the triumphs of the cross in heathen countries, with peculiar delight" (58); here she not only stands in for but stands up for the marvels of manifest domesticity. At the same time, however, I would not want to overlook the ways in which such (manifestly) domestic rhetoric, like the Cherokee rhetoric more generally, could be marshaled against the removalist camp. As Mary Hershberger notes, two women often seen as poster girls for apolitical domesticity were at the forefront of a popular movement on the Cherokees' behalf: "To block removal, Catharine Beecher and Lydia Sigourney organized the first women's petition campaign and flooded Congress with antiremoval petitions, making a bold claim for women's place in national political discourse." Written anonymously by Beecher, the petition rehearsed the standard pieties: women, it announced, "have nothing to do with any struggle for power, nor any right to dictate the decisions of those that rule over them.—But they may *feel* for the distressed; they may stretch out the supplicating hand for them, and by their prayers strive to avert the calamities that are impending over them."[58] Yet such appeals ultimately carve out an expanded role for women in the space that Beecher's own rhetoric insists women disclaim:

And those whose hearts thrill at the magic sound of *home*, and turn with delightful remembrance to the woods and valleys of their childhood and youth, will they allow this helpless race to be forced for ever from such blessed scenes, and to look back upon them with hopeless regret and despair?

You who gather the youthful group around your fireside, and rejoice in their future hopes and joys, will you forget that the poor Indian loves his children too, and would as bitterly mourn over all their blasted hopes? And, while surrounded by such treasured blessings, ponder with dread and awe [the] fearful words of Him, who thus forbids the violence, and records the malediction of those, who either as individuals, or as nations, shall oppress the needy and helpless.[59]

Invoking woman's place to transcend it, Beecher speaks with a political authority not properly hers. (Indeed, this is so in a literal sense: she was inspired to mount her campaign after hearing Evarts speak, and the language of her petition strongly resembles that of his 1830 "Address of the Cherokees.") As Alisse Portnoy writes, "because women's petitions effectively combined essentializing ideologies about womanhood with strategically selected topics of debate, the political intrusion of female antiremoval petitioners seemed a natural extension of their female roles and responsibilities. The result, though, was a rhetorically constructed, distinctly gendered political authority that enabled women's collective participation in national debates for the first time in United States history."[60] A reexamination of Brown's *Memoir* suggests how a *Cherokee* woman may have defied Indian removal by working through similar "essentializing ideologies" of race and gender. Such a reexamination suggests, moreover, how as a Cherokee *woman* Brown's rhetoric may have carried a degree of difference not only from Euro-American ideology but also from a gendered ideology of removal that operated within her own nation.

One way to think of Brown's adoption and adaptation of Christian domesticity is to place her in the role that Michael Coleman attributes to female students at Brainerd: as "cultural brokers," these young women "saw themselves as helping their families to build a new kind of nation, one that could resist white demands for removal." Early in the *Memoir*, Anderson writes that the founding of Brainerd "came to the ears of Catharine, then living at the distance of a hundred miles, and excited in her a desire to attend the school" (13). Though one can only guess at the source of this desire, the uncommonly strong yearning for education expressed in Brown's letters, her "wish to learn as much as I can" (50) and "improve the great privileges, which I now enjoy" (36) in order to be, as she puts it repeatedly, "useful to my poor countrymen" (90), is striking. This quest for "usefulness to our countrymen" (81) can, of course, be read in the parochial terms of an 1819 American Board report, which praised Indian education as a way to "qualify [students] for extending influence, and for important usefulness, in their respective nations."[61] Yet it is also possible to read such "usefulness" in a more actively political sense. A recurrent theme in Brown's fervent prayers, Anderson notes, is her solicitude toward her people: "her desires for the salvation of her people, were now strong and ardent. For them she wept and prayed, in secret places, and in the company of her female friends at their weekly prayer-meetings" (18). Brown's letters echo these sentiments: "My heart bleeds for my people, who are on the brink of destruction" (37). Expressions such as these, it may be, deploy the terms of Christian domesticity in an attempt to effect not only her people's eternal salvation but their rescue from immediate destruction. To say this is not to question Brown's "unfeigned piety" (68) or "true religion" (48), any more than noting Beecher's turns of domestic phrase is to question her commitment to domestic ideology. It is, rather, to suggest that for Brown, as for Beecher, unfeigned piety and true religion—perfect imitation of Christian domesticity—may have been avenues to contesting the removal of Indians from the body (and bodies) of the nation.

The power of Christian domesticity to contest Indian removal emerges even more strongly in Brown's letters to those individuals, Cherokee and white, who were in a better position than she to translate usefulness into political action. For example, her letters to her brother David, which constitute a sizable plurality of the correspondence reproduced in the *Memoir*, suggest a process of grooming him for the work that is denied Cherokee women. In a letter written in the year of the *Memoir*'s publication, Evarts had counseled David to pursue Christian ordination as a means of gaining Euro-American allies: "The prevalence of the Christian religion among your people . . . is the only thing that will secure the public opinion of this country strongly in their favor, and if public opinion is strongly in their favor, . . . indignation would be aroused by any open and flagrant acts of injustice towards your countrymen."[62] Brown, needless to say, couches her own appeals in terms appropriate to her station. Urging her brother to further his religious training so that he will be prepared for "great usefulness in the world" (74), she advises: "I trust you will not return before you are prepared to preach the Gospel. . . . I do not expect you to go through all the studies, that ministers generally do in New England, but wish you to be qualified enough to withstand the enemies of God" (80). Brown's letters, it appears, served as private (domestic) communications that passed the bounds of domesticity:

encouraging David to obtain the education he needs to represent Cherokee Christianity not only to his own people but also to the larger world, Brown calls on her guaranteed "influence" to inspire and deputize her male relative to labor on the Cherokees' behalf. And indeed, David's later activities—which included translating the New Testament into the syllabary designed by Sequoyah, preparing laws for the Cherokee national council, and lecturing on Cherokee progress and affairs—indicate that his studies took on a decidedly political cast. According to Anderson, it was Catharine who had taken the lead in steering David down this path: "David had been desirous, for some time, of being fitted to preach the Gospel to his countrymen, and was encouraged to aim at such a preparation, first by his sister Catharine, and then by the missionaries" (40). Though as a Christian domestic, Brown could not appear on the national stage, she seems to have acted as David's confidante and dialogue coach, helping her brother find his own voice with which to address and redress the needs of their people.

In a somewhat different fashion, the letters of lavish praise and glowing report that Brown penned to her Christian benefactors demonstrate the ways in which her exemplary piety bound advocates to the Cherokee cause. "My sincere desire, and earnest prayer to the throne of grace," she addresses one southern supporter, "is, that your labors may be blessed, and that God would make you the instrument of saving many souls from eternal destruction" (46); to a northern donor, she writes, "I can never express my gratitude to God, for his goodness towards me, and my dear people. Surely it is of his own glorious mercy, that he is sending to us the Gospel of the Lord Jesus, in this distant land, where the people had long sat in darkness, and were perishing for lack of the knowledge of God" (48). Such fervent expressions of devotion to white sponsors and disdain for her own people may strike one as distasteful. Noting that students at the Cherokee Female Seminary in post-Removal Oklahoma authored articles for their newspaper exulting "that many tribe members had progressed past savagery and were on their way to equality with whites," Devon Mihesuah (Choctaw) suggests that these women's hymns of praise to the glories of civilization indicate their despite for Cherokee culture and identity. Yet however legitimate such a reading may be, it is worth recalling that the Cherokee rhetoric functioned through just such oblations of abasement and exaltation; intended specifically for white consumption in Brown's case and for a dual audience of Cherokees and whites in the case of the seminarians, these rituals of praise, humility, and progressive chauvinism publicized the Cherokees' achievements while at the same

time recruiting support for their existence as a people. Virginia Moore Carney (Eastern Cherokee) argues that throughout the Removal years, Brainerd's female students used their letters to "fight for the rights of the
Cherokees"; sidelined by the ideology that supposedly granted them so privileged a role in uplifting their people, these young women, like Brown before
them, applied themselves to the civilized Cherokee woman's favored activity
to weave not garments but a skein of words that buoyed their people's quest
to endure as a nation.[63]

And in this respect, one of the most fascinating aspects of Brown's
*Memoir* is its suggestion that domestic ideology not only served the Cherokee Nation but also served to claim or reclaim a position for women within
it that transcended the domestic role of weaving and spinning. Revisionist
studies of Indian gender relations have argued that, contrary to nineteenth-
century beliefs, Native women enjoyed considerably greater freedom and
authority within tribal societies than within intercultural entities such as the
Cherokee Nation. The stereotype of Indian women as pitiable helots or
shameless wantons, such studies argue, confuses cause and effect, representing not only the limited perspectives of Euro-American (and mostly male)
reporters but also the damaging effects of colonialism, including the programs dedicated to raising Indian women's status. As Paula Gunn Allen puts
it: "When the patriarchal paradigm that characterizes western thinking is
applied to gynecentric tribal modes, it transforms the ideas, significances,
and raw data into something that is not only unrecognizable to the tribes
but entirely incongruent with their philosophies and theories." Though few
critics accept unreservedly Allen's claim that "the physical and cultural
genocide of American Indian tribes is and was mostly about patriarchal fear
of gynocracy," most agree that the roles of women in Indian cultures have
been obscured or altered by patriarchal bias and by Euro-American economic, political, military, and missionary systems. Thus, for example, Carol
Devens argues that "asymmetrical, even antagonistic relations between the
sexes" within Ojibwa society may have been an outgrowth of encounter,
while Regula Schonenberger suggests similarly that a complementarity of
gender roles in pre-contact Delaware society, with "a blurring of realms
which in our cultural context are clearly demarcated as gender-specific and
separate spheres," was disrupted by the fur trade, war, and the revivalist religion of Handsome Lake, which emphasized submission to male leaders
and fomented hunts for female witches.[64] In each case, these critics note the
interdependence of Euro-American discourse and practice: what writers

*made* of Indian women reflected to a great degree what colonialism had *made* of Indian societies.

As with all Indian peoples, the factors that critics identify as impacting Indian women's traditional status make it impossible to state with certainty what the position of Cherokee women was in the years before the rise of their nation. It seems unlikely that Cherokee women ever held the despotic power that trader Alexander Long attributed to them in 1725: "the women rules the roost and wears the breeches and sometimes will beat their husbands within an inch of their lives." Nonetheless, there is evidence that Cherokee women's roles were considerably more varied, active, and substantive than the ideal of Christian domesticity allowed.[65] Throughout the eighteenth century, Perdue writes, Cherokee women had "their own arena of power" beyond the control or even awareness of men; grounded in their role as agriculturalists—a role that was itself grounded in the myth of Selu, the female deity whose death gave rise to corn—Cherokee women's productive (and not merely reproductive) power pervaded the economic, cultural, and spiritual life of their people. This honoring of women's creative energy was represented by the central part they played in the Green Corn Festival, the Cherokees' annual ceremony of communal self-definition and renewal. According to James Adair's 1775 account, the "old beloved women" performed the culminating act of the festival, presenting the new crop in token of women's life-sustaining role. Perdue argues that "the Green Corn Ceremony marked the social and spiritual regeneration of the community, and the role of women in the ceremony symbolized [the role] they played in Cherokee society. . . . By honoring the corn, Cherokees paid homage to women."[66] In the Green Corn Ceremony, according to this reading, Cherokee society dramatized women's role as givers, keepers, and replenishers of tribal life.

Moreover, the (re)generative power of the Cherokee women seems not to have been merely symbolic; rather, pre-Nation Cherokees translated women's sacred power into political authority. Or perhaps one might say that political authority derived from women's sacred power, the matrilineal clan system and matrilocal residence pattern of pre-Nation Cherokee society providing not only that one's identity was dependent on one's female relatives but also that women claimed a voice in tribal affairs through the unit of the local household. Thus eighteenth-century Cherokee women showed no compunction about intervening in their people's political life, as when one woman, Kateuha, addressed a letter to Benjamin Franklin urging him to "mind what a woman says" and expressing her "hopes [that] you have a beloved woman amongst you who will help to put her Children Right if they do wrong, as I shall do the same." The title to which this petitioner, like Adair, alludes was reserved for women who had achieved the pinnacle of political power; most famously held by Nancy Ward, the eighteenth-century War Woman of Chota, the title of Beloved Woman conferred upon the holder the right to speak in tribal, intertribal, and extratribal occasions, as well as the ability to act as mediator in determining the fate of prisoners of war.[67] Ironically, then, women in traditional Cherokee society, far from being the abject wretches of domestic discourse, seem to have held authority within the realms that domestic ideology prohibited women: the economic, the political, the military, and the ceremonial. Or, to phrase this somewhat differently, what Cherokee women claimed was the power, inherited from Selu, to revitalize these realms, to sustain traditional Cherokee society through acts of sacred renewal.

If, however, the role of resacralizing the traditional was prized by Cherokee women in the years before the consolidation of their nation, that prominent social/ceremonial function began to close—ideologically and, to an extent, materially—as a result of the Cherokee Nation's rise. And this was so because the forces that brought the Nation into existence—trade, warfare, diplomacy, and the federal civilization program—favored the power of men as creators and re-creators of Cherokee society over that of women. The deerskin trade magnified male hunting as the source of economic prosperity, while military clashes put a premium on men's prowess as warriors. The transition to private landholding (itself related to the loss of communal lands) dissipated the matrilocal township, while the acquisition of private property (including slaves) enabled the growth of a bourgeois lifestyle compatible with the ideal of true womanhood. Finally, the plan of realigning Cherokee men as farmers (in part a response to the depletion of fur-bearing animals) involved women retreating to the home, while the program of missionary cultivation, as we have seen in the instance of the *Memoir*, emphasized docility, submissiveness, and silence as the Christian woman's proper traits. Commenting on the comparable shift in gender relations among the eighteenth-century Delawares and Mahicans, Jane Merritt suggests that "the balance of power in native communities most likely rested on subtle tensions between female clan lineages and male political needs. Potential for conflict between the two was always present and probably expanded as interactions with white immigrants multiplied."[68] This exaggeration of male social, political, and spiritual power was not sudden among the Cherokees, and neither,

it seems, was it ever as complete as both Cherokee and Euro-American boosters claimed. In 1789, William Bartram provided a portrait of Cherokee
women that, while nowhere near as extreme as Long's, would still have
seemed inexplicable to those fettered to the image of the lowly "squaw":

the condition of the women is as happy, compared with that of the men, as the condition of women in any part of the world. Their business or employment is chiefly in
the house, as it is with other women, except at the season when their crops are grow-
ing, when they generally turn out with their husbands or parents, but they are by no
means compelled to such labor. . . . Besides, you may depend upon my assertion that
there is no people any where who love their women more than these Indians do, or
men of better understanding in distinguishing the merits of the opposite sex, or more
faithful in rendering suitable compensation. . . . I never saw or heard of an instance
of an Indian beating his wife or other female, or reproving them in anger or in harsh
language. And the women make a suitable and grateful return; for they are discreet,
modest, loving, faithful, and affectionate to their husbands.[69]

Even this sunny summary, however, comports to a great degree with the precepts of domestic ideology: though Bartram grants Cherokee women a considerable share of contentment and marital bliss, he omits any reference to
women's political, social, or conjugal authority. Rather, he suggests that
Cherokee women have begun to adopt both Euro-American domestic roles
("their business or employment is chiefly in the house") and the tempera-
ment that rounds out the domestic ideal ("they are discreet, modest, loving,
faithful, and affectionate"). Raymond Fogelson argues that one may read in
commentaries such as Bartram's "subtle changes in the status of women,"
themselves reflective of "significant transformations in local ecology and in
economics, social structure, and political organization." Though I am reluc-
tant to attribute such transparency to textual accounts produced under the
aegis of the Cherokee rhetoric, it is evident that the birth of the Cherokee Nation was attended by upheavals in the representation, if not always the reality, of women's status as bearers of their people's culture and identity.[70]

A quarter-century later, with the Cherokee Nation in full flower,
women's ability to effect the ongoing life of their society—at least as decreed
by the laws of their Nation—had waned to near nothing. As Perdue notes,
"the republic usurped many of the prerogatives of clans and undermined the
principle of matrilineal kinship," as by institutionalizing property inheritance from father to children and by transferring to the new system of courts
the clan's authority to adjudicate disputes.[71] Even the law most often cited as
evidence of women's continuing power within the Nation, that of married

women's retaining their property, can be seen principally as a means of preventing unscrupulous whites from gaining control of national assets, not as a defense of women's rights.[72] The assault on women's participation in political affairs culminated in an 1826 ruling by the General Council of the Cherokee Nation that restricted the franchise to free male citizens, a move ratified the following year by the Constitution of 1827. The role envisioned for Cherokee women by politicians, agents, missionaries, and the leaders of the Nation alike was thus one of drastically reduced autonomy and opportunity; as Ridge put it, women were to be confined to performing the "Duties assigned them by nature as Mothers or Wives." (Tellingly, when in 1835 Ross set out to help the Brainerd missionaries collect Cherokee traditions, he applied not to women but to "the aged men who have been correctly instructed in the traditions of our ancestors.") In the eyes of these men, women's usefulness had been pared down to the basics of biological motherhood; though female influence might be celebrated sentimentally in stories of the Nation's birth, to the men at the helm of the Nation, Cherokee women had lost their life-giving power as guardians of sacred tradition. In this sense, as Gregory Evans Dowd writes, domestic ideology's attempt to turn "Indian women into spinners and weavers . . . threatened to turn the world on its side, to derange the powers that governed fertility of all kinds, even to end life's renewal."[73]

For Cherokee women, then, the acts of "Indian" performance that were played out by their nation occasioned greater ambivalence than was the case for Cherokee men: the nation that sought to safeguard their traditional identity as Cherokees sought to strip their traditional identity as women. As such, it is unsurprising that the transformation in the role of women became a focal point of conflict within the Cherokee Nation throughout the Removal years. William McLoughlin writes that a persistent source of "division among the Cherokees . . . was between those who held to the ideal of a communal ethic and matrilineal kinship and those who were adopting an individualist ethic and the patriarchal family." Wilma Dunaway finds that gender was a key factor in this division: "The majority of Cherokee women did not see the future as did their national leaders." Evidence of Cherokee women's divergence from the Nation's norms, Dunaway notes, appears in the fact that significant numbers of Cherokee women, conscious that the program of domestic instruction would infringe on women's rights, "mounted aggressive and continuous opposition to the missionaries and schools." The Brainerd missionaries describe one such woman whose husband complained that his wife, "being in an uncivilized & heathen state," planned to "take [their children] away [from school], & it would then be out of his power to get them."[74] According to a letter included in the *Memoir*, Brown's own mother, the full-blood (or possibly mixed-blood) Tsa-luh, was of the same mind: she "wished she had never sent me to this school, and that I had never received religious instruction" (45). In this conflict over missionary instruction or indoctrination, one perceives how women's attempts to assert traditional gender roles—or to assert their gender's role in the traditional—posed a challenge to the Nation's rhetorically homogeneous identity.

A particularly dramatic sign of women's refusal to conform to such an enforced identity appeared in the Cherokee revitalization or Ghost Dance movement of 1811–13, in which Cherokee prophets (some of them women) advised their people to reject white culture and to return to the sacred rituals and customs of their ancestors. Precipitated in part by a series of earthquakes that physically shook the Nation during this period—earthquakes that produced not a qualm among Cherokee leaders such as John Ross, who wrote casually in 1813 that "the Earthquakes are still to be felt occasionally about this place"—the Ghost Dance movement, evidence of social upheavals within the Cherokee Nation, shocked Euro-American observers who had never marked the fissures beneath the Nation's outwardly civilized surface. "A large collection of these deluded creatures met at Oostenalee town where they held a grand savage feast and celebrated a great medicine dance which was performed exclusively by women," a horrified Thomas McKenney, who would later serve as Commissioner of Indian Affairs, wrote—his horror amplified, perhaps, by the fact that it was women who had turned their "influence" against the Nation. Indian agent Return J. Meigs, for his part, reported that "some of the [Cherokee] females are mutilating fine muslin dresses" in protest, while Moravian missionaries recorded the prophets' message that Selu was offended because corn was being prepared using white technology: "plant Indian corn and pound it in the manner of your forefathers; do away with the mills. The Mother of the Nation has forsaken you because all her bones are being broken through the grinding [of the mills]." By reconstituting the maternal body of the Cherokee people and by disfiguring the woven dresses that signified fealty to domesticity, those women who participated in the revitalization movement marked their difference from the domestic, dependent identity that had been imposed on them. And in so doing, they honored the traditional not simply by recovering past customs but by asserting their rights, as women, to *reinvent* the past. That is, where Perdue argues that in the Cherokee Nation "women became the conservators of traditional values while men entered a brave new world," women's central role within this Cherokee revitalization movement suggests that the traditional values Cherokee women conserved included most importantly the sacred power to remake the world anew.[75]

This being the case, it would be a mistake to assume that all women's resistance to the Cherokee Nation assumed such overtly traditionalist forms—or that the traditional could be recalled only in such overt ways. At the same time, women's efforts to resuscitate the traditional took the shape that Cherokee people had long cultivated: that of speaking through the voice of the dominant culture. Thus Nancy Ward, petitioning the Cherokee National Council in 1817 and 1818 on behalf of Cherokee women, echoed domestic ideology to convince the leaders of the Nation to preserve common landholding and to outlaw future land sales: "We do not wish to go to an unknown country which we have understood some of our children wish to go [to] over the Mississippi, but this act of our children would be like destroying your mothers. . . . Therefore, children, don't part with any of our lands but continue on it & enlarge your farms & cultivate and raise corn & cotton, and your mothers and sisters will make clothing for you which our father the president has recommended to us all." That these issues were of particular concern to Cherokee women cannot be doubted; as Dunaway notes, "the elimination of matrilineal control over lands" was one of many proposals that threatened "to entrench male dominance and patrilineal descent," while Removal might have meant the death knell of matrilineal and matrilocal traditions. But the success of Ward's speech (the laws for which she petitioned were in fact passed) need not mean, as Karen Kilcup argues, that her words expressed women's power in "traditional Cherokee culture," as opposed to being "a sentimental appeal to motherhood—which in white culture would have been an appeal to 'influence.' "[76] To the contrary, when one compares Ward's address with Beecher's circular, noting not only the remarkably similar sentimental/domestic imagery but also the way in which such devices provided both of these women a platform from which to address their respective nations, it becomes evident that it was *because* Ward employed the terms of female influence that her appeal worked, and worked politically, in a setting where women's traditional powers had come under assault. In the eyes of the Cherokee Nation's leaders, women's traditional and domestic roles may have inhabited separate realms. But women such as Ward, practiced in the art of sacred renewal, found ways to invest the domestic with the traditional, to make the domestic perform sacred work.

It may seem a long way from Beloved Woman Ward to Little Eva Brown—and to be sure, the latter's activities took place on a different, if no less prominent, scale and stage than those of the War Woman of Chota. Yet Brown is similar to Ward in her use of the acceptable discourse of Christian domesticity to tap a gendered authority denied her by that very discourse. Writing in 1830, domestic author Sarah Tuttle adopted the conventional complaint that "the women were miserable slaves and drudges to their fathers and husbands" before the Cherokee Nation's conversion to civilized domesticity; but in Brown's case, the misery, slavery, and drudgery seem to have been attributable in large part to domestic ideology's empowerment of men like her father, while liberation appears to have come by wielding that ideology to place herself on a roughly equal footing with them.[77] The encroachment of domestic ideology in Brown's family, at least as represented by the *Memoir*, was well advanced. Her mother, Anderson writes, was "more attentive to neatness and good order, in the internal arrangements of the family, and more conversant with the duties of domestic life, than her countrywomen generally" (10), while her father appears the quintessential patriarch, moving the nuclear family at will and brandishing the stick of paternal inheritance when Catharine balks at his orders: "if she would not mind him, and go with them now," he warns his daughter during an argument over the family's removal to Arkansas, "he would disown her forever" (26–27). John Brown was, in fact, close enough to the centers of male power to participate in the drafting and ratification of the 1827 constitution, and he seems to have put into practice in his own household the laws of fatherly authority and filial—in particular, female—obedience that were to become mandatory for the Nation as a whole.

If, under these circumstances, submission to the will of a heavenly Father would have seemed all too familiar to Brown, such submission might also have seemed a means of freeing herself from her earthly father's sway, or even of gaining a measure of power over him. After receiving Christian instruction from his daughter, Anderson records, John Brown underwent a revolution not only in his soul's estate but also in his treatment of Catharine and in his respect for her mentors: "Now, he does not ask her [to remove] without our consent; will not take her except by our advice" (43). In time, gaining the ultimate triumph over her father by effecting his conversion, Brown became, as it were, the nominal head of her family: "Ere long she had the joy of beholding her father, mother, a brother, and two or three sisters, unitedly seeking the pardon of their sins" (55). In similar fashion, Brown finds it possible to influence other male leaders through her example and ad-vocacy of Christian domesticity. The "efforts of Catharine" (38) to convince her father of the value of Christian education, Anderson notes, led to the fol-lowing resolution: "We, the headmen, chiefs of the Creek-Path town, Chero-kee nation, have this day assembled ourselves together for the purpose of devising some plan for the education of our children" (38), a plan that ulti-mately provided Brown with her own sphere of influence, removed from the eyes of father and missionaries alike. Brown's victories support Nancy Shoe-maker's argument that, as with her seventeenth-century namesake, Kateri Tekakwitha, Indian women within a colonial world "called upon the symbols of Christianity to assert their own identity and authority within the native community."[78] In this light, Brown's burning desire to become "useful to my dear people," to "be made the means of turning many souls from darkness unto marvellous light" (45), suggests her will to recover, not repudiate, the power that, according to the laws of her nation, women could express only as or through domestic influence.

Consistent with this reading, Brown's daily activities, as well as her grander assignments, were carried out largely within the domestic circle. Whether achieving "a salutary and abiding impression" on individual Chero-kee women (29), "teaching the Lord's Prayer and the catechism to the younger girls in the school" (18), or holding "a weekly prayer-meeting with the female members" of the mission (57), Brown functioned most comfort-ably and effectively with her countrywomen. Thus when the missionaries re-ceived word that the Cherokees near Brown's home settlement of Creek Path "desired another school" for "their daughters" (42)—an outcome, as previ-ously stated, of her influence on the headmen of the region—Brown was tapped for the post: "These facts being known at Brainerd, the missionaries thought it their duty to advise Catharine to go and take charge of the con-templated school" (42). Brown's first independent teaching job placed her in an opportune position to interact with other Cherokee women: "Catharine opened her school with about twenty scholars, and the number soon in-creased. Not only the daughters, but the mothers also, manifested a strong desire to receive instruction" (54). Brown's preference for and persistence in drawing together Cherokee women may indicate that, like many Christian women, she found in the acceptance of a suffering Christ a way of validating "feminine" spirituality, or of projecting into the spiritual realm her own sense of domestic anguish. Alternatively, the practice of female piety within the sanctioned space of the mission may have offered Brown, in Perdue's words, an opportunity to create a "community of women that replicated in some ways the world in which [she] grew up" but that was denied, derided, and suppressed by the official organs of her nation.[79]

This whisper of a Cherokee "female world of love and ritual"[80] operating within the heart of the enterprise that had encouraged the Cherokees to consign women to society's fringes is strengthened by the fact that Brown apparently hosted some of her meetings in private, and in her native tongue: "after a prayer-meeting, conducted by the missionaries," she and "a pious Indian woman of great age, collected a little group of their people, who had come to spend the Sabbath there, and held a religious conference, with prayer and praise, all in the Cherokee language" (40). The significance to Brown of such gatherings is suggested by a letter written during her final illness, in which she instructs an acquaintance to "continue the meetings of females" (93) after her death. And her death, in this respect, can be seen as a furtherance of her life's work: that of resisting the loss of sacred authority vested in the women of the Cherokee Nation. The frontispiece of the American Sunday School edition of the *Memoir* captures the scene of Brown's lasting influence on those of her own gender: a woman (presumably Brown) sits propped in a canopied bed on which an open book rests, telling her life to another who attends at an escritoire, her pen poised to take down every word. This image of the transmission of Brown's inspirational story from woman to woman has a certain internal validity: Brown's diary, Anderson documents, was preserved by missionary women (52), while her legacy lived on in the post-Removal seminarians who eulogized her in their own domestic publications. Suggesting the survival of a women's secret/sacred society largely exempt from male surveillance—even if it runs within the walls of a largely male establishment—this image transforms Brown's domestic influence into an extension of the Cherokee woman's traditional realm. Speaking through the appropriate language of domestic piety, Brown's "persuasive and irresistible eloquence" (121) presses not only for the recovery of her people but, specifically, for the recovery of women's sacred power of healing and renewal.

And in this respect, Brown's life and works intervene in a uniquely gendered fashion in one of the most fiercely contested sites of struggle between Indian and white medicine: the conflict between indigenous and implanted systems of faith and healing. For the Cherokees, as for all eastern Indian peoples, clashes between shamans and missionaries were acute throughout the Removal years. According to Tuttle, shamans would often charge that "the missionaries prevented the success of their charms," while American Board missionary Daniel Butrick (Ross's correspondent on matters of Cherokee tradition) found that his preaching against "idleness, sabbath-breaking and especially conjuring, and my determined public opposition to them, has excited some feeling against me." One way in which the Cherokees expressed hostility toward white medicine was by spreading rumors of mission-sponsored epidemics. According to the journal kept at the Brainerd station, the mission's doctor, Elizur Butler, "met a man who had heard that many of the children [at the mission] were sick & that they were all going home. He expected to take his son home on account of the sickness & said others in his neighborhood were calculating to do the same." In his late nineteenth-century studies of Cherokee healing formulas, James Mooney found that this belief persisted: "white physicians," the healers he contacted averred, "let loose epidemics to ravage the Cherokee settlements. According to some informants, [the physicians] do it simply because they hate the Indians; according to others, in order to enrich themselves at the expense of their victims." The Cherokee term for disease, Mooney writes, can be translated as "the intruder"; if civilization was the disease, then the term was fitting.[81]

And the cure, as the scene of Elias Boudinot's murder in post-Removal Oklahoma indicates, could be a violent one. "He had begun building a house for his family adjacent to Samuel Worcester's mission at Park Hill when the survivors of the 'trail of tears' arrived in the West," Perdue describes the event. "On the morning of June 22, 1839, near the construction site of his new house, several Cherokees approached Boudinot and requested medicine. As he led two of the men to the dispensary at the mission, they attacked with knife and tomahawk and escaped, leaving Boudinot fatally wounded."[82] Executed in the traditional manner of clan revenge, and cut down at the juncture of the twin sites where white medicine was dispensed—the mission and the pharmacy—Boudinot fell victim to the belief that such medicine was indeed a lethal intruder, an epidemic that threatened the body and soul of the Cherokee people.

As with the many instances of Cherokee revitalization I have noted, from the founding of the Nation to the flaring of the Ghost Dance, one should not assume that this distrust of white medicine was confined to traditionalists (however defined); nor should one assume that all who embraced white medicine did so as the missionaries desired. In 1835, a traveler in the Cherokee country, J. P. Evans, wrote that it was only those possessing the "true Indian character" who would not "trust to the operations of medicine alone in the cure of disease; but resort to conjurations etc. with perfect confidence in their efficacy"; the evidence, however, suggests that this preference for shamanistic healing may have been shared by the majority of Cherokees, even by those who professed the Christian religion. The Brainerd journal reports of one convert: "the woman who had been raised almost to health by [Dr. Butler's] instrumentality, had fallen a victim to her imprudence; or perhaps to the mistaken notions of her relatives. She died yesterday. It appears that she had been heated in a Hot house, and while in a high state of perspiration plunged into a river. This is one of the Indian methods of curing the sick: but, in a case like hers, nothing could have been more injudicious. Ignorance and superstition mutually foster each other, as it respects both soul and body."[83] For Christian and pagan Cherokees alike, it seems, when it came to healing body and soul, the "true Indian character" came out.

The same, indeed, could have been said of the mission's favorite daughter. As Perdue notes, "even Catharine Brown, that most Christian of Cherokees, was not immune to the lure of Cherokee religious practice." During her brother John's fatal illness, she accompanied him on a trip to Alabama's sulphur springs to attempt a sweat-bath cure (64), while during her own last days, she consented to her parents' course of shamanistic treatment: "it had been proposed to send again for Dr. Campbell. But her parents were persuaded first to try the skill of some Indian practitioners" (91). Though the missionaries were distressed by Brown's choice of doctors, it is possible that faith in shamanistic healing had been with her all along—had brought her, in fact, to the mission's doors. Raymond Fogelson discovered that twentieth-century Cherokee conjurors "did not feel any inconsistency in combining the professions of Indian conjuror and Methodist or Baptist preacher"; Catherine Albanese, meanwhile, finds that "around the time of the Removal, one Cherokee told Butrick that the same word which meant a power to heal disease also meant a power which atoned for collective moral guilt." It may be, then, that while Butrick and his fellows were railing against the shamans, seeking to drive a wedge between the traditional healing of disease and their own emphasis on moral guilt, Cherokee Christians such as Brown, like a female conjuror described by McLoughlin, had embraced white medicine in a "pragmatic effort to gain the support of the strong spiritual powers of that faith system to add to those of the Cherokee system." By calling on Christian conjuring—on the figure that the missionaries, praying for the cure of another mortally ill Cherokee woman, termed "the Great Physician"—Brown may have sought not only to heal the consumption that was eating away at her own body but to prevent white medicine from consuming her people.[84]

If I seem to be suggesting that Brown, that exemplary Christian convert, convention, or construct, might herself have been a shamanistic healer, such a claim is not without precedent, either in the literature of Cherokee healing or in the *Memoir* itself. The association of women with medicine and healing was deeply rooted in Cherokee belief, as in the myth of Stone Man (or Stoneclad), a cannibalistic giant who ravaged the community before being overcome by a lineup of seven menstruating women, and who, as his dying act, "told them the medicine for all kinds of sickness."[85] Given this belief in the ability of women to give (as well as take) life, it is unsurprising that the profession of shaman was open to members of both sexes. In the years before the Removal, Dunaway writes, "half or more of the conjurers were women; and this professional skill provided them income, influence and standing in their communities." As late as the first third of the twentieth century, while the absolute number of women conjurors had declined, their authority had not: "If a woman practices," Frans Olbrechts reports, "she does not limit herself to patients of her own sex, nor to any set diseases; nor is the treatment by her of any ailments, even in male patients, considered improper. She exercises her profession on a par with her male congeners, enjoys the same rights, and if her knowledge and skill justifies it, she may in time be held in the same reputation as one of the leading members of the faculty."[86] The profession of healing, it seems, provided Cherokee women with a uniquely suitable opportunity to exercise their traditional power to create, sustain, and renew life.

In this respect, it is particularly intriguing that the skill missionaries and leaders alike lauded as the insignia of the Cherokee woman's progress in civilization—and through her, the civilization of her nation—was central to the performance of shamanistic healing. "The consideration which the doctor receives for his services," Mooney writes, "was generally a deer-skin or a pair of moccasins, but is now a certain quantity of cloth, a garment, or a handkerchief. The shamans disclaim the idea that the [cloth] is pay, in our sense of the word, but assert that it is one of the agencies in the removal or banishment of the disease spirit." This belief that "the evil influence of the disease . . . enter[s] into the cloth" is richly suggestive, for it makes it possible to see Cherokee women using their domestic influence, as manifested by their weaving of cloth, not to encourage but to dispel the epidemic disease of colonialism, the disease that threatens their own and their people's removal. Dunaway writes that adopting the arts of weaving served Cherokee women materially, as a way of maintaining "crucial cultural elements of household production and informal exchange" and thus of retaining local power.[87] At the same time, the weaving of cloth into shamanistic healing practices reveals the ties between the traditional and the domestic in the emergence of the Cherokee woman's identity, as it fuses women's medicine power with, or infuses that power into, the most hallowed attainment of domestic propriety.

And the weaving of the Cherokee women, whereby civilized garments become at once the cloak of Christian domesticity and the talisman of Indian healing, provides a final, powerful way of connecting the life of Catharine Brown to the performance of Indian medicine. The missionaries, as I have indicated, found Brown's taste for "displaying the clothing and ornaments in which she was arrayed" (14) the most objectionable residue of heathenism in their young convert. Indeed, Brown's costume and ornamentation became a virtual obsession in writings surrounding the mission, as in American Board historian Joseph Tracy's description of her as "haughty, vain, and loaded with trinkets" or Tuttle's comparable portrait of her as a girl "richly dressed in the habit of her country, [who] appeared highly to value the many ornaments with which her neck, arms and hands were decorated." Yet where Christian writers attributed this fondness for finery to un-Christian self-love and childish coquetry, other reports suggest that Brown's physical appearance may have possessed a larger cultural or ritual significance. The Moravian missionaries who preceded the American Board noted that in the Green Corn Festival, "the Indians, especially the women, are decked out in all their finery," while Ross's friend Payne, witness to a Green Corn ceremonial in the fateful year of 1835, provided a more detailed description of the women dancers: "And now entered a long train of females, all dressed in long gowns, like our ladies, but all with gay colors, and bright shawls of various hues, and beads innumerable upon their necks, and tortoise-shell combs in their hair, and ears bored all around the rim, from top to bottom, and from every bore a massive ear-drop, very long, and generally of silver. A selected number of the dancers wore under their robes, and girded upon their calves, large squares of thick leather, covered all over with terrapin-shells closed together and perforated and filled with pebbles, which rattled like so many sleigh-bells."[88] Intriguing for its glimpse into the ways in which Cherokee women—even those who participated in traditional religious festivals—may have combined elements of Cherokee and Euro-American apparel, this passage simultaneously raises the possibility that Brown's supposed vanity provides a clue to her own participation in Cherokee ceremonies of healing and community renewal.

In their study of Cherokee dance and drama, Frank Speck and Leonard

Broom note the association between dance and healing: "The medical formulas exist to cure maladies and afflictions already manifested in symptoms among sufferers; the dance rites are prophylactic. The principles that insure individual health and social welfare (collective and individual well-being) are inculcated in the dances." Women's central role, through dance, in warding off the symptoms of disease and in promoting social welfare is signified not only by their participation in the Green Corn ceremony but also by their performance in the revitalization movement that gripped the Cherokees when Brown was an adolescent, wherein the women appeared in garb comparable to that which Payne observed during the Removal crisis: "they held a grand savage feast," as McKenney wrote, "and celebrated a great medicine dance which was performed exclusively by women, wearing terrapin shells, filled with pebbles, on their limbs, to rattle in concert with their wild, uncouth songs." Furthermore, as Charles Hicks noted in 1818—the year of Brown's baptism—women were solely responsible for at least one dance associated with Cherokee well-being: "the physic-dance was very much in use formerly, but is partly neglected now. This belongs to the women in particular." Indeed, Speck and Broom argue that women were symbolically if not physically central to the full repertoire of Cherokee dances: "In the center of a room cleared of furnishings is an inverted corn mortar or, as a substitute, a chair. The mortar is vaguely symbolic of economic plenty and is associated with women. This fertility connotation is from the signification of corn as 'old woman' or 'our mother.' "[89] Women's dancing, in short, was integral to Cherokee healing; women were, in a sense, the medicine bundle, the place where the densely woven lines connecting Selu and Stone Coat, the Green Corn ceremony, the ritual payment of cloth, and other acts of Cherokee medicine, of continuity and renewal through sacred performance, met and held.

In this light, Brown's body was loaded not only with trinkets but also (through them) with ritual significance; she bore, invisibly to any but Cherokee eyes, the traditional signs of women's power to effect sacred revitalization. And as such, her continuing to wear a "single drop" in each ear suggests her effort to retain, within the limits of domestic propriety, a link to the Cherokee woman's healing power. Or one might say that domestic ideology, which invested propriety with a ritual significance of its own, provided the link Brown needed between her role as Cherokee healer and Christian martyr. Likening Cherokee women's adoption of civilized performance to their eons-old occupation of basket weaving, Sarah Hill writes that "each new material, and its associated forms, has been added to earlier conventions rather than supplanting them. . . . New materials and forms have been adopted only when they proved useful."[90] As Brown's life suggests, such usefulness could serve her people in ways unlike that which the dominant culture, or the dominant elements of her own, perceived: weaving a cloth of Cherokee and white medicine, women such as Brown adapted colonialist conventions to carry not the form but the force of the traditional.

The implications of Brown's performance for our understanding of nineteenth-century Indian lives and literature are profound. Her works put to rest the lingering notion that tradition and innovation were (if not absolutely opposed) recognizable extremes on a continuum of Indian answers to colonialism. Lee Irwin, for example, has recently argued that the "strategies Native peoples followed in responding to [the] crushing onslaught against their spiritual lives" ran along "a spectrum between two major alternatives: accommodation or resistance. . . . On the religious front, some groups, like the Cherokee and other southeastern peoples, tried to accommodate the new way of life introduced" by whites, while "over against the strategy of accommodation is the resistance or revivalist movements that increasingly emphasized the importance of traditional Native values, indigenous religious orientations, and the need to abandon all dependency on non-Native goods or ideas." Even granting that this model allows for middle-ground positions, its division of responses—with accommodation on one end of the spectrum and resistance, revitalization, or traditionalism on the other—fails to account for numerous factors that Cherokee daughter Catharine Brown makes manifest: the diversity of responses in any Indian group, the limitations of identifying Indian responses *to* Euro-American terms solely *in* Euro-American terms, and, finally, the flexible and fugitive nature of traditionalism, which could be achieved through accommodation as surely as through anything else. As Joanna Brooks writes in her study of late eighteenth-century Indian communities of faith, including those that gathered around Mohegan minister Samson Occom, conversion could be a means of "rearticulating Indianness as a distinctive and powerful religious identity," a means of re-creating sacred communities through the very forces most dedicated to their destruction. If it is true, as Joel Martin suggests, that Brown herself "played a leading role in a Cherokee revitalization movement," then what drapery could the sacred not wear?[91]

And if this is so in the case of Indian communities as a whole, it is equally so in the case of their English-literate spokespersons: rather than plotting these individuals along a continuum from resistance to conciliation, one might better recognize that all were engaged in comparable, if not identical, acts involving the renewal of the sacred/traditional through the invented/imitated. To appreciate this fact, it is necessary only to set William Apess, typically placed on one extreme of the continuum, beside Brown, typically placed on the other. In his initial work on Apess, O'Connell suggested that the Pequot autobiographer was not only an "exceptional person" but literally an exception—an Indian who accomplished the "astonishing act" of producing not just an autobiography, but an autobiography of the sophistication and power of *A Son of the Forest*, without guidance, aid, or tangible model. In this heroic reading, Brown's life can figure only as a counterfactual example: whereas her ghostwritten *Memoir* "might easily have been seen as justification for someone in the New York or Boston publishing scene to take down and edit Apess's reminiscences," O'Connell's conclusion is that Apess's work—once again remarkably—was exclusively his own.[92]

Yet in a later reassessment of Apess, O'Connell raises the unwonted but, to my mind, far more warranted possibility that Apess was not exceptional but representative—that "his books and his life . . . contradict the long unchallenged assumption by historians that there was no significant presence of Native Americans in most of New England (and elsewhere east of the Mississippi) for much of the nineteenth century." And if so, this would lead to the further conclusion that Apess, the highly polished, overtly political Indian autobiographer, did not spring out of nowhere; rather, he relied on a tradition and a support system to foster his voice and vision. "Tempting as it may be to regard Apess as extraordinary in being such a powerful intellectual and writer, it is impossible for him to have achieved all he did in these realms without some form of community," O'Connell insists. "Neither David Walker among African Americans nor Apess among Native Americans is, if I am right, anomalous, a loner, or altogether exceptional. Who did Apess talk to in Boston, in Albany, in Providence, in Hartford, and in New York City? Who lent him books and to whom did he lend? What newspapers did he read? . . . These very basic questions remain unanswered."[93] If O'Connell is right—and I do not see how he could be wrong—then the most striking and, for scholars of antebellum Indian literature, enduring influence that Catharine Brown commanded may have been her influence on William Apess.

There is, I admit, no concrete evidence of which I am aware to support this supposition. However, there is circumstantial evidence aplenty. To begin with, the popularity of Brown's book in the decade after its publication raises the tantalizing possibility that Apess may have read it, or at least known of it.

Apess's familiarity with the works of Elias Boudinot, Euro-American sponsor of the Cherokee author who took his name, makes it even more likely that Apess had encountered the *Memoir*. A story strongly resembling the *Memoir*, the (perhaps) fictionalized dialect auto/biography *The Pious Indian: Or, Religion Exemplified in the Life of Poor Sarah* (1820), has been attributed to the Euro-American Boudinot; in addition to Apess's borrowing from Boudinot's *A Star in the West* (1816) for much of the material in the appendix to the second edition of *A Son of the Forest*, he concludes the appendix with Boudinot's "Indian Hymn," a dialect poem professing to be an Indian's prayer to God.[94] O'Connell, describing the "Indian Hymn" as a "strange, patronizing" poem, is mystified that "Apess would have chosen to reproduce it" to round out his life story. But in actuality, this is no more mysterious than that Apess should have chosen to remove "those parts which some persons deemed objectionable" when he prepared the second edition of his memoir, or, for that matter, that he should have chosen the comfiest of savagist clichés for its title.[95] Apess, like Brown, was working not beyond but *through* Euro-American conventions; casting about for models by which to construct a life, he not only would have been drawn to a text such as Brown's but also would have been in a better position than Euro-American readers—past and present—to perceive the ways in which the *Memoir* establishes an Indian identity via the conventions of "Indian" performance. Apess, I think it is safe to say, makes more of this performative mystery than Brown; freed of an actual interlocutor such as Brown's Anderson, he is able to address his implied interlocutors more openly and critically than his predecessor. But this is the nature of literary (if not domestic) influence: writers surpass those on whom they rely. And so one is left with another mystery that is not such a mystery after all: that an apparently radical Indian voice like Apess's should be indebted to an apparently submissive Indian voice like Brown's.

And in the end, are Apess's and Brown's voices really that different? Do not both draw on a common set of materials—most pertinent here, those that Laura Mielke terms "sentimental language and situations"—to patch together an identity?[96] Are not many of Apess's works similar to Brown's in form (spiritual autobiography) and, at least in the case of the totally neglected *The Increase of the Kingdom of Christ* (1831), function (global evangelization)? It may seem unaccountable that the man who, in the heavily anthologized "An Indian's Looking-Glass for the White Man" (1833), penned a scathing indictment of Euro-American prejudice and a pugnacious assertion of Indian pride also delivered the *Memoir*-worthy paean to domestic imperialism that is *The Increase of the Kingdom of Christ*: "Yes, you would thank your heavenly father day and night could you see the same red men who painted themselves fearfully in the late war, sharpened their hatchets, made their knives keen for the scalp, and sought the blood of your soldiers, your women, and your children, now praying for you and blessing your good missionaries, who have followed them into the shadow of the wilderness and besought them to turn to the precious Savior and become heirs of the kingdom of grace." This embarrassing, flustering piece—an aberration? a mistake? a misattribution?—has bollixed those few critics willing to come near it. O'Connell twists himself into knots trying to explain its "regressive" rhetoric; Robert Allen Warrior (Osage), paying tribute to Apess as a founding Native intellectual, writes that "each of [Apess's] books is remarkable in its own way," but ignores the sermon entirely; and Sandra Gustafson, tracing Apess's use of "Israelite theories of native origins," makes only glancing reference to the sermon in which Apess most fully utilizes these theories, preferring once again to focus on the usual suspects: *A Son of the Forest, Indian Nullification, Eulogy on King Philip*. (I include myself in this critical roster; my marginal notes indicate that on a first reading of *Increase*, all I could stammer out was: "this *really* doesn't sound like Apess.") But such "critical confusion," David Carlson argues in a reading of Apess in relation to antebellum legal discourse, is rooted in "a failure to appreciate fully the relationship between [Apess's] autobiographical acts and the models of self made available through the powerful discursive formations surrounding him"; even this most fiery defender of Indian lives emerges as an imitator mantled in civilized guise.[97] As Jill Lepore sums up, Apess too deals in "Indian speech" that is "invented fiction"; like his Cherokee contemporaries and their pious domestic elder sister, he robs white medicine of its power to destroy Indian identity by robing Indian identity in the power of white medicine.[98]

In 1835—the year in which Elias Boudinot signed away his nation's rights, and in which William Apess's declaration of the Mashpee tribe's nullification of the laws of Massachusetts earned him the reputation of being a latter-day powwow, a "very deceptive imposter" who "has got the entire control and confidence of nearly all the tribe"[99]—another Indian performance was held that attests to the complexities of being and becoming "Indian." Recorded by J. P. Evans, it was a dance conducted by the eastern Cherokees:

I will now bring another company to view:—this consists of three or four men disguised in masks, made of large gourds, with openings for the eyes, nose, and mouth, and painted in a hideous manner. They represent mendicant travellers on a long journey; and their raiment and other equipments, remind me of the crafty Gibeonites, who appeared before Joshua as ambassadors from a distant land. I doubt whether Garrick ever acted a part on the English stage, more in conformity to nature and reality, than I have seen low life, decrepitude and old age, acted by young Cherokees disguised, in a rude dance house. Some person advances & asks them various questions;—where they are from?—Where are they going? etc. The first they generally answer by saying [that] they have come from a distant land. Other questions are propounded, and answers given, which produce great merriment. They are invited to dance, and, accordingly, perform after the singing of the Eagle dancers. Their dancing, and accompanying gestures, are so ludicrous, and at the same time, so exactly in imitation of the characters they represent that the giddy multitude are almost convulsed with laughter.[100]

Evans could not have realized it, but he was watching a stereotypical representation of himself. For what he had witnessed was a Cherokee Booger Dance, a dance dating probably to the first arrival of Europeans in the Cherokee country and dedicated, as Speck and Broom write, to "weakening the harmful powers of alien tribes and races, who, as living beings or ghosts, may be responsible for sickness or misfortune." According to a version of the Stone Coat myth told to Speck and Broom in the twentieth century by Cherokee interpreter and informant Will West Long, Stone Coat had "provided the Cherokee with the Booger Dance as a means of counteracting the social and physical contamination which [whites'] coming brought upon the natives"; the mythical monster who had been compelled by the power of women to relinquish his medicinal lore had granted the Cherokees defense against the agents of colonialism through a ritual performance of mimicry, mockery, and healing laughter. In this traditional, emergent dance, the Cherokees whom Evans believed to be representatives of "the original character of the tribe" performed in the manner of their progressive leaders, enacting whiteness as a means of propitiating the demons of colonial power. That the Cherokees were not wholly successful in immunizing themselves against the epidemic of white medicine is obvious: they failed to halt the Removal of 1838, thousands of their people died along the Trail of Tears, and even before these events transpired as well as after they concluded, the decisions of some of their members to pursue a particular version of Indianness opened up wounds within the body of the Nation that have not fully healed to this day. And yet, as Jill Sweet writes, if one wonders how Indian peoples "have managed to survive culturally in spite of their long history of intruding others," then "certainly [their] performance tradition" is one of the most likely factors.[101] For it was this

evolving bundle of performance that simultaneously made possible adjust-
ment to Euro-American civilization and allegiance to sacred tradition. Or
to put this another way: as the written and unwritten acts of Brown, Apess,
Boudinot, Ross, and their people so powerfully attest, if being and becoming "Indian" was a performance, for them it was the performance of their
lives.

Chapter 3
# The Acts of the Prophets

*Don't talk to me about Indians: there are no Indians left except those in my band.*

*—Sioux medicine man Sitting Bull, in response to the breakup of the Great Sioux Reservation in 1889*

Long before the Wild West exhibitions that transformed him into an international celebrity, William F. Cody ("Buffalo Bill") had dwelt among the Indian dead. As a boy of eleven or twelve in Kansas, he recalled, his "proudest minute" was when he "downed his first Injun!"; as a buffalo hunter, he killed, according to his own count, 4,280 buffalo in a twelve-month stint with the Kansas Pacific Railroad; as a U.S. army scout, he went after not the Indians' game but the Indians' scalps, reporting after one successful trip, in an echo of General Philip Henry Sheridan's famous line, that he "had the satisfaction of showing [off] five '*good*' Indians, that is dead ones."[1] Retiring from the field in 1872, Cody turned to dramatizing scenes of genocidal combat in a series of frontier melodramas; in his first such performance, *The Scouts of the Prairie; or Red Deviltry As It Is* (1872), he vowed, "I'll not leave a Redskin to skim the Prairie." Indeed, the dramas he staged with his theatrical company, the Buffalo Bill Combination, dovetailed with their real-life precedents in more ways than one. On a reprieve from the footlights following the Battle of the Little Bighorn in 1876, and reputedly still wearing his stage costume of black velvet, he slew a Cheyenne subchief, Yellow Hair (Cody persisted in calling him "Yellow Hand"), whose death he promptly exploited—and whose scalp he proudly displayed—in a stage play commemorating the encounter, *The Red Right Hand; Or, Buffalo Bill's First Scalp for Custer* (1877).[2] As Louis Warren writes, in its "deadly real" dimensions of "killing Cheyenne and Sioux Indians and harrying them from their homes" as well as in its representational mode of "presenting himself in ways that reassured, and thereby entertained, a larger public about the heroism of American conquest," Cody fine-tuned a lethal Indian performance culled from the remains of those he both displaced and displayed.[3]

When, moreover, Cody founded Buffalo Bill's Wild West in 1883, the ghostly relic of Yellow Hair became Exhibit A in the reenactment of the scuffle and scalping that formed the centerpiece of his fledgling show. Plainly enough, a prominent source of the pageant's immense popularity lay in its representation of Indians as insubstantial or spectral; even as actual Indian bodies performed before white audiences, by tacit compact between exhibitor and patron these were understood to be, as much as Yellow Hair's scalp, images or icons of a vanished race. From the start, Cody's Wild West had recycled nostalgic scenes of Indian attack on various outposts of white society, all of these raids, of course, foiled by Buffalo Bill and his cavalry. Beginning with the 1886–87 season, a more elaborate spectacle, "The Drama of Civilization," pictured the erasure of the Indians through a series of tableaux: beginning with "The Primeval Forest," a view of savage life before the coming of whites, these snapshots transformed the Indians into museum pieces lost in the rolling tide of modern life. In an 1885 promotional coup, Cody signed the Hunkpapa Sioux medicine man Sitting Bull, supposed villain of the Little Bighorn, to remind his customers of the dangerous mischief and fortunate fall of Indian medicine; in 1893, the year Buffalo Bill's Wild West stormed the World's Columbian Exposition in Chicago (where Frederick Jackson Turner first read his paper "The Significance of the Frontier in American History"), Cody added a vignette recounting the Last Stand—too late, however, to feature the maligned Sitting Bull, who had been killed several years earlier in the preliminaries to the Wounded Knee massacre of 1890. For all its obvious masquerade and imposture, Buffalo Bill's Wild West was predicated on bringing back to life the authentic West: its star refused to term it a *show*, and promotional materials announced it to be "a series of original, genuine and instructive object lessons in which the participants repeat the heroic parts they have played in actual life upon the plains."[4] In this respect, though Cody seems to have maintained more honorable relations with his Pawnee and Sioux performers than was characteristic of the time, what his Wild West suggested to white consumers was that the Indians they saw before their eyes were already ghosts, remnants or revenants who would never know that in reality, their people's actual life on the plains had been laid to rest.[5]

While Buffalo Bill's Wild West was in full swing, there arose another westerner who walked among Indian ghosts: Wovoka (the Cutter), also known by the English name of Jack Wilson. A Paiute (Numu) Indian living near the Walker River Reservation in Mason Valley, Nevada, Wovoka had fallen into a trance during a total eclipse of the sun on New Year's Day, 1889, and had experienced a vision of the afterlife: "Here he saw God, with all the people who had died long ago engaged in their oldtime sports and occupations, all happy and forever young. It was a pleasant land and full of game. After showing him all, God told him he must go back and tell his people they must be good and love one another . . . [and] if they faithfully obeyed his instructions they would at last be reunited with their friends in this other world, where there would be no more death or sickness or old age. He was then given the dance which he was commanded to bring back to his people."[6] Hailed as a prophet upon his awakening, Wovoka instituted the "dance in a circle," soon to be known, infamously, as the Ghost Dance. Within weeks of his vision, emissaries from distant tribes, traveling by foot and by rail car, began to seek out the prophet and to spread the news by mouth and by mail. Indian tribes as far-flung as the Cheyennes, Arapahos, Pawnees, Assiniboines, Shoshones, Kiowas, Mandans, Hidatsas, Kickapoos, Delawares, Wichitas, Apaches, Taos Pueblos, and Teton Sioux attended to the words of hope the prophet bore: participation in the Ghost Dance, the doctrine developed as the word spread, would hasten the coming of an Indian utopia, where the people would be reunited with their ancestors, vast herds of buffalo would once more roam the plains, and the white oppressor would be cast out if not wholly eradicated. The dancers stood in a circle, held hands, and moved in a sunwise direction, singing songs:

The whole world is coming,
A nation is coming, a nation is coming,
. . . . . . . . . . . . . . . . . . . .
Over the whole earth they are coming.
The buffalo are coming, the buffalo are coming,
. . . . . . . . . . . . . . . . . . . . . .
The father says so, the father says so. (1072)

Following the prophet's example, individual dancers fell into trances, from which they awoke to relate encounters with dead relatives, visions of the afterlife, missives from the great mystery. Dismissed at first by whites as harmless fanaticism, the Ghost Dance was later painted by Indian agents, military officers, and newspaper reporters as a potential source of pan-tribal armed revolt when it spread to the Pine Ridge, Standing Rock, and Rosebud reser-

vations under the encouragement of Sitting Bull and other Sioux "hostiles."
On December 29, 1890, almost exactly two years after the date of the
prophet's original vision, the massacre of armed Sioux warriors as well as unarmed men, women, and children at Wounded Knee Creek brought to a close
the most intense and widespread period of Ghost Dancing, as well as, in the
eyes of past and current historians, the possibility of organized, traditionalist Indian resistance to colonialism. In the death field at Wounded Knee, the
narrative of Buffalo Bill's Wild West seemed to have been fulfilled: from that
point forward, Indians could survive—if at all—only in the imagined show
spaces of their conquerors.[7]

Taken together, Buffalo Bill's Wild West and Wovoka's Ghost Dance
seem to mark a climactic moment in the history of Indian performance: as
sacred performance makes a final, futile gesture of defiance before lapsing
into desuetude, the performance of Indianness ascends and triumphs. And
yet, in at least one significant respect, this opposition of Indian medicine (the
Ghost Dance) and white medicine (the Wild West) is inadequate; in at least
one respect, Cody, the Euro-American showman who slew the buffalo and
the way of life dependent on them, and Wovoka, the Native American visionary who foretold the return of the game and the culture it sustained, walked
a common ground. For however different their acts were in form and intent,
both orchestrated performances that helped to consolidate an intertribal Indian identity centered on the costume, ritual, and dance of the Plains, an
identity that persists, in the eyes of Indians and whites alike, to this day.[8] Such
an invented identity, as Ann McMullen notes, has long been viewed as "inappropriate to local native cultures"; given the ascendancy of an anthropological model that privileges the unit of the tribe and that, in Joel Martin's words,
"valorizes only what looks like 'traditional'" beliefs and customs, intertribal
innovations have often been read as deviations at best, perversions at worst.
Lately, however, theoretical models emphasizing the flexible and creative nature of cultural traditions have led scholars to recognize the intertribal as a
development with a much longer history than was previously assumed, a development existing in what William Powers calls a "dialectical relationship"
with the tribal: "the interchange of tribal traits on the Plains or elsewhere is
not so much the result of a breakdown in tribal distinctiveness as it is perhaps the *cause* of the Plains Indian culture, a culture initially made up of the
shreds and patches of earlier cultures." In this respect, modern critics have
seen the intertribal not as a violation of tribal authenticity but, quite the contrary, as a performative adaptation that may have invigorated sacred tribal

traditions (or the sacred tradition of the tribe itself) during a period of esca-
lating Euro-American assault.[9]

In the last quarter of the nineteenth century, federal advocates of assimilation—the so-called Friends of the Indian—had adopted an aggressive program of detribalization. The passage of the Dawes or General Allotment Act
of 1887, the outlawing of Indian dance and ceremony, and the shepherding of
Native youth into off-reservation boarding schools such as Richard Henry
Pratt's Industrial School in Carlisle, Pennsylvania—where, Pratt wrote in
1893, "the Indian in them" was "to be killed"—were all part of a blueprint
dedicated, in the words of one reformer, to "breaking up the tribal mass."
Commissioner of Indian Affairs Thomas Jefferson Morgan laid out this plan
bluntly in 1889: "the logic of events demands the absorption of the Indians
into our national life, not as Indians, but as American citizens. . . . The Indians must conform to 'the white man's ways,' peaceably if they will, forcibly if
they must." In a particularly bizarre—but for the present study, germane—illustration of the reformers' mentality, an 1895 catalogue publicizing the
Carlisle school recycled George Catlin's image of the "evil spirit" from the
okipa to represent "the first Indian boy who applied to Captain Pratt": an
otherworldly figure from tribal ceremony extinguished by assimilationist
education.[10]

Within such a climate of hostility toward tribalism, intertribal performance spaces such as the Ghost Dance and Buffalo Bill's Wild West provided
Indians opportunities to construct, enact, or renew a variant on traditional
tribal identity that emphasized the distinctiveness, unity, and difference of
Indians *as* Indians. Resembling the early nineteenth-century example of the
Cherokees—who participated in both their own ghost dances and their own
medicine shows—yet departing from this example by extending tribal distinctiveness into the intertribal realm, Ghost Dance and Wild West facilitated
a return to sacred tradition, to a common identity or ideal of Indianness, that
was at the same time a branching out into uncharted territory—into a common identity or ideal of Indianness. As L. G. Moses describes this phenomenon in his groundbreaking study of Indian experience in Cody's Wild West,
"one of the things that [Cody's] Show Indians helped to create was a genuine
'Indian' identity that went well beyond ethnic or national affiliation"; in the
Wild West, "as they had done in the Ghost Dance," Indians could "discover
and then nurture a common 'Indian' identity" that persisted in the face of efforts to stamp Indianness out.[11]

To be sure, Buffalo Bill's Wild West, that epitome of colonialist domination and distortion, seems an odd place for such a genuine Indianness to take root. Yet the history of Indian performance, of cross-cultural imitation, initiation, and invention, argues otherwise: for Indians to discover an enduring Native identity by performing white medicine was no stranger than for white Americans to recover a lost authenticity, resurrect a failing covenant, or authorize a crusading national identity by performing Indian. After all, the Ghost Dance was itself as much an act of intercultural performative reinvention as it was a revival of traditional tribal performance; like the Wild West, the Ghost Dance involved the forging of a genuine Indian identity through the reworking of a range of tribal traditions as well as the traditions of the Indians' oppressors. In this sense, Cody's Wild West and the Ghost Dance were indeed comparable in fusing Indian sacred performance with the performance of Indianness: both, in trying to "reproduce authentically something that was dying in the very act of being reproduced," gave birth to a new authenticity that could be (re)produced only *through* performance.[12] This is the function of all ritual, successfully performed: like the okipa and the Green Corn Festival, the Ghost Dance and the Wild West renewed Indian lives, communities, and identities through a ceremonial dying. And in this respect, both the Ghost Dance and the Wild West epitomize the fertile complexity of the medicine bundle: a return to sacred tradition that is simultaneously a departure from it, a recapturing of Indian essence that is simultaneously a disruption of any such essential continuity, a radical, indeed revolutionary, assertion of blood-red indigenism that is simultaneously a work of emergent trading in intercultural performative space.

My final chapter, then, uses the conjunction of the Ghost Dance and Buffalo Bill's Wild West to draw the history of Indian performance to a different conclusion, a conclusion that emphasizes the interaction of diverse performance spaces—(inter)tribal and intercultural—in the complex, contested, and continuing invention of Indian identity and performance (or Indian identity performance). The chapter will conclude by considering these issues in the exemplary case of Wovoka and Cody's contemporary, the Lakota *wicasa wakan*, or holy man, Black Elk, whose mediated autobiography, *Black Elk Speaks* (1932), has been central to ongoing debates concerning Indian identity and sacred tradition. As both Ghost Dancer and Wild West dancer, Lakota visionary and Catholic catechist, collaborator on a book both reviled as a desecration of Indian belief and celebrated as a spiritual behest to all peoples, Black Elk (and the text that bears his name) epitomize the conflictual, creative circumstances through which Indian peoples and prophets performed, and continue to perform, the power of the medicine bundle.

## Real Indians

> *Their model of a man is an Indian. They aspire to be Indians and nothing else.*
> —Doctrine of the Smoholla prophetic movement, from James Mooney, The Ghost-Dance Religion and the Sioux Outbreak of 1890 *(1896)*

The Plains Ghost Dance of 1889–90 was of local origin and regional scope, but it might nonetheless be seen as the culmination of a transcontinental movement that had begun at the latest a century earlier (and that continues, if in radically different forms, more than a century later). As Hazel Hertzberg writes in her study of twentieth-century Indian political movements, though Indian peoples from the early days of contact had responded to the Euro-American presence in terms reflecting "the diversity of Indian societies," at the same time "another theme was at work": "the effort to find a common ground beyond the tribe, a broader identity and unity based on shared cultural elements, shared experiences, shared needs, and a shared common fate." The dawning of intertribal configurations in the era of colonization appears as early as the seventeenth century, with diverse Indian peoples finding common ground within such spaces for conversion and revitalization as the Praying Towns of John Eliot. Beginning in the mid-eighteenth century, however, a more sweeping and self-conscious intertribalism arose among Indian peoples throughout the continent, driven by the visions of charismatic, nativist prophets including Neolin (Delaware), Handsome Lake (Seneca), Kenekuk (Kickapoo), and Tenskwatawa (Shawnee). Each of these spiritual leaders preached variants of a common message comprising the rejection of most or all things non-Indian, the recovery of traditional lifeways, and the discovery of an underlying unity among all Indian peoples. Not all revitalization movements fit this model; the Cherokee Ghost Dance of 1811–13, for example, was one of a number of revivals that focused on tribal rather than intertribal unity. Yet as Gregory Evans Dowd notes, the tradition of intertribal nativist resistance possessed a powerful appeal: "spreading the truly radical message that Indians were one people," these movements convinced Indian peoples across the continent that Euro-American power could be overcome through ritual returns to an aboriginal purity.[13] Prophetic revivals, then, underlay (if they did not entirely initiate) the quest for a modern Indian identity, an identity grounded not solely in tribal affiliation but in a distinctive, separate Indianness.

The revivalist message of separation, purification, and unification appears, to cite one of the earliest and most influential cases, in the teachings of Neolin, the Delaware whose visions inspired Pontiac and his allies in the 1760s (and whose message may have been passed down to subsequent prophets through intertribal contact). According to Moravian missionary David Zeisberger, Neolin preached that the Indians "ought not to have so much to do with the whites but cherish their own customs and not imitate the manners of the whites, else it would not go well with them." This admonition not to imitate whites took corporeal form in Neolin's use of Indian medicine to remove all traces of the intruder from Native bodies: according to trader James Kenny, the prophet prescribed a "Bitter Water . . . to purge out all that they got of y$^e$ White peoples ways & Nature." Moreover, as Zeisberger learned by conversing with one of Neolin's disciples, the program of physical separatism extended to the spiritual realm: "He stated that there were two ways of salvation, one for the white people and one for the Indians. . . . He said, further, that he knew that the Saviour was the way of salvation, that he had known Him many years and had had spiritual communication with Him. I asked him whether he knew the Lord who had been wounded for our transgressions and who had shed His blood. He replied, 'No, I know nothing of Him. Otherwise I know all things.'"[14] This belief in the unbridgeable schism between Indian and white deities and destinies reached its logical culmination in the revolutionary directive that Neolin transmitted from the Great Spirit:

The land on which you are, I have made for you, not for others: wherefore do you suffer the whites to dwell upon your lands? . . . Before those whom you call your brothers [the whites] had arrived, did not your bow and arrow maintain you? You needed neither gun, powder, nor any other object. The flesh of animals was your food, their skins your raiment. But when I saw you inclined to evil, I removed the animals into the depths of the forest, that you might depend on your brothers for your necessities, for your clothing. Again become good and do my will, and I will send animals for your sustenance. . . . Drive [the whites] away; wage war against them. I love them not. They know me not. They are my enemies, they are your brothers' enemies. Send them back to the lands I have made for them. Let them remain there.[15]

In this prophecy, just as Indian wickedness lies in imitating the whites—and especially in sporting civilized garments—so does the restoration of Indian integrity precede, as well as proceed from, the conquest of the invaders. Dowd attributes Neolin's widespread influence to the fact that his message was an extension of indigenous custom: among peoples who observed personal rituals of purgation, as well as annual ceremonies (such as the Green Corn Festival) that effected the renewal of the community, a blueprint for performative reinvention, even to the point of reordering the world, was anything but foreign. As Dowd summarizes: "these prophets, despite their many innovations, offered a solution to Indian problems that came out of Indian traditions. Reform the world through ritual; recapture sacred power. The message," Dowd concludes, "took hold"—and could not have done so if it were alien to deeply rooted convictions and conventions.[16]

At the same time, however, this traditional call was channeled through a host of practices that, as Alfred Cave writes, "had no clear, identifiable antecedent" in Native tradition—even, or especially, those Euro-American practices that the prophets most reviled. This engagement with Euro-America is particularly notable in the case of the Christian religion, to whose powerful effect on the nativist tradition Dowd pays tribute when he groups these movements under the title of "the Indians' Great Awakening." In one respect, this crossover between Indian and Christian awakenings is unsurprising, inasmuch as eighteenth- and nineteenth-century Christian revivals attracted significant numbers of Indians who may have seen therein "some basis in experience for believing that the new world in the making would include them."[17] Yet it might seem unwonted that the school of nativist protest, which envisioned a new world in the making founded on the repudiation of intercultural imitation, should itself have been indebted to Indian contact with, contemplation of, and sacred identity construction through Christianity.

The evidence, however, suggests just the opposite: that nativist prophets may have been more, rather than less, familiar with (and, perhaps for that reason, hostile to) Christianity than was common among their people. Congregationalist minister Samuel Kirkland, who labored among the Iroquois for a half-century beginning in the 1760s, relates that one such spiritual leader contested the supremacy or even the singularity of Christian ritual by pointing out that "the eating of the flesh of the roasted dog in [the Indians'] *ancient rite* was a transaction equally *sacred & solemn with that* which the Christians call the *Lords feast*. The only difference is in the *elements*: the

Christians use *bread & wine*, we use *flesh & Broth*." The confidence with which this prophet locks horns with Kirkland implies a sophistication with his opponent's belief system that could have derived only from careful and interested study of (or, perhaps, long practice with) the Christian faith. As Jane Merritt writes: "To debate or counter its effects, nativist reformers had to understand Christianity's concepts. In doing so, these ideas seeped into the language and beliefs of spiritual leaders."[18] Further evidence of this process appears in the doctrine of a revivalist prophet encountered by eighteenth-century evangelist David Brainerd (who lent his name to the station where Catharine Brown was educated); the prophet's words reveal an intimacy with Christianity in the spirit, if not the letter, that overcomes Brainerd's initial, automatic reproach:

of all the sights I ever saw among them, or indeed anywhere else, none appeared so frightful or so near akin to what is usually imagined of infernal powers; none ever excited such images of terror in my mind, as the appearance of one who was a devout and zealous reformer, or rather restorer, of what he supposed was the ancient religion of the Indians. . . . I discoursed with him about Christianity, and some of my discourse he seemed to like; but some of it he disliked entirely. He told me that God had taught him his religion, and that he would never turn from it, but wanted to find some that would join heartily with him in it; for the Indians, he said, were grown very degenerate and corrupt. . . . It was manifest he had a set of religious notions that he had looked into for himself, and not taken for granted upon bare tradition. . . . I must say, there was something in his temper and disposition that looked more like true religion than anything I ever observed amongst other heathens.[19]

That this prophet could gain such a concession from Brainerd, renowned for his piety and punctiliousness—and wholly intolerant of Indian convictions in all other instances recorded in his journal—suggests that one of the religious notions the prophet had looked into in order to inspire his people's return to their ancient religion was Christianity itself.

Indeed, it is possible to argue that Christian proselytizing such as Brainerd's had prepared the ground for the very kernel of the prophetic message: the belief in a supreme God who deputized prophets on earth to spread his word and to draw all his peoples into the fold. According to Euro-American reports, it was common for nativist prophets to have received their vocation upon visiting an afterlife conspicuously like that of Christians (except without the Christians). The "Imposter," Kenny writes of Neolin, "tells [the Delawares] that he had a Vission of Heaven where there was no White people but all Indians, & wants a total Seperation from us." Furthermore, upon the commencement of their ministries, prophets such as Neolin, Tenskwatawa, and Kenekuk (the latter two of whom Catlin met and painted) set about creating innovative works of intercultural scripture: written or, more commonly, pictographic scrolls that carried the force of the Christian Bible, even as the message encoded within these texts posed a direct challenge to the Bible's teachings and teachers. Zeisberger notes the methods of the Indian "preachers [who] pretended to have received revelations from above, to have traveled into heaven and conversed with God": "These teachers marked off on a piece of parchment made of deerskin two roads, both leading to heaven, one designated by God for the Indians, the other for the white people. . . . This rude parchment is, as it were, their Bible, and lies spread before them when they preach for the Indians."[20] Kenny provides a more detailed description of the text that Neolin had contrived "in order to shew [the Delawares] y$^e$ right way to Heaven":

This plan is Portrayed on a Dress'd Leather Skin & some on paper, fixes y$^e$ Earth at y$^e$ Bottom & heaven at y$^e$ top, having a straight Line from One to y$^e$ Other, by which their forefathers use'd to assend to Hapiness. Abo$^t$ y$^e$ middle is like a Long Square cuting thire way to Hapiness, at right Angles, & stoping them representing y$^e$ White people, y$^e$ outside is a Long Squair like black Stroke Circomscribing y$^e$ Whole within it, & joyning on y$^e$ left Hand Issuing from y$^e$ White peoples place is cut many Strokes parralel to thire Squair or Situation, all these Strokes represents all y$^e$ Sins & Vices which y$^e$ Indians have learned from y$^e$ White people, through which now they must go, y$^e$ Good Road being Stopt. Hell being fixed not far off, there they are Led irrevocibly.—Y$^e$ Doctrine Issued on this & y$^e$ way to help it, is said to be, to learn to live without any Trade or Connections with y$^e$ White people, Clothing & Supporting themselves as their forefathers did.[21]

A forerunner of the cartoons that George Catlin's Indian performers produced, Neolin's bible offered his proselytes a plain choice: pursue the traditional path to happiness or become hopelessly ensnared in the white man's ways. Merritt writes that when "native religious leaders adopted books of images and written works, hoping to revitalize traditional religious practices, these new devices also changed the nature of their religions."[22] But by the same token, when nativist prophets adapted the book to their own purposes, the nature of the text was changed by its involvement in Indian sacred traditions.

Merritt's comment represents the standard form in which scholars have plotted the prophets' relationship to Christianity: however they "hoped" for traditionalist revitalization, these critics argue, what the prophets achieved was to hasten the changes they sought to arrest. Richard White set the tone for such an ironic reading: "what all of these religious leaders had in common was the assimilation of segments of Christian doctrine that they used to effect an ostensible return to traditional customs." Echoing White's construction—where assimilation effects a merely "ostensible" recovery of the past—Sandra Gustafson writes that "although nativists stressed the return to tradition, emphasized cultural difference, and even developed a theory of separate creations, they nonetheless incorporated elements of Christianity and shared certain spiritual practices characteristic of evangelical revival culture, notably reliance on prophets and dreams." Catherine Desbarats similarly contends that "Christianity ironically supplied some of the language that Indians such as Tenskwatawa would use to help dig deeper, and deeply consequential, boundaries between white Americans and Indians."[23] That Indians should claim as traditional what was patently imitated or invented, these critics seem to suggest, makes revitalization movements not only peculiar but (if not precisely self-deluded) at least unselfconscious, unable to perceive that what the prophets and their followers took to be traditional was not actually traditional at all.

I find these articulations unsatisfying for a number of reasons. To begin with, I question the decision to cast this or any process of cultural transfer in the ironic mode; why should it be a source of wonder that nativists used Christianity to reject Christianity, any more than that the Cherokees used white nationalism to remain Indian? By the same token, I question the tendency of the previous expressions to view Christianity as a graft, a transportable "segment" or "element" that can take the place of an equally reified tradition. The trouble with this construction is not simply that it smacks unhealthily of the medicine show, with cultural products lined up for bottling and sale, but also that in treating culture in this way, it mistakes the nature of traditionalist revitalization itself. That is to say, tradition cannot be revitalized *without* what Dowd terms cultural "borrowings"; indeed, inasmuch as traditionalist revitalization movements arise only within cultures confronted by an alien other that they wish to dispel (even if that other is the self), tradition cannot be revitalized without borrowings that appear irreconcilable with the movement's own aims.[24] Or, to drop the term *borrowings*—a term that implies a concreteness to cultural traditions that I wish to avoid—one might say that traditionalist revitalization is necessarily a process of intercultural reinvention; though differing from everyday cultural processes in the circumstances that give rise to it as well as in its heightened dramatization of the reinventive acts without which cultures could not exist, the revitalization of tradition names the fact that cultures ceaselessly, and simultaneously, change and stay stable, remain what they are by becoming what they are not. In this sense, there is nothing surprising or out of joint about a culture revitalizing its own traditions through imitation of another's. What but this, after all, was the medicine show?

And this process of cultural emergence through revitalization (or revitalization through emergence) was, moreover, one with which native revivalists would have been deeply familiar, whether modern Euro-American critics are or not; for it was a process inherent in native formulations of the traditional and the sacred. As I have argued in the case of the Mandans and the Cherokees, the sacred in Indian life arises less from abstraction than from enactment; in belief systems where, as Lee Irwin writes of Plains religions, the sacred is "grounded in personal experience and explicitly manifested in ceremonial and ritual behavior," sacred tradition resides not in a discrete body of doctrine fixed through time but in the process of iteration, variation, and renewal to which each performance gives rise.[25] In such religions, then, the traditional is not opposed to the ongoing and the inventive (as it tends to be, at least hypothetically, in religions of original revelation and scriptural authority); rather, in such religions the traditional relies for its existence on the ongoing and the inventive. Thus it was that for Indian peoples living under conditions of colonialism, the traditional/sacred could be—and in the case of the nativist prophets was—secured through the performance of Euro-American culture and religion. Indeed, one might say that the occasion of revivalist prophecy was the sine qua non of Indian sacred performance, which is based in the conviction that revitalization is not only possible but ever present, latent in each act. This is not ironic; it is iconic. For it is the nature and function of the medicine bundle to claim the emergent in the service of the sacred, to restore the old by becoming the new.

It is in this respect, too, that I would read the most seemingly paradoxical facet of the nativists' call for sacred solidarity: their invocation of an essential difference between Indians and whites. When Magua, the fork-tongued prophet of James Fenimore Cooper's *The Last of the Mohicans* (1826), inflames an Indian audience with an oration that begins, "the Spirit that made men, colored them differently," he picks up a theme that echoes through the literature of nativist prophecy.[26] Stories of the separate creation of the races—or of separate deities responsible for those creations—appear to have been widespread among Indian peoples in the eighteenth and nineteenth centuries. Even that exemplary convert (and prophet?) Catharine

Brown, as reported by editor Anderson, had once harbored a belief in racial difference: "She supposed, that the Cherokees were a different race from the whites, and therefore had no concern in the white people's religion" (16).[27] As this example suggests, Indian racial thought and despite for Christianity went hand in hand.

In the teachings of the prophets, however, such stories took on tones that could be termed not only "racial" but specifically racist. In Lewis Henry Morgan's account of the Handsome Lake code, for example, the theory of separate racial origins grounds what appears to be nothing less than an antimiscegenation law: "Listen further to what the Great Spirit has been pleased to communicate to us:—He has made us, as a race, separate and distinct from the pale-face. It is a great sin to intermarry, and intermingle the blood of the two races. Let none be guilty of this transgression." Even more strikingly, a multiple-origins story told by the Shawnee prophet Tenskwatawa seems to call for all-out racial war:

When the Great spirit made this Island he thought it necessary to make also human beings to inhabit it, and with this view he formed an Indian. . . . The Great spirit then opened a door, and looking down [the Indians] saw a white man seated upon the ground. . . . The great Spirit told them that this white man was not made by himself but by another spirit who made & governed the whites & over whom or whose subjects he had no controul. That as soon as they reached their Island and had got comfortably situated, this great white spirit would endeavour to thwart his designs. . . . If it be foreordained that every thing is to belong to the whites, . . . then the Indians grown desperate by a consciousness that their end is approaching will suffer the [sacred] fire to burn and to destroy the whites, upon whom they will call, tauntingly, to quench it.[28]

When one recalls that the Shawnee prophet took the name "Tenskwatawa"—"the open door"—upon acquiring his powers, one glimpses the significance of this story: granting the Indians a prophetic vision rooted in separate origins and destinies, the open door leads inexorably to racial conflict.

Of course, when Tenskwatawa or Handsome Lake (or even, through Anderson, Catharine Brown) speaks of race, it is by no means certain that the term held meanings identical to those it possessed for Euro-Americans. Dowd, for one, considers it "anachronistic" to label prophetic discourse "racial"; he argues that however the prophets may have "sought Indian unity," they "saw Indians as having spiritual differences with American citizens," not racial ones. Nancy Shoemaker, attempting to understand the prevalence of apparently racial terms in eighteenth-century Cherokee discourse, argues that for Brown's people, "red and white symbols" designated "a dualism between war and peace"; thus Indians who distinguished between "red" and "white" people "may have meant people who advocated war and people who advocated peace." Shoemaker notes, however, that by the end of the eighteenth century at latest, "the color-based categories that grew out of Cherokee color symbolism had become racial categories because the Cherokees described the origins of difference as being innate, the product of separate creations, and they spoke of skin color as if it were a meaningful index of difference." Circe Sturm (Choctaw) finds similarly that "by the late eighteenth century," the Cherokees "had internalized an understanding of racial difference and racial prejudice that articulated with Western views"; as evidenced not only by the growth of plantation slavery but also by the use of race in "the process of nation building," the Cherokees' national revitalization movement made use of Euro-American racial theory as a means of claiming a distinctive Indian identity. And in this respect, it should not be surprising if nativist prophets too found racial theory attractive, for its basic propositions were amenable to precisely the Indian unity they sought. When craniologist Samuel George Morton, one of the founders of nineteenth-century racial science, argued "that all the American [Indian] nations . . . are of one race" and that "this race is peculiar, and distinct from all others," his assertion dovetailed perfectly with prophetic calls for Indian separateness, distinctiveness, and unity.[29] As with the prophets' use of Christianity, the core of their intertribal message, the assertion of a radical/racial difference between Indians and whites, was itself a result of negotiation with the people, the nation, and the beliefs whose rejection that message espoused.

And in this instance, such a negotiation had particularly profound implications for Indian identity. For the revised or revived version of Indianness disseminated by the nativist prophets mirrored not just the specialized field of antebellum racial science but the oldest, firmest, and deadliest of Euro-American inventions: what Robert Berkhofer, in his classic *The White Man's Indian* (1978), terms "the idea and the image of the Indian" itself. In the process of creating an intertribal Indianness immune to white influence—an Indianness that not only eschewed all white imitation but also rejected the very construct and constructs of whiteness—prophetic revitalization movements took on the dominant culture's central conceptual and representational category, the category by which Euro-American culture most aggressively defined itself: the category of an essential Indianness that was everything whites were not. This Indian was a heathen, not a Christian; savage, not civilized; a red man, not a white;—this Indian, to quote Berkhofer again, "must be conceived of as ahistorical and static," beyond the possibility of change because, as Morton had it, the "characteristics which distinguish the different Races, are independent of external causes."[30] Such a model of racial fixity was, of course, no more true of Morton's people than it was of Tenskwatawa's; whether in the ethnologic museum or in the intertribal movement, the "external cause" of the other accounted powerfully for the characteristics of Indians and whites alike. But as an explanatory tool and a rallying cry, this shared belief in the eternal and invariable hostility between the races served Morton's and Tenskwatawa's causes equally well.

That Indians could claim such a category by adopting usages that both they and whites agreed real Indians could not adopt—and that, moreover, Indians could use such an adopted identity to revitalize rather than ossify real Indianness—signifies both the complexity and the power of Indian sacred performance, its formation through even the most seemingly antipathetic (not to mention bathetic) of vehicles. Thus Tenskwatawa's brother Tecumseh, sounding uncannily like his archfoe Andrew Jackson—as well as any number of vanishing-Indian poems, plaints, and paeans of the heyday of Euro-American racial science—called on the language of innate racial difference to spur his people to resistance: "Where today are the Pequot? Where are the Narragansett, the Mohican, the [Pokanoket], and other powerful tribes of our people? They have vanished before the avarice and oppression of the white man, as snow before the summer sun. . . . Will we let ourselves be destroyed in our turn, without making an effort worthy of our race? Shall we, without a struggle, give up our homes, our lands, bequeathed to us by the Great Spirit? The graves of our dead and everything that is dear and sacred to us?"[31] Race, in this address, becomes the master term of Indian identity, subsuming and breathing new life into the tribe, an affiliation that has been unable to preserve "everything that is sacred to us." Tecumseh should not be seen as the voice of all Indian peoples (particularly when his exhortation was recorded by a white writer and, in all likelihood, sympathizer with Jacksonian ideology). Yet his address, like those of the earlier prophets, symbolizes the emergence of an ethnic category that, crossing the racial divide it erects, produces even as it enacts a powerful, new, sacred Indian identity.

As an intertribal movement, the 1890 Ghost Dance partook of this character of sacred reinvention; like its predecessors, it spawned a separate, distinctive Indian identity by marshaling and coordinating a range of disparate tribal and extratribal sources. Indeed, it is possible that the prophetic message of the previous century was carried, through Tenskwatawa, to the Plains and far western tribes, thus establishing "a continuous line of development of North American nativistic movements from the Delaware Prophet of 1760 through the Ghost Dance of 1890."[32] As with its precursors, the most evident point of contact between the Ghost Dance and the invading force from whom its adherents sought relief lies in its relationship to Christianity. Contemporary reports focused almost exclusively on the Ghost Dance's Christian parallels; indeed, to one military observer, the Ghost Dance was little better than a "perversion of the Christian religion as taught by missionaries." References to Wovoka as "the Christ" were universal in newspaper coverage, much of which recycled the story that this Indian Messiah had "showed [his followers] the scars on his hands and feet where he had been nailed to the cross." Equally common were reports that Wovoka, though not claiming to be the Messiah himself, professed to have "been to heaven" and to have prophesied "that the Messiah is coming to earth again." Army Lieutenant Hugh Lenox Scott, who met with Ghost Dancers in December 1890, expressed the prevailing wisdom: "That this dance is intended as a worship of the white man's God there can be no doubt in the mind of any intelligent person who hears what [the Indians] have to say on the subject."[33] Though it would not take long for the same sources to conclude that the Ghost Dance was a direct threat *against* Christians, they were nonetheless convinced that there was no force strong enough in the Indians' own faith to inspire such devotion and millennial aspiration.

The professional and amateur anthropologists who studied the Ghost Dance in the years after Wounded Knee lent scholarly cachet to this supposition. Indian enthusiast George Bird Grinnell, writing of his experience with the Cheyennes, argued that the Christian character of the Dance ran so deep that its common appellation was a misnomer: "I never heard of the dance of the Indians called the 'Ghost Dance' until I returned to the East. In the Indian country it is known as the 'Dance to Christ.'" Though the principal anthropological source on the Wovoka religion, James Mooney, who had spent years seeking out the Ghost Dance prophet and reconstructing the movement he had initiated, insisted that Wovoka "makes no claim to be Christ, the Son of God, as has been so often asserted in print" (773), he too bolstered the dominant interpretation in his *The Ghost-Dance Religion and the Sioux Outbreak of 1890* (1896), titling the first chapter of his narrative "Paradise Lost" and writing therein that "the belief in the coming of a messiah, who should restore them to their original happy condition, was well nigh universal among the American tribes" (658). In 1891, Alice Fletcher of the American Folklore Society voiced the majority opinion when she hypothesized that "in a rudely dramatic but pathetic manner this 'Messiah craze' presents a picture of folk suffering, and their appeal for the preservation of their race, to the God of their oppressors." Indeed, to this day, many popular and scholarly accounts of the Ghost Dance take its Christian character for granted. Dee Brown, for example, writes that the Dance was "entirely Christian. Except for a difference in rituals, its tenets were the same as those of any Christian church." L. G. Moses, similarly, notes the continuities between the Ghost Dance and "the Judeo-Christian tradition," explaining that "Wovoka believed himself to be a prophet ordained by Providence." In his fictionalized biography of Wovoka, Paul Bailey speculates that the prophet "wished he were a white man," a "miracle worker like Jesus"; in his biography of Buffalo Bill, Louis Warren contends that "the most remarkable and uniform characteristic" of the Ghost Dance "was its announcement of an Indian messiah"; and in her study of the Ghost Dancers who traveled with Buffalo Bill's Wild West, Sam Maddra writes that these performers were adherents of "a faith based on the teachings of Christianity."[34] For modern writers, as for their sources, the power of the Christian faith was so great that even a movement dedicated to its overthrow had become its consort.

As with the earlier prophetic movements, there are a number of ways to explain the crazy quilt of Christian allusions surrounding (some might say suffocating) the Ghost Dance. To begin with, issues of translation must be taken into account in investigations of prophetic utterance as transmitted through white amanuenses; terms such as *Messiah, God, heaven,* and the like—not to mention *prophet*—may represent Euro-American glosses of Indian concepts for which there is no exact Christian equivalent. In his remarks on the emissaries who brought Wovoka's word to the Lakota people, Jeffrey Ostler notes that the most widely cited Lakota-language account of the meeting "consistently uses the term *Wakan Tanka Cinca*" to refer to Wovoka, "which the translator sometimes rendered as Son of God and other times as Messiah. . . . [But] neither God nor the commonly used Great Spirit are very good translations for *Wakan Tanka*. Great Mystery is better, though the important point is that *Wakan Tanka* is not a person; instead the term refers to the collective spiritual powers of the universe, which can be manifested in myriad ways." Thus Ostler reasons that what the emissaries believed they had met was not "the Second Person of a triune God" but "a specific manifestation of *Wakan Tanka* (i.e., of the sacred, mysterious, spiritual powers of the universe)."[35]

At the same time, Ostler's analysis reminds us that whatever Wovoka's original revelation may have been, the nature of its dissemination—the fact that it was circulated by a variety of Indian ambassadors and adopted rapidly by a range of tribes—complicates the question of its Christian dimensions. As Thomas Overholt notes, "virtually every report we have of Wovoka's teaching is second- or third-hand, mediated to us through delegates from the various tribes who visited him and brought his teachings back to their own people," and these couriers may have introduced "embellishments and even substantive changes in the doctrine." Thus, for example, one of Mooney's principal informants, a Cheyenne Indian named Porcupine, who visited Wovoka in the early days of his mission, seems to have been a promoter of the story fusing Wovoka with Christ, stigmata and all: "Just before sundown I saw a great many people, mostly Indians, coming dressed in white men's clothes. The Christ was with them. . . . I had heard that Christ had been crucified, and I looked to see, and I saw a scar on his wrist and one on his face, and he seemed to be the man" (795). Taking these factors into consideration, John Kucich is inclined to dismiss the supposed Christianity of the Ghost Dance as an artifact of white incomprehension and chauvinism: "While contemporary white observers tended to read the Ghost Dance as bastardized Christianity—with a messiah preaching a gospel of an Indian Father colored by the apocalyptic strains of the Book of Revelation—and while James Mooney himself stressed what he saw as the universal elements of the movement, the Ghost Dance was nevertheless fashioned out of Native American materials."[36]

The available evidence suggests, however, that Kucich's reading is too precipitate and conclusive—that while many of the contemporary and current sources doubtless overemphasize the Christian quality of the Ghost Dance, Christianity was indeed one of many threads, and perhaps a prominent one, from which the Ghost Dance religion, both as originally received by Wovoka and as broadcast thereafter, was woven. To understand the intercultural contours of the Dance, it is necessary to consider the "materials" from which the Dance was fashioned within their own, Native American, contexts—to recognize, that is, that the indigenous traditions involved in the Ghost Dance almost certainly did not draw the hard-and-fast distinctions between the traditional and the emergent that Kucich's comment suggests. In his analysis of the Ghost Dance as a principal source of an emergent late century Indian identity, Gregory Smoak argues that if "indigenous concepts" of "shamanism and prophecy" drove the Ghost Dance, the same concepts "created a flexible religious milieu open to the incorporation of new elements and doctrines through the process of direct revelation."[37] As such, for its prophets and practitioners, there may have been no contradiction, or even contradistinction, between the "indigenous" and "new" varieties of religious experience that gave birth to, or were given birth through, the Ghost Dance. Lee Irwin, in his study of Plains visionary traditions, elaborates on this point. Noting that among Plains peoples "dreams and visions are a fundamental means for social and cultural transformation," Irwin provides a basis for understanding the performance of sacred tradition within such intertribal, intercultural visionary experiences as the Ghost Dance:

Dreams and visions are a means for both the confirmation and the elaboration of the spiritual potentials of the religious world. They expressively communicate the reality of their potency through the process of enactment—not through verbal report. The confirmation comes through the experience of dreaming; the elaboration comes about through the reenactment of the specific contents of the vision in acts of power. Thus it is possible for religious values to evolve spontaneously within a unified but unbounded mythic-religious context that is constantly undergoing subtle change and transformation. And yet that transformation is such that it maintains a certain pragmatic continuity with past experience and belief. Tradition in this sense is a process of gradual transformation of the historical and reflective consciousness of the individual and community over long periods of time. It is a dialogical process by which meaning, symbols, actions, and objects all reflect past interactions and present elaborations. . . . Therefore, dreaming among the Plains peoples acts both to validate cultural traditions and to facilitate their dynamic transformation.[38]

This redefinition of tradition within the context of visionary religions is vital to an understanding of the development of the Ghost Dance and of the role that Christianity played within that development. Such a definition makes it plain that it is fallacious to boil the prophet's visionary acts down to a singular Ghost Dance "doctrine"; as even those messengers who accepted the standard image of Wovoka as a man with "the nail-prints in his hands and feet and the spear wound in his side, of the crucified Savior" insisted, this embodiment of sacred power spoke no inviolable Sermon on the Mount: "many different versions of his teachings were given." Furthermore, just as the Ghost Dance emerged through the traditional-innovative vision(s) of the prophet Wovoka—and was reenvisioned through the traditional-innovative experiences of envoys such as Porcupine and the Lakota emissaries—so did each performance of the Dance host opportunities for the dialectical process described by Irwin, whereby past interactions and present elaborations shape and inform one another. As Overholt demonstrates, the Ghost Dance "was able to undergo shifts in response to feedback from the people," with the trance visions of individual dancers frequently forming the basis of "new ghost songs that were used in subsequent dancing." In this respect, the Ghost Dance confirms Irwin's argument concerning the role of individual visionary experience in collective ceremonial performance: "The vision . . . serves as a primary religious means for cultural innovations of the most essential type. This function not only strengthens the centrality of the vision in the religious life of the people, but it also helps give definition to the religious topology. Each vision experience contributes its contents to the totality of the mythic discourse and helps give form and substance to religious thought and action."[39] Characteristic of the medicine bundle, the Ghost Dance reproduced the sacred (traditional, tribal) by performing the new (intertribal, intercultural).

A closer consideration of the various streams of individual and collective experience that poured into the Ghost Dance affirms this process of traditional emergence. As a young man, Wovoka had worked for the Wilson family, Presbyterians from whom, Mooney reports, the youth had received not only his English name but "a confused idea of the white man's theology" (765). It is possible as well that Wovoka had been exposed at some point to Mormonism, whether prior to his revelation or during the early occurrences of the Ghost Dance, in which Mormons were said to have participated; though one can dismiss as slander late century accusations that the Mormons had incited the Ghost Dance "in order to increase their influence with the Indians," Mormonism may nonetheless have "fanned the fire of Indian revivalism that had already begun to rage in the west."[40] It is of course reductive to see Christianity as having simply been deposited into the Ghost Dance; as is made evident by a story related to Mooney by George Sword, an Oglala Lakota of the Pine Ridge Reservation, the traditional shaped the emergent as surely as the reverse: "When coming we come to a herd of buffaloes. We killed one and took everything except the four feet, head, and tail, and when we came a little ways from it there was the buffaloes come to life again and went off. This was one of the messiah's word come to truth" (821–22). Such a "confounding of aboriginal and Christian ideas," as Mooney saw it (1088)—with the resurrected buffalo at once evocative of Christ, demonstrative of Wovoka's prophetic authority, and indicative of the Ghost

Dance's continuity with rituals of renewal—indicates the fluidity and, in practical terms, indistinguishability of the various threads of which the Ghost Dance bundle was constituted or to which it gave rise.

The complexity of this emergent process becomes even more evident when one considers additional tribal antecedents and variations of the Ghost Dance. For example, the religious movement founded in the 1870s by the prophet Smoholla of the Columbia River Valley—a movement that likewise prophesied the return of the Indian dead and the removal of the whites—shows evidence of an intercultural gestation; Smoholla, Mooney reports, "had frequented the Catholic mission" among the Yakima Indians (717) and had in the manner of earlier prophets constructed a pictographic bible from which to read his prophecies. Mooney likewise speculated that the Ghost Dance may have received an infusion of belief and ritual from the Indian "Shakers" of Puget Sound, who practiced "a mixture of Catholic, Presbyterian, and old Indian ceremonies" (750) and who may have met with Wovoka on one occasion (763). Further Paiute sources for the Ghost Dance seem to have included the visions of an earlier prophet, Wodziwob, who like Wovoka awoke from a trance to report that "his soul had journeyed over the mountains to the land of the dead, had seen the dead happy in this land, and had extracted promises from the souls to return to their loved ones";[41] the private or public lessons of Wovoka's father, Tavibo, who was referred to as a "'dreamer' with supernatural powers" if not a prophet (765);[42] and preexisting Paiute dances such as the Round Dance, on which the "dance in a circle" seems to have been modeled.

Once the Ghost Dance began its spread to other tribes, further innovations developed. For example, the Sun Dance, which had long served as "an intense reaffirmation of tribal and group identity" on the Plains—and as such had become an equally intense target of white ire—survived in the addition of "a tree or pole planted in the center [of the Ghost Dance] and variously decorated" (921).[43] In one intriguing case described by Mooney, this decoration consisted of "an American flag," the national standard of those who pursued the suppression of Indian dance (823). Meanwhile, in Lakota performances of the Ghost Dance, Mooney reported, "a sacred redstone pipe" (823), which (as George Catlin had discovered) was "the most sacred thing in Sioux mythology" (789), played a central role, notwithstanding its transformation into a symbol associated with both Indian and Christian deities: "I have seen a man hold up the pipe to the sky, saying, 'Smoke, Sinti' (Sinti being their great mythologic trickster), and then in the same way,

'Smoke, Jesus'" (1064). As with the Christian dimensions of the Ghost Dance, this sacred act defies (or deifies) its origins in intercultural, intertribal innovation.

One of the principal means by which the Ghost Dance was spread indicates the futility of parsing it for distinct religious sources. Students from the Carlisle Indian School, whose literacy and familiarity with Euro-American rail systems made them ideal couriers, not only "acted as interpreters, wrote down the words of the messiah, and delivered his message to their people" (900) but also, according to Mooney, took part in the Ghost Dance: "Paul Boynton, a particularly bright Carlisle student, who acted as my interpreter . . . told how Sitting Bull [an Arapaho prophet of the Ghost Dance, not the Sioux medicine man] had hypnotized him with the eagle feather and the motion of his hands, until he fell unconscious and did really see his [dead] brother. . . . He embodied his experience in a song which was afterward sung in the dance" (923). Here, an Anglo-educated, literate, Christian Indian, his presence among the Ghost Dancers facilitated by the transportation system that had helped men like Cody drive the buffalo to near extinction, adds his own vision to the Ghost Dance. The complexity of this episode indicates once more the capacity of sacred tradition to work through even those agencies, such as the boarding school, whose purpose was to launch "an uncompromising hegemonic assault on [the Indians'] cultural identity."[44] The Ghost Dance, Edward Huffstetler concludes, served as "a point of dialogic exchange between the religions of a variety of cultures, and it clearly functioned as a nexus, or conduit, between these shifting and differing contexts."[45] Drawing from and combining into novel patterns an astonishing array of tribal, intertribal, and extratribal sources, the Ghost Dance can be seen both as an object lesson in indigenous performative reinvention and as a veritable microcosm of American interculturalism itself.

As with earlier prophetic movements, however, the performers of the Ghost Dance articulated from this heterogeneous mix a system of beliefs and practices emphasizing their singularity as Indians and their separation from whites. Though Wovoka himself cultivated an intercultural persona, living, Mooney wrote, in a traditional wickiup bereft of all "articles of civilized manufacture" (770) yet appearing "well dressed in white man's clothes, with the broad-brimmed white felt hat common in the west" (769), his teachings, as Mooney understood them, drew an inviolable line between Indians and whites in the present time and for all eternity: "the great underlying principle of the Ghost dance doctrine is that the time will come when the whole

Indian race, living and dead, will be reunited upon a regenerated earth. . . . The white race, being alien and secondary and hardly real, has no part in this scheme of aboriginal regeneration, and will be left behind with the other things of earth that have served their temporary purpose, or else will cease entirely to exist" (777).[46] This emphasis on a distinctive intertribal identity cordoned off from the white world pervaded the practice of the Ghost Dance as well as the principle. For instance, regardless of individual tribes' tailoring of the Dance to suit their unique ritual systems, all placed special emphasis on "the sacred red paint" provided by the prophet (778), which was used to decorate the faces of the dancers; delegates to Wovoka were invariably granted a handful of the red clay from which this paint was mixed. Though the color red carried ritual significance for Indian peoples before and beyond the Ghost Dance, being in the words of late century Lakota holy men "the color that spirits like best," in this particular application it served a unifying purpose, signifying the prophet's favor and providing a symbolic linkage between performances distant in space and diverse in practice.[47]

Likewise, the choreography of the Ghost Dance, though varying from tribe to tribe, adhered to a core configuration that joined Indian persons and peoples within a sacred circle from which outside influences were barred. "As the song rises and swells," Mooney writes, "the people come singly and in groups from the several tipis, and one after another joins the circle until any number from fifty to five hundred men, women, and children are in the dance. When the circle is small, each song is repeated through a number of circuits. If large, it is repeated only through one circuit, measured by the return of the leaders to the starting point" (920). The songs themselves enhance this sense that with the closing and turning of the circle the people are effecting a symbolic return to the starting point, a ritual recovery of Indian identity: "We shall surely be put again (with our friends)" (959); "I have come because I want to see them, / The people, all my children" (1097); "We are all going up, / To the great village" (1102). Commenting on the emergent quality of the Ghost Dance songs, Mooney writes that "there is no limit to the number of these songs, as every trance at every dance produces a new one, the trance subject after regaining consciousness embodying his experience in the spirit world in the form of a song, which is sung at the next dance and succeeding performances until superseded by other songs originating in the same way. . . . While songs are thus born and die, certain ones which appeal especially to the Indian heart . . . live and are perpetuated" (953). This suggestive précis tells not only about the process by which individual songs arise, "die," and are reproduced but also about the analogous process by which Indian subjects are conceived through the singing; far from being mere commentary on the singers' experience of dying into life, the songs are at once products and productive of the new Indian identities that "live and are perpetuated." Patricia Penn Hilden sums up the relationship between prophetic revitalization and performative reinvention: "By dancing and undertaking the other essential ceremonies, [the Ghost Dancers] were *creating* an *Indian* world, an Indian self, a Native people, a Native politics."[48] In the words of one song, "*E'yehe'* ! they are new— / *E'yehe'* ! they are new" (963), the Indian dead and their living representatives joined in a ritual return to Indianness.

And that process, that politics, takes its most explicit shape through the prohibition of whiteness from the Ghost Dance and from its outcome—a prohibition that, as I have said, denies even as it relies on a cross-fertilization of beliefs both Indian and white. In this regard, the universality of the red paint in the Ghost Dance can be seen as serving not only a unifying but also a differentiating function, the color highlighting the physical difference between Indian and white and thus emphasizing whites' inability to participate in the Ghost Dance or partake of its fruits. (This despite the fact that, as Alice Kehoe notes, Wovoka distributed the red clay in "rinsed-out tomato cans," an alien technology that made the sacred material transportable over long distances. In what can be seen as an anticipatory inversion of the modern-day reproof of assimilationist Indians as "apples"—red on the outside but white on the inside—these containers, though white on the outside, were deep red at the core.) One Sioux participant in both the Sun Dance and the Ghost Dance described the difference between Indians and whites in these terms: "The Indians are red, so they are the favorite people of the Sun," as opposed to the "white people," who "have no mercy on the red people."[49] Similarly, a Sioux performance of the Ghost Dance reported by Mooney emphasized the racial function of the color symbolism: having "discarded everything they could which was made by white men," the dancers donned "shirts and leggings painted in red" and adorned their faces to match (916).

Eliminating white objects from the Ghost Dance was coupled with the exclusion of whites from hearing its message. For example, the so-called Messiah Letter containing the prophet's instructions to the Arapahoes, taken down by Carlisle students, carried both the promise that "every body is alive again" and the explicit directive, "dont tell no white man" (780). In similar fashion, on one of his visits to witness an Arapaho dance, Mooney found his plans routed by a united front of suspicion and separatism: "my hopes were dashed to the ground the first night by hearing the old priest, Weasel Bear, making the public announcement in a loud voice throughout the camp that a white man was among them to learn about their sacred things, but that these belonged to the religion of the Indian and a white man had no business to ask about them" (961). In the manner of the okipa, the inner mystery of the medicine bundle refuses penetration by white investigators; the "sacred things" of the Ghost Dance are for Indians alone.

And the songs themselves, once again, play a vital role in this construction of Indianness as that which rejects all things white. "At first I liked the whites," the Arapahoes sing (961), but a change has come:

The yellow-hide, the white-skin (man).
I have now put him aside—
I have now put him aside—
I have no more sympathy with him,
I have no more sympathy with him. (978)

And another Arapaho song prophesies the erasure of whites from the Indian world:

I'yehe' ! my children—*Uhi'yeye'heye* !
I'yehe' ! my children—*Uhi'yeye'heye* !
I'yehe' ! we have rendered them desolate—*Eye'ăe'yuhe'yu*!
I'yehe' ! we have rendered them desolate—*Eye'ăe'yuhe'yu*!
The whites are crazy—*Ahe'yuhe'yu*! (972)

The Ghost Dance, in sum, constituted a performance space in which diverse tribes could be—or become—Indians, divorced in spirit from the intercultural arena within which that spirit had emerged. In this light, it is neither inappropriate nor disrespectful to suggest that the Ghost Dancers were what whites and Indians alike termed their cousins in Buffalo Bill's Wild West: "show Indians," who not only showed their Indianness through intercultural performance but also constructed Indianness through that show.

In the years after Wounded Knee, a number of Ghost Dancers, including two of the Sioux emissaries to Wovoka, Kicking Bear and Short Bull, carried on careers *as* show Indians in Buffalo Bill's Wild West. The apparent curiosity of imprisoned Ghost Dancers being paroled to tour with Buffalo Bill is but one of many ways in which these twin Indian performance spaces overlapped in the final decade of the nineteenth century. From the first signs of trouble, Cody and his Indian players had been involved in the unfolding history of the Ghost Dance, with Sioux performers sent by the United States Army to "persuade their families and friends to awaken from their fevered dreams" and Cody himself hastily dispatched on (and just as quickly recalled from) a mission to treat with his former acquaintance and employee, Sitting Bull.[50] In the period immediately before Wounded Knee, Cody, in Louis Warren's words, "began to play up the threat of the Ghost Dance," telling reporters that "a religious Indian is the most dangerous kind" and that "this is very likely to be the most gigantic uprising of Indians ever known." Reflecting on the Ghost Dance years later, he reiterated his conviction that "the religious ghost-dance festivities [had] fanned the flames of war," necessitating the armed response at Wounded Knee. Moreover, in a story that gained popularity years later, it was reported that Sitting Bull's horse, a present from Cody trained to fall and stomp the ground on hearing a gunshot, went into its act when the bullets that killed Sitting Bull were fired. Some Indian onlookers, the story further went, were convinced that the spirit of Sitting Bull had entered the horse's body, inducing it to perform one final, futile Ghost Dance.[51] All of these stories, and more, have passed into national mythology. For in all, the Wild West serves as both counterpoint and corrective to the Ghost Dance; Cody's show becomes a disciplinary mechanism by which those engaged in an outlawed and outlandish form of Indian medicine are either destroyed or domesticated, transformed into players of a polite, acceptable version of their formerly recalcitrant selves. The popularity, to this day, of the story of Sitting Bull's show horse exemplifies the appeal of this narrative of Indian dispossession: while Sitting Bull himself, representative in the white mind of resistant Indian identity, is cut down, his horse, a dumb animal groomed to prance on command, unthinkingly reenacts a dance now leeched of its power and, literally, carried on only by ghosts.

Interestingly, while anthropologists and Indian enthusiasts of the time tended to read Wild West entertainment as an assault on traditional Indian performance and identity—as did Mooney, who wrote sourly in 1898 that the last vestiges of tribal dance and ceremony had "degenerated into a wild west show with the sole purpose of increasing gala receipts"[52]—reformers condemned the shows not for destroying tribal tradition but for *preserving* it, for miring Indians in former ways that militated against their entrance into citizenship. Thus the Indian Rights Association, writing in 1899, decried the shows for their furtherance of traditional practices: "This is the foster-father of those barbarous customs, modes of life, and habits of thought which Indian education justly aims to destroy. . . . It is worse than folly for the Government to say to the Indian child, through the school: Think, dress, act like a civilized white man; and then to say, through the show business: Think, dress, act like a savage Indian." Commissioner of Indian Affairs Thomas Jefferson Morgan was of the same mind, writing in 1890, against the backdrop of the Ghost Dance and Wounded Knee: "The schools encourage Indians to abandon their paint, blankets, feathers, and savage customs, while the retention and exhibition of these is the chief attraction of the shows."[53] The reformers, knowingly or not, thus rehearsed the philosophy and policy of Morgan's famous namesake, who at the start of the nineteenth century had fingered an analogous form of medicine performance as the backbone of Indian resistance to assimilation:

> But the endeavors to enlighten them on the fate which awaits their present course of life, to induce them to exercise their reason, follow its dictates, and change their pursuits with the change of circumstances have powerful obstacles to encounter; they are combated by the habits of their bodies, prejudices of their minds, ignorance, pride, and the influence of interested and crafty individuals among them who feel themselves something in the present order of things and fear to become nothing in any other. These persons inculcate a sanctimonious reverence for the customs of their ancestors; that whatsoever they did must be done through all time; that reason is a false guide, and to advance under its counsel in their physical, moral, or political condition is perilous innovation; that their duty is to remain as their Creator made them.[54]

Naming prophetic revitalization as the seedbed of traditionalism, Jefferson set the precedent for the reformers' attack on the shows, which, they claimed, acted prophetlike to debar the Indians' adoption of nontraditional identities. On the face of things, the reformers' charge could not be further from the anthropologists' lament: where the former deplore the survival of traditional Indian performance, the latter rue its loss. But on closer inspection, both positions appear fundamentally alike: both ultimately, and identically, divorce the traditional from the intercultural contexts in which it operated, treating it as an item to be salvaged or suppressed rather than a process to be reinvented.

Neither of these positions has really gone away. Thus, some critics have read the role-playing of Cody's Indians as a violation of the sacred identities expressed within the Ghost Dance: while Cody's show "cemented roles for Indians who play Indian," it denied them the right "to act out their real traditional roles on the American landscape," reducing Indians to "imitating imitations of themselves." In an analysis of the comparable case of Australian aborigines who toured in wild-west-type entertainment, Roslyn Poignant phrases this argument as follows: "Although the performances they gave were grounded in their own cultural practices," native players in Euro-American spectacle were "ensnared in a hall of distorting mirrors," forced to enact "European fantasies in a performance that [was] destroying them." Increasingly, however, it has become popular to read Cody's Wild West as a vehicle for the preservation of tribal tradition. Reformist condemnation turning to revisionist celebration, critics write that Buffalo Bill's Wild West, like the Ghost Dance, helped Indians to "protect vital traditions of music and dance that had been driven underground on the reservation," to "maintai[n] their own religious and cultural practices," and to "perpetuate aspects of traditional culture": by participating in sweat baths, by dancing social (though apparently not ceremonial) dances, and more generally by carrying out roles that had been constricted if not prohibited by the agencies of detribalization, show Indians, the argument goes, were able to achieve what the Ghost Dance promised, the resumption of their old-time sports and occupations. As L. G. Moses concludes, the Wild West "provided an opportunity for Indians, not so much to play a role, but simply to be themselves."[55]

I agree with these latter critics that Buffalo Bill's Wild West, like the Ghost Dance, played an important part in late century Indian identity formation. To say this, however, is not the same as saying that it protected or perpetuated "aspects of traditional culture"; one has only to recall the circumstances under which these persons performed—away from home, thrown together with strangers, required to enact a drama not of their choice, and in some cases on leave from prison for an attempt to recover sacred tradition—to perceive the logical impossibility of them carrying "aspects" of tribal traditions through such a process of challenge and change. What is needed in our analysis of Wild West entertainment is a language that eschews the medicine-show notion of culture (or tribe) as a collection of aspects to be preserved, protected, or perpetuated, a language that, instead, recognizes cultural perpetuation in the terms of the Ghost Dance: a ritual death yielding to revitalization, a recovery of the past through its ever-changing reenactment. In this light, where Moses tends to oppose the traditional to the emergent in the previous quotation, I prefer to say that, as in the Ghost Dance, Indians in Buffalo Bill's Wild West became themselves *by* playing a role: they became members of an Indian collective by wearing store-bought costumes, following scripted dramas, earning salaries, traveling to eastern and European cities, selling signed photographs, playing Ping-Pong between sets, and forging intercultural as well as intertribal ties.[56] It is not that tribal tradition in Euro-American shows was transmitted not transformed, or transformed not transmitted. Rather, as in the Ghost Dance, tribal tradition in Euro-American shows was transmitted through transformation, transformed through transmission.

William Powers's distinction between "preservationist" and "reservationist" approaches to Plains dance, song, and ceremony provides a language for these processes. Powers explains: "By 'preservationist,' I mean an attitude towards fieldwork and analysis that is largely generated by individual or disciplinary concerns, if not fears, that American Indian [performance] is vanishing. . . . The preservationist approach consciously or unconsciously suggests that *real* American Indian culture is pre-reservation, and therefore dead; only modified, impure, bastardized, tainted remnants or vestiges survive." By contrast, the reservationist views "culture as an ongoing phenomenon capable of transmitting values over generations"; thus the reservationist is "largely concerned with contemporary" performance, with those acts—whether deemed traditional or not by those who perform them—that continue to be performed, and hence with those acts that, like any performance, emerge in relation to their others.[57] According to these terms, if the Wild West audience and impresario, the anthropological establishment, the Friends of the Indian, and critics past and present were to a greater or lesser degree preservationists, the show Indians—like Catlin's troupes, Catharine Brown's nation, and Wovoka's Ghost Dancers—were reservationists, living according to the rites of the medicine bundle, people who revitalized sacred tradition through intercultural, intertribal performance.

## Show Indians

> We look at the Indian congress as a spectacle, but who can tell what it may mean to the Indians themselves?
> —Review of the Omaha Exposition (1898), from the American Monthly Review

The life story of one of Buffalo Bill's show Indians, the Lakota autobiographer Luther Standing Bear, provides a compelling example of this process of performative identity formation. Owing, perhaps, to his close ties to the engines of late century detribalization—his education at the Carlisle school, his career in Buffalo Bill's Wild West (and later in the motion picture industry), and his employment with the Indian Bureau and advocacy of Indian citizen-ship—Standing Bear has most commonly been read in relation to his or his people's degree of assimilation. Thus Frederick Hale reads Standing Bear as a man who possessed a "generally though by no means categorically positive attitude towards assimilation in European-American society"; H. David Brumble sees Standing Bear as representative of those autobiographers who suggest that "in moving from prereservation Indian life to the white world," Indians were "passing over a great divide" from which there was no return; and Dan Moos, in his analysis of the ways in which cultural outsiders sought to write themselves into the American national narrative during the late nineteenth century, considers Standing Bear in light of the efforts of Cody's performers to effect "their Americanization through employment as actors in the show." Yet Standing Bear's 1928 autobiography, *My People the Sioux*, the first of a series of reflections on traditional and transitional Sioux life and culture, is not in any simple sense an account of personal and cultural detrib-alization, of "change from the old way of life."[58] Rather, it is a complex rumi-nation on (or enactment of) the politics of Indian performance, a work that reveals the emergence of a show Indian identity. Indeed, in the view of Ger-ald Vizenor (Anishinabe), Standing Bear heralds the rise of a modern (or postmodern) Indian identity: "Standing Bear seemed to envision the onset of the postindian warriors of simulations; that sensation of a new tribal pres-ence in the very ruins of the representations of invented Indians."[59] In this light, Standing Bear appears neither as an assimilationist nor as a tradition-alist but as a reservationist, who suggests that, if Indian identity is to be pre-served within the contexts of colonialism, it must be performed.

Standing Bear's insights into the perils and promise of Indian perfor-mance are illustrated by twin incidents during his school days that anticipate his later involvement with Buffalo Bill's Wild West. In one of these episodes, relating his visit to the theater on an eastern recruitment tour for the Carlisle school, Standing Bear recalls the mistreatment of his countryman, Sitting Bull, at the hands of white managers: "A white man came on stage and intro-duced Sitting Bull as the man who had killed General Custer (which, of course, was absolutely false). Sitting Bull arose and addressed the audience in the Sioux tongue, as he did not speak or understand English. . . . He never even mentioned General Custer's name. Then the white man who had intro-duced Sitting Bull arose again and said he would interpret what the chief had said. He then started in telling the audience all about the battle of the Little Big Horn. . . . He told so many lies that I had to smile" (185). Concluding the

episode in terms that critique the exploitative nature of Wild West–type entertainment, Standing Bear writes indignantly: "As I sit and think about that
incident, I wonder who that crooked white man was, and what sort of Indian
agent it could have been who would let these Indians leave the reservation
without even an interpreter, . . . and then cart them around to different Eastern cities to make money off them by advertising that Sitting Bull was the
Indian who slew General Custer!" (187). In this context, Standing Bear's later,
huffy reflection that "it did not seem right for Indians who cannot understand a word of the English language to leave the reservation to engage in the
show business" (261)—as well as his own efforts as an interpreter with Cody's
show to protect the performers from abuse and disadvantage—can be read
straightforwardly as proof of his disdain for, if not hostility toward, Indian
performance in white spectacle. Consistent with the position of Morgan and
the reformers—as well as of his countryman and fellow Carlisle student,
Chauncey Yellow Robe, who wrote scathingly in a 1914 editorial of "the evil
and degrading influence of commercializing the Indian before the world"—
it seems that Standing Bear considers the Wild West show a theater of abuses,
where Indians are not only encouraged but, as in Sitting Bull's case, forced to
play the part of the unredeemed, irreclaimable savage.[60]

This reading of Standing Bear's attitude toward Indian performance in
the Wild West show is, however, complicated by a parallel episode concerning his own speaking appearance before a white audience, in this case a group
of visitors to Carlisle. Asked by one eager member of the audience to say
something in his native language, Standing Bear responds: " '*Lakota iya woci
ci yakapi queyasi oyaka rnirapi kte sni tka le ha han pe lo*,' which, interpreted
into English, means, 'If I talk in Sioux, you will not understand me anyhow.'
But I did not understand exactly how to interpret this properly at that time,
so I was pleased when there was a clapping of hands, so I could sit down
again. Just then," he continues, "the [white] man stood up again, and while I
was shivering in my shoes for fear of what he might again ask me, he said,
'Can that boy interpret what he said into English?' I knew I had to say something, so I replied that it meant, 'We are glad to see you all here to-night' "
(167). This episode adopts a far more complex attitude toward Indian performance than was evident in the case of the Sitting Bull farce. For if the previous story suggested Standing Bear's resistance to Indian performers being
sent out into a world where they would be left to the mercy of white interpreters of their life and language, this story finds Standing Bear contributing

to, indeed orchestrating, the farce, the misrepresentation of Indian words at the expense, this time, of the white consumer.

To say this is not to cast Standing Bear as a simple trickster—a man who, as Moos writes, "puts on a costume" within his writings "as he does in Cody's show," or, as Alan Trachtenberg suggests in an analysis of Standing Bear's later autobiography, *Land of the Spotted Eagle* (1933), a man whose "disguise" may have been "a crafted irony, a way of mocking prevailing stereotypes of 'savage' and 'civilized,' inverting the terms and undermining the credulity of those nonnatives who took themselves to be 'real' Americans." As with the Cherokee authors or William Apess, this slide from performance to subterfuge slights not only the depth and complexity of intercultural imitation but also, most importantly for my purposes, the ways in which the performance of Indianness works to *enhance*, not simply to ironize, a "real" Indian identity. "Don't tell no white man," the Messiah Letter of the prophet Wovoka read; this is precisely what Standing Bear does (or does not do), and in so (not) doing he reveals his affinity with the Carlisle students who performed both in the Ghost Dance and in Cody's Wild West, as well as with the Ghost Dancers (Sitting Bull included) who likewise crossed over into white performance spaces. Standing Bear's preface, in which he terms his book "a message to the white race," promising "to bring my people before their eyes in a true and authentic manner" but then hedging that "no one is able to understand the Indian race like an Indian" (n. pag.), reflects the ambiguity of his position as Indian interpreter. "The nature of the 'message' offered to white audiences by Standing Bear," Lucy Maddox writes, "was, of necessity, performative."[61] And as such, that message, like Wovoka's prophetic word, (with)holds the possibility of an Indianness beyond the white audience's vigilance, awareness, or control: "you will not understand me anyhow."

Viewed in this light, Standing Bear's autobiography becomes a sustained meditation on the performance of Indian identity, a performance that revitalizes that identity through processes of intercultural adoption and adaptation. A realization of the interplay between Indian and white medicine dawns on the reader of *My People the Sioux*—and, perhaps, on its author—only gradually, as in the early pages Standing Bear seems to privilege a neat opposition between traditional life and an intruding white civilization. For example, when the railroad first enters Lakota territory, it appears as "a big snake . . . crawling across the prairie" (6), and this serpent in the aboriginal garden is literally derailed by the Indians, who "tear up some of the rails" on which the train is traveling and watch as "it ran off the track and was badly wrecked" (7). Similarly, when during a discussion of Indian pastimes Standing Bear refers to "American baseball," he is prompt to assert a fundamental difference between the Indian origin of this sport and the adulterated game with which readers identify: "Remember, I say AMERICAN baseball—not English. WE were the only real Americans" (43). According to these terms, if Indianness is "real," civilization is a simulacrum, a contemptible effort to copy the real Americans: "A tipi would probably seem queer to a white child," Standing Bear muses, "but if you ever have a chance to live in one you will find it very comfortable—that is, if you get a *real* tipi; not the kind used by the moving-picture companies" (13). Of politicians, he offers a comparable red-white opposition: "the Indian chief, without any education, was at least honest. . . . There was no hand-shaking, smiling, and 'glad-handing' which meant nothing. The chief was dignified and sincere" (59). Even in matters of religion, Standing Bear maintains, the most whites can do is imitate a prior reality that Indians once embodied. Thus, concluding a discussion of the Sun Dance, he writes: "We were then true Christians" (122)—that is, they practiced what Christ preached—but now "things have changed, even among the white people. They tear down their churches and let playhouses be built on the spot. What can be your feeling of reverence when you think of the house of God, in which you worshiped, being used to make fun in?" (122). Invoking the aura of Indian artlessness that critics back to Catlin had found at once admirable and unsustainable, Standing Bear here associates traditional Indianness with that which can neither mimic nor be mimicked.

The greatest outrage in these early sketches, accordingly, appears when Indians attempt to perform whiteness. In one such instance, Standing Bear is duped by an ambiguously gendered priest: "He was dressed in a long skirt, like a woman, but he was a man. . . . Whatever he did, I imitated him, not understanding what it meant" (92–93). Even more egregious is the case of Standing Bear's father, who returns from a trip to Washington in no better shape than Catlin's hapless Wi-jun-jon: "my father was so dressed up that he could not remove his boots all the way back to Dakota. When he got home, we children did not recognize him at all as he started to walk to his tipi. As he went inside, we children all ran to see who the white man was who had just gone into our tipi. . . . He looked so funny to us—more like a real curiosity. He even had kid gloves and a cane, but with all this white man's stylish make-up, he still wore his long hair" (69). The sideshow term *curiosity* signifies the sin that Standing Bear's father has committed in allowing himself to be "made up" by whites. Incongruous in his combination of traditional hair-style and civilized clothing, and pathetic in his inability to shake off, much less take up, the trappings of the white world, Standing Bear's father appears at this point in the autobiography the direct antithesis of his people's traditional hero, Crazy Horse. "The greatest chief the Sioux ever had" (87), Crazy Horse made his reputation not by "getting into the show business" (87) but by quietly and faithfully serving his people, a quality signified by the fact that he "never cared to dress up in gaudy clothes, but was a very plain man" (87–88). In both an implicit rebuke of his father, who was lured by the false promise of gaudy clothes, and a direct condemnation of the dirty business of the Wild West show, Standing Bear casts the show Indian as a traitor to tradition who ends up trapped, not empowered, by his attainments in the white world.

Yet notably, Standing Bear's father is offered a chance at redemption not by embarking on a heroic campaign of resistance such as Crazy Horse's but by dressing up once again in the accouterments of civilization. Thus the book's pivotal tenth chapter, "My Father's Store," begins to establish a more complex understanding of the uses of Indian performance for Indian persons. Standing Bear writes: "At this time my father was accounted a great man in his tribe and a chief who had the welfare of his people at heart. But he saw that the white men were pushing toward the West, and that sooner or later they would occupy the whole country. He realized that fighting would not get the Indians anywhere, and that the only recourse was to learn the white man's way of doing things, get the same education, and thus be in condition to stand up for his rights" (98). Putting this new philosophy to practice, "he took the money the Government had just paid me and started off on a trip. He was gone about ten days, and then he returned all dressed up. He wore a collar, a necktie, a stiff shirt, and even carried a watch and chain" (98). Here, the father's quest to learn the white man's way of doing things—in particular, his way of imitating that which he is not—differs significantly from the earlier account of his prostration (if not prostitution) by white performance. Whereas in the prior incidence Standing Bear's father was little more than a puppet tricked out by whites, here he grasps the tools of the actor's trade as a means of furthering "the welfare of his people," sustaining the real of Indian life through play in white clothes. From this later vantage, it appears that the opening sections of the book represented the young Standing Bear's naive, nostalgic (mis)understanding of the dynamics of Indian performance; his opposition of tradition to innovation or imitation, no matter how romantically appealing or viscerally satisfying, is exposed not only as an over-simplification but also, crucially, as a direct impediment to the identity he wishes to preserve. In this revised frame of reference, his father's imitative acts become signs not of repudiation but of revitalization, actions dedicated to the survival of "the only real Americans," whose realness must from this point on be performed in contact with white civilization.

This revised consciousness of the possibilities of Indian performance animates the chapters in which Standing Bear himself enters the orbit of the white world. In Chapter 14, "First Days at Carlisle," he relates an experience that was universal among Indian schoolchildren: the replacement of the child's Indian name with one chosen by whites. Standing Bear writes: "Then the teacher took a piece of white tape and wrote the name on it. Then she cut off a length of the tape and sewed it on the back of the boy's shirt. . . . Soon we all had the names of white men sewed on our backs" (137). Yet if, by the terms of the earlier tale of his father's clownish appearance in white clothing, this enforced masquerade would have been either utterly ridiculous or utterly intolerable, through Standing Bear's revised perspective it initiates the emergence not only of a new identity but of a new conceptualization *of* identity: "Now, after having had my hair cut, a new thought came into my head. I felt that I was no more Indian, but would be an imitation of a white man. And we are still imitations of white men, and the white men are imitations of the Americans" (141). Here imitation is no longer identified with the loss of the real, but more ambivalently with its invention. Thus, if his feeling that "I was no more Indian" evidences the traumatic nature of the transformation he has undergone, his concluding sentence marks a newfound conviction that *all* peoples within the intercultural realm exist through their others, that his Indian ("American") identity must henceforth go under a new name. When, therefore, Standing Bear next refers to himself and his brethren as the only "*real American*" people (171), that real has shifted; no longer defined by physical or ontological distance from the white world, the Indian real now consists both in a self-conscious act of racial identification and in a determination to use his imitative powers on behalf of his people. Retaining at once a sense of racial pride—as when he asks a fellow student ashamed to be called an Indian, "you are an Indian, aren't you?" (183)—and a complementary awareness that Indianness must be constantly reinforced and reinvented, Standing Bear commits to deploying his newly traditional identity to revitalize a race into which, like a Ghost Dancer, he has been less born than reborn.

Standing Bear's belief in the power of Indian performance to redeem Indian identity is suggested by two episodes late in the autobiography in which he describes his enactment of Indianness within two different, yet interconnected, public spaces. The first of these events occurs during his travels with Buffalo Bill, whose troupe Standing Bear understands, somewhat sardonically, in the terms contemporary Cody biographer Louis Warren applies to it: as "a forum for the creation of Indian identities."[62] Commenting that "all the [show] Indians belonged to the Sioux tribe," yet "we were supposed to represent four different tribes, each tribe to ride animals of one color" (252), Standing Bear exposes the stagecraft of the show, its ability to generate for an uninitiated audience a portrait of real Indianness that the performers know is but a ploy. In addition, writing of the show Indians' playful assumption of white disguise in a department store like that in which he held his first job in the white world, Standing Bear represents show Indian performance as a transcultural (indeed transgendered) riot of mimicry: "When we reached Chicago I took all the Indian men up to Marshall Field & Company's store. They all wanted to buy fur overcoats. . . . Some of the boys even indulged in some 'make-up,' such as they had seen white girls using, and it was not long before they could decorate their lips, cheeks, eyebrows, etc., as expertly as any white girl" (268–69). Yet in contrast to the episodes of racial and gendered cross-dressing from his youth, Buffalo Bill's Wild West emerges not simply as a ludicrous or lugubrious costume ball. During the show's sojourn in England, Standing Bear embraces the opportunity to get in on the act:

> Buffalo Bill came to me several times and said, "Don't forget, now, Standing Bear, to have your boys do their very best. And dance your very best before the King."
> I promised to carry out his wishes faithfully, and the show started. Everything worked splendidly. When it came time for the Indians to come in with their village in the center of the arena, we started the dance in which I was to appear before the King of England. I had a beautiful lance, and as the dance proceeded I worked over toward the King's box. There I shook the lance in his face and danced my very prettiest, you may be sure. The King had been very dignified thus far and had not even smiled. But when I got down to doing my fancy steps and gave a few Sioux yells, he had to smile in spite of himself. I saw that I had made a hit with him, and was very happy. (255–56)

Patently a canned routine (the "fancy steps," in particular, mark this solo as a precursor of the "fancy dancing" of twentieth-century intertribal powwows), Standing Bear's moment in the spotlight dramatizes the ways in which Indian identity was invented through the spectacle of Buffalo Bill's Wild West.

Plainly enough, this performance is comparable to his speech to the Carlisle visitors; unable to recognize the staged nature of the performance, his British audience takes his dance for the real. But for Standing Bear himself, the dance possesses a reality beyond its artifice; if Cody had reason to exult in this performance, this authentication of American character for the nation's former colonial overlords, Standing Bear too uses his private audience with the king to liberate himself from a relationship of colonial power, to authenticate (through fabrication) his own version of the true American. Performing before the English throne, that is, Standing Bear grasps the possibility that Wovoka and the Ghost Dancers, including those of Standing Bear's own people who joined Cody's troupe, had put into practice: the possibility of the dance to invent a distinctively Indian reality. As Standing Bear wrote in a later autobiographical statement, *Land of the Spotted Eagle* (1933), while "outwardly I lived the life of the white man, . . . all the while I kept in direct contact with tribal life. . . . I kept the language, tribal manners and usages, sang the songs and danced the dances."[63] Dancing in Buffalo Bill's Wild West enables Standing Bear to invent an Indian identity beyond the reach of the ringleader who requisitioned his steps, indeed beyond the reach of the show that, outwardly, made such an invention possible. Like the Ghost Dance, his dance uses intercultural imitation to shape a circle from which prying whites are outcast.

The potential of Indian performance in Standing Bear's reinvention of tribal life is capped by a final episode, the approximate climax of the book, in which he recounts his elevation to the position of chief. Recalling his address to his people during the installation ceremony, Standing Bear writes: "I told them . . . that I would do all in my power to help my people at all times, regardless of where I might be. That was the oath I took when I became chief of the Oglala Sioux, the greatest Indian tribe in the United States" (274). To certify his commitment, he is called on, once again, to dance: "The chiefs then began to sing a brave song, and all got up to dance. Now that I was one of them, I had to dance with them. That was the first time in my life that I had the honor of dancing with the old chiefs" (274–75). After the dance, he reminisces, "There were many tribes present that day—Omahas, Pawnees, Winnebagoes, Crows, Cheyennes, Arapahoes, as well as the Sioux. So I was made a chief in the Indian custom in front of all these different tribes; therefore the title of 'Chief' is now right and proper for me to use, whether in California or in any other part of the United States; and my people know that as long as I live I will do what is right and proper for them." He concludes, "Whenever an Indian leaves his reservation and comes among the white people to-day, either to go on the stage or in the moving pictures or with a Wild West show, he is always greeted with 'Hello, Chief.' This is most decidedly wrong" (276). Standing Bear wraps up his remembrance of the ceremony and his recrimination of showmanship with the defiant line: "It would be well for the white race to learn who is the true American. It is high time they knew the difference" (277).

In this climactic recollection, Standing Bear returns in some measure to the discourse of the book's early pages: he contends that he is a *real* chief—one authenticated by an intertribal collective—and not an imitation "chief"—one authenticated merely by stage, screen, or show. Yet as with the instance of his dancing *in* the show, the "difference" between the white race and the true American on which Standing Bear insists is a fugitive one, elastic rather than essential—as is evidenced by the fact that "my people," in the foregoing passage, have expanded to include not only the Sioux but all the "different tribes" who have invented a common identity. Standing Bear's discussion of the Ghost Dance is generally dismissive; though he writes that the massacre at Wounded Knee "made my blood boil" (224), he adopts the dominant culture's attitude toward the Dance itself, using his newfound allegiance to a western system of cosmogony to refute his people's beliefs as superstition (218) and priding himself on having sided with "the Progressives" who helped put down the Ghost Dance (229). Yet the previously cited line—"Now that I was one of them, I had to dance with them"—could well have been the Ghost Dance credo. As with the Ghost Dance, Standing Bear secures through intertribal performance an Indian identity that is at once a part of and apart from the show: in the spaces of white domination and spectacle, in Buffalo Bill's Wild West and on the reservation, Standing Bear steps into a dance that performs the real.

Any reading of Standing Bear as a performer of Indian identity must be cautious neither to endorse nor to trust his rhetoric unreservedly; as a man whose political activities put him at odds with some of the people he claimed to represent, there is no question that his autobiography contains a strong element of self-justification.[64] Nor, for that matter, is his portrayal entirely consistent. When, for instance, his book's final page urges that "with education and learning [the Indian] will make a real American citizen of whom the white race will be justly proud" (288), the meaning of the American (and of the real) appears to have shifted yet again, this time in a way that leaves the Indian behind. Similarly, when Standing Bear writes that, on a visit home from the Carlisle school, "I heard several of [my people] remark that I looked more like a white boy, because my skin had become lighter from my work in-side," and recalls that "it made me feel very proud to have them compare me to a white boy" (191), one is perhaps inclined to question his commitment to an Indian identity. Yet even this passage reveals a sense of the invented nature of racial discriminations: "But I have to laugh now at my appearance," he concludes wryly. "I looked like one of those Jew comedians on the stage" (191–92). In a comparable illustration of the intricacies of interracial performance, he describes a drama held at Carlisle: "One evening I recall that we gave a little play called 'The Landing of Columbus.' My brother Henry played the part of Columbus. Of course the acting was not very good, but we did the best we knew how at that time, and it brought out one point in Amer-ican history of which the people knew but little" (235). If this seems a clear case of the type of drama favored by Buffalo Bill—Indians reenacting their own dispossession—one might ask what the "one point" was that the play brought out, or more importantly, *who* "the people" were for whom this point was brought out.

Vine Deloria Jr.'s favorable assessment of Indian performers in Buffalo Bill's Wild West might be taken as a commentary on the life story of Luther Standing Bear: "Wild West shows performed a very important function in the closing decades of the last century. Indian leaders were generally carted to Washington, kept enclosed in a hotel room until they were ushered in to see the President or the Secretary of the Interior, sternly admonished to sign the treaty or agreement that ceded large tracts of tribal lands, and then un-ceremoniously sent home to the reservations. . . . The Wild West shows—particularly Cody's troupe—offered a great deal more. . . . Knowledge of white society gained in tours with Cody stood many of the Indians in good stead in later years."[65] If on his initial return from Washington, Standing Bear's father is the archetype of the Indian leader Deloria describes, a would-be headman become pawn to white power, Standing Bear is the contrasting figure of the show Indian, who finds in Wild West-type entertainment the knowledge of white society necessary to control to some degree his own and his people's representation. Judging these Indian players not on fidelity to a putative original but on the acts of self-determination embodied and enabled by their performance in Buffalo Bill's Wild West, the contemporary Sioux activist-critic, like his predecessor, perceives intertribal, intercultural perfor-mance as a fundamental tool in the revitalization of Indian tradition.

In his introduction to the 1979 reissue of John G. Neihardt's *Black Elk Speaks* (1932), Deloria speaks on behalf of another Lakota Indian whose life and life story were bound up in Euro-American practices of staged performance. Deloria's frequently duplicated (and disputed) introduction concludes: "Present debates center on the question of Neihardt's literary intrusions into Black Elk's system of beliefs and some scholars have said that the book reflects more of Neihardt than it does of Black Elk." But, Deloria wonders, "can it matter? The very nature of great religious teachings is that they encompass everyone who understands them and personalities become indistinguishable from the transcendent truth that is expressed. So let it be with *Black Elk Speaks*. . . . It is good. It is enough."[66] Deloria's tribute to *Black Elk Speaks* responds, though perhaps with insufficient critical consideration, to Sally McCluskey's 1972 disclosure that despite the book's "ring of authenticity," in significant respects the words of *Black Elk Speaks*, including its famous beginning and ending, were not the words that Black Elk spoke. They were, instead, as Neihardt told McCluskey, "what [Black Elk] would have said if he had been able."[67] The extent to which Neihardt had spoken for Black Elk was clarified in 1984, with Raymond J. DeMallie's publication of *The Sixth Grandfather*, which made available the Black Elk–Neihardt interview transcripts. It now emerged that Neihardt had edited, rephrased, and rearranged Black Elk's memories with considerable license. Furthermore, DeMallie's book dropped another bombshell, subsequently confirmed by Michael Steltenkamp's interviews with members of Black Elk's family: the Lakota holy man had been a practicing Catholic, a catechist and evangelist to his own and neighboring tribes, for nearly thirty years when Neihardt met him.[68]

If, however, these revelations have had the salutary effect of complicating responses to *Black Elk Speaks* and to Indian autobiography generally, they have had the unfortunate effect of steering Black Elk criticism down twin, equally unproductive, paths: on the one hand, a debate over whether Neihardt's book is an authentic representation of Black Elk's Lakota voice, on the other, a tempest over whether Black Elk's voice had been leeched of its Lakota character long before Neihardt arrived on the scene. Critics who have challenged the validity of *Black Elk Speaks* include G. Thomas Couser, who terms the book a work of "cultural imperialism" that "reenacts the process it so eloquently condemns: the appropriation and erasure of Lakota culture by whites," and William Powers, who accuses the narrative of misleading contemporary Lakota peoples into accepting an adulterated version of their own faith "manufactured in the literary workshops of the white man." Conversely, *Black Elk Speaks* has been defended by Amanda Porterfield, who writes that the belief system reflected in the book "is first and foremost a Lakota theology," and by Julian Rice, who argues that when Black Elk is "disentangled from Neihardt," it is plain that he remained a spokesman for "a Lakota culture independent of adopted Christianity," a man who became a Catholic only "for reasons of social expediency." In perhaps the strongest statement of this latter position, Neil Schmitz asserts that to separate Black Elk from Neihardt is to be faithful to the holy man's own intentions: "Black Elk puts into English sacred Lakota texts, his own and his tribe's, legitimizing a space for traditional tribal narrative in American literature." Schmitz thus sees Black Elk as representative of the Indian narrator's power to force a traditional vision past the white poet's lines: "What is 'Indian' in American literature, captured or bestowed, is still somehow 'Indian,' has its special mode, retains its sacredness, keeps its distinct identity. Romantic idealizing Euro-American frames can be detached."[69]

It is not my purpose to minimize the problematics of *Black Elk Speaks*; given the withering assaults on Lakota culture and religion that Black Elk witnessed and withstood, it is certainly valid to examine the ways in which his life—and the text of his life—participated in that history. Yet the terms within which Black Elk's life has been cast, I believe, circumvent such an inquiry. Schmitz's position, valuable though it is for its suggestion of a distinctive, indigenous identity operating within the Black Elk text, typifies the problem. Even if it were *possible* in Black Elk's case to detach the Euro-American "frame" from the Native American "identity," it would still be worth asking whether it is *worthwhile* to do so—whether, in fact, to do so would not be to sacrifice what is special, distinct, and most of all sacred about Black Elk's identity as a Native American visionary prophet. As the examples of the Ghost Dance and Buffalo Bill's Wild West indicate, not only was the traditional identity of the Plains Indians itself an ongoing process of performative reinvention that cannot be pinned down in the manner that Schmitz and other critics suggest, but that process, that performance, was generated in contact with the very Euro-American frames one might wish to detach. For as I have said, prophetic revitalization implies the presence and pressure of such frames; prophetic revitalization arises from the conflictual, productive bundling of Indian medicine with white.

The attempt to separate Black Elk from the text of his life, then, does not represent an advance over the authenticity-versus-appropriation debate; if anything, it further obscures the traditionalism it seeks to evoke. Thus, if Black Elk's speaking cannot be divorced from *Black Elk Speaks*—if, as Moos puts it, "the overlay of white editorship is so thorough" that "one cannot

clearly distinguish between Black Elk's self-representation and the construc-
tions of his white editor"—one should see this not as an obstacle to avoid but
as an avenue through which to enter: as in the Ghost Dance and Buffalo Bill's
Wild West, traditional and emergent Indian performance are *not* clearly dis-
tinguishable, for each exists via its relationship to its apparent other.[70] As Eric
Cheyfitz's recent intervention into the debate illustrates, viewing the text in
terms rooted in the theory and practice of indigenous, prophetic performance opens up a way to reframe the issues that *Black Elk Speaks* raises:

> Deloria's reading of *Black Elk Speaks* focuses discussion not on the identity of the au-
> thors but on the text, as a political or social performance rather than as a referent or
> key to transcendent identities. Deloria is in effect treating the text as social act, not
> aesthetic object, that is, as Native oral performance, not Western writing. . . . *Black
> Elk Speaks*, then, claims its Indian identity not through essence—the sorting out of
> European from Native American, of the written from the oral, of Neihardt from Black
> Elk—for such sorting, in any absolute sense, is impossible. Rather, it claims its iden-
> tity through practice—of a particular pantribal, Indian community's resistance to the
> erosion [in Deloria's words] "of the continuing substance of Indian tribal life."[71]

The impossibility of sorting out Black Elk from Neihardt, the traditional
from the Westernized, the holy man from the Catholic, is apparent when one
considers the source material of this (or any) Indian life: the published transcripts of *The Sixth Grandfather* do not offer what DeMallie terms "direct access to Black Elk" (*SG*, xxiii) any more than does Neihardt's book, for these
records were from the beginning textual interpretations of translated speech,
and neither do subsequent reflections on Black Elk's life and character, such
as those offered by his son Ben Black Elk or his granddaughter Lucy Looks
Twice, capture the bodily Black Elk, for these too are scribal mediations of a
tribal original. (Moreover, these familial stories are conflicting, as when Lucy
tells Steltenkamp that Black Elk "put all his medicine away" after his conversion yet recalls to Neihardt's daughter Hilda that "before he passed away"
Black Elk told his family, "The only thing I really believe is the pipe religion."[72]) One will never recover Black Elk through these sources, or through
any other that may emerge in the future, if by this one means recovering a
stable entity that exists outside the intercultural matrix in which Black Elk's
narrative was and is received. If, however, one places the Lakota prophet's
life—by which I mean not only his physical life but the texts based on it—
within the sacred bundle of medicine acts in which he performed, then one
will be able to appreciate the ways in which *Black Elk Speaks* ritually produces
an emergent, revitalized Indian identity.

Viewing Black Elk's life in this way is consistent with the understanding of Plains religions that I have noted of the Ghost Dance: the lifelong transformation of Black Elk's vision is emblematic of Lakota belief and ritual, which relied, like the Dance, on revisions of existing traditions. According to interviews with Lakota holy men conducted by James R. Walker, whose service as physician on the Pine Ridge reservation from 1896 to 1914 overlapped the period of Black Elk's conversion to Catholicism, the apparent conservatism of Lakota religion was belied by the central role of innovation and individual initiative in religious practice. Thus, though one of Walker's principal sources, George Sword, told him that the religious ceremonies of the Lakotas "must be done exactly as they are taught. Every word and every motion said or done in the ceremony must be right," he also stressed the flexibility and adaptability built into the ceremonial structure: "The medicine men governed all ceremonies of medicine. But a shaman could change any custom or ceremony." (Sword maintains the traditional distinction between the *wicasa wakan*, holy man or shaman, and the *pejuta wicasa*, or medicine man.)[73] Another of Walker's interviewees, Thomas Tyon, told him that such revisionary power extended to the point of inventing ceremonies anew: "A shaman is a wise man who has intercourse with the spirits. . . . He may promulgate ceremonies of a new kind. If he does this he must prepare himself by the sweat bath according to the customs and seek a vision. If his vision is right he will be told what to do. Then he may organize a new ceremony according to the directions he receives in the vision." Moreover, given the importance of the *hanbleceyapi*, or "crying for a vision" experience for male (and some female) members of Lakota culture, it was possible for individuals outside the community of medicine or holy men to contribute to the evolution of ritual and belief. Visions, the Sword interview continues, "may come at any time or in any manner to anyone," and when they did, according to another of Walker's sources, Thunder Bear, they were often of such a nature as to require communal interrogation and negotiation: "When [a vision] comes, it will tell [the visionary] something which will be a knowledge of some medicine or what to do in the future or a warning against some evil or to make another quest or to cease from seeking a vision. The communication is apt to be ambiguous and require an interpretation," involving "much time and consultation" among the society of holy men.[74]

This dialectical structure of belief, allowing both for the alteration of traditional practices and for the reclamation of emergent forms along traditional lines, affirms that Lakota religion, in common with the religious traditions of the Plains, was inherently open to revitalization, to the sorts of prophetic acts that Short Bull, one of the emissaries who had brought the Ghost Dance to the Sioux, told Walker existed within the Dance itself: "Each one described his vision. Each vision is different. Men, women, children have visions." As De-Mallie sums up: "The content of [Lakota] religious beliefs and rituals was not conceived of as static, but rather as continually changing, infused with new revelations from visions that might modify older forms." Thus when Hertha Wong, in her reading of *Black Elk Speaks*, writes that "for Black Elk," the "traditional . . . means pre-reservation," she makes the same mistake that both Walker and Neihardt did, the former proclaiming that "the last of the order of holy men among the Oglalas has gone before his final judge and the progress of civilization has extinguished the order" and the latter infamously concluding *Black Elk Speaks* with a comparable elegy for a dying creed.[75] This is the logic of the preservationist: the opposition of the traditional and the intercultural, the dying of the old without the rebirth of the new. But the life of Black Elk, a life faithful to the religious tradition(s) he both transmitted and transformed, speaks with the voice of the reservationist.

The major phases of Black Elk's life—the great vision of his childhood; the tribal, intertribal, and extratribal dances of his young adulthood; the activities as a Catholic convert and catechist of his maturity; and finally, the interviews with Neihardt and other white interpreters of his latter years—can thus be seen, for all their obvious differences, as constituting a single, unbroken practice and reassessment of a traditional, sacred Indian performance. Or, to put this another way, if Black Elk's great vision launches a career of prophetic revitalization, his later acts, both among his own people and among whites, become, as Brian Holloway puts it, diverse "means of expressing a central illumination," literally re-visions of a continuous, emergent prophetic process.[76] Yet this being the case, it is important to repeat that, in the recursive process of Lakota traditionalism, as in the Ghost Dance, additions and variations are at once informed by and informative of prior structures of belief and ritual; new visions are fed back into the existing system, which provides sanction for those re-visions while simultaneously being reinvented through them. The significance of this forging of tradition via variation can be appreciated when one recalls that everything we know about Black Elk from his own recitation—including the information we have on his great vision, healing practices, and participation in tribal ceremonies—has been recorded *after* additional intertribal/intercultural performances (Buffalo Bill's Wild West, the Ghost Dance, Catholic conversion) have occurred.

At its simplest, this helps explain what appears to be Christian ideation in the written texts of Black Elk's life: "Many are called but few are chosen," he reflects in his telling of a Thunder-vision, preliminary to a *heyoka*, or sacred clown ceremony (*SG,* 231), while a passage from the great vision fuses the iconography of traditional medicine and Catholic communion: "the grandfather of the west had given me a wooden cup of water. . . . With the wooden cup of water I was to save mankind. This water was clear and with it I was to raise a nation (like medicine)" (*SG,* 119). But the picture is not so simple, since, as is evident in Black Elk's participation in the Ghost Dance, one cannot separate his performances into distinct threads: traditional beliefs, Christian beliefs within the Dance, the mature Black Elk's recollection of the Dance, Neihardt's reading of Black Elk, and so on. Black Elk reports that in his vision of Wovoka, "He did not resemble Christ. He looked like an Indian, but I was not sure of it" (*SG,* 263). He goes on to say, "At that time I had never had anything to do with white men's religion and I had never seen any picture of Christ" (*SG,* 263)—but this is, as DeMallie points out, "not strictly true, in that Black Elk was clearly familiar with Christianity while he was in Europe" with Buffalo Bill (*SG,* 263n10). Thus, understanding Black Elk's life and texts as constituents of a complex, traditional-transitional medicine bundle enables one not to isolate particular elements but, quite the contrary, to see in his life and texts a consummation of the process of prophetic reinvention: to witness the emergence of a distinctive Indian identity through the intersection of diverse tribal, intertribal, and intercultural (re)visionary acts.

The great vision of Black Elk's youth contains the seeds of this process, as Black Elk, like Wovoka, enters the spirit world (the realm of the six grandfathers) and is named the renewer, the reinventer, of the Lakota people: "Behold the circle of the nation's hoop," Neihardt's version reads, "for it is holy, being endless, and thus all powers shall be one power in the people without end" (*BES,* 35). Consistently less ornate, orotund, or oracular in its diction, but fundamentally similar in its evocation of the rehabilitative properties of the vision, the interview transcript renders this image: "The circle represented the old people that represented the nation. The center of it represented the prosperity of the nation" (*SG,* 123). The underlying symbolism of the great vision—the sacred hoop, the flowering tree, the good red road—emphasizes the capacity for performative renewal. For example, recalling how he encounters Buffalo Woman, deliverer of the sacred pipe to the Sioux people, Black Elk relates: "One of the old men said (showing me the sacred hoop): 'Behold a good nation, a sacred nation, again they will walk toward good land, the land of plenty, and no suffering shall there be. A nation you shall create and it shall be a sacred nation' (meaning that I was given the power to raise a nation)" (*SG*, 125–26). Irwin notes of Plains visionary experience that "the symbolism of rebirth is quite apparent. . . . To move into that [spiritual] reality through an altered awareness meant to be revitalized and renewed through the practical application of visionary knowledge."[77] Black Elk's great vision exemplifies this quality of the visionary complex: foreshadowing "how the nation's hoop would be broken and the flowering tree be withered" (*BES*, 147) by the machinations of the whites, who "came on this continent and put us Indians in a fence and they put another fence somewhere else and put our game into it" (*SG*, 127), Black Elk's vision, like Wovoka's, promises triumph over cultural death through the rebirth of traditional lifeways and identity.

Yet as the previous quotation from Irwin indicates, new life from death cannot be achieved without "practical application"—that is, without public, ritual performance. Thus at the age of seventeen, eight years after his great vision, Black Elk is again visited by spirit voices, who command him to "do your duty and perform this vision for your people upon earth" (*BES*, 161). Relating his first public appearance as organizer and enactor of the Horse Dance, the interview transcript similarly emphasizes the obligation of performing as a means of bringing the vision to life: "I had to perform my duty according to my vision. Of course you know what I have told you and I did it to show my people that I had this vision and to show the people what I would be among them" (*SG*, 220). Too, both transcript and autobiography stress the theme of transformation through enactment, as in the passage that concludes the Horse Dance, which Neihardt adapted closely from the transcribed record: "After the horse dance was over [this ceremony was completed], it seemed that I was above the ground [earth] and did not touch it when I walked [I did not touch the earth]. I felt very happy, for I could see that my people were all happier [and I was also happy to see my people, as it looked like they were renewed and happy]" (*BES*, 175 [*SG*, 225]). In similar fashion, Black Elk's career as a medicine man, from age eighteen to twenty-one, is both authorized by and a fulfillment of his sacred vision: "The power vision cannot be used until the duty we got with the part of the vision has been performed upon the earth. After that the power may be used" (*SG*, 238); "I think I have told you . . . that a man who has a vision is not able to use the power of it until after he has performed the vision on earth for the people to see" (*BES*, 204). Manifested as healing ritual, Black Elk's vision of power sustains Lakota tradition through performative elaboration.

That process of reenactment, moreover, does not come to a close once Black Elk transitions from tribal ceremonies to the world of intertribal and intercultural performance. On the contrary, his Wild West and Ghost Dance period (1886–90) can be seen as coextensive with his earlier visionary performances, indeed as further visitations of those performances within an expanded arena. Just as his first public performances were meant "to show my people that I had this vision and to show the people what I would be among them," so can his activities as a Ghost Dancer and show Indian be seen as demonstrations of his ability to sustain his people through re-vision. Frank Fools Crow, a Lakota healer of the generation after Black Elk's, described an encounter he had with Black Elk upon the commencement of his own show career: "he told me that as a medicine man I would learn many sacred secrets and perform countless ceremonies for people. . . . Black Elk went on to say that, as I traveled to competitions and toured with Wild West shows, word of my healing and prophetic power would spread. Then people who were doubters would ask me to prove what I could do by telling my visions and performing my ceremonies for them."[78] Though the accounts of Black Elk's show days recorded in *The Sixth Grandfather* and *Black Elk Speaks* offer little insight into the sacred secrets he may have learned or the ceremonies he may have performed among non-Indian peoples, they are nonetheless consistent with this portrait of the Wild West as an opportunity to reinforce the great vision's revitalizing power within intertribal and intercultural performance spaces.

Of the two principal written versions of Black Elk's life, that which Neihardt formulated draws more direct parallels between the vision and the show. "I thought I ought to go [with Buffalo Bill]," Black Elk says, "because I might learn some secret of the Wasichu that would help my people somehow. In my great vision, when I stood at the center of the world, the two men from the east had brought me the day-break-star herb and they had told me to drop it on the earth; and where it touched the ground it took root and bloomed. . . . Maybe if I could see the great world of the Wasichu, I could understand how to bring the sacred hoop together and make the tree bloom again at the center of it" (*BES*, 214–15). While its language—and its view of the white man's medicine—is considerably more prosaic than in Neihardt's narrative, the interview transcript still expresses an implicit connection between the vision and this new, intercultural performance ground: "I wanted to see the great water, the great world and the ways of the white men; this is why I wanted to go. So far I looked back on the past and recalled the people's ways. They had a way of living, but it was not the way we had been living. I got disgusted with the wrong road that my people were doing now and I was trying to get them to go back on the good road; but it seemed as though I couldn't induce them, so I made up my mind I was going away from them to see the white man's ways. If the white man's ways were better, why I would like to see my people live that way" (*SG*, 245). As with Luther Standing Bear, Black Elk's desire to investigate, and potentially embrace, the white man's ways might seem a simply pragmatic choice, a quest for material, not spiritual, power. Yet the references to his people's falling away from tradition suggest as well that Buffalo Bill's Wild West may have offered Black Elk, as it did Standing Bear, an opportunity to renew a sense of Indianness that had been stifled by reservation life. In Black Elk's case, too, Wild West performance may have been, as Neihardt's additions suggest, a way of restoring the sacred compact imposed upon him by his great vision. A later passage in the transcript, which reads, "I thought, 'I am going to try my best to get my people back into the hoop again.' At this time, when I had these things in my mind, I was abroad with strange people" (*SG*, 294), intimates that for Black Elk, Lakota tradition, in the characteristic manner of visionary experience, was to be seen through, not replaced by, intercultural performance.

Brief, suggestive comments that Neihardt derived from the transcript lend credence to this hypothesis. Writing of the show Indians' performance in New York, Black Elk says (according to the transcript), "I enjoyed the Indian part of the shows that we put on here at Madison Square Garden, but I did not care much about the white people's parts" (*SG*, 246), or (in the words of the published narrative), "I liked the part of the show we made, but not the part the Wasichus made" (*BES*, 217). These remarks imply that Black Elk objected to the white-orchestrated spectacle of Indian immolation, while reveling in the dances that were, for the most part, under the Indians' control. If so, then it is possible to read Black Elk's preference for Indian dance over Codyesque narrative in the manner that I have read Standing Bear's Carlisle speech or his own Wild West performance: as an embodiment of Indian distinctiveness and autonomy, of sacred secrets and ceremonies that operated within, yet without, the white man's ways. Summing up his own demonstration of Indian dance before British royalty, Black Elk recalls, through Neihardt, "I was young and limber then and could dance many ways" (*BES*, 221) ["I was limber at this time and I could dance many ways"

(*SG*, 249)]. In this portrayal, Indian dance under the auspices of Cody's Wild West retains the flexibility of visionary reenactment; conforming to the white man's ways yet utilizing those ways to carry forward the work of his people's traditions, Black Elk's Wild West interlude appears as yet another of the vision's offspring or offshoots.

One of the ways in which the limber Black Elk danced, on his return from a European sojourn of some two years with and without Cody's show, was in the sacred, ceremonial manner of Wovoka's disciples. Bridging his participation in Buffalo Bill's Wild West and the Ghost Dance is another vision that occurs while Black Elk is abroad: picturing "far off the Black Hills and the center of the world where the spirits had taken me in my great vision" (*BES*, 226), and where "the people were all gathered . . . and there was quite an excitement" (*SG*, 253), Black Elk's trance vision, like Wovoka's, brings him at once to the site of the Indians' greatest loss (the reservation) and to the site of their potential recovery (the spirit world). In this respect, Ghost Dancing is distinctly, and not ironically, reservationist: like Buffalo Bill's Wild West, it offers a revival of tradition through a performance that is at once circumscribed and motivated by that which is not (in any traditional sense) traditional. "I had had a great vision that was to bring the people back into the nation's hoop," Neihardt's text reads, "and maybe this sacred man had had the same vision and it was going to come true, so that the people would get back on the red road" (*BES*, 234). In the transcript, Black Elk recalls: "it looked as though my vision were really coming true and that if I helped, probably with my power that I had I could make the tree bloom and that I would get my people back into that sacred hoop again where they would prosper" (*SG*, 257). Reading Wovoka himself as a re-vision of the great vision—"so much of my vision seemed to be in it [it seemed that I could recall all my vision in it]" (*BES*, 237 [*SG*, 258])—Black Elk becomes once more an "intercessor for my people" (*SG*, 258), a vehicle for carrying on the work of visionary renewal.

A prophet reborn, Black Elk relates the oncoming of a Ghost Dance vision: "Then there came a strong shivering all over my body, and I knew that the power was in me" (*BES*, 240). The vision follows: "I could see a beautiful land where many, many people were camping in a great circle. I could see that they were happy and had plenty. Everywhere there were drying racks full of meat. The air was clear and beautiful with a living light that was everywhere. All around the circle, feeding on the green, green grass, were fat and happy horses; and animals of all kinds were scattered all over the green hills, and singing hunters were returning with their meat" (*BES*, 242; the closely analogous passage occurs in *SG*, 261). This vision, it is perhaps needless to say, is not identical to the great vision of Black Elk's youth; it far more closely resembles the vision of the other world attributed to Wovoka. Yet it is for all that a traditional vision—or, to put this more precisely, it is an exemplification of the Lakota visionary process wherein new or even foreign traditions are integrated into a prior system of belief, broadening what counts as sanctioned visionary experience while adapting to the terms and needs of Lakota social and ceremonial identity. "I told my vision through songs," the published narrative reads, "and the older men explained them to the others" (*BES*, 247); in the transcript: "I told my vision through songs. As I sang one song, there were older men [*than I*] there to tell what they meant to the others" (*SG*, 264). Black Elk's Ghost Dance vision and performance, in short, symbolize the process of emergent identity formation that characterized the Dance as well as the Wild West: the very difference of these visions, songs, and dances from their originals made possible a return to origin, to the sacred center of the medicine bundle.

In Neihardt's telling, of course, this revision of Indian identity is stillborn: coming to see the promise of the Ghost Dance as a betrayal of his tribal vision—"I had had a very great vision, and I should have depended only upon that to guide me to the good. But I followed the lesser visions that had come to me while dancing on Wounded Knee Creek" (*BES*, 250)—Black Elk witnesses the death of the tribal tradition he sought to rescue: "And I, to whom so great a vision was given in my youth," the final page of the book's narrative portion reads, "you see me now a pitiful old man who has done nothing, for the nation's hoop is broken and scattered. There is no center any longer, and the sacred tree is dead" (*BES*, 270). That Neihardt apparently invented this concluding passage from whole cloth does not preclude the possibility that Black Elk himself felt that his great, tribal vision had been weakened by intertribal and intercultural performance. Though its language is far less despairing than that of the Neihardt version, the interview transcript does suggest that Black Elk harbored misgivings about the Ghost Dance's relationship to his prophetic mission: "All through this I depended on my Messiah vision whereas perhaps I should have depended on my first great vision which had more power and this might have been where I made my great mistake" (*SG*, 266). Yet whatever Black Elk's personal verdict on his Ghost Dance and Wild West days, neither the tragic/preservationist conclusion of *Black Elk Speaks* nor the less melancholic but comparably partitioned understanding of Black Elk's personal history provided by DeMallie in *The Sixth Grandfather*—wherein the former holy man "turned his back on the vision" of his youth in his later days (*SG*, 53)—can account for the record of Black Elk's life. In that life, tribal, intertribal, and intercultural performance coexist in such intimate and intricate relation that none can be sacrificed without the loss of the others.

The last and longest phase of Black Elk's life, from his conversion in 1904 to his death in 1950, confirms this vision (or re-vision). Writing of the late century Catholic missions to the Lakota people, Harvey Markowitz notes the emphasis on replacement, not reinvention, that predominated in the days of Black Elk's conversion: "the early crisis in Catholic missionary efforts among the [Sioux] revolved around the failure of a missiological paradigm that sought to replace Sioux cultural and religious traditions with the institutions of Euro-American society and Catholicism." This paradigm was exemplified by the event that, according to Black Elk's daughter Lucy, convinced him to convert to Catholicism: while doctoring a dying child, he was confronted by a priest, Father Lindebner, who "had already baptized the boy and had come to give him the last rites. . . . He took the drum and rattle and threw them outside the tent. Then he took my father by the neck and said, 'Satan, get out!' "[79] In his discussion of this episode, DeMallie argues that the conversion that followed shortly thereafter signified Black Elk's recognition of a power "greater than his own" (*SG*, 14) and his consequent retreat from the power vision of his youth: "Black Elk's conversion was unquestionably genuine. By accepting Catholicism he at last put himself beyond the onerous obligations of his vision, and he never practiced the Lakota religious ceremonies again" (*SG*, 14). Yet not only is this interpretation challenged by the outcome of the incident—the boy recovered, whereas the priest died shortly thereafter in an accident involving, fittingly in light of Black Elk's power vision, a horse (*SG*, 239)—but a parallel incident at a later point in Black Elk's life, as recalled by his granddaughter Esther, suggests an alternative reading both of his conversion and of his obligation to his vision:

I was at my grandfather's house, and he was sitting down, getting his pipe ready early in the morning, and here was Father Sialm knocking on the door. They opened the door, and he came in, and he saw my grandfather with the pipe. Father Sialm grabbed the pipe and said, "This is the work of the devil!" And he took it and threw it out the door on the ground.

My grandfather didn't say a word. He got up and took the priest's prayer book and threw it out on the ground. Then they both looked at each other, and nobody said one word that whole time.

And then they both went out, and I saw Father Sialm pick up the prayer book, and Grandfather picked up his pipe. Each one picked up his own.[80]

Black Elk's recovery of the pipe—not only his retrieval but his retention of it—supports Clyde Holler's argument that "Black Elk's commitment to Christianity" did not "necessarily imply any lessening of his commitment to traditional Lakota religion." For in that religion, the traditional was not incompatible with—indeed, was enabled by—visionary replenishment and renewal. In Lakota practice, George Sword told Walker, the healer "may have only one kind of medicine" in his bag "or he may have a great many kinds"; Black Elk seems to have preferred to hold a great many kinds of medicine in his bag, each gaining power through the presence of the others.[81]

Yet in embracing Christian-Lakota innovation, Black Elk was anything but an innovator. As Robert Hilbert notes of the twentieth-century Lakota experience of Catholicism, "a number of medicine men are also practicing Catholics in good standing. They experience no opposition between the two religious systems." Lucy, though in Steltenkamp's account a faithful Catholic and, as such, adamant that Black Elk "put all his medicine practice away" after his conversion, nonetheless provides an example of the ways in which Lakota Catholics may have conjoined ostensibly distinct religious traditions: "My father got the permit for the church gathering, but he had also told the people to bring their Indian costumes to Mass so that afterward they could have a feast and dance. He knew they liked the dancing. So some of them even wore their Indian costumes to church. That was the only way they could have their dances for a while. A lot of them joined the church and got baptized." Lucy's language, characteristically, is somewhat belittling: the term *costumes* and the offhand remark "he knew they liked the dancing" suggest that in her view Black Elk had coaxed or even conned his people into entering a sanctum they would otherwise have shunned. But the scene she describes of Indians' dancing forbidden dances in church—complement to the Ghost Dancers putting Christianity to traditional use—offers a more complex image of Lakota church membership than Lucy may have allowed. It is in this sense that David Murray's reading of Black Elk as a "born-again traditionalist" gains resonance: the traditionalism of Black Elk and his people inhered in their ability to breathe old life into a series of performances, even the performance of being "born again" into the Christian faith.[82]

I am mindful that my reading of Black Elk's Catholicism relies heavily on the recollections of his descendants, whose memories of their progenitor's relationship to Christianity may have been shaped by their need to negotiate their own beliefs. This personalizing of the holy man's example is evident in the words of his son Ben, interpreter at the Neihardt interview sessions, who announces: "I used to lead two lives: one, Indian religion, and one as a Christian. . . . It used to be that when I would speak about the pipe, when I used the pipe, it seemed to me that it clashed with Christianity. But now, I know they come together in our church. . . . Now, I live only one way." But to suggest that these memories tell us as much about their speakers as about Black Elk is not to dismiss them; it is, rather, to receive them as evidence of the success of Black Elk's medicine performance, a success measured by its ongoing ability to affect (or effect) a Lakota identity. The memories—or more importantly, the practices—of Black Elk's circle become further revisions of his original vision, further instances of ritual transformation. Thus when another of Black Elk's granddaughters, Olivia, states proudly that "my kids are all going traditional. Some of them are dancing, some of them are in sun dancing, and some of them are competing in powwows," the limberness of the traditional, its reenactment through a variety of acts running the gamut from the canonical Sun Dance to the modern-day powwow, vouches once more for the power of Black Elk's evolving, sacred vision.[83]

In the final act of his life, Black Elk himself, according to Olivia, "danced traditional" as "part of the pageant." The pageant to which she refers was the Sioux Indian pageant organized as a tourist attraction in 1935 by Rapid City businessman Alex Duhamel; Black Elk, DeMallie reports, joined the show upon its inception and participated "every season for most of the rest of his life" (*SG*, 63). In the show, Alice Kehoe writes, Black Elk danced and performed a series of rituals, "including offering the pipe to the Almighty and drumming, rattling, and singing his old healing prayers over a pretend patient." Noting that the pageant "was a secular show," Kehoe argues that Black Elk's decision "to casually go through what he once believed to be potent rituals" suggests that he had rejected Lakota religion, a conclusion strengthened in her view by the fact that in 1935, he also sat for a "photograph of himself offering the rosary and crucifix to an Oglala child." Lucy similarly discounted her father's appearance in the pageant: "it was just a show, and he never meant it." But the history of Indian show, or of the show Indian, suggests a different conclusion—suggests, in fact, that such rituals were no less potent than the rites the holy man had performed before, during, and after his days with Buffalo Bill. Commenting on Black Elk's stage career, Schmitz calls attention to "the theatrical Black Elk, the Black Elk comfortable with show business types, with dancers and artists, a Black Elk comfortably traversing the line between ritual and theatrical performances."[84] In this view, Black Elk the pageant showpiece was neither a naif nor a stooge, overawed by the white man's medicine; he knew how to act.

And like any good actor, he knew how to draw a crowd. In 1947, three years before his death and while still performing in the Sioux pageant, Black Elk related the "seven rites of the Oglala Sioux" to Joseph Epes Brown, who published his account as *The Sacred Pipe* (1953). In the book's foreword, Brown quotes Black Elk as saying "I have wished to make this book through no other desire than to help my people in understanding the greatness and truth of our own tradition."[85] That this tradition has, as DeMallie observes, been calibrated to accord with the Catholic sacraments (*SG*, 71) is no more surprising than that, in Lucy Black Elk's account of her father's teachings, Catholicism has been reinvented to further Lakota tribalism:

Ever since I was six years old he trained me in prayers—Indian prayers—and Indian Catholic hymns. There's one song—the first song he ever taught me was this song here. I'll sing it right now. . . .

O God most good
Who wants to make himself known,
All rejoice rightly,
He asks of you your hearts.
You Lakota are a nation,
Quickly may they come together;
Jesus would have it so,
Because he has called you all.[86]

A song worthy of the Ghost Dance, this Indian Catholic hymn calls together the people within the sacred circle of their nation. During his career as a catechist, Lucy recalls, Black Elk was sent by the Jesuit fathers to "different tribes": "He instructed Arapahoes, Winnebagoes, Omahas, and others." As an emissary or evangelist, Black Elk thus continued the work of the prophet who had inspired him; like Wovoka, he became a central figure in the unification and differentiation of an Indian people. As in the Ghost Dance, suggestively described by his son as "a prayer that was danced," Black Elk combined Christian prayer and Lakota performance to fulfill Wovoka's prophecy of return through renewal.[87]

Thus we come full circle to the Ghost Dance prophet, who ended his life, as did the Lakota seer who followed in his footsteps, moving in and out of both Indian and white show spaces. According to Mooney, "when last heard from [in 1894] Wovoka was on exhibition as an attraction at the Mid-winter fair in San Francisco. By this time [1896] he has doubtless retired into his original obscurity" (927). But in fact, though Wovoka did appear briefly as a show Indian, such a performance, far from signaling or sealing the loss of his power, was but one of many forms through which the move-ment he had founded ramified in the consciousness of Indian peoples in the years thereafter. Throughout the first decade of the 1900s, Indians from the Assiniboine, Sioux, and Arapaho reservations continued to write to the prophet, addressing him with the honorific "father" and applying to him for canisters of the sacred red clay to be "used [as] the medicines." These supplicants continued, moreover, to see themselves as spreading the prophet's message, telling Wovoka in one letter that "when I got [the paint] I make a pray meeting with a good-men who have re[s]pect of you, and also we have a fest [feast or festival] over it," and announcing in another: "I am staying with the news you tell me all the time till now [and] I have been as far north to a place called Prince Albert and I am telling them about the news. . . . Help me that I want the people on earth to think and go into the road of life."[88] Additional evidence of the survival/revival of the Ghost Dance comes from Mooney, who wrote that "the dance still exists (in 1896) and is developing new features at every performance" (653); although he considered the Dance "extinct" among most tribes, he noted that "the Paiute were yet dancing a year ago" and that the Kiowas "have recently taken up the dance again" (927).

For that matter, Mooney's belief that the Ghost Dance had fizzled out among the majority of tribes was likely mistaken. In 1917, an agent from Nevada reported that Wovoka still "has considerable influence among distant tribes" and "seemingly keeps in close touch with them," with "delegations [having] paid him a visit." Even among the Lakotas, hardest hit by the Ghost Dance's suppression, there is evidence that "Pine Ridge and Rosebud tribes-men continued the Ghost Dance despite Wounded Knee, just as tribesmen from other reservations did. In the end, the Ghost Dance became a part of the enduring religious heritage of the Lakota." In 1933—the year after the prophet's long life came to an end and his teachings were reborn in *Black Elk Speaks*, and the year before Franklin Delano Roosevelt's commissioner of In-dian affairs, John Collier, lifted the long-standing ban on tribal and inter-tribal dances—Alexander Lesser termed the Ghost Dance a "cultural

stimulant" that had brought about a "renaissance of [Plains] culture," helping Indian peoples throughout the Plains to weather the policies of detribalization that had reigned for the half-century previous. In his analysis of the
demographics of the Ghost Dance, Russell Thornton argues that "it is . . .
possible to say that [the Dance] actually 'worked'—not, of course, by returning deceased American Indian populations to life, but by strengthening tribal
identity and distinctions between American Indian and European populations."[89] According to this reading, the Ghost Dance did in fact play a vital
role in bringing Indian ghosts back to life, ensuring that emergent forms of
sacred identity/performance would survive to this day.

In the last quarter of the twentieth century, the Ghost Dance reemerged
yet again as a symbol of intertribal consciousness and resistance: the American Indian Movement's (AIM) 1973 occupation of the Wounded Knee massacre site,[90] as well as the movement's rediscovery of *Black Elk Speaks* as (in
Vine Deloria's words) "a North American bible of all tribes" (*BES*, xiii),
evince the undying relevance of the Ghost Dance to the invention of modern
Indian identity.[91] Writing of contemporary Indian activism such as the
Wounded Knee protest, Chadwick Allen suggests the connection between
such acts and prophetic performance: "Activist events—demonstrations,
marches, and occupations—employ ideological interpretive frames . . . that
help assign meaning to movement participation and to specific protest activities. Designed to highlight ethnic differences between the majority settler
population and the particular indigenous minority people, these events also
tend to have an immediately discernable dramatic structure. They stage the
'facts' of persistent indigenous presences and a version of contemporary indigenous 'reality.' . . . As drama, these events routinely mobilize powerful
emblematic representations of Native identity, whether along tribal, pan-
tribal, or pan-indigenous lines, that respond to the expectations—and that
often are shaped by the expressed needs—of particular audiences." Though
protest events tend to be more immediate, limited, and pointed than
prophetic revitalization movements, all of these elements pertain to both: applying "interpretive frames," whether mystical, millennial, or militant, to "assign meaning" to the performance, "highlighting ethnic difference" between
Native participants and Euro-American onlookers, "staging the facts of persistent indigenous presence" and offering a "version of indigenous reality"
within a "discernable dramatic structure," and employing "emblematic representations of Native identity" drawn from a range of tribal, intertribal, and
extratribal sources, revitalization movements and activist events alike charge

Indian identity and tradition with a heightened political, typological, and semiotic significance that transforms the old to the new. In this regard, it is telling that modern Indian authors such as Vizenor have suggested that the "language of tribal poets and novelists could be the new ghost dance literature." Indeed, in the words of Ward Churchill, the "worldview" of the Ghost Dance "is integral at some important level to the outlook of any traditionalist Indian," for "it is this worldview which defines the continuing traditions of the indigenous peoples of this hemisphere in the contemporary setting."[92] As Elizabeth Rich sums up, in contemporary Indian political, literary, and community consciousness, "the language and rhetoric used during the Ghost Dance Movement persists."[93]

The same could be said of the Ghost Dance's secular partner, Buffalo Bill's Wild West. Though Cody's show slipped from his grasp in 1913 and the old showman himself died, weary and bankrupt, in 1917, the traditions of Indian performance that the show had helped to cultivate persist in forms as diverse as the intertribal powwow, the western rodeo, and the Mardi Gras Indian pageants.[94] The powwow, in particular, which Moses terms "both an evocation of culture and a means of creating an adaptive culture for those Indian nations long separated from their landed heritage," remains a forum not only for the exhibition of Indian dance and music but also for the assertion of Indian identity. As Mark Mattern writes, in the powwow, Indians "define a sense of 'who we are,' of what it means to be both a member of a particular tribe and an American Indian." In this respect, Powers comments, the powwow functions in the manner of Buffalo Bill's Wild West and the Ghost Dance as a means of producing an Indian difference from the dominant culture: "Music and dance still serve, as in the past, to maintain distance from the otherwise unavoidable white man's world. Singers still speak in song of things unmentionable in ordinary discourse, and dancers strut before their captive audience in a manner distinctly Indian. The white world is on the horizon, but in the dance arbor the singers shout courage to the dancers and onlookers." Mattern further notes that the powwow serves this differentiating function, as did the Ghost Dance and the Wild West, not merely by *announcing* Indianness but by consciously and continuously *articulating* it: "Indians do not simply reaffirm and reinforce their mutual identity and commitments through powwow practices; they negotiate them."[95] And as ever, one of the principal forces that contemporary Indian identity must negotiate remains the white world from which powwow performers seek to establish distance: as festivals that draw significant numbers of non-Indian persons, and as traditions forged in part through contact with non-Indian cultures, contemporary tribal and intertribal powwows forge a distinctive Indianness in and through an intercultural arena. Thus, like the Ghost Dance and the Wild West from which they sprang—or, more distantly, like the Algonquian medicine man from whom the contemporary powwow takes its title—modern-day Indian performance retains the visionary capacity of erecting living Indian traditions upon the ghosts of intercultural performances past.

In the closing years of their lives, both Wovoka and Cody put in time with a new form of Indian performance: the medium of the motion pictures. Cody, increasingly plagued by financial difficulties as the years wore on, concocted a scheme to shoot and star in a film, *The Indian Wars* (1914), a lavish production to feature key scenes in his personal history as well as in the history of the subduing of the West, including the scalping of Yellow Hair, the Ghost Dance movement, and the massacre at Wounded Knee. The film, however, performed poorly at the box office and has since disappeared save for a handful of stills.[96] Wovoka, meanwhile—who was portrayed by a double in *The Indian Wars* preaching a Christ-like sermon on a mountain peak—was invited by cowboy actor Tim McCoy to visit the set of the 1924 silent film *The Thundering Herd*; the prophet, Michael Hittman reports, availed himself of the opportunity to preach to the Arapaho Indians, "participants in Wovoka's religion," who acted in the film. The history of Indian performance in the motion pictures was (and is) no more praiseworthy than that of its stage and stadium counterparts: both Luther Standing Bear, who pursued a career in the movies but lamented that "white 'imitators'" got all the good parts (284), and whose vow to "make some real Indian pictures" (284) was left unfulfilled, and Black Elk, whose life story was slated for a cinematic treatment that never materialized (*SG*, 50), attest to the role of film, like all such performances, in rehearsing the Indians' dispossession. The first edition of *My People the Sioux*, in fact, was introduced by western actor William S. Hart, who offered a sneering, condescending portrait of Standing Bear as a "blanket Indian" who "may be a bit short on education" and whose "people [were] whipped by a stronger race—like dumb animals—for deeds beyond their understanding."[97] For Hart, Standing Bear's life was no better than a Wild West melodrama, a tale of stronger races and Indian traces.

Yet the participation of these shrewd prophets and performers in the early history of film suggests an alternative reading. With its uncanny ability to raise the spirits of the dead, to preserve them reenacting their old-time sports and occupations, and to disseminate these images to a countrywide audience, film might have seemed to Indian actors another iteration of the Ghost Dance, another medium of revitalization. In this respect, film hearkened back to Cody's earliest stage play, *The Scouts of the Prairie*, in which costumed extras performed both the Indians' death and their resurrection: "'The Scouts of the Plains' was an Indian drama, of course," Cody wrote, "and there were between forty and fifty 'supers' dressed as Indians. . . . [T]he way [we] killed Indians was 'a caution.' We would kill them all off in one act, but they would come up again ready for business in the next." Similarly, as Joy Kasson notes, the schema of Buffalo Bill's Wild West guaranteed both that Indian performers would be defeated and that they would endure: "In its fictionalized historical representation, Americans could savor the thrill of danger without risking its consequences, could believe that struggle and conflict inflicted no lasting wounds, and could see for themselves that the enemy 'other' would rise from the dust, wave to the crowd, and sell souvenir photographs at the end of the day."[98] From the point of view of white Americans, these simulated deaths may indeed have done no more than assuage guilty consciences and countenance further atrocities. But from the perspective of those other Americans who participated in such spectacles as both actors and witnesses, this cycle of death and rebirth may have held a different meaning. These ghosts, these players, rise from the ground.

# Conclusion

*A man who is full of tricks can do many things!*
—*Conclusion to a Mandan Coyote story, in Martha Warren Beckwith,*
Mandan-Hidatsa Myths and Ceremonies *(1937)*

In his final book, *The World We Used to Live In: Remembering the Powers of the Medicine Men* (2006), published after his death in 2005, the Sioux activist-critic Vine Deloria Jr. returned to the struggle over Indian medicine that had shaped American life and literature from the beginning. "Nothing seems to stem the tide of abuse and misuse of Indian ceremonies," Deloria wrote. "The consumer society is indeed consuming everything in its path." Deloria's last act caps a chorus of Native American protest against the burgeoning array of Euro-American peddlers, preachers, and poets capitalizing on an ever more lucrative commerce in Indian healing. Wendy Rose (Hopi/Miwok) depicts Indian spirit selling as an attempt "to occupy and consume other cultures just as surely as their land and resources have been occupied and consumed." Leslie Marmon Silko (Laguna Pueblo) argues that such avaricious medicine play is fundamentally racist, fed by the arrogant persuasion that "the white man, through some innate cultural or racial superiority, has the ability to perceive and master the essential beliefs, values and emotions of persons from Native American communities." Yet even such gall, these writers charge, carries its own vindication: those who co-opt the Indian spirit convince themselves that they are, Catlin fashion, sympathizing with those they displace, preserving that which would otherwise be lost. And so, Ward Churchill concludes, "the charade by which [whites] cloak themselves in the identity of their victims is their best and ultimately most compulsive hedge against the psychic consequences of acknowledging who and what they really are. . . . This pattern of emotional/psychological avoidance embedded in the ritual role-playing of Indians . . . represents no alternative to the status quo. To the contrary, it has become a steadily more crucial ingredient in an emergent complex of psychosocial mechanisms allowing North American business-as-usual to sustain, stabilize, and reenergize itself."[1] The commodi-fication and consumption of Indian medicine, these critics insist, is—has al-ways been—a matter of power.

That power touches all who traffic, for good or ill, in medicine ways. Ed-ward Hale, the Mandan medicine man whom I met years ago, turned up shortly after in an article accusing him of "practicing spiritual fraud." Ac-cording to some, the article explained, Hale is not a real medicine man but a city slicker who "returned to the [Mandan] reservation sometime during the early 80s and demanded a certain tribal bundle" with which to carry on his business.[2] His subsequent employment as spiritual intercessor on behalf of incarcerated Native Americans, the article continued, was seen by his critics as the hustle of a flimflam artist who had assumed the mantle of Indian med-icine to hoodwink unsuspecting customers and to bilk the taxpayers of Penn-sylvania. In this light, Hale's offer to me—"I'll set you up"—appears the pitch of the perfect con man, eager to pick whatever pocket his medicine can lay bare.

Whatever the truth of such accusations, they follow an old pattern of treating Indian medicine men as charlatans while lavishing praise and reward on Euro-American marketers of Indian mysteries. Thus Hale—who reaped precisely $1,920 for a year's work with a despised and desperately under-served population—is lambasted for failing to adhere to a traditional stan-dard of asceticism, while Euro-American mystics who cater to white CEOs are celebrated on the covers of *Time* and *Newsweek* and toasted by Bill Moy-ers on PBS. William Apess, Neolin, Elias Boudinot, John Ross, Catharine Brown, Tenskwatawa, Wovoka, Luther Standing Bear, Black Elk: all have been accused, by critics in their own day or ours, of being un-Indian, unworthy of the medicine they claim, nontraditional, false. Recently, when Churchill made injudicious comments about the September 11 terrorist attacks, critics set out to prove that he too was a fraud, that his medicine was bad.[3] Such is the power of Indian medicine, which signifies the struggle for spiritual and material authority in our tangled cultural history.

"The medicine man is everybody's resource," states Al Logan Slagle (Cherokee). "There is no one else likely to help us survive as a people." Delo-ria agrees; his book ends: "We would do well to return to those roots."[4] The question, of course, is not only how we will survive as a people but as what people we will survive. Medicine is a resource and a roots, to be sure. But it is too late by far to imagine a return that will not involve the other. The lesson of the medicine show and the medicine bundle is plain: we cannot go back to the world we used to live in but must re-member the medicine man as a central figure (perhaps *the* central figure) in a world of emergent, intercultural performance.

On a recent trip to New Mexico to visit college friends, I was reminded of this. The church we entered (more to escape the blazing sun than anything else) was ancient—built, I believe, shortly after the Pueblo prophetic revolt of 1680 put a temporary halt to the Spanish conquest. A scaffold had been erected in the interior, and a man was painting kachinas upon the smooth mud-daub walls. The figures paraded along at a height of ten or fifteen feet, their journey ending at the altar where the tabernacle and crucifix were. The artist was a local man, Ken Seowtewa, a Zuni Christian who explained that there was nothing remarkable about Zuni deities lining the walls of a church built by Spanish missionaries. The Zuni religion, he told us, had always been consistent with Christianity, only the Zunis had not realized this until the Spanish came. His work was incomplete, some of the figures rendered in full color, others half-finished, others mere outlines. He had been at it, he told us, for the better part of twenty years, interrupted time and again by lack of funds, speculation that the church might come down, health reasons. He would be grateful for any contribution we could make.

The thought crossed my mind—how could it not?—that this might be some sort of scam, that this grand, Sisyphean project might have been contrived to gain—what? Cash? A chuckle at the whiteman? Spiritual victory over the sons of the conquerors? But the paintings possessed a beauty that made such thoughts seem boorish. They were beautiful like Catlin's paintings, like mystery, like medicine. They spoke of a history both inconceivable and inescapable. They represented at once the tragedy and the possibility of that centuries-old bundle of performance.

We stayed in the church a long time, listening to Seowtewa's narration, admiring his paintings, enjoying the cool. When we left, we gave him a twenty. In return, he gave us his blessing, and his business card.

# Notes

## Introduction

1. P. Allen, "Sacred Hoop," 19.

2. Jennings, *Invasion of America*, 52–53; John Eliot, in Shepard, *Clear Sun-shine*, 115. Colonial attacks on Indian medicine men are discussed by Cave, "Indian Shamans"; and Nash, "'Antic Deportments.'" For a study of seventeenth-century shamanism, see Simmons, "Southern New England Shamanism."

3. Niezen et al., *Spirit Wars*, 5; Calhoun, "Creation of a Bureau of Indian Affairs in the War Department" (1824), in Prucha, *Documents of Indian Policy*, 38; Monroe, "Message of President Monroe on Indian Removal" (1825), in Prucha, *Documents of Indian Policy*, 40.

4. Irwin, "Freedom, Law, and Prophecy," 301; Teller, "Courts of Indian Offenses" (1883), in Prucha, *Documents of Indian Policy*, 160, 161; T. Morgan, "Rules for Indian Courts" (1892), in Prucha, *Documents of Indian Policy*, 187. On the contemporaneous assault on Indian shamanism by the Euro-American medical establishment, see Niezen et al., *Spirit Wars*, 92–137; and Trennert, *White Man's Medicine*.

5. Collier, quoted in Mann, "Earth Mother," 196. On ongoing threats to Indian religious freedom, see Vecsey, "Prologue," 7–25.

6. On Revolutionary-era white Indian play, see P. Deloria, *Playing Indian*, 10–70; Kamrath, "American Indian Oration"; and Marienstras, "Common Man's Indian."

7. T. Morton, *New English Canaan*, 276–77. On the colonial phenomenon of the "white Indian," see Axtell, "White Indians"; and Ingersoll, *To Intermix with Our White Brothers*, 53–67.

8. For recent studies of the conversion accounts of Eliot's converts, see Bross, *Dry Bones and Indian Sermons*, esp. 52–83; and Wyss, *Writing Indians*, esp. 17–51.

9. Krupat, *For Those Who Come After*, 40.

10. Ortiz, "National Indian Literature," 65.

11. On the significance of context in the analysis of oral performance, see Dundes, "Texture, Text, and Context"; on the emergent quality of performance, see Bauman, *Verbal Art*, 37–45; and Hymes, "Breakthrough into Performance."

12. Vecsey, "Prologue," 15; Kohl, *Kitchi-Gami*, 254; Schechner, *Between Theater and Anthropology*, 15. For a consideration of translation, context, and displacement in Euro-American accounts of Indian performance, see Cheyfitz, *Poetics of Imperialism*.

13. Worthen, "Disciplines of the Text," 23; Schechner, *Between Theater and Anthropology*, 39.

14. Blau, "Universals of Performance," 258; Roach, *Cities of the Dead*, 6, 30.

15. Of the works I have named, neither Fliegelman's *Declaring Independence* nor Waldstreicher's *Perpetual Fetes* is centrally concerned with the encounter of Native and Euro-American peoples. Yet by revealing that print media, far from serving as simple replacements of original, oral performances, "surrounded these events and gave them extralocal meaning" (Waldstreicher, 11), these studies propose models of oral/written interaction that have helped me to develop my thinking on these issues.

16. Gustafson, *Eloquence Is Power*, xvi, xviii, xvi; Round, "Indigenous Illustration," n. pag. Scholars of Mesoamerican societies have been particularly active in exploring alternative literacies and the oral-literate interface; see, for example, Boone and Mignolo, eds., *Writing without Words*; Burkhart, "Nahuatl Song of Santiago"; and Mary Louise Pratt's well-known analysis of Guamán Poma de Ayala's *New Chronicle and Good Government* (1613), "Arts of the Contact Zone."

17. Gustafson, *Eloquence Is Power*, 12.

18. White, *Middle Ground*, ix; Michaelsen, *Limits of Multiculturalism*, 38–39, xvii; Clifford, *Predicament of Culture*, 23; Bank, "Staging the 'Native,'" 463. On the dangers of equating the middle ground with the leveling of hierarchies, see also Cohen, "A Mutually Comprehensible World?"; and Herman, "Romance on the Middle Ground." White and other ethnohistorians have also been criticized for ignoring Native American oral history in their reconstructions of the middle ground; see, for example, Bohaker, "*Nindoodemag*"; and S. Miller, "Licensed Trafficking." White's response to this critique appears in "Creative Misunderstandings," 13.

19. White, *Middle Ground*, xv; White, "Creative Misunderstandings," 10.

20. White, *Middle Ground*, 523; Abrahams, "White Indians," 180, 181, 180.

21. Diamond, "Introduction," 2.

22. Peacock, "Ethnographic Notes," 208.

23. D. Walker, "Indian Sacred Geography," 103; Vecsey, "Prologue," 15.

24. V. Deloria, *We Talk, You Listen*, 57; Guerrero, "Academic Apartheid," 56; Womack, *Red on Red*, 5, 49, 67. Additional calls for an indigenous literary criticism include Robert Allen Warrior (Osage), *Tribal Secrets*; and Jace Weaver (Cherokee), *That the People Might Live*. On the role and responsibilities of non-Indian scholars who study Indian languages and literatures, see also Littlefield, "American Indians."

25. Sarris, *Keeping Slug Woman Alive*, 29.

26. Speaking of the damage anthropological study has done to Indian communities, V. Deloria advises, "Each anthro desiring to study a tribe should be made to apply to the tribal council for permission to do his study. He would be given such permission only if he raised as a contribution to the tribal budget an amount of money equal to the amount he proposed to spend in his study. Anthropologists would thus become productive members of Indian society instead of ideological vultures" (*Custer Died*, 95). Attempting to fulfill what I see as a just demand, I have committed to the following: though I cannot apply for permission from the long-dead Indian peoples who play a role in this study, I intend to dedicate whatever revenue this book generates to the living descendants of those peoples.

*Chapter 1*

1. Catlin, *Letters and Notes*, 1:155. All further references to *Letters and Notes* will be cited parenthetically in the text.

2. Catlin did, in fact, enter into a brief, mutually distrustful partnership with Barnum, whose early ventures included the exhibiting of Indians; see Dippie, *Catlin and His Contemporaries*, 102–5. For Catlin biography, see also Haberly, *Pursuit of the Horizon*. The mercurial Catlin's life, yawing precipitately from the ludic to the tragic, has proved fascinating to many; those who have sparked or sustained my interest include Goetzmann and Goetzmann, *West of the Imagination*, 15–35; Mulvey, "Catlin in Europe"; Reddin, *Wild West Shows*, 1–52; and Truettner, *Natural Man*. For beautiful full-color reproductions of Catlin's artwork, see Gurney and Heyman, eds., *George Catlin*.

3. The modern reader recognizes in this scene the homoeroticism that Catlin either could not or would not name. Catlin does address this aspect of the ceremony in his later account, *O-Kee-Pa: A Religious Ceremony and Other Customs of the Mandans* (1867), where his scientific stance helps distance him from the events he reports: "mounting on to one of the dancing buffaloes, [the evil spirit] elevated his wand, and consequently the [artificial] penis, which was inserted under the skin of the animal, whilst the man underneath continued to dance, with his body in a horizontal position" (84). Even here, however, Catlin's reticence shows through; this description is printed not in the text proper but on a "detached page, which is proposed to be used at the discretion of the purchaser" (83). For an invaluable study of the okipa, see Bowers, *Mandan Social and Ceremonial Organization*, 111–63, 347–65.

4. P. Deloria, *Playing Indian*, 4, 5. On the performance of race and ethnicity during the antebellum period, see also Browder, *Slippery Characters*, esp. 13–74; and, on the runaway theatricality of antebellum culture, with its twin icons, the self-made man and the confidence man, see Halttunen, *Confidence Men*.

5. See, for example, Joel Martin: "The actual living Indian had been exiled; the fictive dead Indian was romanticized. The former was the precondition for the latter, if not the cause" ("'My Grandmother,'" 138); also Green: "for anyone to play Indian successfully, real Indians have to be dead" ("'Tribe Called Wannabee,'" 49). Sundquist provides a comparable context for Catlin: "His Indian Gallery . . . effectively marked the absorption or elimination of much Indian life from the eastern United States" ("Indian Gallery," 45). For a broader study of Indian Removal and American literature, see Maddox, *Removals*.

6. Catlin, *Adventures*, 1:291. A convenient collection of American and European "vanishing-Indian" statements, most of which accept Catlin's theory of Mandan extinction, can be found in the reviews of his Gallery reprinted in this narrative of his European travels (1:53–59, 205–40).

7. For a twentieth-century reconstruction of the 1837 smallpox epidemic, including evidence of the Mandans' cultural survival, see Jensen, "Mandan Tragedy." Catlin's father, more frank than the artist could afford to be, wrote in 1838 of his son's response to the tribe's fate: "He mourns the dreadful destiny of the indian tribes by the small pox, which report is verified, but unquestionably that shocking calamity will greatly increase the value of his enterprize & his works" (Putnam to Francis Catlin, 18 March

1838, in Roehm, *Letters*, 127). On Catlin's misrepresentation of the Mandans as a doomed people, see also Hight, "'Doomed to Perish.'"

8. Mazel, "'Beautiful and Thrilling Specimen,'" 140.

9. Roach, *Cities of the Dead*, 4, 5, 6–7.

10. Ibid., 3, 78.

11. Mather, quoted in Starr, *Social Transformation*, 48. On early contacts between Indian and Euro-American medicine, see Calloway, *New Worlds for All*, 24–33; and Vogel, *American Indian Medicine*, 36–110. Robinson offers one theory as to why whites could embrace Indian medicine while maligning Indian medical practice: "Although the English expected to find remedies among the Indians, they did not expect to find medical systems. When such systems were apparent, as when Indians incorporated ritual and prayer in their healing practices, colonists were inclined to regard these practices as superstitious at best, demonic at worst" ("New Worlds," 97).

12. Barton, *Materia Medica*, xv; Rush, "Medicine among the Indians," 257, 276.

13. *Health Journal and Advocate of Physiological Reform* (1840), quoted in Albanese, *Nature Religion*, 125; Vogel, *American Indian Medicine*, 131; Wright, *Hawkers and Walkers*, 120; Benes, "Itinerant Physicians," 101. My list of "Indian" healing manuals comes from Pickard and Buley, *Midwest Pioneer*, 72–73.

14. Tufts, *Narrative*, 96, 97. On the selling of "Indian" medicine in the nineteenth century, see also Lears, *Fables of Abundance*, 142–48; and Steele, "Reduced to Images."

15. Irving, "Traits of Indian Character," 226; J. Hall, "Mr. Catlin's Exhibition," 536, 537. On the Removal-era belief that civilized Indians were, in effect, diseased Indians, see Dippie, *Vanishing American*, 25.

16. Catlin, *Breath of Life*, 3, 17, 23, 6, 76, 75.

17. Thoreau, *Walden*, 77, 78–79, 317.

18. Thoreau, *Maine Woods*, 156.

19. Ibid., 182. For a fuller analysis of Thoreau's assumption of Indian medicine, see my "Taking the Indian Cure."

20. Spence, *Dispossessing the Wilderness*, 11.

21. Drinnon, *Facing West*, 195; Jones, quoted in D. Smith, *Sacred Feathers*, 202; P. Deloria, *Playing Indian*, 187; Dippie, *Catlin and His Contemporaries*, 117. For a nuanced study of Catlin's national park scheme, see Weber, "Catlin and a Nation's Park." On the removal of Indians as a prerequisite to the formation of America's national parks, see J. Sears, *Sacred Places*, 149–55.

22. Cawelti, "Frontier and the Native American," 152. The Hudson River school and its connection to American national identity are discussed by Barringer, "Course of Empires"; and A. Miller, *Empire of the Eye*.

23. Cass, "Indian Treaties," 391.

24. Berkhofer, who uses the Wi-jun-jon painting as the cover of his classic *The White Man's Indian*, discusses how this image reflects Catlin's belief that "civilization destroyed the noble Indian" (89). For an extended reading of the Wi-jun-jon episode as expressive of Catlin's wavering, and ultimately ineffectual, sympathy for the Indians, see Mielke, *Moving Encounters*.

25. Boime, *Magisterial Gaze*; John, "Cultural Nationalism," 178, 191. On landscape as

an engine of imperialism, see also W. Mitchell, "Imperial Landscape"; and Truettner, "Ideology and Image."

26. L. Morgan, *League of the Iroquois*, 444.

27. P. Deloria, *Playing Indian*, 73, 77, 78.

28. Schoolcraft, *Address*, 29; Fenton, introduction to *League of the Iroquois*, ix; L. Morgan, *League of the Iroquois*, 125, 225. On Morgan's relationship with fictionalized and real Indians, see also Bieder, *Science Encounters the Indian*, 199–205; and Michaelsen, *Limits of Multiculturalism*, 85–106. I am indebted to Roger Abrahams for pointing out to me the complexity of the relationship between Morgan and Ely S. Parker.

29. Catlin, *O-Kee-Pa*, 37; Catlin, *Adventures*, 1:34; *London Atlas*, quoted in Catlin, *Adventures*, 1:56. On Catlin as a founding father of ethnology, see Mielke, *Moving Encounters*; and, for an intriguing study of Catlin's Gallery as an example of the "encyclopedic" mode of antebellum display, one "driven by the encyclopedia's emphasis on classification and *objectification*," see Masters, "Book of Nature," 65.

30. Stocking,"Introduction," 5. The Indian museum's roots in eighteenth-century British imperialism are discussed by Bickham, "Indians and Empire." For a discussion of the American imperialist context, see Hendry, *Reclaiming Culture*, 4–8.

31. Catlin, *Adventures*, 2:301, 1:296.

32. King, *Colonial Discourses*, 5; Ewers, "Clark's Indian Museum," 53; Maximilian, Prince of Wied-Neuwied, quoted in Ewers, "Clark's Indian Museum," 62. Thomas L. McKenney, head of the Office of Indian Affairs in the decade before Catlin's travels, and coauthor, with James Hall, of a collection of Indian biographies illustrated by Charles Bird King, maintained a similar museum/council chamber/portrait gallery in Washington; see Viola, "Washington's First Museum." Approving of Catlin's decision not to provide the illustrations for McKenney and Hall's magnum opus, Richard Drinnon suggests that this "great painter of the North and South American Indian disdainfully refused to be hanged in the necrological McKenney-Hall gallery" (*Facing West*, 195). As should be clear by now, however, it is reductive to suppose that Catlin's Gallery was any friendlier to living Indians than was McKenney and Hall's.

33. Clifford, *Predicament of Culture*, 220, 250; Clifford, "On Ethnographic Allegory," 112, 113.

34. On Catlin's representation of Osceola and the Seminoles as museum artifacts, see Johnson, "'Rising from the Stain.'"

35. Cass, quoted in Catlin, *Adventures*, 1:252; Catlin, *Adventures* 1:62. Remnants of the medicine show lingered in the 2002 exhibition of Catlin's works hosted by the Renwick Gallery of the Smithsonian American Art Museum. A number of devices tended to transform Indians into static, pristine, natural beings: for instance, in a room that promised a view of the plains as Catlin experienced them, there were nature sights and sounds on a series of wraparound screens—but no people. In addition, though the exhibit occasionally placed Indians within a historical context, as when a placard noted that "the Mandan had been in direct recorded contact with Europeans since the 1730s," the tour guide I followed undercut this information, stating that the Mandans were the tribe "least touched by European influence." Nor did the exhibit question the prominently displayed quotation from Catlin that termed the In-

dians of the West "true, noble, unspoiled." Interesting, too, was the tendency to present Catlin's works as definitive of Indian realities; the same tour guide repeatedly told her group that "you can see" various historical facts about the Indians based on Catlin's paintings—that the paintings were "realistic" and "captured . . . all the details." Based on my visit, I would not go so far as Hilden does in her critique of the National Museum of the American Indian, which she terms "a vast mausoleum" where Native peoples become "'our' Indians, America's quaint and exotic past," and where "non-Native visitors come . . . to spend a few hours playing 'Indian'" ("Race for Sale," 24). I would, however, endorse Luke's general point about museum art displays: "Art exhibitions in the last analysis are elaborate and expensive works of educational theater with their own special rhetorical agendas and peculiar political teachings. And, for this reason alone, they merit thorough investigation" (*Shows of Force*, 1). On the practice of ethnographic allegory in the modern museum, see also Brumble, "Indian Sacred Materials"; and, for a modern anthropologist's attempt to mediate the competing demands of Native and non-Native populations concerning museum collections, see M. Brown, *Who Owns Native Culture?*

36. Studies of the antebellum Indian drama are numerous. See, for example, M. Anderson, "Image of the Indian"; E. Jones, *Native Americans*; and P. Sears, *Pillar of Fire*. For a checklist of plays, see Wilmeth, "Noble or Ruthless Savage?"

37. Paulding, "American Drama," 339, 342, 356.

38. Neal, "Late American Books," 190, 198–99, 199–200.

39. Ibid., 200; Catlin, *Adventures*, 1:72, 71, 88, 78.

40. Alger, *Edwin Forrest*, 1:17, 39, 127, 138, 139, 239, 240. I first learned of the Forrest/Push-ma-ta-ha story through Moody's biography, *Edwin Forrest*, 40–48 (which rephrases and condenses Alger's report). More critical assessments of Forrest's (and *Metamora*'s) relationship to the Indian peoples and policies of the time can be found in Gaul, "'Genuine Indian'"; and Grose, "Edwin Forrest."

41. Catlin, *Adventures*, 1:107; Stone, *Metamora*, 12.

42. Bernard Hewitt, *Theatre U.S.A.*, 1; Meserve, *Emerging Entertainment*, 5; Drummond and Moody, "Indian Treaties," 15; Mason, "Politics of *Metamora*," 93; Scheckel, *Insistence of the Indian*, 125; L. Morgan, *League of the Iroquois*, 4; Bank, *Theatre Culture*, 64. For a critique of the tendency to explain the plays' emergence in terms of Indian disappearance, see Flynn, "Academics on the Trail"; for Bank's own rereading of the Indian drama in light of the Indian presence, see "Staging the 'Native.'" An alternative reading of the plays as repositories of revolutionary utterance appears in Sayre, *Indian Chief*, 99–125.

43. James Mackay, quoted in Meyer, *Village Indians*, 29. For the Mandans' history of European contact, see Wood and Thiessen, eds., *Early Fur Trade*, 18–69. Charles McKenzie, who visited the Mandans in the early nineteenth century, paints a picture of them vastly different from Catlin's renderings: "their dress . . . in many instances consisted of Articles foreign to these distant Tribes—viz. Russia Sheeting trowsers, swans down Vests, Corduroy Jackets, Calico shirts, &c. all resembling Canadian Voyageurs clothing" ("Some account," 242). This is not to ignore that McKenzie, a trader, was as motivated by pecuniary considerations as was Catlin to present a decidedly selective (if not wholly spurious) portrait of the tribe.

44. Catlin, *O-Kee-Pa*, 42.

45. Ibid., 37, 40. Catlin subscribes to the batty theory, popular during his time, that the Mandans "have sprung from some other origin than that of the other North American tribes, or that they are an amalgam of natives with some civilized race" (1:93), a race he goes on to name as the Welsh (2:259–61). Though this would seem to render his prize less purely American, at the same time, the theory of Welsh origins enhances the Mandans' marketability as nonpareils or nondescripts. For a study of the rise, peak, and decline of the Welsh-origins theory, see Williams, *Madoc*.

46. Cass, "Indians of North America," 54. The attack on medicine men in nineteenth-century periodical literature is covered by Wilson, "Shamans and Charlatans."

47. *Philadelphia Saturday News*, quoted in Catlin, *Adventures*, 1:230; *American Sentinel*, quoted in Catlin, *Adventures*, 1:228.

48. Cass, "Indians of North America," 54–55.

49. Masters, "Book of Nature," 85.

50. *Edinburgh Review*, quoted in Catlin, *Adventures*, 1:52.

51. Dunlap, "Mr. Catlin's Lectures," 126.

52. Late nineteenth-century ethnographer Garrick Mallery dismisses Catlin's story of the Dog as a fabrication based on the fact that "the people referred to, before and after and at the time of the visit of Catlin to them, were in the habit of drawing the human face in profile, and, indeed, much more frequently than the full or front face" (*Picture-Writing*, 741).

53. M. Pratt, *Imperial Eyes*, 7. On Catlin as imperialist geographer, see also John, "Benevolent Imperialism." John, somewhat surprisingly, overlooks the pipestone quarry in his analysis of the "imperialist and expansionist teleology" of Catlin's works (610), focusing instead on the artist's depiction of the Mandans.

54. Drinnon, *Facing West*, 168 (caption); Laubin and Laubin, *Indian Dances*, 41; "Iowa Indians," 91.

55. Kirshenblatt-Gimblett, "Objects of Ethnography," 420.

56. Dickens, "Noble Savage," 337; "Ojibbeway Indians," 401; Catlin, *Adventures*, 1:145, 147. For the "jolly fat dame's" appearances, see Catlin, *Adventures*, 1:156, 162. On blackface imitation, see Abrahams, *Singing the Master*, esp. 131–53; and Lott, *Love and Theft*. Given Catlin's transatlantic appeal, Meer's *Uncle Tom Mania*, which explores the minstrel tradition in America and England, is especially pertinent here.

57. Catlin, *Adventures*, 2:227.

58. Ibid., 1:116; Powers, *War Dance*, 18; the Doctor and Jim, quoted in Haberly, *Pursuit of the Horizon*, 166. For a further examination of the experiences and writings of Catlin's dancers, see my "Savage Tour."

59. I am tempted to propose, indeed, that Catlin's Indian dancers may have intentionally sabotaged his performances, in the manner of the Navajo dancers who, refusing to allow photographer Edward S. Curtis to film a sacred dance, may have "secularized it by dancing it backwards" (Lyman, *Vanishing Race*, 69). Curtis, intriguingly, followed Catlin in achieving artistic rebirth via Indian play: "For the time being Curtis became an 'Indian,'" a contemporary article reported. "He lived 'Indian,' he talked it, he was 'heap

white brother.' The best years of his life were spent, like the renegades of old, among the Indians" (*Seattle Times*, 1903, quoted in Lyman, *Vanishing Race*, 53).

60. For what it may be worth, I offer the observation that there seems to be a particularly strong temptation among those who study Indian dance to throw themselves into that which they study. Thus early anthropologist Alice C. Fletcher, in *Indian Games and Dances* (1915), expresses a hope that her collection will spur "our young people" to "enjoy and share in the spirit of the olden life upon this continent" (xxii); toward that end, she concocts a ceremony by which white children, in the manner of Morgan's "Inindianation" converts, may assume Indian identities (132–39). And then there are the Laubins, adopted by the family of Sitting Bull because, they announce in *Indian Dances of North America* (1977), the Indians considered them "more Indian than our own Indian children" (xi). It is not surprising that the Laubins's frankly embarrassing book—more a celebration of their own medicine play than a consideration of Indian dance, as indicated by the fact that most of the book's photographs are of themselves cavorting in Indian costume—contains a paean to their progenitor, Catlin (41–43).

61. Dippie, *Catlin and His Contemporaries*, 327, 328; Dunlap, "Mr. Catlin's Lectures," 126; Hall, "Mr. Catlin's Exhibition," 536–37; Catlin, *O-Kee-Pa*, 90.

62. Interestingly, in one version of the okipa origin myth, the ceremony emerges as a drama taught by the gods: "They showed these people how to give the ceremony, paint, and dress" (Bowers, *Mandan Social and Ceremonial Organization*, 158). Even more suggestively, ritual preparation focuses on the medium of *painting*: "They thought, 'How will we paint to make them good-looking? We might use some of the color of the snakes; they look nice.' . . . When he was painted, he was very beautiful" (159). If Catlin was aware of such origin stories, however, he did not mention them.

63. Irwin, *Dream Seekers*, 228.

64. Bowers, *Mandan Social and Ceremonial Organization*, 75, 106; Beckwith, *Mandan-Hidatsa Myths*, xv; Densmore, *Mandan and Hidatsa Music*, 13; Bowers, *Mandan Social and Ceremonial Organization*, 107.

65. Schmitz, *White Robe's Dilemma*, 68.

66. Bowers, *Mandan Social and Ceremonial Organization*, 144. One might also consider Catlin in relation to a Mandan Coyote (Trickster) myth, "Coyote and Sun," in which the titular antihero, who "had a habit of wandering from place to place," admires "how Sun was dressed and thought that he could imitate him. During the night by means of his power he got all the things together that Sun wore," but ultimately he is unmasked and punished for his presumption (Beckwith, *Mandan-Hidatsa Myths*, 269). Again, this tale underscores the importance the Mandans placed on the legitimate inheritance and use of medicine power.

67. Lévi-Strauss, *Savage Mind*, 55.

68. Halpin, introduction to *Letters and Notes*, 1:xiv. Part of the problem with such assessments lies in their untenable privileging of the visual over the verbal, expressed overtly by L. Mitchell: "Catlin for the most part succeeded in painting what he saw, rather than what he said he saw" (*Witnesses to a Vanishing America*, 104–5). In similar fashion, Lubbers confesses his disappointment that "a man of so keen and unerring an eye [as Catlin] fell prey to the grossest cliches when he exchanged paint brush for

pen" (*Born for the Shade*, 158). This belief in the primacy of visual representation—a belief that Catlin himself promotes when he writes that viewers "will learn vastly more from lines and colours than they could from oral or written delineations" (1:192)—has been rebuked by numerous critics who cite the role of plastic conventions and political agendas in pictorial representations of Indians. See, for example, Ewers, "Fact and Fiction"; Gerdts, "Marble Savage"; and Schimmel, "Inventing the 'Indian.'"

69. I take the phrase "masking Indian realities" from Fairchild's essay, "George Sand and George Catlin." Other critics who fault Catlin's accuracy include Davis and Thacker, "Pictures and Prose"; and Wasserman, "Artist-Explorers."

70. Crapanzano, "Hermes' Dilemma," 53, 76, 51.

71. Ewers, "White Man's Strongest Medicine," 40.

72. Ibid.

73. Haberly, *Pursuit of the Horizon*, 2; Catlin, *Adventures*, 2:194, 56 n.

74. Bowers, *Mandan Social and Ceremonial Organization*, 75; C. Allen, *Blood Narrative*, 171, 170.

75. Beckwith, *Mandan-Hidatsa Myths and Ceremonies*, 309, 314, 319. Catlin, not surprisingly, fashioned himself something of an authority on Indian pictographs. Illustrating his mastery of the Indians' representational mode, he provides a pictograph-by-pictograph reading of the images on the shirt of the Mandan chief Mah-to-toh-pa or Four Bears (1:148–54). The same shirt—or, according to Holm, the artist's clever forgery of it—traveled in Catlin's exhibition ("Four Bears's Shirt"). Whether pictographs shaped Catlin's developing art is a question too large for an endnote; it is worth noting, at least, that the artist missed no opportunity to work them into his portraits, featuring them as adornment on many an Indian outfit. On Catlin's response to Indian pictography, see also Kolodny, "Fictions of American Prehistory," 697.

*Chapter 2*

1. Moulton, *John Ross*, 87; John Ross to John Howard Payne, 27 January 1838, *Papers of Chief John Ross*, 1:587 [cited hereafter as *Papers*]. For the letter cited in my epigraph, see Ross to Elizabeth Milligan, 10 April 1838, *Papers*, 1:626.

2. On the supposed Cherokee performance and Ross's denial, see Amacher, "Behind the Curtain," 106.

3. Ross to George Lowrey, after 20 October 1837, *Papers*, 1:529.

4. Hall, "Mr. Catlin's Exhibition," 537.

5. Catlin, *Letters and Notes*, 2:119, 120, 121. Cherokee "arts" would prove far more helpful to Catlin than his to them. In 1838, a Cherokee delegation had approached the rebellious Seminoles to treat for peace; as Ross reconstructed the event, the chiefs "accompanyed the Cherokee mediators under the white flag of peace into the lines of the American Army—but alas! they have all been seized and confined as prisoners of

war" and taken to Fort Moultrie, where Catlin scored one of the greatest triumphs of his artistic career: the painting of Osceola (Ross to Payne, *Papers*, 1:588).

6. Lewis Ross to John Ross, 18 February 1837, *Papers*, 1:469; Ross to Martin Van Buren, 16 March 1837, *Papers*, 1:483; Ross to John Mason, Jr., 11 August 1837, *Papers*, 1:515; Ross to a gentleman of Philadelphia, 6 May 1837, *Papers*, 1:497.

7. Krupat, *Voice in the Margin*, 152; Gilmore, "Indian in the Museum," 27; Owens, "As If an Indian," 17.

8. See Clifton, ed., *Being and Becoming Indian*. Clifton most directly accuses Indians of deceptive play in *Invented Indian*. For an unbiased analysis of purposeful deception among colonized peoples, see Scott, *Domination and the Arts of Resistance*.

9. Clifford, *Predicament of Culture*, 11, 12. On the concept of invented ethnicity, see also Nagel, "Constructing Ethnicity." On the related concept of the "invention of tradition," see Mauzé, "On Concepts of Tradition."

10. P. Deloria, *Playing Indian*, 189; Clifford, *Predicament of Culture*, 338; Garroutte, *Real Indians*, 81; Clifford, *Predicament of Culture*, 10; Garroutte, *Real Indians*, 7. For a further discussion of identity issues among present-day Indian peoples, see H. Weaver, "Indigenous Identity."

11. Writing of indigenous suspicion of the concept of invented tradition, Linnekin notes that "what many anthropologists view as an advance in cultural theory can be read popularly as 'destructive' of native claims to cultural distinctiveness" ("Cultural Invention," 447). Given the history of the medicine show (and of anthropology's part in it), I do not think that this popular reading is far off the mark.

12. Roach, *Cities of the Dead*, 28; Garroutte, *Real Indians*, 10, 103–4, 10; Butler, *Gender Trouble*, 147; Garroutte, *Real Indians*, 120, 137.

13. What little work exists on Brown is of a principally biographical (or hagiographical) nature. For an early reading of Brown as Christian "saint," see R. Walker, *Torchlights to the Cherokees*, 175–85; for a later analysis of her within a classificatory scheme of Indian converts, see Freeman, "Indian Convert." Modern biographies include Perdue, "Catharine Brown"; and Higginbotham, "Creek Path." Brief notice appears in Bataille, *Native American Women*, 44–45; Johnston, *Cherokee Women in Crisis*, 42–43; and Perdue, *Cherokee Women*, 169–70. For background on the American Board, see McLoughlin, *Cherokees and Missionaries*, 102–23.

14. Justice, *Our Fire Survives*, 6.

15. For example, whereas Krupat had originally argued that Apess's writings lacked an "indigenous, Pequot sense" (*Voice in the Margin*, 145), he later suggested that Apess reveals the "synecdochic self-definition" "typical" of Native expression (*Ethnocriticism*, 229). Though Krupat adds that "all autobiographies by Native people" need not "take synecdoche as their defining figure" (*Ethnocriticism*, 230), the implication remains that this putatively traditional element affirms Apess's bona fides as Indian autobiographer. For a critique of the way in which such models of identity make Indians "intelligible [only] on the colonizer's terms," see Sarris, *Keeping Slug Woman Alive*, 90.

16. R. Anderson, *Memoir of Catharine Brown*, 52. All further references to the *Memoir* will be cited parenthetically in the text.

17. Patterson, *Life of Black Hawk*, 35; Seaver, *Life of Jemison*, xxvi.

18. Complicating the question of editorial involvement is the fact that successive

printings of the *Memoir* reveal considerable variability. In the case of Brown's letters, it is difficult to say whether the words attributed to her are hers; though her letters reprinted in the *Memoir* are identical to those published during her lifetime (e.g., the letter in *Memoir*, 76–77, matches the letter cited under Brown's name in my bibliography), this does not preclude the possibility of editorial intervention in her published correspondence.

19. Krupat, *Voice in the Margin*, 147, 147n9; O'Connell, "Introduction," xln34.

20. Krupat, ed., *Native American Autobiography*, 115; Powell, "Rhetorics of Survivance," 405. The citations in the passage by Powell are from Michel de Certeau.

21. C. Walker, *Indian Nation*, 3–4.

22. On the rise of Cherokee nationalism, see especially McLoughlin, *Cherokee Renascence*.

23. Cherokee delegation to Senate and House of Representatives, 15 April 1824, *Papers*, 1:77; Hallock, *From the Fallen Tree*, 223.

24. Boudinot, "Address to the Whites," 69.

25. Ridge, "Cherokee Civilization," 88; Ross to David Brown, 13 July 1822, *Papers*, 1:43.

26. On the stadial theory of human development favored by the philosophers of the Scottish Enlightenment, see Bieder, *Science Encounters the Indian*; and Sheehan, *Seeds of Extinction*. For a recent consideration of the place of the American Indians in this theory, see Bickham, *Savages within the Empire*, 171–209.

27. Entry of 24 June 1818, in Phillips and Phillips, eds., *Brainerd Journal*, 65 [cited hereafter as *Brainerd Journal*].

28. Entry of 19 November 1818, *Brainerd Journal*, 93; entry of 30 May 1822, *Brainerd Journal*, 269–70.

29. Ridge, "Cherokee Civilization," 86; [Cheever], *Removal of the Indians*, 49; Payne, "Green Corn Dance," 175, 195.

30. Ridge, "Cherokee Civilization," 88; Ross to John Q. Adams, 12 March 1825, *Papers*, 1:105; Gaul, "Introduction," 17; David Brown to Jeremiah Evarts, 1826, quoted in Gaul, "Introduction," 17. For Brown's letter in defense of slavery, see McLoughlin, *Cherokee Renascence*, 342–43. Though McLoughlin argues that American Board members tended to be even guiltier of racism than the norm (*Cherokees and Missionaries*, 128–43), he also notes the presence of cultural relativism among their ranks ("Missionaries as Cultural Brokers"). On Cherokee racism, see Sturm, who writes that "the new Cherokee state would increasingly replicate the racial ideologies and practices of the U.S. federal and state governments," including their support of the institution of African slavery (*Blood Politics*, 54). Boudinot, though a nonslaveholder, assented to the system, if only by remaining silent about it; see Peyer, *Tutor'd Mind*, 188–89.

31. Boudinot, "Address to the Whites," 72; Ross to United States Senate and House of Representatives, 21 June 1836, *Papers*, 1:442; Boudinot, "Address to the Whites," 78, 79.

32. Denson, *Demanding the Cherokee Nation*, 51; [Cheever], *Removal of the Indians*, 10, 39.

33. Evarts, *Essays*, 56, 75.

34. Ross wrote in 1836 that treaties proved the Cherokees to be "a distinct people, sovereign *to some extent*," with "a separate political existence as a society, or body politic, and a capability of being contracted with in a national capacity" (to Senate and House, 21 June 1836, *Papers*, 1:429, my emphasis). Ross's apparent hedging over Cherokee sovereignty is magnified by the fact that the same memorial grounds the Cherokees' rights as much in their civilized progress as in their inherent nature.

35. Evarts, "Address of the Cherokees," 260; Evarts, *Essays*, 56.

36. Boudinot, editorial of 12 November 1831 in *Cherokee Phoenix*, 142, 143.

37. Marshall, *Cherokee Nation v. State of Georgia*, 167; Cass, "Removal of the Indians," 75.

38. Jackson, quoted in McLoughlin and Conser, "Cherokee Censuses," 217n2; Cass, "Removal of the Indians," 71; Lumpkin, in "House Debate on the Indian Removal Question, May 15, 26, 1830," in Washburn, ed., *American Indian and the United States*, 2:1073–74. On the removalist inner circle's coordinated attacks against Cherokee mixed-bloods, see Ingersoll, *To Intermix with Our White Brothers*, 221–29; and, on the historic distrust of the Indian mixed-blood in American culture and literature, see H. Brown, *Injun Joe's Ghost*. Modern studies of the Cherokees have demonstrated that the equation of white blood with progressive attitudes is, whatever else it may be, historically inaccurate. As Sturm argues, the "standard dichotomies of mixed-blood vs. full-blood and traditional vs. progressive . . . obscure the diversity of the Cherokee community, both historically and at present" (*Blood Politics*, 57).

39. Perdue, "Introduction," 33, 32, 33, 32, 33; Rifkin, "Representing the Cherokee Nation," 48, 72, 48n2. Rifkin's argument is in large part a reaction against Krupat's postcolonial analysis of Cherokee political rhetoric: when the Cherokees "offer a narrative of identity in which they describe themselves not only as politically analogous to Americans in regard to independence and sovereignty, but as like them in sharing a morally, religiously, and socially progressive future," Krupat writes, they "take possession of the master's 'books'" and "obtain some important part of the master's power—which then, to be sure, may be turned to [their] own purposes" (*Ethnocriticism*, 162, 156). As Rifkin sees it, such an argument overlooks the fact that Cherokee leaders exerted significant power over their *own* people through their duplication of the master's "books."

40. On the heterogeneity of the Cherokee Nation, see Perdue, "'Rising from the Ashes'" and "Traditionalism"; McLoughlin, "Cherokee Antimission Sentiment"; and Dunaway, "Rethinking Cherokee Acculturation."

41. O'Connell, "Introduction," xxii; Bhabha, "Of Mimicry and Man," 86, 91; Cantwell, *Ethnomimesis*, 5.

42. Ross to James Monroe, 19 January 1824, *Papers*, 1:59; Ross to Payne, 5 March 1836, *Papers*, 1:391.

43. Ross to Cherokee General Council, 24 October 1823, *Papers*, 1:54; Ross to the Cherokees, 14 April 1831, *Papers*, 1:217.

44. Ross to Payne, 4 July 1837, *Papers*, 1:505.

45. Schmitz, *White Robe's Dilemma*, 49.

46. Washington, quoted in Perdue, *Cherokee Women*, 111; entry of 11 June 1823, *Brainerd Journal*, 361; Hicks, quoted in E. Evans, ed., "Jedidiah Morse's Report," 69;

Ridge, "Cherokee Civilization," 81. On the missionary program of domestic instruction among the Cherokees, see also Perdue, "Southern Indians"; and Young, "Women, Civilization, and the Indian Question." Letters from Cherokee schoolgirls emphasizing their domestic duties are collected in Perdue, "Letters from Brainerd." On domestic education in the Cherokee Female Seminary in Oklahoma, see Mihesuah, *Cultivating the Rosebuds*, esp. 37–47; and on domestic education throughout the Indian boarding school system, see Paxton, "Learning Gender."

47. Simonsen, *Making Home Work*, 72; Ridge, "Cherokee Civilization," 82, 87, 86; Boudinot, "Address to the Whites," 77; Ross to Senate and House, 22 February 1837, *Papers*, 1:471.

48. Stearns, "Discourse on Female Influence," 50; Beecher, *Essay on Slavery*, 37; Melder, "Ladies Bountiful," 9. Though the ideology of domesticity has been written about perhaps more extensively than any other subject of its time, three early studies remain among the best introductions to the topic: Douglas, *Feminization of American Culture*; and Welter, "Cult of True Womanhood" and "Feminization of American Religion."

49. On the Euro-American image of the Indian woman, see Green, "Pocahontas Perplex"; and Smits, "'Squaw Drudge.'"

50. J. Hall, "An Essay on the History of the North American Indians," in McKenney and Hall, *History of the Indian Tribes*, 3:249.

51. Beecher, *Treatise on Domestic Economy*, 155; Stearns, "Discourse on Female Influence," 47.

52. Johnston, *Cherokee Women in Crisis*, 42–43.

53. Marshall, *Cherokee Nation v. State of Georgia*, 165, 167, 166, my emphasis. On the sentimental contexts of federal Indian policy, see Sheehan, *Seeds of Extinction*, 123; and Wald, *Constituting Americans*, 26.

54. Sigourney, *Traits of the Aborigines*, 180.

55. Kaplan, "Manifest Domesticity," 591. Comparable treatments of domestic imperialism include Sánchez-Eppler, "Raising Empires"; and Wexler, "Tender Violence." The phrase "manifest domesticity" was first used, to the best of my knowledge, in Gillian Brown's valuable study of the intersection of domestic ideology and the capitalist individualism it claimed to contest, *Domestic Individualism*.

56. On the role of literary sentimentalists such as Sigourney in promoting Removal, see Burnham, *Captivity and Sentiment*, 92–117.

57. Lomawaima, "Domesticity in the Indian Schools." On the American Board's resistance to Cherokee Removal, see McLoughlin, *Cherokees and Missionaries*, 239–65; on debates among American Board missionaries concerning the proper Christian response to the Removal crisis, see McLoughlin, "Civil Disobedience." During the early years covered by the *Memoir*, Brown's people struggled against a treaty, extorted from them by Andrew Jackson, that would have removed them to the Arkansas Territory (*Cherokees and Missionaries*, 107–12); thus the references to Brown fulfilling her "filial duty" by so removing seem especially unfortunate. Ironically, Jackson had spoken in favor of the Brainerd station during the 1816 council at which the American Board gained Cherokee leaders' approval to conduct missionary work among their people.

58. Hershberger, "Mobilizing Women," 15; [Beecher], "Circular to Benevolent Ladies," 65.

59. [Beecher], "Circular to Benevolent Ladies," 65. Given Beecher's involvement in Cherokee politics, it is intriguing to conjecture that Brown may in fact have been a model for Little Eva. As Hershberger writes, "the only political references in the letters of young Harriet Beecher [Stowe] are enthusiastic reports of her work in [her sister's] petition campaign," and it seems likely that she would have read Brown's *Memoir* in conjunction with this work ("Mobilizing Women," 22). The fact that Harriet's father, Lyman, was a founder of the Cornwall Mission School and a critic of the Boudinot-Gold affair strengthens this hypothesis (see Rugoff, *Beechers*, 65–66).

60. Portnoy, *Their Right to Speak*, 77–78. Portnoy argues that Beecher's subsequent opposition to women's antislavery activism, rather than representing a retreat to domestic orthodoxy, reflected the common preference for gradualism over immediate abolition: "to conclude that Beecher refused women the right to petition on behalf of African Americans because she embraced traditional gender roles is to strip this historical moment of nearly all its complexity and explanatory force" (243). Portnoy's argument thus intervenes in the perennial debate over whether domestic ideology was empowering or debilitating for women. Though I can hardly delve into that debate here, I can second Nancy Hewitt's argument that an essential step toward grasping the complexity of domestic discourse and practice lies in the recovery of the specific contexts within which specific women lived, wrote, and acted; the alternative, to accept domestic ideology as an all-encompassing ideal, serves to "extend the hegemony of the antebellum bourgeoisie" and thus to disguise the fact that "diversity, discontinuity, and conflict were as much a part of the historical agency of women as of men" ("Beyond the Search," 316). Such a recovery project seems particularly urgent in the case of Indian women.

61. Coleman, "Cherokee Girls at Brainerd," 135; E. Evans, "Jedidiah Morse's Report," 67.

62. Evarts to David Brown, 1824, quoted in McLoughlin, *Cherokees and Missionaries*, 301.

63. Mihesuah, *Cultivating the Rosebuds*, 41; Carney, *Eastern Band Cherokee Women*, 16–17. Samples of the post-Removal seminarians' essays appear in Kilcup, ed., *Native American Women's Writing*, 401–14. These women identified themselves with Brown sufficiently to devote an issue of their paper, *Cherokee Rose Buds*, to her; see Mihesuah, *Cultivating the Rosebuds*, 38.

64. P. Allen, *Sacred Hoop*, 223, 3; Devens, *Countering Colonization*, 4; Schonenberger, *Lenape Women*, 161. The image of the "squaw drudge" persisted well into the twentieth century, ultimately crumbling under the assault of Marxist and feminist studies of the 1970s, which argued that Indian women's considerable power in pre-contact times, a power linked to their vital role in subsistence economies, was disrupted by capitalism. For a review of such studies, see Leacock, "Origins of Gender Inequality." For summaries of current scholarship on Indian women, see Perdue, "Writing the Ethnohistory"; and Shoemaker, "Introduction." Bibliographies include Ford, "Native American Women"; and Welch, "American Indian Women."

65. Long, "Small Postscript," 30. On Cherokee women's status prior to the Nation's

rise, see Fogelson, "On the 'Petticoat Government' "; Hatley, *Dividing Paths*, 52–63; and Perdue, *Cherokee Women*, 13–59. Sattler's comparative study of the Cherokees and Creeks finds that the greater degree of autonomy among Cherokee women reflected their enhanced role in their people's economic system ("Women's Status"); Rodning, meanwhile, musters archaeological evidence to advance his claims for gender complementarity in pre-Nation Cherokee society ("Archaeological Perspectives").

66. Perdue, *Cherokee Women*, 30; Adair, *History of the American Indians*, 107; Perdue, *Cherokee Women*, 26. Additional pre-Removal accounts of the Cherokee Green Corn Festival include Payne, "Green Corn Dance"; and Bartram, "Observations." For versions of the Selu myth, see Mooney, *Myths of the Cherokee*, 242–49.

67. Kateuha to Franklin, quoted in Shoemaker, "Introduction," 9. Perdue argues that the titles of War Woman and Beloved Woman were not identical, Beloved Woman being reserved for "postmenopausal women who had acquired unusual spiritual power by surviving both menstruation and warfare" ("Nancy Ward," 89). Thus a woman of Ward's stature held, consecutively, both titles. On the role of the War Woman and Beloved Woman, see also Carney, "'Woman Is the Mother.' "

68. Merritt, *At the Crossroads*, 55. On the forces that shaped Cherokee society in the eighteenth and nineteenth centuries, see Goodwin, *Cherokees in Transition*; Hudson, "Southeastern Indians"; and O'Donnell, "Southern Indians." On the transformation of gender roles specifically, see Hill, *Weaving New Worlds*, 89–109; and Perdue, *Cherokee Women*, 65–113.

69. Bartram, "Observations," 80–81.

70. Fogelson, "On the 'Petticoat Government,' " 170. In "Cherokee Women," Perdue accepts Cherokee leaders' and missionaries' claims for the revolution in women's roles; in her later *Cherokee Women*, she questions such claims, arguing that most women continued to exercise their pre-Nation roles after the Nation's rise (109–84). For a similar argument, see Dunaway, "Rethinking Cherokee Acculturation."

71. Perdue, *Cherokee Women*, 139.

72. Strickland argues that "the inheritance laws of the Cherokees indicated that equality of women was still a basic social goal" of the Nation (*Fire and the Spirits*, 100). Yet the wording of the law concerning intermarriage, which protects the woman's property in order to "avoid imposition on the part of any white man" (quoted in E. Evans, "Jedidiah Morse's Report," 73), suggests that securing women's rights may have been more a happy *result* than a *goal*. As evidence for this, Ridge waffles considerably in his description of the laws concerning married women's property: "The laws of our Nation from time immemorial recognizes a separate property in the wife and husband, and this principle is universally cherished among the less informed Class and in fact in every grade of intelligence. If they are so disposed, the law secures to the Ladies, the control of their own property" ("Cherokee Civilization," 84). In a passage deleted from his final report, he continues to hedge: "Property belonging to the wife is not exclusively at the control & disposal of the husband, and in many respects she has exclusive & distinct control over her own, particularly among the less civilized & in fact in every class & grade of intelligence, the law is in favor of the females in this respect" (84). Though Ridge may be trying to craft a portrait that will not offend white sensibilities, he too appears unwilling to grant women full property rights.

73. Ridge, "Cherokee Civilization," 81; Ross to Cherokee antiquarians, 15 September 1835, *Papers*, 1:354; Dowd, "Spinning Wheel Revolution," 272.

74. McLoughlin, *Cherokee Renascence*, 326–27; Dunaway, "Rethinking Cherokee Acculturation," 182, 172; entry of 23 September 1818, *Brainerd Journal*, 82.

75. Ross to Return J. Meigs, 3 January 1813, *Papers*, 1:18; McKenney and Hall, *History of the Indian Tribes*, 1:386–87; Meigs, "Record of the Cherokee Indian Agency in Tennessee, 1801–1835," quoted in McLoughlin with Conser and McLoughlin, *Cherokee Ghost Dance*, 148; Moravian mission diary, 1811–12, quoted in *Cherokee Ghost Dance*, 142; Perdue, *Cherokee Women*, 64. McLoughlin covers the revitalization movement in "Cherokee Ghost Dance," and *Cherokees and Missionaries*, 82–101. Additional considerations include Dowd, *Spirited Resistance*, 173–79; and May, "Nativistic Movements among the Cherokees."

76. Nancy Ward, "Petition to the Cherokee National Council, May 2, 1817," in Kilcup, *Native American Women's Writing*, 29; Dunaway, "Rethinking Cherokee Acculturation," 170; Kilcup, *Native American Women's Writing*, 26. Perdue argues similarly that for Ward, "references to motherhood evoked power rather than sentimentality" (*Cherokee Women*, 101); but this is to overlook the power *of* sentimentality in Euro-American and Cherokee discourse.

77. Tuttle, *Letters and Conversations*, 2:97.

78. Shoemaker, "Kateri Tekakwitha," 51.

79. Perdue, "Catharine Brown," 82.

80. I take this phrase from Smith Rosenberg, "Female World."

81. Tuttle, *Letters and Conversations*, 2:78–79; Butrick, quoted in McLoughlin, *Cherokees and Missionaries*, 205; entry of 25 July 1821, *Brainerd Journal*, 228; Mooney, *Swimmer Manuscript*, 39, 14. Mooney makes additional comments on late century conflicts between shamans and missionaries in "Sacred Formulas," 336.

82. Perdue, "Introduction," 30.

83. J. Evans, "Sketches," 10, 12; entry of 3 July 1822, *Brainerd Journal*, 284.

84. Perdue, "Catharine Brown," 87; Fogelson, "Conjuror in Eastern Cherokee Society," 61; Albanese, "Exploring Regional Religion," 351; McLoughlin, *Cherokees and Missionaries*, 206; entry of 3 June 1822, *Brainerd Journal*, 273. On the conjunction of Cherokee and Christian healing, see also McLoughlin, "Fractured Myths": "The Cherokees [seem] to have found at last a way to use the power of the Anglo-American invader to save their own people" (187).

85. Mooney, *Myths of the Cherokee*, 320. Another version of the Stone Coat myth appears in Speck and Broom, *Cherokee Dance and Drama*, 14–15. For a fascinating examination of the role the myth plays in another site of overlap between Cherokee and white medicine—the invention of Sequoyah's syllabary—see Bender, "Framing the Anomalous."

86. Dunaway, "Rethinking Cherokee Acculturation," 177; Olbrechts, in Mooney, *Swimmer Manuscript*, 84.

87. Mooney, "Sacred Formulas," 337, 338; Dunaway, "Rethinking Cherokee Acculturation," 164.

88. Tracy, *History of the American Board*, 70; Tuttle, *Letters and Conversations*, 2:7;

ks

Spring Place Mission diaries, 26 August 1803, in Baillou, "Mythology and Conceptual World," 97; Payne, "Green Corn Dance," 191–92.

89. Speck and Broom, *Cherokee Dance and Drama*, 19; McKenney and Hall, *History of the Indian Tribes*, 1:386–87; Hicks, 16 April 1818, in *Brainerd Journal*, 54; Speck and Broom, *Cherokee Dance and Drama*, 20.

90. Hill, *Weaving New Worlds*, 316.

91. Irwin, "Freedom, Law, and Prophecy," 297–98; Brooks, *American Lazarus*, 55; Joel Martin, "Visions of Revitalization," 62. On Christian Indian communities as extensions of the traditional, see also Gustafson, *Eloquence Is Power*, 90–101. For additional studies of the complexity of Indian conversion, see Brightman, "Toward a History"; Griffiths, "Introduction"; Salisbury, "Embracing Ambiguity"; and Axtell's still indispensable "Some Thoughts," which argues in terms that anticipate Brooks's: "Rather than achieving a nativistic revitalization at the hands of a charismatic prophet," some Indian communities "used the religion of Christ to the same end" (51).

92. O'Connell, "Introduction," xl, xlv, xlii.

93. O'Connell, "'Once More,'" 169, 174–75. Wyss points out one type of community of which Apess was both member and inheritor: "Hailed as a radical, Apess has been praised for his unique challenge to European assumptions about Native Americans. But literary scholars' accolades, while well deserved, deny the extensive tradition of Native American Christian writing that existed well over a century before Apess" (*Writing Indians*, 155). As Wyss notes in another place, Apess's eclipsing of a female contemporary was not unique either: unlike her famous husband, Mary Occom "teetered on the periphery of the evolving world of Native literacy" ("Mary Occom," 412).

94. Considerable doubt surrounds the authorship of *Poor Sarah*. Wiget, taking the work to be the creation of the Cherokee Boudinot, writes that "in 1823 Elias Boudinot . . . decided to create a fiction" ("Elias Boudinot," 4). Ruoff states that Boudinot "translated into Cherokee a short fictional work entitled *Poor Sarah*, published in 1833" ("Old Traditions," 148). And Peyer argues that the Cherokee Boudinot's Euro-American sponsor was responsible for the work, which "first appeared anonymously in the *Religious Intelligencer* on January 1, 1820" before the younger man "finally made use of it in 1823" (*Tutor'd Mind*, 222). My research has turned up a version of the story as early as 1818, the year the fifteen-year-old Cherokee Boudinot entered the Cornwall mission school. Peyer is almost certainly correct, therefore, that he was not the text's author, though the question of the elder Boudinot's authorship remains uncertain. What is certain is that *Poor Sarah* arises from the same blend of missionary fervor and Christian domesticity that marks the *Memoir*, with the Indian woman Sarah determining to "give my heart all away to Jesus, tell him I be all his; serve him all my life; beg Holy Spirit come fill all my heart, make it all clean and white like Jesus" (*Pious Indian*, 7).

95. O'Connell, in Apess, *Son of the Forest*, 97–11; Apess, *Son of the Forest*, 3.

96. Mielke, "'Native to the Question,'" 262. On the presence of domestic discourse in Apess's writings, see also Gussman, "'O Savage, Where Art Thou?'"

97. Apess, *Increase of the Kingdom of Christ*, 111; O'Connell, headnote to Apess, *In-*

*crease of the Kingdom of Christ*, 99; Warrior, "Eulogy on William Apess," 1; Gustafson, "Nations of Israelites," 42; Carlson, *Sovereign Selves*, 69. On Apess's use of legal discourse to critique racist categories, see also Doolen, *Fugitive Empire*, 156–83; on his use of Christian discourse for the same purpose, see Haynes, "'A Mark for Them All'"; and Tiro, "Denominated 'SAVAGE.'"

98. Lepore, *Name of War*, 220. On Apess as "Indian" performer, see also Dannenberg, "Apess's *Eulogy*."

99. Josiah Fiske, quoted in Nielsen, "Mashpee Indian Revolt," 411. On Apess's part in the Mashpee affair, see also Gaul, "Apess's *Indian Nullification*"; and Mandell, "Mashpee's Struggle," 319–22.

100. J. Evans, "Sketches," 19.

101. Speck and Broom, *Cherokee Dance and Drama*, 37, 38; J. Evans, "Sketches," 10; Sweet, "Burlesquing 'The Other,'" 73.


## Chapter 3

1. Cody, *True Tales*, 6; Cody, *Life*, 169. On Cody's buffalo-hunting prowess, see *True Tales*, 68. Of the various Cody autobiographies, the only one that is likely the work of Cody himself is the 1879 *Life of Hon. William F. Cody*, published before his Wild West days. Because, however, my interest lies more in the Cody persona than in Cody the person—and as he and his press agents devoted considerable energy to blurring the two—I treat all such works as equivalent.

2. *The Scouts of the Prairie* (1872), quoted in Kasson, *Buffalo Bill's Wild West*, 23. On Cody's career as a stage performer before the Wild West, see R. Hall, *Performing the American Frontier*, 54–67; and Wickstrom, "Buffalo Bill." On the Yellow Hair episode, see Cody, *Life*, 340–47; and Russell's detailed reconstruction of the event (*Lives and Legends*, 214–35).

3. Warren, *Buffalo Bill's America*, 93.

4. Wild West playbill, quoted in Slotkin, *Gunfighter Nation*, 84.

5. Warren, arguing that Cody's Indian-killer persona was moderated by sustained contact with Indians during his Wild West years, writes that "of all Cody's characteristics, it is [his] profound ambivalence about Indians that seems most impenetrable" (*Buffalo Bill's America*, 199). In a similar vein, Reddin writes that though Cody may have seen himself as an "advocate for Indians," his private philanthropy contrasted starkly with his public performances, which "depicted Indians as warlike, misguided, and frightening opponents" (*Wild West Shows*, 140). For additional treatments of Wild West shows as extensions of colonial power over Indian persons and performances, see Clark, "Menace of the Wild West"; and Jonathan Martin, "'Most Cosmopolitan Object Teacher.'" On the ongoing colonial work of the Buffalo Bill Museum in Cody, Wyoming, see Dickinson, Ott, and Aoki, who write that the museum uses artifacts from the shows to "carnivalize the violent conflicts between Anglo Americans and Native Americans" ("Memory and Myth," 87).

6. Mooney, *Ghost-Dance Religion*, 771–72. All further references to *Ghost-Dance Religion* will be cited parenthetically in the text.

7. Studies of Wovoka and the Ghost Dance include, in addition to Mooney's unparalleled work, Hittman's meticulously researched biography, *Wovoka and the Ghost Dance*; Kehoe's invaluable analysis of the Ghost Dance's antecedents and offspring, *Ghost Dance*; Smoak's exploration of ethnic identity formation in the 1890 Ghost Dance and its 1870 predecessor, *Ghost Dances and Identity*; and Thornton's intriguing if untestable hypothesis that the Ghost Dance represented a conscious attempt by Indian peoples ravaged by catastrophic population loss to "increase their numbers through regaining populations of the dead" (*We Shall Live Again*, 19).

8. I follow Powers in my use of the term *intertribal* rather than the more familiar *pan-Indian*: whereas *pan-Indian* suggests the emergence of a single, overarching Indian identity that does away with tribal affiliation, *intertribal* implies the recognition or forging of common ties across tribal lines, thus preserving the tribal even while transforming it. See Powers, *War Dance*, esp. 86–110. For studies of twentieth-century intertribal movements, see Ewers, "Emergence of the Plains Indian"; Hertzberg, *Search for an Indian Identity*; and Thomas, "Pan-Indianism." Ewers mentions Cody's Wild West as a significant force behind contemporary Indian identity; Thomas names the Ghost Dance; Hertzberg references both. Ewers, by the way, mentions Catlin's paintings as a prominent force in popularizing the image of the Plains Indian ("Emergence of the Plains Indian," 535–36).

9. McMullen, "What's Wrong," 127; Joel Martin, "Before and Beyond," 678; Powers, *War Dance*, 12. The intertribal ideal can, of course, be abused in scholarly discourse that fails to appreciate tribal differences; for a critique of this tendency, see Hochbruck, "Cultural Authenticity."

10. R. Pratt, "Remarks on Indian Education," 279; Gates, "Addresses," 342; T. Morgan, "Statement on Indian Policy," 75; catalogue of Carlisle Indian School, quoted in Malmsheimer, "'Imitation White Man,'" 68. Studies of the late nineteenth-century attack on Plains tribalism are numerous. On the Dawes Act, see Hoxie, *Final Promise*; and Washburn, *Assault on Indian Tribalism*. On the suppression of Indian dance and ceremony, see C. Ellis, *Dancing People*, 55–77; and Ostler, *Plains Sioux*, 174–82. Finally, on the boarding school movement, see Adams, *Education for Extinction*; and the essays in Trafzer, Keller, and Sisquoc, eds., *Boarding School Blues*.

11. Moses, *Wild West Shows*, xiv, 279.

12. Schwartz, "Wild West Show," 664.

13. Hertzberg, *Search for an Indian Identity*, 6; Dowd, *Spirited Resistance*, xix. Considerations of eighteenth- and nineteenth-century prophetic revivals include Joel Martin, *Sacred Revolt*; Sayre, *Indian Chief*; and Wallace, *Death and Rebirth*.

14. Zeisberger, "Diary," 24–25; Kenny, "Journal," 188; Zeisberger, "Diary," 27–28. On Neolin, see Cave, *Prophets of the Great Spirit*, 22–44; Dowd, *Spirited Resistance*, 33–36; and White, *Middle Ground*, 279–85.

15. Schoolcraft, *Algic Researches*, 118–19.

16. Dowd, *Spirited Resistance*, 35. On the practice of the Green Corn Festival throughout the eastern woodlands, see Witthoft, *Green Corn Ceremonialism*.

17. Cave, *Prophets of the Great Spirit*, 9; Dowd, *Spirited Resistance*, 27; Simmons, "Red Yankees," 265.

18. Kirkland, *Journals*, 360; Merritt, *At the Crossroads*, 92.

19. Edwards, *Life of Brainerd*, 329, 330. On Brainerd's encounters with Indian prophets, see also Gustafson, *Eloquence Is Power*, 78–90; and Pointer, "'Poor Indians,'" who suggests that the evangelist's doctrinal positions may have been modified by contact with his Native counterparts.

20. Kenny, "Journal," 175; Zeisberger, "History," 133.

21. Kenny, "Journal," 175.

22. Merritt, *At the Crossroads*, 126.

23. White, *Middle Ground*, 280; Gustafson, *Eloquence Is Power*, 88; Desbarats, "Following *The Middle Ground*," 88.

24. Dowd, *Spirited Resistance*, 129.

25. Irwin, *Dream Seekers*, 71.

26. Cooper, *Last of the Mohicans*, 300.

27. On Cherokee multiple-origins stories, see McLoughlin and Conser, "'First Man.'"

28. L. Morgan, *League of the Iroquois*, 251–52; Trowbridge, *Shawnese Traditions*, 1, 3, 56.

29. Dowd, *Spirited Resistance*, 239n49; Shoemaker, "How Indians Got to Be Red," 632, 643; Sturm, *Blood Politics*, 50; S. Morton, *Inquiry*, 4. On Euro-American racial theory in the nineteenth century, see Bieder, *Science Encounters the Indian*; and Horsman, *Race and Manifest Destiny*, 116–86.

30. Berkhofer, *White Man's Indian*, 1, 29; S. Morton, *Crania Americana*, 3.

31. Tecumseh, in Armstrong, ed., *I Have Spoken*, 45.

32. Thurman, "Shawnee Prophet's Movement," 531. Ostler argues that it is erroneous to consider the Ghost Dance a revitalization movement, for "this category . . . fails to account for the movement's oppositional character" (*Plains Sioux*, 262). Though I accept Ostler's argument that Wovoka should be seen as a "prophet of rebellion," who "looked to spiritual power to overthrow colonial rule" (250), I do not believe that such a role is incompatible with the process of revitalization—if, that is, one sees revitalization as a renewal of sacred tradition through emergent performance.

33. Maus, "New Indian Messiah," 947; "New Indian Messiah," 11; John S. Mayhugh, quoted in Logan, "Ghost Dance," 273; Hugh Lenox Scott, quoted in Moses, "Jack Wilson," 306.

34. Grinnell, "Account of the Northern Cheyennes," 62; Fletcher, "Indian Messiah," 60; D. Brown, *Bury My Heart*, 435; Moses, "'Father Tells Me,'" 335, 339; Bailey, *Ghost Dance Messiah*, 18; Warren, *Buffalo Bill's America*, 376; Maddra, *Hostiles?* 34.

35. Ostler, *Plains Sioux*, 253.

36. Overholt, "Ghost Dance," 41; Kucich, *Ghostly Communion*, 65. For what it is worth, Sioux missionaries saw the Ghost Dance as an abomination, not as an approximation of their faith; see Kerstetter, "Spin Doctors."

37. Smoak, *Ghost Dances and Identity*, 80.

38. Irwin, *Dream Seekers*, 189, 199.

39. Interview of Philip F. Wells, 6 October 1906, in Ricker, *Voices of the American West*, 144, 143; Overholt, "Ghost Dance," 56; Irwin, *Dream Seekers*, 193.

40. Maus, "New Indian Messiah," 947; Barney, *Mormons, Indians and the Ghost Dance*, 155. Barney's study, the fullest to date on Mormon influence on the Ghost Dance, concludes that though there were numerous points of contact between the two religions—including the Mormons' conviction that the Indians were descendants of the Lost Tribes of Israel, a common belief in the return of the dead, and a similarity between Mormon Endowment Robes and Sioux Ghost Shirts—"there is little empirical evidence that would lead to the conclusion that the Mormons and Mormon doctrine were in fact the forces that produced the Ghost Dance Religion" (155). For further consideration of the Mormons' role in the Ghost Dance and earlier prophertic movements, see Smoak, *Ghost Dances and Identity*, 71–80, 166–67.

41. Kehoe, *Ghost Dance*, 33.

42. An unfortunate if understandable lapse in Mooney's study is his confusion of Wodziwob with Tavibo (701–3, 765). On the spiritual abilities of Wovoka's father, see Hittman, *Wovoka and the Ghost Dance*, 29–35; on Wodziwob, see Kehoe, *Ghost Dance*, 32–34.

43. Lewis, *Medicine Men*, 52. On the centrality of the Sun Dance to Plains identity and ritual renewal, see also Ostler, *Plains Sioux*, 168–72.

44. Adams, *Education for Extinction*, 223. Recent reassessments of the boarding schools suggest that they may have unintentionally served tribal and intertribal interests. Smoak, for instance, writes that "the attempted imposition of white culture often functioned as a shared experience that reinforced similarities among Indian peoples as well as magnifying their differences with whites," so that "many of the students sent away to boarding schools returned with a new sense of Indianness" (*Ghost Dances and Identity*, 154). C. Ellis agrees: "writing [about the schools] from the vantage point of assimilation models tells us about policy and its failures, but it tells us almost nothing about [the students'] experience" ("Rainy Mountain Boarding School," 68).

45. Huffstetler, "Spirit Armies," 5.

46. Some scholars argue that Wovoka's original vision was "distorted" (Kehoe, *Ghost Dance*, 39) by other Indian peoples, especially the Lakotas, and thus that Mooney's influential depiction of the Ghost Dance as a separatist movement is flawed. Citing versions of Wovoka's message that emphasize a reunion of Indians *and* whites in the afterlife, for example, Hittman faults "Mooney's Plains bias" (*Wovoka and the Ghost Dance*, 98) for popularizing Sioux and Kiowa versions that foresaw the restoration of a terrestrial Indian paradise following the destruction of whites. Overholt, by contrast, argues that it is "reasonable to assume" that "the elimination of the Whites formed an important part of the original doctrine" ("Ghost Dance," 43). And, indeed, certain early versions of the prophet's creed, including that reported (though admittedly at second hand) by Paiute spokeswoman Sarah Winnemucca, reference the return of a deity who will "exterminate [the whites] from the earth" (quoted in Hittman, *Wovoka and the Ghost Dance*, 259). Because, however, my purpose is not to recover the original intentions of the Ghost Dance "author" but to discuss the Dance's cultural work among the various peoples who took it up, this debate becomes moot: though the details of Wovoka's vision(s) are disputable, there is little question that

many—perhaps most—Indian peoples made the separation of Indians and whites a central component of the Dance. For a reasoned discussion of this controversy, see Smoak, *Ghost Dances and Identity*, 168–70. For analyses of the ways in which the Sioux Ghost Dance has itself been distorted by critics who treat it as militaristic rather than prophetic, see DeMallie, who argues that such a view ignores "the basic religious nature of the movement" ("Lakota Ghost Dance," 388); Ostler, who finds that "the thesis that the Sioux transformed a peaceful teaching into a militant one originated in the army's attempts to justify its campaign to suppress the Sioux Ghost Dance" (*Plains Sioux*, 261); and Maddra, who writes similarly that "the dominant interpretation that the Lakota Ghost Dance leaders 'perverted' Wovoka's doctrine of peace into one of war is based on primary source material derived from the testimony of those who had actively worked to suppress the religion" (*Hostiles?* 44).

47. Thomas Tyon et al., in J. Walker, *Lakota Belief and Ritual*, 108.

48. Hilden, "Race for Sale," 27.

49. Kehoe, *Ghost Dance*, 9; Tyon et al., in J. Walker, *Lakota Belief and Ritual*, 108.

50. Moses, *Wild West Shows*, 105. On the attempts of Cody's troupe to intervene in the Ghost Dance, see also Maddra, who suggests that Cody and his performers were seeking to ingratiate themselves to the Bureau of Indian Affairs officials who had threatened to prohibit Indian participation in the Wild West (*Hostiles?* 86–111).

51. Warren, *Buffalo Bill's America*, 378; Cody, quoted in Warren, *Buffalo Bill's America*, 378, 379; Cody, *True Tales*, 253. The story of Sitting Bull's horse, Lemons reveals, was invented as late as 1932—coincidentally, the year of the publication of *Black Elk Speaks*—by a Euro-American historian and his Sioux informant ("History by Unreliable Narrators"). For a popular version of the story, see Russell, *Lives and Legends*, 363.

52. Mooney, quoted in Kosmider, "Refracting the Imperial Gaze," 325. On the anthropological critique of the Wild West, see Elliott, "Problem of the Real," 202–3; and S. Smith, *Reimagining Indians*, 7–12.

53. Indian Rights Association, "Condemnation of Wild West Shows," 314; T. Morgan, "Wild West Shows," 311. On the reformers' crusade against the Wild West, see C. Ellis, *Dancing People*, 79–101; and Moses, *Wild West Shows*, 60–79.

54. Jefferson, "Second Inaugural Address," 368.

55. Green, "Tribe Called Wannabee," 38, 50; White, "Turner and Buffalo Bill," 35; Poignant, *Professional Savages*, 8, 141; Warren, *Buffalo Bill's America*, 363; Maddra, *Hostiles?* 146; Kasson, *Buffalo Bill's Wild West*, 191; Moses, *Wild West Shows*, 272.

56. For comparable thoughts on show Indian identity, see Trachtenberg's review of Moses's book. A parallel study of performance and cultural authenticity among late nineteenth-century Northwest Coast "show Indians" is Paige Raibmon's *Authentic Indians*, esp. 34–73.

57. Powers, *War Dance*, 4.

58. Hale, "Luther Standing Bear," 28; Brumble, *American Indian Autobiography*, 64; Moos, *Outside America*, 150; R. Ellis, introduction to *My People the Sioux*, xi. All further references to *My People the Sioux* will be cited parenthetically in the text.

59. Vizenor, *Manifest Manners*, 3. On Standing Bear's centrality to the Sioux "liter-

ary renaissance" of the late nineteenth and early twentieth centuries, see also Heflin, "*I Remain Alive*," 79–103.

60. Yellow Robe, "Menace of the Wild West Show," 224. Recent readings of Sitting Bull's Wild West career argue that he was far less the exploited innocent than Standing Bear makes him out to be. Moos, for example, sees Sitting Bull as a canny manipulator of Indian imagery: "With little to trade in a white world, Sitting Bull turned toward the popular creation of himself" (*Outside America*, 170). Kasson argues similarly that Sitting Bull was "an actor every bit as much as Cody" (*Buffalo Bill's Wild West*, 178), who played off his reputation as the man who had killed Custer to amass personal and cultural capital. On Sitting Bull's own autobiographical works, the pictographic records of his deeds as a warrior, see Moos, *Outside America*, 177–83; and Risch, "Picture Changes."

61. Moos, *Outside America*, 193; Trachtenberg, *Shades of Hiawatha*, 283; Maddox, *Citizen Indians*, 8.

62. Warren, *Buffalo Bill's America*, 407.

63. Standing Bear, *Land of the Spotted Eagle*, 235.

64. Powers, seeking to discredit Standing Bear in an article dedicated to debunking *Black Elk Speaks*, writes that "Luther Standing Bear's 'autobiographies'" were "all obviously written by a New York editor" ("When Black Elk Speaks," 52). Although Standing Bear did obtain editorial assistance for *My People the Sioux*, there is no evidence that the editor's role was as significant as Powers claims. R. Ellis does have cause to question Standing Bear's claim to the chieftainship: "if [it] is true" that he was made a chief, "he did not actively fill the role for very long, for in succeeding years he resided on the reservation only intermittently" ("Luther Standing Bear," 148).

65. V. Deloria, "Indians," 54.

66. V. Deloria, introduction to *Black Elk Speaks*, xiv. All further references to *Black Elk Speaks* will be cited parenthetically in the text, prefaced *BES*.

67. McCluskey, "*Black Elk Speaks*," 237; Neihardt, quoted in McCluskey, 238.

68. See DeMallie, ed., *The Sixth Grandfather*; and Steltenkamp, *Black Elk*. All further references to *The Sixth Grandfather* will be cited parenthetically in the text, prefaced *SG*.

69. Couser, "*Black Elk Speaks*," 87, 74; Powers, "When Black Elk Speaks," 55; Porterfield, "Black Elk's Significance," 56; Rice, *Black Elk's Story*, x, 2; Schmitz, *White Robe's Dilemma*, 12, 165. Commenting on this debate, Forbes suggests that "many of the historical interpretations of Black Elk's religious views [may] reveal more about the assumptions of the interpreters than about Black Elk" ("Which Religion Is Right?" 25). For a study that seeks not to weigh in on the debate but to illustrate how the debate has facilitated the text's rise to canonical status, see Silvio, "*Black Elk Speaks*."

70. Moos, *Outside America*, 195.

71. Cheyfitz, "(Post)Colonial Construction," 87.

72. Lucy Looks Twice, quoted in Steltenkamp, *Black Elk*, 34; Lucy Looks Twice, quoted in H. Neihardt, *Black Elk and Flaming Rainbow*, 119. For further comments on the mediated nature of Black Elk's life, see Arnold, "Black Elk and Book Culture."

73. George Sword, in J. Walker, *Lakota Belief and Ritual*, 75, 81. Black Elk practiced

both as a holy man and as a medicine man; on the possibility of a single man serving as both, see Sword, in J. Walker, *Lakota Belief and Ritual*, 92.

74. Tyon et al., in J. Walker, *Lakota Belief and Ritual*, 104; Sword, in J. Walker, *Lakota Belief and Ritual*, 79; Thunder Bear, in J. Walker, *Lakota Belief and Ritual*, 131.

75. Short Bull, in J. Walker, *Lakota Belief and Ritual*, 143; DeMallie, "Lakota Belief and Ritual," 43; Wong, *Sending My Heart Back*, 138; J. Walker, *Lakota Belief and Ritual*, 50. Interestingly, both Walker and Neihardt stand in relation to the Lakotas somewhat in the manner that George Catlin stood to the Mandans. Though both boasted of their spiritual adoption by the tribe, Walker writing that "to get the desired information, I became an Oglala medicine man, complying with the requirements of their order" (*Lakota Belief and Ritual*, 46), and Neihardt similarly claiming adoption as "Flaming Rainbow," after a figure from Black Elk's great vision, neither seems to have gained access to the performative secret that the tribe held in reserve (or in reservation): "I sought information from the holy men," Walker continues, "and was told that they taught their mystic lore only to candidates for admission to their order who were acceptable to the Gods and that no other than a full-blooded Oglala had ever been ordained as a holy man" (47).

76. Holloway, *Interpreting the Legacy*, 80.

77. Irwin, *Dream Seekers*, 97.

78. Mails, assisted by Chief Eagle, *Fools Crow*, 88.

79. Markowitz, "Catholic Mission and the Sioux," 136; Lucy Looks Twice, quoted in Steltenkamp, *Black Elk*, 34.

80. Esther Black Elk DeSersa, in Neihardt and Utrecht, eds., *Black Elk Lives*, 137.

81. Holler, "Black Elk's Relationship," 39; Sword, in J. Walker, *Lakota Belief and Ritual*, 91. For a further argument that Christianity was not incompatible with traditional Lakota religion, see Howard, "Incommensurability and Nicholas Black Elk."

82. Hilbert, "Catholic Mission Work," 143; Lucy Looks Twice, quoted in Steltenkamp, *Black Elk*, 34, 67; Murray, *Forked Tongues*, 72.

83. Benjamin (Ben) Black Elk, in Neihardt and Utrecht, *Black Elk Lives*, 9; Olivia Black Elk, in Neihardt and Utrecht, *Black Elk Lives*, 57.

84. Olivia Black Elk, in Neihardt and Utrecht, *Black Elk Lives*, 134; Kehoe, *Ghost Dance*, 67; Lucy Looks Twice, quoted in Steltenkamp, *Black Elk*, 114; Schmitz, *White Robe's Dilemma*, 123.

85. J. Brown, *Sacred Pipe*, xx.

86. Lucy Looks Twice, quoted in Steltenkamp, *Black Elk*, 56–57.

87. Ibid., 62; Ben Black Elk, in Neihardt and Utrecht, *Black Elk Lives*, 8.

88. Unnamed Arapaho Indian to Jack Wilson, 31 March 1910, in Dangberg, ed., "Letters to Jack Wilson," 295; Fred Robinson (Assiniboine) to Jack Wilson, 17 January 1909, in Dangberg, "Letters to Jack Wilson," 288. The northern tours described by the latter supplicant bore fruit among Canadian Dakota Indians, who, as Kehoe's field research indicates, were yet performing the Ghost Dance as late as the 1980s (*Ghost Dance*, 41–50).

89. L. A. Dorrington, 12–13 May 1917, in Stewart, "Contemporary Document on Wovoka," 221; Clow, "Lakota Ghost Dance," 323; Lesser, "Significance of the Ghost Dance," 114, 112; Thornton, *We Shall Live Again*, 45.

90. On AIM and Wounded Knee, see Rich, "'Remember Wounded Knee.'"

91. As with all aspects of Black Elk's life, his continuing relevance to Lakota (and other Indian) peoples has been hotly contested. Powers argues that Black Elk's teachings "have not impressed the average Lakota, who today wonders why so many people would be interested in the life of, what to them, was just another Oglala" ("When Black Elk Speaks," 52). Trimble, by contrast, writes that "the reputation of the holy man" and "his descendants in [both] the traditional [and] Christian communities" remains undiminished "on the reservation today," while "*Black Elk Speaks* remains an important document in the preservation and practice of Lakota belief and ritual" ("Introduction," xv). Though I am in no position to weigh the merits of these claims, I would point out that a fact often cited against Black Elk—that "the only language to which *Black Elk Speaks* . . . has not been translated is Lakota" (Powers, "When Black Elk Speaks," 53)—does not mean that "the circulation of this autobiography . . . continues only in non-Native circles" (Moos, *Outside America*, 203). Most Native peoples today read English, and as a further comment by Deloria suggests, many Native peoples today read *Black Elk Speaks*: "More than one Indian political organization has based its approach to modern problems on *Black Elk Speaks*" (*God Is Red*, 51).

92. C. Allen, *Blood Narrative*, 11–12; Vizenor, *Manifest Manners*, 106; Churchill, "Generations of Resistance," 162–63. On the imagery of the Ghost Dance as "one of the more audacious evocations for Native writers to convey complexities of survival and to reclaim representation of their cultures," see also Moore, "Return of the Buffalo," 57.

93. Rich, "'Remember Wounded Knee,'" 79. On the "persistence of Indian communities and tribal identities" in the twentieth century, see also D'Arcy McNickle (Cree/Salish/Kootenai), *Native American Tribalism*, 8. Published in the year of the Wounded Knee occupation, McNickle's book, in its rejection of the majority opinion that "the only cultures that remain pristine and therefore viable are those that remain in hostile isolation from all outside cultural encounters" (13), helped pave the way for a view of tribalism as intercultural performative reinvention.

94. On the influence of Buffalo Bill's Wild West on the Mardi Gras Indian gangs, see M. Smith, *Mardi Gras Indians*, 96–106.

95. Moses, *Wild West Shows*, 275; Mattern, "Powwow as a Public Arena," 191; Powers, *War Dance*, 167; Mattern, "Powwow as a Public Arena," 192. On the connection between Buffalo Bill's Wild West and the powwow, see also C. Ellis, *Dancing People*, 79–101; and Whitehorse, *Pow-Wow*, 4–12.

96. Cody's brief film career is discussed by Kasson, *Buffalo Bill's Wild West*, 255–63; Moses, *Wild West Shows*, 229–48; and Warren, *Buffalo Bill's America*, 537–40. For a study of the backbreaking production and disappointing reception of *The Indian Wars*, see Paul, "Buffalo Bill and Wounded Knee."

97. Hittman, *Wovoka and the Ghost Dance*, 131; Hart, introduction to *My People the Sioux*, xiii, xiv.

98. Cody, *Life*, 327; Kasson, *Buffalo Bill's Wild West*, 265.

*Conclusion*

1. V. Deloria, *World We Used to Live In*, xvii; Rose, "Great Pretenders," 407; Silko, "Old-Time Indian Attack," 211; Churchill, *Indians Are Us?* 228. On the contemporary selling of Indian spirituality, see also Churchill, "Spiritual Hucksterism"; and Whitt, "Cultural Imperialism." On modern white Indian play generally, see Huhndorf, *Going Native*. For a statement of how deeply offensive contemporary Native peoples consider white medicine play, and a manifesto to combat its spread, see the "Declaration of War against Exploiters of Lakota Spirituality" (1993), in Churchill, *Indians Are Us?* 273–77.

2. D. Jones, "Maligning the Magic," C1.

3. Churchill claims Cherokee ancestry but is not an enrolled member of the tribe, a revelation that emerged during the backlash against his controversial essay that ultimately cost him his tenured professorship.

4. Slagle, quoted in Lincoln with Slagle, *Good Red Road*, 225; V. Deloria, *World We Used to Live In*, 214.

# Bibliography

Abrahams, Roger D. *Singing the Master: The Emergence of African American Culture in the Plantation South*. New York: Pantheon, 1992.

———. "White Indians in Penn's City: The Loyal Sons of Saint Tammany." In *Riot and Revelry in Early America*, ed. William Pencak, Matthew Dennis, and Simon P. Newman, 179–204. University Park: Pennsylvania State University Press, 2002.

Adair, James. *Adair's History of the American Indians*. Ed. Samuel Cole Williams. Johnson City, Tenn.: Watauga, 1930.

Adams, David Wallace. *Education for Extinction: American Indians and the Boarding School Experience, 1875–1928*. Lawrence: University of Kansas Press, 1995.

Albanese, Catherine L. "Exploring Regional Religion: A Case Study of the Eastern Cherokee." *History of Religions* 23.4 (May 1984): 344–71.

———. *Nature Religion in America: From the Algonkian Indians to the New Age*. Chicago: University of Chicago Press, 1990.

Alger, William Rounseville. *Life of Edwin Forrest, the American Tragedian*. 2 vols. Philadelphia: J. B. Lippincott, 1877.

Allen, Chadwick. *Blood Narrative: Indigenous Identity in American Indian and Maori Literary and Activist Texts*. Durham, N.C.: Duke University Press, 2002.

Allen, Paula Gunn. "The Sacred Hoop: A Contemporary Perspective." In *Studies in American Indian Literature: Critical Essays and Course Designs*, ed. Paula Gunn Allen, 3–22. New York: Modern Language Association, 1983.

———. *The Sacred Hoop: Recovering the Feminine in American Indian Traditions*. Boston: Beacon, 1992.

Amacher, Richard E. "Behind the Curtain with the Management of Indian Plays, 1825–1860." *Theatre Survey* 7 (1966): 101–14.

Anderson, Marilyn J. "The Image of the Indian in American Drama during the Jacksonian Era, 1829–1845." *Journal of American Culture* 1 (1978): 800–810.

Anderson, Rufus. *Memoir of Catharine Brown, a Christian Indian, of the Cherokee Nation*. 1824. 2nd ed. Boston: Crocker and Brewster, 1825. Reprint, Signal Mountain, Tenn.: Mountain Press, n.d.

Apess, William. *The Increase of the Kingdom of Christ: A Sermon*. In *On Our Own Ground: The Complete Writings of William Apess, a Pequot*, ed. Barry O'Connell, 99–112. Amherst: University of Massachusetts Press, 1992.

———. *A Son of the Forest*. In *On Our Own Ground*, 1–97.

Armstrong, Virginia Irving, ed. *I Have Spoken: American History through the Voices of the Indians*. Chicago: Swallow, 1971.

Arnold, Philip P. "Black Elk and Book Culture." *Journal of the American Academy of Religion* 67.1 (March 1999): 85–111.

Axtell, James. "Some Thoughts on the Ethnohistory of Missions." In *After Columbus: Essays in the Ethnohistory of Colonial North America*, 47–57. New York: Oxford University Press, 1988.

———. "The White Indians of Colonial America." *William and Mary Quarterly* 32 (1975): 55–88.

Bailey, Paul. *Ghost Dance Messiah*. Los Angeles: Westernlore, 1970.

Baillou, Clemens de. "A Contribution to the Mythology and Conceptual World of the Cherokee Indians." *Ethnohistory* 8 (1961): 93–102.

Bank, Rosemarie K. "Staging the 'Native': Making History in American Theatre Culture, 1828–1838." *Theatre Journal* 45 (1993): 461–86.

———. *Theatre Culture in America, 1825–1860*. Cambridge: Cambridge University Press, 1997.

Barney, Garold D. *Mormons, Indians and the Ghost Dance Religion of 1890*. Lanham, Md.: University Press of America, 1986.

Barringer, Tim. "The Course of Empires: Landscape and Identity in America and Britain, 1820–1880." In *The American Sublime: Landscape Painting in the United States, 1820–1880*, by Andrew Wilton and Tim Barringer, 39–65. Princeton, N.J.: Princeton University Press, 2002.

Barton, Benjamin Smith. *Collections for an Essay towards a Materia Medica of the United States*. Philadelphia: Way and Groff, 1798–1804.

Bartram, William. "Observations on the Creek and Cherokee Indians." Ed. E. G. Squier. *Transactions of the American Ethnological Society* 3.1 (1853): 3–81.

Bataille, Gretchen M. *Native American Women: A Biographical Dictionary*. New York: Garland, 1993.

Bauman, Richard. *Verbal Art as Performance*. Rowley, Mass.: Newbury, 1977.

Beckwith, Martha Warren. *Mandan-Hidatsa Myths and Ceremonies*. New York: American Folk-Lore Society, 1937.

Beecher, Catharine. *An Essay on Slavery and Abolitionism, with Reference to the Duty of American Females*. Philadelphia: Henry Perkins, 1837.

———. *A Treatise on Domestic Economy. For the Use of Young Ladies at Home and at School*. Rev. ed. New York: Harper, 1855.

[Beecher, Catharine]. "Circular Addressed to Benevolent Ladies of the U. States." *Christian Advocate and Journal and Zion's Herald*, 25 December 1829, 65–66.

Bellin, Joshua David. "The Savage Tour: Indian Performance across the Atlantic." In *The Indian Atlantic: Native Americans and Anglo-American Culture, 1755–1850*, ed. Tim Fulford and Kevin Hutchings. Forthcoming.

———. "Taking the Indian Cure: Thoreau, Indian Medicine, and the Performance of American Culture." *New England Quarterly* 79 (2006): 3–36.

Bender, Margaret. "Framing the Anomalous: Stoneclad, Sequoyah, and Cherokee Ethnoliteracy." In *New Perspectives on Native North America: Cultures, Histories, and Representations*, ed. Sergei A. Kan and Pauline Turner Strong, 42–62. Lincoln: University of Nebraska Press, 2006.

Benes, Peter. "Itinerant Physicians, Healers, and Surgeon-Dentists in New England and New York, 1720–1825." In *Medicine and Healing*, ed. Peter Benes, 95–112. Dublin Seminar for New England Folklife Annual Proceedings, 1990. Boston: Boston University Press, 1992.

Berkhofer, Robert F., Jr. *The White Man's Indian: Images of the American Indian from Columbus to the Present.* New York: Vintage, 1978.

Bhabha, Homi K. "Of Mimicry and Man: The Ambivalence of Colonial Discourse." In *The Location of Culture*, 85–92. London: Routledge, 1994.

Bickham, Troy. "'A Conviction of the Reality of Things': Material Culture, North American Indians and Empire in Eighteenth-Century Britain." *Eighteenth-Century Studies* 39.1 (Fall 2005): 29–47.

———. *Savages within the Empire: Representations of American Indians in Eighteenth-Century Britain.* Oxford: Oxford University Press, 2005.

Bieder, Robert E. *Science Encounters the Indian, 1820–1880: The Early Years of American Ethnology.* Norman: University of Oklahoma Press, 1986.

Blau, Herbert. "Universals of Performance; Or, Amortizing Play." In *By Means of Performance: Intercultural Studies of Theatre and Ritual*, ed. Richard Schechner and Willa Appel, 250–72. Cambridge: Cambridge University Press, 1990.

Bohaker, Heidi. "*Nindoodemag*: The Significance of Algonquian Kinship Networks in the Eastern Great Lakes Region, 1600–1701." *William and Mary Quarterly* 63 (2006): 23–52.

Boime, Albert. *The Magisterial Gaze: Manifest Destiny and American Landscape Painting c. 1830–1865.* Washington, D.C.: Smithsonian, 1991.

Boone, Elizabeth Hill, and Walter D. Mignolo, eds. *Writing without Words: Alternative Literacies in Mesoamerica and the Andes.* Durham, N.C.: Duke University Press, 1994.

Boudinot, Elias. "An Address to the Whites Delivered in the First Presbyterian Church, on the 26th of May, 1826." In *Cherokee Editor: The Writings of Elias Boudinot*, ed. Theda Perdue, 67–83. Knoxville: University of Tennessee Press, 1983.

———. Editorial of 12 November 1831 in *Cherokee Phoenix.* In *Cherokee Editor*, 140–43.

Bowers, Alfred W. *Mandan Social and Ceremonial Organization.* Chicago: University of Chicago Press, 1950.

Brightman, Robert. "Toward a History of Indian Religion: Religious Changes in Native Societies." In *New Directions in American Indian History*, ed. Colin G. Calloway, 223–49. Norman: University of Oklahoma Press, 1988.

Brooks, Joanna. *American Lazarus: Religion and the Rise of African-American and Native American Literatures.* New York: Oxford University Press, 2003.

Bross, Kristina. *Dry Bones and Indian Sermons: Praying Indians in Colonial America.* Ithaca, N.Y.: Cornell University Press, 2004.

Browder, Laura. *Slippery Characters: Ethnic Impersonators and American Identities.* Chapel Hill: University of North Carolina Press, 2000.

Brown, Catharine. "Letter from Catharine Brown to her brother, David Brown, at the For. Mis. School, at Cornwall, dated Creek-Path, Feb. 21." *Missionary Herald* 17.8 (August 1821): 258–59.

Brown, Dee. *Bury My Heart at Wounded Knee: An Indian History of the American West.* New York: Holt, 1970.

Brown, Gillian. *Domestic Individualism: Imagining Self in Nineteenth-Century America.* Berkeley: University of California Press, 1990.

Brown, Harry J. *Injun Joe's Ghost: The Indian Mixed-Blood in American Writing.* Columbia: University of Missouri Press, 2004.

Brown, Joseph Epes. *The Sacred Pipe: Black Elk's Account of the Seven Rites of the Oglala Sioux.* Norman: University of Oklahoma Press, 1953.

Brown, Michael F. *Who Owns Native Culture?* Cambridge, Mass.: Harvard University Press, 2003.

Brumble, H. David, III. *American Indian Autobiography.* Berkeley: University of California Press, 1988.

————. "Indian Sacred Materials: Kroeber, Kroeber, Waters, and Momaday." In *Smoothing the Ground: Essays on Native American Oral Literature*, ed. Brian Swann, 283–300. Berkeley: University of California Press, 1983.

Burkhart, Louise M. "The Amanuenses Have Appropriated the Text: Interpreting a Nahuatl Song of Santiago." In *On the Translation of Native American Literatures*, ed. Brian Swann, 339–55. Washington, D.C.: Smithsonian, 1992.

Burnham, Michelle. *Captivity and Sentiment: Cultural Exchange in American Literature, 1682–1861.* Hanover, N.H.: University Press of New England, 1997.

Butler, Judith. *Gender Trouble: Feminism and the Subversion of Identity.* New York: Routledge, 1990.

Calloway, Colin G. *New Worlds for All: Indians, Europeans, and the Remaking of Early America.* Baltimore: Johns Hopkins University Press, 1997.

Cantwell, Robert. *Ethnomimesis: Folklife and the Representation of Culture.* Chapel Hill: University of North Carolina Press, 1993.

Carlson, David J. *Sovereign Selves: American Indian Autobiography and the Law.* Urbana: University of Illinois Press, 2006.

Carney, Virginia Moore. *Eastern Band Cherokee Women: Cultural Persistence in Their Letters and Speeches.* Knoxville: University of Tennessee Press, 2005.

————. "'Woman Is the Mother of All': Nanye'hi and Kitteuha: War Women of the Cherokees." In *Native American Speakers of the Eastern Woodlands: Selected Speeches and Critical Analyses*, ed. Barbara Alice Mann, 123–43. Westport, Conn.: Greenwood, 2001.

Cass, Lewis. "Indians of North America." *North American Review* 22 (1826): 53–119.

————. "Removal of the Indians." *North American Review* 30 (1830): 62–121.

Castillo, Susan. *Colonial Encounters in New World Writing, 1500–1786: Performing America.* London: Routledge, 2006.

Catlin, George. *The Adventures of the Ojibbeway and Ioway Indians in England, France, and Belgium; Being Notes of Eight Years' Travels and Residence in Europe with His North American Indian Collection.* 2 vols. 3rd ed. 1852. Reprint, Scituate, Mass.: Digital Scanning, 2001.

————. *Breath of Life or Mal-Respiration. And Its Effects upon the Enjoyments & Life of Man.* New York: John Wiley, 1872.

———. *Letters and Notes on the Manners, Customs, and Conditions of the North American Indians.* 2 vols. 1841. Reprint, New York: Dover, 1973.

———. *O-Kee-Pa: A Religious Ceremony and Other Customs of the Mandans.* Ed. John C. Ewers. New Haven, Conn.: Yale University Press, 1967.

Cave, Alfred A. "Indian Shamans and English Witches in Seventeenth-Century New England." *Essex Institute Historical Collections* 128 (1992): 239–54.

———. *Prophets of the Great Spirit: Native American Revitalization Movements in Eastern North America.* Lincoln: University of Nebraska Press, 2006.

Cawelti, John G. "The Frontier and the Native American." In *America as Art*, by Joshua C. Taylor, 133–83. New York: Harper and Row, 1976.

[Cheever, George B.] *The Removal of the Indians. An Article from the American Monthly Magazine: An Examination of the Advancement of the Southern Tribes, in Civilization and Christianity.* Boston: Peirce and Williams, 1830.

Cheyfitz, Eric. *The Poetics of Imperialism: Translation and Colonization from "The Tempest" to "Tarzan."* New York: Oxford University Press, 1991.

———. "The (Post)Colonial Construction of Indian Country: U.S. American Indian Literatures and Federal Indian Law." In *The Columbia Guide to American Indian Literatures of the United States Since 1945*, ed. Eric Cheyfitz, 3–124. New York: Columbia University Press, 2006.

Churchill, Ward. "Generations of Resistance: American Indian Poetry and the Ghost Dance Spirit." In *Coyote Was Here: Essays on Contemporary Native American Literary and Political Mobilization*, ed. Bo Schöler, 161–79. Aarhus, Denmark: SEK-LOS, 1984.

———. *Indians Are Us? Culture and Genocide in Native North America.* Monroe, Maine: Common Courage, 1994.

———. "Spiritual Hucksterism: The Rise of the Plastic Medicine Men." In his *Fantasies of the Master Race: Literature, Cinema and the Colonization of the American Indians*, ed. M. Annette Jaimes, 215–28. Monroe, Maine: Common Courage, 1992.

Clark, Susan F. "The Menace of the Wild West Shows." In *The Cultures of Celebrations*, ed. Ray B. Browne and Michael T. Marsden, 145–55. Bowling Green, Ohio: Bowling Green State University Popular Press, 1994.

Clifford, James. "On Ethnographic Allegory." In *Writing Culture: The Poetics and Politics of Ethnography*, ed. James Clifford and George E. Marcus, 98–121. Berkeley: University of California Press, 1986.

———. *The Predicament of Culture: Twentieth-Century Ethnography, Literature, and Art.* Cambridge, Mass.: Harvard University Press, 1988.

Clifton, James, ed. *Being and Becoming Indian: Biographical Studies of North American Frontiers.* Prospect Heights, Ill.: Waveland, 1993.

———. *The Invented Indian: Cultural Fictions and Government Policies.* New Brunswick, N.J.: Transaction, 1990.

Clow, Richmond L. "The Lakota Ghost Dance after 1890." *South Dakota History* 20 (1990): 323–33.

Cody, William F. *The Life of Hon. William F. Cody, Known as Buffalo Bill, the Famous Hunter, Scout and Guide.* Hartford: Frank E. Bliss, 1879. Reprint, Lincoln: University of Nebraska Press, 1978.

————. *True Tales of the Plains.* New York: Cupples and Leon, 1908.

Cohen, Kenneth. "A Mutually Comprehensible World? Native Americans, Europeans, and Play in Eighteenth-Century America." *American Indian Quarterly* 26 (2002): 67–93.

Coleman, Michael C. "American Indian School Pupils as Cultural Brokers: Cherokee Girls at Brainerd Mission, 1828–1829." In *Between Indian and White Worlds: The Cultural Broker*, ed. Margaret Connell Szasz, 122–35. Norman: University of Oklahoma Press, 1994.

Cooper, James Fenimore. *The Last of the Mohicans.* New York: Penguin, 1986.

Couser, G. Thomas. "*Black Elk Speaks* with Forked Tongue." In *Studies in Autobiography*, ed. James Olney, 73–88. New York: Oxford University Press, 1988.

Crapanzano, Vincent. "Hermes' Dilemma: The Masking of Subversion in Ethnographic Description." In *Writing Culture: The Poetics and Politics of Ethnography*, ed. James Clifford and George E. Marcus, 51–76. Berkeley: University of California Press, 1986.

Dangberg, Grace M., ed. "Letters to Jack Wilson, the Paiute Prophet, Written between 1908 and 1911." In *Bureau of American Ethnology, Bull.* 164, 279–96. Washington, D.C.: Bureau of American Ethnology, 1957.

Dannenberg, Anne Marie. "'Where, Then, Shall We Place the Hero of the Wilderness?': William Apess's *Eulogy on King Philip* and Discourses of Racial Destiny." In *Early Native American Writing: New Critical Essays*, ed. Helen Jaskoski, 66–82. Cambridge: Cambridge University Press, 1996.

Davis, Ann, and Robert Thacker. "Pictures and Prose: Romantic Sensibility and the Great Plains in Catlin, Kane, and Miller." *Great Plains Quarterly* 6 (Winter 1986): 3–20.

Deloria, Philip J. *Playing Indian.* New Haven, Conn.: Yale University Press, 1998.

Deloria, Vine, Jr. *Custer Died for Your Sins: An Indian Manifesto.* Norman: University of Oklahoma Press, 1988.

————. *God Is Red.* New York: Grossett and Dunlap, 1973.

————. "The Indians." In *Buffalo Bill and the Wild West*, 45–56. Pittsburgh, Pa.: University of Pittsburgh Press, 1981.

————. Introduction to *Black Elk Speaks: Being the Life Story of a Holy Man of the Oglala Sioux*, as told through John G. Neihardt, xi–xiv. 1932. Reprint, Lincoln: University of Nebraska Press, 1979.

————. *We Talk, You Listen: New Tribes, New Turf.* New York: Macmillan, 1970.

————. *The World We Used to Live In: Remembering the Powers of the Medicine Men.* Golden, Colo.: Fulcrum, 2006.

DeMallie, Raymond J. "Lakota Belief and Ritual in the Nineteenth Century." In *Sioux Indian Religion: Tradition and Innovation*, ed. Raymond J. DeMallie and Douglas R. Parks, 25–43. Norman: University of Oklahoma Press, 1987.

————. "The Lakota Ghost Dance: An Ethnohistorical Account." *Pacific Historical Review* 51 (1982): 385–405.

————, ed. *The Sixth Grandfather: Black Elk's Teachings Given to John G. Neihardt.* Lincoln: University of Nebraska Press, 1984.

Densmore, Frances. *Mandan and Hidatsa Music.* Smithsonian Institution Bureau of American Ethnology, Bull. 80. Washington, D.C.: U.S. Government Printing Office, 1923.

Denson, Andrew. *Demanding the Cherokee Nation: Indian Autonomy and American Culture, 1830–1900.* Lincoln: University of Nebraska Press, 2004.

Desbarats, Catherine. "Following *The Middle Ground.*" *William and Mary Quarterly* 63 (2006): 81–96.

Devens, Carol. *Countering Colonization: Native American Women and Great Lakes Missions, 1630–1900.* Berkeley: University of California Press, 1992.

Diamond, Elin. "Introduction." In *Performance and Cultural Politics*, ed. Elin Diamond, 1–12. London: Routledge, 1996.

Dickens, Charles. "The Noble Savage." *Household Words* 7 (1853): 337–39.

Dickinson, Greg, Brian L. Ott, and Eric Aoki. "Memory and Myth at the Buffalo Bill Museum." *Western Journal of Communication* 69.2 (April 2005): 85–108.

Dippie, Brian W. *Catlin and His Contemporaries: The Politics of Patronage.* Lincoln: University of Nebraska Press, 1990.

———. *The Vanishing American: White Attitudes and U.S. Indian Policy.* Middletown, Conn.: Wesleyan University Press, 1982.

Doolen, Andy. *Fugitive Empire: Locating Early American Imperialism.* Minneapolis: University of Minnesota Press, 2005.

Douglas, Ann. *The Feminization of American Culture.* New York: Anchor, 1977.

Dowd, Gregory Evans. "Spinning Wheel Revolution." In *The Revolution of 1800: Democracy, Race, and the New Republic*, ed. James Horn, Jan Ellen Lewis, and Peter S. Onuf, 267–87. Charlottesville: University of Virginia Press, 2002.

———. *A Spirited Resistance: The North American Indian Struggle for Unity, 1745–1815.* Baltimore: Johns Hopkins University Press, 1992.

Drinnon, Richard. *Facing West: The Metaphysics of Indian-Hating and Empire-Building.* New York: Schocken, 1990.

Drummond, A. M., and Richard Moody. "Indian Treaties: The First American Dramas." *Quarterly Journal of Speech* 39 (1953): 15–24.

Dunaway, Wilma. "Rethinking Cherokee Acculturation: Agrarian Capitalism and Women's Resistance to the Cult of Domesticity, 1800–1838." *American Indian Culture and Research Journal* 21.1 (1997): 155–92.

Dundes, Alan. "Texture, Text, and Context." *Southern Folklore Quarterly* 28 (1964): 251–65.

Dunlap, William. "Mr. Catlin's Lectures." *New-York Mirror* 15 (14 October 1837): 126.

Edwards, Jonathan. *The Life of David Brainerd.* Ed. Norman Pettit. Vol. 7 of *The Works of Jonathan Edwards.* New Haven, Conn.: Yale University Press, 1985.

Elliott, Michael. "Ethnography, Reform, and the Problem of the Real: James Mooney's *Ghost-Dance Religion.*" *American Quarterly* 50 (1998): 201–33.

Ellis, Clyde. *A Dancing People: Powwow Culture on the Southern Plains.* Lawrence: University Press of Kansas, 2003.

———. "'We Had a Lot of Fun, But of Course, That Wasn't the School Part': Life at the Rainy Mountain Boarding School, 1893–1920." In *Boarding School Blues: Re-*

*visiting American Indian Educational Experiences*, ed. Clifford E. Trafzer, Jean A. Keller, and Lorene Sisquoc, 65–98. Lincoln: University of Nebraska Press, 2006.

Ellis, Richard N. Introduction to *My People the Sioux*, by Luther Standing Bear, ix–xx. Ed. E. A. Brininstool. 1928. Reprint, Lincoln: University of Nebraska Press, 1975.

———. "Luther Standing Bear: 'I Would Raise Him to Be an Indian.'" In *Indian Lives: Essays on Nineteenth- and Twentieth-Century Native American Leaders*, ed. L. G. Moses and Raymond Wilson, 139–58. Albuquerque: University of New Mexico Press, 1985.

Evans, E. Raymond, ed. "Jedidiah Morse's Report to the Secretary of War on Cherokee Indian Affairs in 1822." *Journal of Cherokee Studies* 6.2 (Fall 1981): 60–78.

Evans, J. P. "Sketches of Cherokee Characteristics." *Journal of Cherokee Studies* 4.1 (1979): 10–20.

Evarts, Jeremiah. "Address of the Cherokees." In *Cherokee Removal: The "William Penn" Essays and Other Writings*, ed. Francis Paul Prucha, 254–62. Knoxville: University of Tennessee Press, 1981.

———. *Essays on the Present Crisis in the Condition of the Indians*. In *Cherokee Removal*, 43–199.

Ewers, John C. "The Emergence of the Plains Indian as the Symbol of the North American Indian." In *Smithsonian Institution Annual Report for 1964*, 531–44. Washington, D.C.: Smithsonian Institution, 1965.

———. "Fact and Fiction in the Documentary Art of the American West." In *The Frontier Re-examined*, ed. John Francis McDermott, 79–95. Urbana: University of Illinois Press, 1967.

———. "The White Man's Strongest Medicine." *Bulletin of the Missouri Historical Society* 24 (October 1967): 36–46.

———. "William Clark's Indian Museum in St. Louis 1816–1838." In *A Cabinet of Curiosities: Five Episodes in the Evolution of American Museums*, ed. Walter Muir Whitehill, 49–72. Charlottesville: University Press of Virginia, 1967.

Fairchild, Sharon L. "George Sand and George Catlin—Masking Indian Realities." *Nineteenth-Century French Studies* 22 (1994): 439–49.

Fenton, William N. Introduction to *League of the Ho-De'-No-Sau-Nee, Iroquois*, by Lewis Henry Morgan, v–xviii. Rochester: Sage, 1851. Reprint, Secaucus, N.J.: Citadel, 1962.

Fletcher, Alice C. *Indian Games and Dances with Native Songs*. 1915. Reprint, Lincoln: University of Nebraska Press, 1994.

———. "The Indian Messiah." *Journal of American Folk-Lore* 4.12 (January–March 1891): 57–60.

Fliegelman, Jay. *Declaring Independence: Jefferson, Natural Language, and the Culture of Performance*. Stanford, Calif.: Stanford University Press, 1993.

Flynn, Joyce. "Academics on the Trail of the Stage 'Indian': A Review Essay." *Studies in American Indian Literatures* 11.1 (Winter 1987): 1–16.

Fogelson, Raymond D. "The Conjuror in Eastern Cherokee Society." *Journal of Cherokee Studies* 5.2 (Fall 1980): 60–87.

———. "On the 'Petticoat Government' of the Eighteenth-Century Cherokee." In *Personality and the Cultural Construction of Self: Papers in Honor of Melford E.*

*Spiro*, ed. David K. Jordan and Marc J. Swartz, 161–81. Tuscaloosa: University of Alabama Press, 1990.

Forbes, Bruce David. "Which Religion Is Right? Five Answers in the Historical Encounter between Christianity and Traditional Native American Spiritualities." *Neihardt Journal* 2 (2000): 18–26.

Ford, Ramona. "Native American Women: Changing Statuses, Changing Interpretations." In *Writing the Range: Race, Class, and Culture in the Women's West*, ed. Elizabeth Jameson and Susan Armitage, 42–68. Norman: University of Oklahoma Press, 1997.

Freeman, John F. "The Indian Convert: Theme and Variation." *Ethnohistory* 12.2 (Spring 1965): 113–28.

Garroutte, Eva Marie. *Real Indians: Identity and the Survival of Native America.* Berkeley: University of California Press, 2003.

Gates, Merrill E. "Addresses to the Lake Mohonk Conferences." In *Americanizing the American Indians: Writings by the "Friends of the Indian," 1880–1900*, ed. Francis Paul Prucha, 331–44. Cambridge, Mass.: Harvard University Press, 1973.

Gaul, Theresa Strouth. "Dialogue and Public Discourse in William Apess's *Indian Nullification.*" *ATQ*, n.s. 15.4 (December 2001): 275–92.

———. "'The Genuine Indian Who Was Brought Upon the Stage': Edwin Forrest's *Metamora* and White Audiences." *Arizona Quarterly* 56.1 (Spring 2000): 1–27.

———. "Introduction." In *To Marry an Indian: The Marriage of Harriett Gold and Elias Boudinot in Letters, 1823–1839*, ed. Theresa Strouth Gaul, 1–76. Chapel Hill: University of North Carolina Press, 2005.

Gerdts, William H. "The Marble Savage." *Art in America* 62 (July–August 1974): 64–70.

Gilmore, Paul. "The Indian in the Museum: Henry David Thoreau, Okah Tubbee, and Authentic Manhood." *Arizona Quarterly* 54.2 (Summer 1998): 25–63.

Goetzmann, William H., and William N. Goetzmann. *The West of the Imagination.* New York: Norton, 1986.

Goodwin, Gary C. *Cherokees in Transition: A Study of Changing Culture and Environment Prior to 1775.* University of Chicago Department of Geography, Research Paper No. 181. Chicago: University of Chicago Press, 1977.

Green, Rayna. "The Pocahontas Perplex: The Image of Indian Women in American Culture." *Massachusetts Review* 16 (1975): 698–714.

———. "The Tribe Called Wannabee: Playing Indian in America and Europe." *Folklore* 99 (1988): 30–55.

Griffiths, Nicholas. "Introduction." In *Spiritual Encounters: Interactions between Christianity and Native Religions in Colonial America*, ed. Nicholas Griffiths and Fernando Cervantes, 1–42. Lincoln: University of Nebraska Press, 1999.

Grinnell, George Bird. "Account of the Northern Cheyennes Concerning the Messiah Superstition." *Journal of American Folk-Lore* 4.12 (January–March 1891): 61–69.

Grose, B. Donald. "Edwin Forrest, *Metamora*, and the Indian Removal Act of 1830." *Theatre Journal* 37 (1985): 181–91.

Guerrero, M. Annette Jaimes. "Academic Apartheid: American Indian Studies and 'Multiculturalism.'" In *Mapping Multiculturalism*, ed. Avery F. Gordon and Christopher Newfield, 49–63. Minneapolis: University of Minnesota Press, 1996.

Gurney, George, and Therese Thau Heyman, eds. *George Catlin and His Indian Gallery*. Washington, D.C.: Smithsonian American Art Museum, 2002.

Gussman, Deborah. "'O Savage, Where Art Thou?': Rhetorics of Reform in William Apess's *Eulogy on King Philip*." *New England Quarterly* 77 (2004): 451–77.

Gustafson, Sandra M. *Eloquence Is Power: Oratory and Performance in Early America*. Chapel Hill: University of North Carolina Press, 2000.

———. "Nations of Israelites: Prophecy and Cultural Autonomy in the Writings of William Apess." *Religion and Literature* 26.1 (1994): 31–53.

Haberly, Lloyd. *Pursuit of the Horizon: A Life of George Catlin, Painter and Recorder of the American Indian*. New York: Macmillan, 1948.

Hale, Frederick. "Acceptance and Rejection of Assimilation in the Works of Luther Standing Bear." *Studies in American Indian Literatures* 5.4 (Winter 1993): 25–41.

Hall, James. "Mr. Catlin's Exhibition of Indian Portraits." *Western Monthly Magazine* 1 (November 1833): 535–38.

Hall, Roger A. *Performing the American Frontier, 1870–1906*. Cambridge: Cambridge University Press, 2001.

Hallock, Thomas. *From the Fallen Tree: Frontier Narratives, Environmental Politics, and the Roots of a National Pastoral, 1749–1826*. Chapel Hill: University of North Carolina Press, 2003.

Halpin, Marjorie. Introduction to *Letters and Notes on the Manners, Customs, and Conditions of the North American Indians*, by George Catlin, 1:vii–xiv. New York: Dover, 1973.

Halttunen, Karen. *Confidence Men and Painted Women: A Study of Middle-Class Culture in America, 1830–1870*. New Haven, Conn.: Yale University Press, 1982.

Hart, William S. Introduction to *My People the Sioux*, by Luther Standing Bear, xiii–xiv. Ed. E. A. Brininstool. Boston: Houghton Mifflin, 1928.

Hatley, Tom. *The Dividing Paths: Cherokees and South Carolinians through the Era of Revolution*. New York: Oxford University Press, 1993.

Haynes, Carolyn. "'A Mark for Them All to . . . Hiss At': The Formation of Methodist and Pequot Identity in the Conversion Narrative of William Apess." *Early American Literature* 31.1 (1996): 25–44.

Heflin, Ruth J. *"I Remain Alive": The Sioux Literary Renaissance*. Syracuse, N.Y.: Syracuse University Press, 2000.

Hendry, Joy. *Reclaiming Culture: Indigenous People and Self-Representation*. New York: Palgrave Macmillan, 2005.

Herman, Daniel J. "Romance on the Middle Ground." *Journal of the Early Republic* 19 (1999): 279–91.

Hershberger, Mary. "Mobilizing Women, Anticipating Abolition: The Struggle against Indian Removal in the 1830s." *Journal of American History* 86 (1999): 15–40.

Hertzberg, Hazel W. *The Search for an American Indian Identity: Modern Pan-Indian Movements*. Syracuse, N.Y.: Syracuse University Press, 1971.

Hewitt, Bernard. *Theatre U.S.A., 1665 to 1957*. New York: McGraw-Hill, 1959.

Hewitt, Nancy A. "Beyond the Search for Sisterhood: American Women's History in the 1980s." *Social History* 10 (1985): 299–321.

Higginbotham, Mary Alves. "The Creek Path Mission." *Journal of Cherokee Studies* 1 (1976): 72–86.

Hight, Kathryn S. "'Doomed to Perish': George Catlin's Depictions of the Mandan." *Art Journal* 49 (1990): 119–24.

Hilbert, Robert. "Contemporary Catholic Mission Work among the Sioux." In *Sioux Indian Religion: Tradition and Innovation*, ed. Raymond J. DeMallie and Douglas R. Parks, 139–47. Norman: University of Oklahoma Press, 1987.

Hilden, Patricia Penn. "Race for Sale: Narratives of Possession in Two 'Ethnic' Museums." *TDR* 44.3 (Fall 2000): 11–36.

Hill, Sarah. *Weaving New Worlds: Southeastern Cherokee Women and Their Basketry.* Chapel Hill: University of North Carolina Press, 1997.

Hittman, Michael. *Wovoka and the Ghost Dance.* Expanded ed. Ed. Don Lynch. Lincoln: University of Nebraska Press, 1997.

Hochbruck, Wolfgang. "Cultural Authenticity and the Construction of Pan-Indian Metanarrative." In *Cultural Difference and the Literary Text: Pluralism and the Limits of Authenticity in North American Literatures*, ed. Winfried Siemerling and Katrin Schwenk, 18–28. Iowa City: University of Iowa Press, 1996.

Holler, Clyde. "Black Elk's Relationship to Christianity." *American Indian Quarterly* 8 (1984): 37–49.

Holloway, Brian. *Interpreting the Legacy: John Neihardt and "Black Elk Speaks."* Boulder: University Press of Colorado, 2003.

Holm, Bill. "Four Bears's Shirt: Some Problems with the Smithsonian Catlin Collection." In *Artifacts/Artifakes: The Proceedings of the 1984 Plains Indian Seminar*, 43–59. Cody, Wyo.: Buffalo Bill Historical Center, 1992.

Horsman, Reginald. *Race and Manifest Destiny: The Origins of American Racial Anglo-Saxonism.* Cambridge, Mass.: Harvard University Press, 1981.

Howard, Scott J. "Incommensurability and Nicholas Black Elk: An Exploration." *American Indian Culture and Research Journal* 23.1 (1999): 111–36.

Hoxie, Frederick E. *A Final Promise: The Campaign to Assimilate the Indians, 1880–1920.* Lincoln: University of Nebraska Press, 1984.

Hudson, Charles M., Jr. "Why the Southeastern Indians Slaughtered Deer." In *Indians, Animals, and the Fur Trade: A Critique of "Keepers of the Game,"* ed. Shepard Krech III, 155–76. Athens: University of Georgia Press, 1981.

Huffstetler, Edward. "Spirit Armies and Ghost Dances: The Dialogic Nature of American Indian Resistance." *Studies in American Indian Literatures* 14.4 (Winter 2002): 1–17.

Huhndorf, Shari M. *Going Native: Indians in the American Cultural Imagination.* Ithaca, N.Y.: Cornell University Press, 2001.

Hymes, Dell. "Breakthrough into Performance." In *Folklore: Performance and Communication*, ed. Dan Ben-Amos and Kenneth S. Goldstein, 11–74. Paris: Mouton, 1975.

Indian Rights Association. "Condemnation of Wild West Shows." In *Americanizing the American Indians: Writings by the "Friends of the Indian," 1880–1900*, ed. Francis Paul Prucha, 313–16. Cambridge, Mass.: Harvard University Press, 1973.

Ingersoll, Thomas N. *To Intermix with Our White Brothers: Indian Mixed Bloods in the United States from Earliest Times to the Indian Removals*. Albuquerque: University of New Mexico Press, 2005.

"Iowa Indians." *Illustrated London News*, 10 August 1844, 91.

Irving, Washington. "Traits of Indian Character." In *Sketch Book of Geoffrey Crayon, Gent.*, 225–33. New York: Penguin, 1988.

Irwin, Lee. *The Dream Seekers: Native American Visionary Traditions of the Great Plains*. Norman: University of Oklahoma Press, 1994.

———. "Freedom, Law, and Prophecy: A Brief History of Native American Religious Resistance." In *Native American Spirituality: A Critical Reader*, ed. Lee Irwin, 295–316. Lincoln: University of Nebraska Press, 2000.

Jefferson, Thomas. "Second Inaugural Address, March 8, 1805." In *A Compilation of the Messages and Papers of the Presidents*, ed. James D. Richardson, 1:366–70. New York: Bureau of National Literature, 1897.

Jennings, Francis. *The Invasion of America: Indians, Colonialism, and the Cant of Conquest*. New York: Norton, 1975.

Jensen, Marguerite. "The Mandan Tragedy." *Indian Historian* 5.3 (Fall 1972): 18–22.

John, Gareth E. "Benevolent Imperialism: George Catlin and the Practice of Jeffersonian Geography." *Journal of Historical Geography* 39 (2004): 597–617.

———. "Cultural Nationalism, Westward Expansion and the Production of Imperial Landscape: George Catlin's Native American West." *Ecumene* 8.2 (2001): 175–203.

Johnson, Kendall. "'Rising from the Stain on a Painter's Palette': George Catlin's Picturesque and the Legibility of Seminole Removal." *Nineteenth Century Prose* 29.2 (Fall 2002): 69–93.

Johnston, Carolyn Ross. *Cherokee Women in Crisis: Trail of Tears, Civil War, and Allotment, 1838–1907*. Tuscaloosa: University of Alabama Press, 2003.

Jones, Diana Nelson. "Maligning the Magic." *Pittsburgh Post-Gazette*, 13 June 1993, C1–C2.

Jones, Eugene H. *Native Americans as Shown on the Stage, 1753–1916*. Metuchen, N.J.: Scarecrow, 1988.

Justice, Daniel Heath. *Our Fire Survives the Storm: A Cherokee Literary History*. Minneapolis: University of Minnesota Press, 2006.

Kamrath, Mark L. "American Indian Oration and Discourses of the Republic in Eighteenth-Century American Periodicals." In *Periodical Literature in Eighteenth-Century America*, ed. Mark L. Kamrath and Sharon M. Harris, 143–78. Knoxville: University of Tennessee Press, 2005.

Kaplan, Amy. "Manifest Domesticity." *American Literature* 70 (1998): 581–606.

Kasson, Joy S. *Buffalo Bill's Wild West: Celebrity, Memory, and Popular History*. New York: Hill and Wang, 2000.

Kehoe, Alice Beck. *The Ghost Dance: Ethnohistory and Revitalization*. New York: Holt, Rinehart, & Winston, 1989.

Kenny, James. "Journal of James Kenny, 1761–1763." Ed. John W. Jordan. *Pennsylvania Magazine of History and Biography* 37 (1913): 1–47, 152–201.

Kerstetter, Todd. "Spin Doctors at Santee: Missionaries and the Dakota-Language Reporting of the Ghost Dance and Wounded Knee." *Western Historical Quarterly* 28 (Spring 1997): 45–67.

Kilcup, Karen L., ed. *Native American Women's Writing, 1800–1924: An Anthology.* Oxford: Blackwell, 2000.

King, C. Richard. *Colonial Discourses, Collective Memories, and the Exhibition of Native American Cultures and Histories in the Contemporary United States.* New York: Garland, 1998.

Kirkland, Samuel. *The Journals of Samuel Kirkland: Eighteenth-Century Missionary to the Iroquois, Government Agent, Father of Hamilton College.* Ed. Walter Pilkington. Clinton, N.Y.: Hamilton College, 1980.

Kirshenblatt-Gimblett, Barbara. "Objects of Ethnography." In *Exhibiting Cultures: The Poetics and Politics of Museum Display*, ed. Ivan Karp and Steven D. Lavine, 386–443. Washington, D.C.: Smithsonian, 1991.

Kohl, Johann Georg. *Kitchi-Gami: Life among the Lake Superior Ojibway.* Trans. Lascelles Wraxall. 1860. Reprint, St. Paul: Minnesota Historical Society, 1985.

Kolodny, Annette. "Fictions of American Prehistory: Indians, Archeology, and National Origin Myths." *American Literature* 75 (2003): 693–721.

Kosmider, Alexia. "Refracting the Imperial Gaze onto the Colonizers: Geronimo Poses for the Empire." *ATQ*, n.s. 15.4 (December 2001): 317–31.

Krupat, Arnold. *Ethnocriticism: Ethnography, History, Literature.* Berkeley: University of California Press, 1992.

———. *For Those Who Come After: A Study of Native American Autobiography.* Berkeley: University of California Press, 1985.

———, ed. *Native American Autobiography: An Anthology.* Madison: University of Wisconsin Press, 1994.

———. *The Voice in the Margin: Native American Literature and the Canon.* Berkeley: University of California Press, 1989.

Kucich, John J. *Ghostly Communion: Cross-Cultural Spiritualism in Nineteenth-Century American Literature.* Hanover, N.H.: University Press of New England, 2004.

Laubin, Reginald, and Gladys Laubin. *Indian Dances of North America: Their Importance to Indian Life.* Norman: University of Oklahoma Press, 1977.

Leacock, Eleanor. "Interpreting the Origins of Gender Inequality: Conceptual and Historical Problems." *Dialectical Anthropology* 7 (1983): 263–84.

Lears, Jackson. *Fables of Abundance: A Cultural History of Advertising in America.* New York: Basic, 1994.

Lemons, William E. "History by Unreliable Narrators: Sitting Bull's Circus Horse." *Montana: The Magazine of Western History* 2 (1995): 64–74.

Lepore, Jill. *The Name of War: King Philip's War and the Origins of American Identity.* New York: Vintage, 1998.

Lesser, Alexander. "Cultural Significance of the Ghost Dance." *American Anthropologist* 35 (1933): 108–15.

Lévi-Strauss, Claude. *The Savage Mind.* Trans. George Weidenfeld. Chicago: University of Chicago Press, 1966.

Lewis, Thomas H. *The Medicine Men: Oglala Sioux Ceremony and Healing.* Lincoln: University of Nebraska Press, 1990.

Lincoln, Kenneth, with Al Logan Slagle. *The Good Red Road: Passages into Native America.* San Francisco: Harper and Row, 1987.

Linnekin, Jocelyn. "Cultural Invention and the Dilemma of Authenticity." *American Anthropologist,* n.s. 93 (1991): 446–49.

Littlefield, Daniel F., Jr. "American Indians, American Scholars and the American Literary Canon." *American Studies* 33 (Fall 1992): 95–111.

Logan, Brad. "The Ghost Dance among the Paiute: An Ethnohistorical View of the Documentary Evidence, 1889–1893." *Ethnohistory* 27.3 (Summer 1980): 267–88.

Lomawaima, K. Tsianina. "Domesticity in the Federal Indian Schools: The Power of Authority over Mind and Body." *American Ethnologist* 20 (1993): 227–40.

Long, Alexander. "A Small Postscript of the Ways and Maners of the Indians Called Charikees." Ed. David H. Corkran. *Southern Indian Studies* 21 (1969): 3–49.

Lott, Eric. *Love and Theft: Blackface Minstrelsy and the American Working Class.* New York: Oxford University Press, 1993.

Lubbers, Klaus. *Born for the Shade: Stereotypes of the Native American in United States Literature and the Visual Arts, 1776–1894.* Amsterdam: Rodopi, 1994.

Luke, Timothy W. *Shows of Force: Power, Politics, and Ideology in Art Exhibitions.* Durham, N.C.: Duke University Press, 1992.

Lyman, Christopher M. *The Vanishing Race and Other Illusions: Photographs of Indians by Edward S. Curtis.* New York: Pantheon, 1982.

Maddox, Lucy. *Citizen Indians: Native American Intellectuals, Race, and Reform.* Ithaca, N.Y.: Cornell University Press, 2005.

———. *Removals: Nineteenth-Century American Literature and the Politics of Indian Affairs.* New York: Oxford University Press, 1991.

Maddra, Sam A. *Hostiles? The Lakota Ghost Dance and Buffalo Bill's Wild West.* Norman: University of Oklahoma Press, 2006.

Mails, Thomas E., assisted by Dallas Chief Eagle. *Fools Crow.* Lincoln: University of Nebraska Press, 1990.

Mallery, Garrick. *Picture-Writing of the American Indians.* Tenth Annual Report of the Bureau of Ethnology. 1893. Reprint, New York: Dover, 1972.

Malmsheimer, Lonna M. "'Imitation White Man': Images of Transformation at the Carlisle Indian School." *Studies in Visual Communication* 11.4 (Fall 1985): 54–75.

Mandell, Daniel R. "'We, As a Tribe, Will Rule Ourselves': Mashpee's Struggle for Autonomy, 1746–1840." In *Reinterpreting New England Indians and the Colonial Experience,* ed. Colin G. Calloway and Neal Salisbury, 299–340. Boston: Colonial Society of Massachusetts, 2003.

Mann, Henrietta. "Earth Mother and Prayerful Children: Sacred Sites and Religious Freedom." In *Native Voices: American Indian Identity and Resistance,* ed. Richard A. Grounds, George E. Tinker, and David E. Wilkins, 194–208. Lawrence: University Press of Kansas, 2003.

Marienstras, Elise. "The Common Man's Indian: The Image of the Indian as a Promoter of National Identity in the Early National Era." In *Native Americans and the Early Republic*, ed. Frederick E. Hoxie, Ronald Hoffman, and Peter J. Albert, 261–96. Charlottesville: University Press of Virginia, 1999.

Markowitz, Harvey. "The Catholic Mission and the Sioux: A Crisis in the Early Paradigm." In *Sioux Indian Religion: Tradition and Innovation*, ed. Raymond J. DeMallie and Douglas R. Parks, 113–37. Norman: University of Oklahoma Press, 1987.

Marshall, John. *The Cherokee Nation v. the State of Georgia*. In *The Cherokee Cases: Two Landmark Federal Decisions in the Fight for Sovereignty*, by Jill Norgren, 165–69. Norman: University of Oklahoma Press, 2003.

Martin, Joel W. "Before and Beyond the Sioux Ghost Dance: Native American Prophetic Movements and the Study of Religion." *Journal of the American Academy of Religion* 59 (1991): 677–701.

———. "'My Grandmother Was a Cherokee Princess': Representations of Indians in Southern History." In *Dressing in Feathers: The Construction of the Indian in American Popular Culture*, ed. S. Elizabeth Bird, 129–47. Boulder, Colo.: Westview, 1996.

———. *Sacred Revolt: The Muskogees' Struggle for a New World*. Boston: Beacon, 1991.

———. "Visions of Revitalization in the Eastern Woodlands: Can a Middle-Aged Theory Stretch to Embrace the First Cherokee Converts?" In *Reassessing Revitalization Movements: Perspectives from North America and the Pacific Islands*, ed. Michael E. Harkin, 61–87. Lincoln: University of Nebraska Press, 2004.

Martin, Jonathan. "'The Greatest and Most Cosmopolitan Object Teacher': *Buffalo Bill's Wild West* and the Politics of American Identity, 1883–1899." *Radical History Review* 66 (1996): 92–123.

Mason, Jeffrey D. "The Politics of *Metamora*." In *The Performance of Power: Theatrical Discourse and Politics*, ed. Sue-Ellen Case and Janelle Reinelt, 92–110. Iowa City: University of Iowa Press, 1991.

Masters, Joshua J. "Reading the Book of Nature, Inscribing the Savage Mind: George Catlin and the Textualization of the American West." *American Studies* 46.2 (Summer 2005): 63–89.

Mattern, Mark. "The Powwow as a Public Arena for Negotiating Unity and Diversity in American Indian Life." *American Indian Culture and Research Journal* 20.4 (1996): 183–201.

Maus, Marion P. "The New Indian Messiah." *Harper's Weekly* 34 (1890): 947.

Mauzé, Marie. "On Concepts of Tradition: An Introduction." In *Present Is Past: Some Uses of Tradition in Native Societies*, ed. Marie Mauzé, 1–15. Lanham, Md.: University Press of America, 1997.

May, Katja. "Nativistic Movements among the Cherokees in the Nineteenth and Twentieth Centuries." *Journal of Cherokee Studies* 15 (1990): 27–39.

Mazel, David. "'A Beautiful and Thrilling Specimen': George Catlin, the Death of Wilderness, and the Birth of the National Subject." In *Reading the Earth: New Directions in the Study of Literature and Environment*, ed. Michael P. Branch et al., 129–43. Moscow: University of Idaho Press, 1998.

McCluskey, Sally. "*Black Elk Speaks*: And So Does John Neihardt." *Western American Literature* 6.4 (Winter 1972): 231–42.

McKenney, Thomas L., and James Hall. *History of the Indian Tribes of North America.* 1836–44. Reprinted as *The Indian Tribes of North America, with Biographical Sketches and Anecdotes of the Principal Chiefs.* Edinburgh: J. Grant, 1933.

McKenzie, Charles. "Some account of the Mississouri Indians in the years 1804, 5, 6, & 7." 1809–10. In *Early Fur Trade on the Northern Plains: Canadian Traders among the Mandan and Hidatsa Indians, 1738–1818. The Narratives of John Macdonell, David Thompson, François-Antoine Larocque, and Charles McKenzie,* ed. Raymond D. Wood and Thomas D. Thiessen, 221–96. Norman: University of Oklahoma Press, 1985.

McLoughlin, William G. "Cherokee Antimission Sentiment, 1823–1824." In *Cherokee Ghost Dance,* by William G. McLoughlin with Walter H. Conser Jr. and Virginia Duffy McLoughlin, 385–93.

———. "The Cherokee Ghost Dance Movement, 1811–1813." In *Cherokee Ghost Dance,* 111–35.

———. *Cherokee Renascence in the New Republic.* Princeton, N.J.: Princeton University Press, 1986.

———. *Cherokees and Missionaries, 1789–1839.* New Haven, Conn.: Yale University Press, 1984.

———. "Civil Disobedience and Social Action among the Missionaries, 1829–1839." In *Cherokee Ghost Dance,* 423–48.

———. "Fractured Myths: The Cherokees' Use of Christianity." In *The Cherokees and Christianity, 1794–1870: Essays on Acculturation and Cultural Persistence,* ed. Walter H. Conser Jr., 152–87. Athens: University of Georgia Press, 1994.

———. "Missionaries as Cultural Brokers." In *Cherokees and Christianity,* 109–26.

McLoughlin, William G., and Walter H. Conser Jr. "The Cherokee Censuses of 1809, 1825, and 1835." In *Cherokee Ghost Dance,* 215–50.

———. "'The First Man Was Red': Cherokee Responses to the Debate over Indian Origins." *American Quarterly* 41 (1989): 243–64.

McLoughlin, William G., with Walter H. Conser Jr. and Virginia Duffy McLoughlin. *The Cherokee Ghost Dance: Essays on the Southeastern Indians, 1789–1861.* Macon, Ga: Mercer University Press, 1984.

McMullen, Ann. "What's Wrong with This Picture? Context, Coversion, Survival, and the Development of Regional Native Cultures and Pan-Indianism in Southeastern New England." In *Enduring Traditions: The Native Peoples of New England,* ed. Laurie Weinstein, 123–50. Westport, Conn.: Bergin and Garvey, 1994.

McNickle, D'Arcy. *Native American Tribalism: Indian Survivals and Renewals.* New York: Oxford University Press, 1993.

Meer, Sarah. *Uncle Tom Mania: Slavery, Minstrelsy and Transatlantic Culture in the 1850s.* Athens: University of Georgia Press, 2005.

Melder, Keith E. "Ladies Bountiful: Organized Women's Benevolence in Early Nineteenth-Century America." *New York History* 48 (1967): 231–54.

Merritt, Jane T. *At the Crossroads: Indians and Empires on a Mid-Atlantic Frontier, 1700–1763.* Chapel Hill: University of North Carolina Press, 2003.

Meserve, Walter J. *An Emerging Entertainment: The Drama of the American People to 1828.* Bloomington: Indiana University Press, 1977.

Meyer, Roy. *The Village Indians of the Upper Missouri: The Mandans, Hidatsas, and Arikaras.* Lincoln: University of Nebraska Press, 1977.

Michaelsen, Scott. *The Limits of Multiculturalism: Interrogating the Origins of American Anthropology.* Minneapolis: University of Minnesota Press, 1999.

Mielke, Laura L. *Moving Encounters: Sympathy and the Indian Question in Antebellum Literature.* Amherst: University of Massachusetts Press, forthcoming.

———. "'Native to the Question': William Apess, Black Hawk, and the Sentimental Context of Early Native American Autobiography." *American Indian Quarterly* 26 (2002): 246–70.

Mihesuah, Devon A. *Cultivating the Rosebuds: The Education of Women at the Cherokee Female Seminary, 1851–1909.* Urbana: University of Illinois Press, 1993.

Miller, Angela. *The Empire of the Eye: Landscape Representation and American Cultural Politics, 1825–1875.* Ithaca, N.Y.: Cornell University Press, 1993.

Miller, Susan A. "Licensed Trafficking and Ethnogenetic Engineering." In *Natives and Academics: Researching and Writing about American Indians,* ed. Devon A. Mihesuah, 100–10. Lincoln: University of Nebraska Press, 1998.

Mitchell, Lee Clark. *Witnesses to a Vanishing America: The Nineteenth-Century Response.* Princeton, N.J.: Princeton University Press, 1981.

Mitchell, W. J. T. "Imperial Landscape." In *Landscape and Power,* ed. W.J.T. Mitchell, 5–34. Chicago: University of Chicago Press, 1994.

Moody, Richard. *Edwin Forrest: First Star of the American Stage.* New York: Knopf, 1960.

Mooney, James. *The Ghost-Dance Religion and the Sioux Outbreak of 1890. Fourteenth Annual Report (Part 2) of the Bureau of Ethnology to the Smithsonian Institution.* Washington, D.C.: U.S. Government Printing Office, 1896. Reprinted as *The Ghost-Dance Religion and Wounded Knee.* New York: Dover, 1973.

———. *Myths of the Cherokee. Nineteenth Annual Report (Part 1) of the Bureau of American Ethnology, 1897–98.* Washington, D.C.: U.S. Government Printing Office, 1900. Reprinted in *History, Myths, and Sacred Formulas of the Cherokees.* Asheville, N.C.: Bright Mountain, 1992.

———. "The Sacred Formulas of the Cherokees." *Seventh Annual Report of the Bureau of American Ethnology, 1885–86.* Washington, D.C.: U.S. Government Printing Office, 1891. Reprinted in *History, Myths, and Sacred Formulas.*

———. *The Swimmer Manuscript: Cherokee Sacred Formulas and Medicinal Prescriptions.* Ed. Frans M. Olbrechts. Smithsonian Institution Bureau of American Ethnology, Bull. 99. Washington, D.C.: U.S. Government Printing Office, 1932.

Moore, David L. "Return of the Buffalo: Cultural Representation as Cultural Property." In *Native American Representations: First Encounters, Distorted Images, and Literary Appropriations,* ed. Gretchen M. Bataille, 52–78. Lincoln: University of Nebraska Press, 2001.

Moos, Dan. *Outside America: Race, Ethnicity, and the Role of the American West in National Belonging.* Hanover, N.H.: University Press of New England, 2005.

Morgan, Lewis Henry. *League of the Ho-De'-No-Sau-Nee, Iroquois.* Rochester: Sage, 1851. Reprint, Secaucus, N.J.: Citadel, 1962.

Morgan, Thomas Jefferson. "Statement on Indian Policy." In *Americanizing the American Indians: Writings by the "Friends of the Indian," 1880–1900*, ed. Francis Paul Prucha, 74–76. Cambridge, Mass.: Harvard University Press, 1973.

———. "Wild West Shows and Similar Exhibitions." In *Americanizing the American Indians*, 309–12.

Morton, Samuel George. *Crania Americana; Or, a Comparative View of the Skulls of Various Aboriginal Nations of North and South America.* Philadelphia: J. Dobson, 1839.

———. *An Inquiry into the Distinctive Characteristics of the Aboriginal Race of America.* 2nd ed. Philadelphia: John Pennington, 1844.

Morton, Thomas. *New English Canaan of Thomas Morton.* Ed. Charles Francis Adams Jr. Boston: Prince Society, 1883. Reprint, New York: Burt Franklin, 1967.

Moses, L. G. "'The Father Tells Me So!' Wovoka: The Ghost Dance Prophet." *American Indian Quarterly* 9 (1985): 335–57.

———. "Jack Wilson and the Indian Service: The Response of the BIA to the Ghost Dance Prophet." *American Indian Quarterly* 5 (1979): 295–316.

———. *Wild West Shows and the Images of American Indians, 1883–1933.* Albuquerque: University of New Mexico Press, 1996.

Moulton, Gary E. *John Ross, Cherokee Chief.* Athens: University of Georgia Press, 1978.

Mulvey, Christopher. "George Catlin in Europe." In *George Catlin and His Indian Gallery*, ed. George Gurney and Therese Thau Heyman, 63–91. Washington, D.C.: Smithsonian American Art Museum, 2002.

Murray, David. *Forked Tongues: Speech, Writing and Representation in North American Indian Texts.* Bloomington: Indiana University Press, 1991.

Nagel, Joane. "Constructing Ethnicity: Creating and Recreating Ethnic Identity and Culture." In *New Tribalisms: The Resurgence of Race and Ethnicity*, ed. Michael W. Hughey, 237–72. Washington Square: New York University Press, 1998.

Nash, Alice. "'Antic Deportments and Indian Postures': Embodiment in the Seventeenth-Century Anglo-Algonquian World." In *A Centre of Wonders: The Body in Early America*, ed. Janet Moore Lindman and Michele Lise Tarter, 163–75. Ithaca, N.Y.: Cornell University Press, 2001.

Neal, John. "Late American Books." In *American Writers: A Series of Papers Contributed to Blackwood's Magazine, 1824–1825*, ed. Fred Lewis Pattee, 190–229. Durham, N.C.: Duke University Press, 1937.

Neihardt, Hilda. *Black Elk and Flaming Rainbow: Personal Memories of the Lakota Holy Man and John Neihardt.* Lincoln: University of Nebraska Press, 1995.

Neihardt, Hilda, and Lori Utrecht, eds. *Black Elk Lives: Conversations with the Black Elk Family.* Lincoln: University of Nebraska Press, 2000.

Neihardt, John G. *Black Elk Speaks: Being the Life Story of a Holy Man of the Oglala Sioux.* 1932. Reprint, Lincoln: University of Nebraska Press, 1979.

"The New Indian Messiah." *New York Times*, 16 November 1890, 11.

Nielsen, Donald M. "The Mashpee Indian Revolt of 1833." *New England Quarterly* 58 (1985): 400–20.

Niezen, Ronald, et al. *Spirit Wars: Native North American Religions in the Age of Nation Building.* Berkeley: University of California Press, 2000.

O'Connell, Barry. "Introduction." In *On Our Own Ground: The Complete Writings of William Apess, a Pequot*, ed. Barry O'Connell, xiii–lxxvii. Amherst: University of Massachusetts Press, 1992.

———. "'Once More Let Us Consider': William Apess in the Writing of New England Native American History." In *After King Philip's War: Presence and Persistence in Indian New England*, ed. Colin G. Calloway, 162–77. Hanover, N.H.: University Press of New England, 1997.

O'Donnell, James H., III. "The Southern Indians and the War for American Independence, 1775–1783." In *Four Centuries of Southern Indians*, ed. Charles M. Hudson, 46–64. Athens: University of Georgia Press, 1975.

"The Ojibbeway Indians." *Illustrated London News* 3.86 (23 December 1843): 401–2.

Ortiz, Simon J. "The Historical Matrix towards a National Indian Literature: Cultural Authenticity in Nationalism." In *Critical Perspectives on Native American Fiction*, ed. Richard F. Fleck, 64–68. Washington, D.C.: Three Continents, 1993.

Ostler, Jeffrey. *The Plains Sioux and U.S. Colonialism from Lewis and Clark to Wounded Knee.* Cambridge: Cambridge University Press, 2004.

Overholt, Thomas W. "The Ghost Dance of 1890 and the Nature of the Prophetic Process." *Ethnohistory* 21 (1974): 37–63.

Owens, Louis. "As If an Indian Were Really an Indian: Native American Voices and Postcolonial Theory." In *Native American Representations: First Encounters, Distorted Images, and Literary Appropriations*, ed. Gretchen M. Bataille, 11–24. Lincoln: University of Nebraska Press, 2001.

Patterson, J. B. *Life of Ma-Ka-Tai-Me-She-Kia-Kiak or Black Hawk.* 1833. Reprinted as *Black Hawk: An Autobiography*, ed. Donald Jackson. Urbana: University of Illinois Press, 1990.

Paul, Andrea I. "Buffalo Bill and Wounded Knee: The Movie." *Nebraska History* 71.4 (Fall 1990): 182–90.

Paulding, James Kirke. "American Drama." *American Quarterly Review* 1 (1827): 331–57.

Paxton, Katrina A. "Learning Gender: Female Students at the Sherman Institute, 1907–1925." In *Boarding School Blues: Revisiting American Indian Educational Experiences*, ed. Clifford E. Trafzer, Jean A. Keller, and Lorene Sisquoc, 174–86. Lincoln: University of Nebraska Press, 2006.

Payne, John Howard. "The Green Corn Dance." Ed. John R. Swanton. *Chronicles of Oklahoma* 10 (1932): 170–95.

Peacock, James L. "Ethnographic Notes on Sacred and Profane Performance." In *By Means of Performance: Intercultural Studies of Theatre and Ritual*, ed. Richard Schechner and Willa Appel, 208–20. Cambridge: Cambridge University Press, 1990.

Pearce, Roy Harvey. *Savagism and Civilization: A Study of the Indian and the American Mind.* Berkeley: University of California Press, 1988.

Perdue, Theda. "Catharine Brown: Cherokee Convert to Christianity." In *Sifters: Native American Women's Lives*, ed. Theda Perdue, 77–91. New York: Oxford University Press, 2001.

———. "Cherokee Women and the Trail of Tears." *Journal of Women's History* 1.1 (Spring 1989): 14–30.

———. *Cherokee Women: Gender and Culture Change, 1700–1835.* Lincoln: University of Nebraska Press, 1998.

———. "Introduction." In *Cherokee Editor: The Writings of Elias Boudinot,* ed. Theda Perdue, 3–38. Knoxville: University of Tennessee Press, 1983.

———. "Letters from Brainerd." *Journal of Cherokee Studies* 4.1 (1979): 4–9.

———. "Nancy Ward." In *Portraits of American Women: From Settlement to the Present,* ed. G. J. Barker-Benfield and Catherine Clinton, 83–100. New York: St. Martin's, 1991.

———. "'Rising from the Ashes': The *Cherokee Phoenix* as an Ethnohistorical Source." *Ethnohistory* 24 (1977): 207–18.

———. "Southern Indians and the Cult of True Womanhood." In *The Web of Southern Social Relations: Women, Family, and Education,* ed. Walter J. Fraser Jr., R. Frank Saunders Jr., and Jon L. Wakelyn, 35–51. Athens: University of Georgia Press, 1985.

———. "Traditionalism in the Cherokee Nation: Resistance to the Constitution of 1827." *Georgia Historical Review* 66 (1982): 159–70.

———. "Writing the Ethnohistory of Native Women." In *Rethinking American Indian History,* ed. Donald L. Fixico, 73–86. Albuquerque: University of New Mexico Press, 1997.

Peyer, Bernd C. *The Tutor'd Mind: Indian Missionary-Writers in Antebellum America.* Amherst: University of Massachusetts Press, 1997.

Phillips, Joyce B., and Paul Gary Phillips, eds. *The Brainerd Journal: A Mission to the Cherokees, 1817–1823.* Lincoln: University of Nebraska Press, 1998.

Pickard, Madge E., and R. Carlyle Buley. *The Midwest Pioneer: His Ills, Cures, and Doctors.* Crawfordsville, Ind.: R. E. Banta, 1945.

*The Pious Indian; Or, Religion Exemplified in the Life of Poor Sarah.* Newburyport, Mass.: W. and J. Gilman, 1820.

Poignant, Rosyln. *Professional Savages: Captive Lives and Western Spectacle.* New Haven, Conn.: Yale University Press, 2004.

Pointer, Richard W. "'Poor Indians' and the 'Poor in Spirit': The Indian Impact on David Brainerd." *New England Quarterly* 67 (1994): 403–26.

Porterfield, Amanda. "Black Elk's Significance in American Culture." In *The Black Elk Reader,* ed. Clyde Holler, 39–58. Syracuse, N.Y.: Syracuse University Press, 2000.

Portnoy, Alisse. *Their Right to Speak: Women's Activism in the Indian and Slave Debates.* Cambridge, Mass.: Harvard University Press, 2005.

Powell, Malea. "Rhetorics of Survivance: How American Indians *Use* Writing." *College Composition and Communication* 53.3 (February 2002): 396–434.

Powers, William K. *War Dance: Plains Indian Musical Performance.* Tucson: University of Arizona Press, 1990.

———. "When Black Elk Speaks, Everybody Listens." *Social Text* 24 (1990): 43–56.

Pratt, Mary Louise. "Arts of the Contact Zone." In *Ways of Reading: An Anthology for Writers,* ed. Donald Bartholomae and Anthony Petrosky, 605–19. 6th ed. Boston: Bedford, 2002.

———. *Imperial Eyes: Travel Writing and Transculturation.* London: Routledge, 1992.

Pratt, Richard Henry. "Remarks on Indian Education." In *Americanizing the American Indians: Writings by the "Friends of the Indian," 1880–1900*, ed. Francis Paul Prucha, 277–80. Cambridge, Mass.: Harvard University Press, 1973.

Prucha, Francis Paul, ed. *Documents of United States Indian Policy*. 2nd ed., expanded. Lincoln: University of Nebraska Press, 1990.

Raibmon, Paige. *Authentic Indians: Episodes of Encounter from the Late-Nineteenth-Century Northwest Coast*. Durham, N.C.: Duke University Press, 2005.

Reddin, Paul. *Wild West Shows*. Urbana: University of Illinois Press, 1999.

Rice, Julian. *Black Elk's Story: Distinguishing Its Lakota Purpose*. Albuquerque: University of New Mexico Press, 1991.

Rich, Elizabeth. "'Remember Wounded Knee': AIM's Use of Metonymy in Twenty-first Century Protest." *College Literature* 31.3 (Summer 2004): 70–91.

Ricker, Eli S. *Voices of the American West*. Vol. 1: *The Indian Interviews of Eli S. Ricker, 1903–1919*. Ed. Richard E. Jensen. Lincoln: University of Nebraska Press, 2005.

Ridge, John. "John Ridge on Cherokee Civilization in 1826." Ed. William G. Sturtevant. *Journal of Cherokee Studies* 6.2 (Fall 1981): 79–91.

Rifkin, Mark. "Representing the Cherokee Nation: Subaltern Studies and Native American Sovereignty." *boundary* 2 32.3 (2005): 47–80.

Risch, Barbara. "The Picture Changes: Stylistic Variation in Sitting Bull's Biographies." *Great Plains Quarterly* 20 (2000): 259–80.

Roach, Joseph. *Cities of the Dead: Circum-Atlantic Performance*. New York: Columbia University Press, 1996.

Robinson, Martha. "New Worlds, New Medicines: Indian Remedies and English Medicine in Early America." *Early American Studies* 3.1 (2005): 94–110.

Rodning, Christopher B. "Archaeological Perspectives on Gender and Women in Traditional Cherokee Society." *Journal of Cherokee Studies* 20 (1999): 3–27.

Roehm, Marjorie Catlin. *The Letters of George Catlin and His Family: A Chronicle of the American West*. Berkeley: University of California Press, 1966.

Rose, Wendy. "The Great Pretenders: Further Reflections on Whiteshamanism." In *The State of Native America: Genocide, Colonization, and Resistance*, ed. M. Annette Jaimes, 403–21. Boston: South End, 1992.

Ross, John. *The Papers of Chief John Ross*. Ed. Gary E. Moulton. 2 vols. Norman: University of Oklahoma Press, 1985.

Round, Phillip H. "Indigenous Illustration: Native American Artists and Nineteenth-Century U.S. Print Culture." *American Literary History* (forthcoming).

Rugoff, Milton. *The Beechers: An American Family in the Nineteenth Century*. New York: Harper, 1981.

Ruoff, A. LaVonne Brown. "Old Traditions and New Forms." In *Studies in American Indian Literature: Critical Essays and Course Designs*, ed. Paula Gunn Allen, 147–68. New York: Modern Language Association, 1983.

Rush, Benjamin. "Medicine among the Indians of North America." In *The Selected Writings of Benjamin Rush*, ed. Dagobert D. Runes, 254–92. New York: Philosophical Library, 1947.

Russell, Don. *The Lives and Legends of Buffalo Bill*. Norman: University of Oklahoma Press, 1960.

Salisbury, Neal. "Embracing Ambiguity: Native Peoples and Christianity in Seventeenth-Century North America." *Ethnohistory* 50 (2003): 247–59.

Sánchez-Eppler, Karen. "Raising Empires Like Children: Race, Nation, and Religious Education." *American Literary History* 8 (1996): 399–425.

Sarris, Greg. *Keeping Slug Woman Alive: A Holistic Approach to American Indian Texts.* Berkeley: University of California Press, 1993.

Sattler, Richard A. "Women's Status among the Muskogee and Cherokee." In *Women and Power in Native North America*, ed. Laura F. Klein and Lillian A. Ackerman, 214–29. Norman: University of Oklahoma Press, 1995.

Sayre, Gordon. *The Indian Chief as Tragic Hero: Native Resistance and the Literatures of America, from Moctezuma to Tecumseh.* Chapel Hill: University of North Carolina Press, 2005.

Schechner, Richard. *Between Theater and Anthropology.* Philadelphia: University of Pennsylvania Press, 1985.

Scheckel, Susan. *The Insistence of the Indian: Race and Nationalism in Nineteenth-Century American Culture.* Princeton, N.J.: Princeton University Press, 1998.

Schimmel, Julie. "Inventing the 'Indian.'" In *The West As America: Reinterpreting Images of the Frontier, 1820–1920*, ed. William H. Truettner, 149–89. Washington, D. C.: Smithsonian, 1991.

Schmitz, Neil. *White Robe's Dilemma: Tribal History in American Literature.* Amherst: University of Massachusetts Press, 2001.

Schonenberger, Regula Trenkwalder. *Lenape Women, Matriliny, and the Colonial Encounter: Resistance and Erosion of Power (c. 1600–1876): An Excursus in Feminist Anthropology.* Bern: Peter Lang, 1991.

Schoolcraft, Henry Rowe. *An Address, Delivered before the Was-Ah-Ho-De-Ne-Son-Ne or New Confederacy of the Iroquois, Aug. 14, 1846.* Rochester, N.Y.: Jerome and Brother, 1846.

———. *Algic Researches.* 1839. Reprinted as *Schoolcraft's Indian Legends*, ed. Mentor L. Williams. East Lansing: Michigan State University Press, 1991.

Schwartz, Joseph. "The Wild West Show: 'Everything Genuine.'" *Journal of Popular Culture* 3.4 (Spring 1970): 656–66.

Scott, James C. *Domination and the Arts of Resistance: Hidden Transcripts.* New Haven, Conn.: Yale University Press, 1990.

Sears, John F. *Sacred Places: American Tourist Attractions in the Nineteenth Century.* Amherst: University of Massachusetts Press, 1998.

Sears, Priscilla. *A Pillar of Fire to Follow: American Indian Dramas, 1808–1859.* Bowling Green, Ohio: Bowling Green University Popular Press, 1982.

Seaver, James E. *A Narrative of the Life of Mrs. Mary Jemison.* Syracuse, N.Y.: Syracuse University Press, 1990.

Sheehan, Bernard W. *Seeds of Extinction: Jeffersonian Philanthropy and the American Indian.* Chapel Hill: University of North Carolina Press, 1973.

Shepard, Thomas. *The Clear Sun-shine of the Gospel Breaking Forth upon the Indians in New-England.* In *The Eliot Tracts, with Letters from John Eliot to Thomas Thorowgood and Richard Baxter*, ed. Michael P. Clark, 101–39. Westport, Conn.: Praeger, 2003.

Shoemaker, Nancy. "How Indians Got to Be Red." *American Historical Review* 102 (1997): 625–44.

———. "Introduction." In *Negotiators of Change: Historical Perspectives on Native American Women*, ed. Nancy Shoemaker, 1–25. New York: Routledge, 1995.

———. "Kateri Tekakwitha's Tortuous Path to Sainthood." In *Negotiators of Change*, 49–71.

Sigourney, L[ydia]. H[oward]. *Traits of the Aborigines of America, a Poem.* Cambridge, Mass.: Hillard and Metcalf, 1822.

Silko, Leslie Marmon. "An Old-Time Indian Attack Conducted in Two Parts. Part One: Imitation 'Indian' Poems. Part Two: Gary Snyder's *Turtle Island.*" In *The Remembered Earth: An Anthology of Contemporary Native American Literature*, ed. Geary Hobson, 211–16. Albuquerque: University of New Mexico Press, 1979.

Silvio, Carl. "*Black Elk Speaks* and Literary Disciplinarity: A Case Study in Canonization." *College Literature* 26.2 (Spring 1999): 137–50.

Simmons, Williams S. "Red Yankees: Narragansett Conversion in the Great Awakening." *American Ethnologist* 10 (1983): 253–71.

———. "Southern New England Shamanism: An Ethnographic Reconstruction." *Papers of the 7th Algonquian Conference, 1975*, 218–56. Ottawa: Carleton University Press, 1976.

Simonsen, Jane E. *Making Home Work: Domesticity and Native American Assimilation in the American West, 1860–1919.* Chapel Hill: University of North Carolina Press, 2006.

Slotkin, Richard. *Gunfighter Nation: The Myth of the Frontier in Twentieth-Century America.* New York: Harper, 1993.

Smith, Donald. *Sacred Feathers: The Reverend Peter Jones (Kahkewaquonaby) and the Mississauga Indians.* Lincoln: University of Nebraska Press, 1987.

Smith, Michael P. *Mardi Gras Indians.* Gretna, La.: Pelican, 1994.

Smith, Sherry L. *Reimagining Indians: Native Americans through Anglo Eyes, 1880–1940.* New York: Oxford University Press, 2000.

Smith Rosenberg, Carroll. "The Female World of Love and Ritual: Relations between Women in Nineteenth-Century America." *Signs* 1 (1975): 1–29.

Smits, David D. "The 'Squaw Drudge': A Prime Index of Savagism." *Ethnohistory* 29 (1982): 281–306.

Smoak, Gregory E. *Ghost Dances and Identity: Prophetic Religion and American Indian Ethnogenesis in the Nineteenth Century.* Berkeley: University of California Press, 2006.

Speck, Frank G., and Leonard Broom. *Cherokee Dance and Drama.* Norman: University of Oklahoma Press, 1983.

Spence, Mark David. *Dispossessing the Wilderness: Indian Removal and the Making of the National Parks.* New York: Oxford University Press, 1999.

Standing Bear, Luther. *Land of the Spotted Eagle.* 1933. Reprint, Lincoln: University of Nebraska Press, 1978.

———. *My People the Sioux.* Ed. E. A. Brininstool. 1928. Reprint, Lincoln: University of Nebraska Press, 1975.

Starr, Paul. *The Social Transformation of American Medicine.* New York: Basic, 1982.

Stearns, Jonathan. "Discourse on Female Influence." In *Up from the Pedestal: Selected Writings in the History of American Feminism*, ed. Aileen S. Kraditor, 47–50. Chicago: Quadrangle, 1968.

Steele, Jeffrey. "Reduced to Images: American Indians in Nineteenth-Century Advertising." In *Dressing in Feathers: The Construction of the Indian in American Popular Culture*, ed. S. Elizabeth Bird, 45–64. Boulder, Colo.: Westview, 1996.

Steltenkamp, Michael F. *Black Elk: Holy Man of the Oglala*. Norman: University of Oklahoma Press, 1993.

Stewart, Omer C. "Contemporary Document on Wovoka (Jack Wilson), Prophet of the Ghost Dance in 1890." *Ethnohistory* 24.3 (Summer 1977): 219–22.

Stocking, George W., Jr. "Introduction: Essays on Museums and Material Culture." In *Objects and Others: Essays on Museums and Material Culture*, ed. George W. Stocking Jr., 3–14. Madison: University of Wisconsin Press, 1985.

Stone, John Augustus. *Metamora; Or, the Last of the Wampanoags*. In *Metamora and Other Plays*, ed. Eugene R. Page, 5–40. Princeton, N.J.: Princeton University Press, 1941.

Strickland, Rennard. *Fire and the Spirits: Cherokee Law from Clan to Court*. Norman: University of Oklahoma Press, 1975.

Sturm, Circe. *Blood Politics: Race, Culture, and Identity in the Cherokee Nation of Oklahoma*. Berkeley: University of California Press, 2002.

Sundquist, Eric J. "The Indian Gallery: Antebellum Literature and the Containment of the American Indian." In *American Literature, Culture, and Ideology: Essays in Memory of Henry Nash Smith*, ed. Beverly R. Voloshin, 37–64. New York: Peter Lang, 1990.

Sweet, Jill D. "Burlesquing 'The Other' in Pueblo Performance." *Annals of Tourism Research* 16 (1989): 62–75.

Thomas, Robert K. "Pan-Indianism." In *The American Indian Today*, ed. Stuart Levine and Nancy Oestreich Lurie, 77–85. DeLand, Fla.: Everett/Edwards, 1968.

Thoreau, Henry David. *The Maine Woods*. Ed. Joseph J. Moldenhauer. Princeton, N.J.: Princeton University Press, 1972.

———. *Walden*. Ed. J. Lyndon Shanley. Princeton, N.J.: Princeton University Press, 1971.

Thornton, Russell. *We Shall Live Again: The 1870 and 1890 Ghost Dance Movements as Demographic Revitalization*. Cambridge: Cambridge University Press, 1986.

Thurman, Melburn D. "The Shawnee Prophet's Movement and the Origins of the Prophet Dance." *Current Anthropology* 25 (1984): 530–31.

Tiro, Karim M. "Denominated 'SAVAGE': Methodism, Writing, and Identity in the Works of William Apess, a Pequot." *American Quarterly* 48 (1996): 653–79.

Trachtenberg, Alan. Review of *Wild West Shows and the Images of American Indians*, by L. G. Moses. *Journal of American History* 84.2 (September 1997): 604–6.

———. *Shades of Hiawatha: Staging Indians, Making Americans 1880–1930*. New York: Hill and Wang, 2004.

Tracy, Joseph. *History of the American Board of Commissioners for Foreign Missions*. 2nd ed. New York: M. W. Dodd, 1842.

Trafzer, Clifford E., Jean A. Keller, and Lorene Sisquoc, eds. *Boarding School Blues: Revisiting American Indian Educational Experiences.* Lincoln: University of Nebraska Press, 2006.

Trennert, Robert A. *White Man's Medicine: Government Doctors and the Navajo, 1863–1955.* Albuquerque: University of New Mexico Press, 1998.

Trimble, Charles. "Introduction." In *Black Elk Lives: Conversations with the Black Elk Family,* ed. Hilda Neihardt and Lori Utrecht, xiii–xvii. Lincoln: University of Nebraska Press, 2000.

Trowbridge, C. C. *Shawnese Traditions: C. C. Trowbridge's Account.* Ed. Vernon Kinietz and Erminie W. Voegelin. Occasional Contributions from the Museum of Anthropology of the University of Michigan, No. 9. Ann Arbor: University of Michigan Press, 1939.

Truettner, William H. "Ideology and Image: Justifying Westward Expansion." In *The West as America: Reinterpreting Images of the Frontier, 1820–1920,* ed. William H. Truettner, 27–53. Washington, D.C.: Smithsonian, 1991.

———. *The Natural Man Observed: A Study of Catlin's Indian Gallery.* Washington, D.C.: Smithsonian, 1979.

Tufts, Henry. *A Narrative of the Life, Adventures, Travels, and Sufferings of Henry Tufts.* Dover, N.H.: Samuel Bragg, 1807.

Tuttle, Sarah. *Letters and Conversations on the Cherokee Mission.* 2 vols. in 1. Boston: T. R. Marvin, 1830.

Vecsey, Christopher. "Prologue." In *Handbook of American Indian Religious Freedom,* ed. Christopher Vecsey, 7–25. New York: Crossroad, 1991.

Viola, Herman J. "Washington's First Museum: The Indian Office Collection of Thomas L. McKenney." *Smithsonian Journal of History* 3.3 (Fall 1968): 1–18.

Vizenor, Gerald. *Manifest Manners: Postindian Warriors of Survivance.* Middletown, Conn.: Wesleyan University Press, 1994.

Vogel, Virgil J. *American Indian Medicine.* Norman: University of Oklahoma Press, 1970.

Wald, Priscilla. *Constituting Americans: Cultural Anxiety and Narrative Form.* Durham, N.C.: Duke University Press, 1995.

Waldstreicher, David. *In the Midst of Perpetual Fetes: The Making of American Nationalism, 1776–1820.* Chapel Hill: University of North Carolina Press, 1997.

Walker, Cheryl. *Indian Nation: Native American Literature and Nineteenth-Century Nationalisms.* Durham, N.C.: Duke University Press, 1997.

Walker, Deward E., Jr. "Protection of American Indian Sacred Geography." In *Handbook of American Indian Religious Freedom,* ed. Christopher Vecsey, 100–115. New York: Crossroad, 1991.

Walker, James R. *Lakota Belief and Ritual.* Ed. Raymond J. DeMallie and Elaine A. Jahner. Lincoln: University of Nebraska Press, 1991.

Walker, Robert Sparks. *Torchlights to the Cherokees: The Brainerd Mission.* New York: Macmillan, 1931.

Wallace, Anthony F. C. *The Death and Rebirth of the Seneca.* New York: Vintage, 1972.

Warren, Louis S. *Buffalo Bill's America: William Cody and the Wild West Show.* New York: Knopf, 2005.

Warrior, Robert Allen. "Eulogy on William Apess: His Writerly Life and His New York Death." In *The People and the Word: Reading Native Nonfiction*, 1–47. Minneapolis: University of Minnesota Press, 2005.

———. *Tribal Secrets: Recovering American Indian Intellectual Traditions*. Minneapolis: University of Minnesota Press, 1995.

Washburn, Wilcomb E. *The Assault on Indian Tribalism: The General Allotment Law (Dawes Act) of 1887*. Ed. Harold M. Hyman. Philadelphia: Lippincott, 1975.

———, ed. *The American Indian and the United States: A Documentary History*. 2 vols. New York: Random House, 1973.

Wasserman, Emily. "The Artist-Explorers." *Art in America* 60 (July–August 1972): 48–57.

Weaver, Hilary N. "Indigenous Identity: What Is It, and Who *Really* Has It?" *American Indian Quarterly* 25 (2001): 240–55.

Weaver, Jace. *That the People Might Live: Native American Literatures and Native American Community*. New York: Oxford University Press, 1997.

Weber, Ronald. "'I Would Ask No Other Monument to My Memory': George Catlin and a Nation's Park." *Journal of the West* 38.1 (January 1999): 15–21.

Welch, Deborah. "American Indian Women: Reaching Beyond the Myth." In *New Directions in American Indian History*, ed. Colin G. Calloway, 31–48. Norman: University of Oklahoma Press, 1988.

Welter, Barbara. "The Cult of True Womanhood: 1820–1860." *American Quarterly* 18 (1966): 151–74.

———. "The Feminization of American Religion: 1800–1860." In *Clio's Consciousness Raised: New Perspectives on the History of Women*, ed. Mary S. Hartman and Lois Banner, 137–57. New York: Harper, 1974.

Wexler, Laura. "Tender Violence: Literary Eavesdropping, Domestic Fiction, and Educational Reform." In *The Culture of Sentiment: Race, Gender, and Sentimentality in Nineteenth-Century America*, ed. Shirley Samuels, 9–38. New York: Oxford University Press, 1992.

White, Richard. "Creative Misunderstandings and New Understandings." *William and Mary Quarterly* 63 (2006): 9–14.

———. "Frederick Jackson Turner and Buffalo Bill." In *The Frontier in American Culture*, ed. James R. Grossman, 7–65. Berkeley: University of California Press, 1994.

———. *The Middle Ground: Indians, Empires, and Republics in the Great Lakes Region, 1650–1815*. Cambridge: Cambridge University Press, 1991.

Whitehorse, David. *Pow-Wow: The Contemporary Pan-Indian Celebration*. San Diego: San Diego State University Press, 1988.

Whitt, Laurie Anne. "Cultural Imperialism and the Marketing of Native America." *American Indian Culture and Research Journal* 19.3 (1995): 1–31.

Wickstrom, Gordon M. "Buffalo Bill the Actor." *Journal of the West* 34.1 (January 1995): 62–69.

Wiget, Andrew. "Elias Boudinot, Elisha Bates and *Poor Sarah*: Frontier Protestantism and the Emergence of the First Native American Fiction." *Journal of Cherokee Studies* 8.1 (Spring 1983): 4–21.

Williams, Gwyn A. *Madoc: The Making of a Myth*. New York: Oxford University Press, 1987.

Wilmeth, Don B. "Noble or Ruthless Savage? The American Indian on Stage and in the Drama." *Journal of American Drama and Theatre* 1.1 (Spring 1989): 39–78, 1.2 (Fall 1989): 34–54.

Wilson, Charles Reagan. "Shamans and Charlatans: The Popularization of Native American Religion in Magazines, 1865–1900." *The Indian Historian* 12.3 (1979): 6–13.

Witthoft, John. *Green Corn Ceremonialism in the Eastern Woodlands.* Occasional Contributions from the Museum of Anthropology of the University of Michigan, No. 13. Ann Arbor: University of Michigan Press, 1949.

Womack, Craig S. *Red on Red: Native American Literary Separatism.* Minneapolis: University of Minnesota Press, 1999.

Wong, Hertha Dawn. *Sending My Heart Back Across the Years: Tradition and Innovation in Native American Autobiography.* New York: Oxford University Press, 1992.

Wood, Raymond D., and Thomas D. Thiessen, eds. *Early Fur Trade on the Northern Plains: Canadian Traders among the Mandan and Hidatsa Indians, 1738–1818. The Narratives of John Macdonell, David Thompson, François-Antoine Larocque, and Charles McKenzie.* Norman: University of Oklahoma Press, 1985.

Worthen, W. B. "Disciplines of the Text/Sites of Performance." *TDR* 39.1 (1995): 13–28.

Wright, Richardson. *Hawkers and Walkers in Early America: Strolling Peddlers, Preachers, Lawyers, Doctors, Players, and Others, from the Beginning to the Civil War.* Philadelphia: Lippincott, 1927.

Wyss, Hilary E. "Mary Occom and Sarah Simon: Gender and Native Literacy in Colonial New England." *New England Quarterly* 79 (2006): 387–412.

———. *Writing Indians: Literacy, Christianity, and Native Community in Early America.* Amherst: University of Massachusetts Press, 2000.

Yellow Robe, Chauncey. "The Menace of the Wild West Show." *Quarterly Journal of the Society of American Indians* 11.2 (July–September 1914): 224–25.

Young, Mary E. "Women, Civilization, and the Indian Question." In *Clio Was a Woman: Studies in the History of American Women,* ed. Mabel E. Deutrich and Virginia C. Purdy, 98–110. Washington, D.C.: Howard University Press, 1980.

Zeisberger, David. "David Zeisberger's History of the Northern American Indians." Ed. Archer Butler Hulbert and William Nathaniel Schwarze. *Ohio Archaeological and Historical Quarterly* 19 (1910): 1–189.

———. "Zeisberger's Diary of a Journey to the Ohio, September 20–November 16, 1767." *Ohio Archaeological and Historical Publications* 21 (1912): 8–32.

# Index

# Acknowledgments

Many fellow scholars have played a role in this book's creation. Foremost among them are Eric Cheyfitz, Betsy Erkkila, Lisa New, Myra Jehlen, and Peter Conn, whose example of perceptiveness, integrity, and commitment will always inform my work. Tom Hallock, Laura Mielke, and Tim Sweet read various incarnations of the Catlin chapter and provided both positive feedback and constructive critique. Joe Fichtelberg chose my paper on Indian performance for a panel he chaired at the Society of Early Americanists conference and encouraged me thereafter both by sharing his own work and by reading mine. Zubeda Jalalzai and Dan Moos have given me tips on everything from John Eliot's missions to Buffalo Bill's Wild West. Kris Bross and I continue to debate the role of the Indian voice in American literature; her comments and criticism have kept me both informed and honest. Phillip Round generously allowed me to read his works in progress. Laura Stevens and Dennis Moore invited me to participate on a panel with Joseph Roach. Lynn Rhoads polished my work on Thoreau. Barry O'Connell has provided general support and encouragement over the years. Finally, the manuscript's first two readers, who remain anonymous to me, offered praise where the book worked and tough questions where it didn't, while the book's final reader, Roger Abrahams, saw what I was trying to say even better than I did and helped me to see it as well. I hope that all of these readers, critics, and friends see their impact on these pages and that they are pleased with what I have done.

La Roche College, where I work, is a small teaching institution with neither the history nor the resources to promote faculty scholarship. Nonetheless, numerous members of the La Roche community have provided me with encouragement, opportunity, and material aid in the completion of this project. My department chair, Sr. Rita Yeasted, made sure that my teaching schedule would allow room for both research and family. My colleagues, especially Chris Abbott, Linda Jordan Platt, Janine Bayer, Ed Stankowski, and Jeff Ritter, offered emotional support during some very tough times both professionally and personally. The library wizards at La Roche—LaVerne Collins,

Darlene Veghts, Jackie Bolte, Marilyn McHugh, and Christy Sarver—provided invaluable assistance. (In particular, Christy tracked down every single interlibrary loan request—fifty thousand at last count—that I made.) La Roche's vice president for academic affairs, Dr. Howard Ishiyama, approved travel funds for the various conferences at which I first tested portions of the book. And the members of the Faculty Development Committee recommended—and Dr. Ishiyama secured—a precious two-semester teaching reduction during the final phase of writing and revision.

The University of Pennsylvania Press has been unfailingly supportive of this project from the start—when editor Jerry Singerman saw promise in *Medicine Bundle* even in its embryonic state—to the finish, when a dedicated staff consisting of acquisitions assistant Mariana Martinez, associate managing editor Erica Ginsburg, copyeditor Mary Tederstrom, and art director John Hubbard saw the book through the closing stages of its development. I am deeply thankful for the interest, acumen, and care shown by all.

And, of course, where would I be without those who share my life outside academia? This is the first time that Lilly can read for herself the acknowledgments page (sorry, Jonah, but your time will come!), so I thank her for her spunk, her love, and her own budding career as an artist. I also thank both her and Jonah for understanding why Daddy was so busy this final semester; as promised, I finished by Christmas! My parents, Judith and Marvin Bellin, have always helped me realize my dreams and reach my goals. I have thanked my wife, Christine Saitz, in each of my two previous scholarly books; I have also made her a promise about this one, and I intend to keep it. For life.

This book is dedicated to my undergraduate advisor and writing teacher. When I graduated, she told me that she would be watching for my byline. Though she did not live to see it, I never would have seen it either without her.